Contents

Preface

It is twenty years since William Empson, just a year after his retirement from Sheffield University, truly turned his mind to collecting his essays and articles. Uncharacteristically invoking the gospel of St John (9, 4) – or maybe he was thinking more immediately of John Donne's Satire III, line 84 – he wrote to his old friend and publisher Ian Parsons in 1972: 'I well know that the night cometh when no man can work, and that I had much better be getting my affairs in order. In fact I meant to do it when I retired, but the inflation is so alarming that it seems better to keep in employment while I may. Besides, I am always finding mistakes in my old articles while having to read some book again for a lecture.'[1]

As that letter suggests, whenever he tried to gather up his writings he invariably felt it necessary to review the argument and ammunition he had originally marshalled for any particular piece. In addition, he found it imperative, not merely to substantiate points of old controversy, but to drive forward into new areas; he was not one to rest on his offprints. He willingly granted in the introductory remarks to his Clark Lectures, given at Trinity College, Cambridge, in 1974: 'I am usually saying things that other people disagree with, and I need to present a much stronger case in print than I do in a lecture. It has been getting pretty near the point of just calling each other liars...' At about this time, in 1972, for instance, he began intensive work on *Doctor Faustus* in relation to both the English and the German Faust-books; and by January 1979 he had amassed so many hundreds of pages of notes and typescript drafts that he knew he had in prospect not just an essay, but a substantial book (*Faustus and the Censor: The English Faust-book and Marlowe's 'Doctor Faustus'* has been edited by John Henry Jones, 1987), so it is not in the least surprising that he was reluctant to face the day when it would be necessary to take ultimate stock of the growing number of his occasional essays. Not idleness, but an ever-enquiring mind: that was the problem. 'Kind of you to enquire', he wrote to Parsons in 1975,

I have been delayed by various things but am going on quite well now, and if I keep it up will finish 'Elizabethan Plays' within a year at least. One keeps finding soft bits that need more information to carry the needed weight, but most of it is just re-writing now. A good deal of the Clark Lecture material comes in, but by no means all. There are a number of old articles I was planning to bring in at the end, but the thing is getting so long I am not sure there will be room. If not they can join the rag-book [*sic*]; we can settle that later.[2]

In the event, he concentrated his energies on three specific volumes – *Using Biography*, *Essays on Shakespeare*, and a collection of essays on other Elizabethan and Jacobean writers (as well as the extended study of *Doctor Faustus*). Yet at his death in April 1984 he had finished only the first, containing essays on Marvell, Dryden, Fielding, Yeats, T. S. Eliot, and Joyce, which was published by Chatto and Windus later that year. In 1986 David B. Pirie edited for Cambridge University Press *Essays on Shakespeare*, a volume that was almost complete when Empson died; with the single exception of an essay on *A Midsummer Night's Dream*, which survives in several confusing drafts and was accordingly left out of the book, the contents are those that Empson had decided to include. The following year, the present editor assembled a volume that is distinct from the canon; *Argufying: Essays on Literature and Culture*, containing both substantial items and a plethora of occasional pieces, constitutes what I believe Empson would have considered his 'rag-book'. Apart from specifying the theme and contents of *Using Biography*, Empson had made known his intentions only in respect of the Shakespeare volume and of the collection of essays on 'other Elizabethan playwrights', as he sometimes vaguely called the companion collection; so it was not hard to design the *omnium gatherum* of *Argufying*: it was necessary only *not* to include those articles which had to be tagged for the Renaissance tome.

There is no substantial guidance, whether preferred or inferred, about the outstanding Elizabethan and Jacobean collection. 'There are several other puzzles which I need to clear my mind and record my opinion about, before I die or become ga-ga, and I know I must hurry up', he wrote to CUP ('Guy Fawkes Night 1981'). 'The plan of one Shakespeare book and then one Jonson etc. book seems to me an admirable one, settling a whole area, and I had much better do that next. But of course I must arrange them as real books...' We know that the Shakespeare collection added up to a 'real book' in his estimation; we cannot be at all certain just how he meant to compose the remaining Renaissance essays. 'The next one is about other Elizabethan playwrights, and perhaps a poet or two', he told Christopher Ricks in 1981; and then, in September 1982: 'The book on Shakespeare and one on other Elizabethan playwrights are to be done by CUP, and... there is stuff I want to hold back for further works, such as the Donne argument...'[3] One title that occurred to him in 1982 was *Some Elizabethan Plays and their Stage* – though 'of course I would be glad to be advised of brisker titles', he sensibly allowed.[4] What is evident is that he wanted to collect his essays on Kyd, Marlowe, Jonson, and Webster, substantially revised (if necessary) since their first periodical appearances; also the several pieces he had written on John Donne and his poetry – which he had loved for a lifetime. (It is not otherwise evident what he meant by 'a poet or two', unless he had it in mind to write more about Herbert or Vaughan.) Moreover, on top of all his other extensive writings – about *Doctor Faustus*, the secret marriage of Andrew Marvell, and further projects – he undertook in the 1970s to do even more research on the urgent business of establishing the context of John Donne's interest in cosmology, and to draft a number of extra pieces – on the astronomer Thomas Digges, on the place of Copernicanism in the Elizabethan world, and especially on the precocious, sky-flying science fiction of Francis Godwin, *The Man in the Moone*. (For reasons which will be made clear as you read on, he thought at one time of entitling this last essay 'Young Donne and Godwin's Man in the Moon'.) All in all, he wrote such a sizeable body of passionate, closely argued essays on the subject of John Donne that it has become irresistible to gather them into a single volume augmented by these other pieces. Only by reading Empson on all aspects of the Donne controversy – biographical, bibliographical, ideological, and aesthetic – is it possible to appreciate the full burden of his commitment to the poetry. For reasons of space and economy, therefore, Empson's pieces on Elizabethan and Jacobean drama will now take their place in the second instalment of a two-volume edition of his essays on Renaissance literature. To say the least, all of the pieces in the present volume are interdependent.

Maybe Empson had an inkling of this happily cogent consequence as long ago as January 1973, when he told Ian Parsons that, of all the essays he had to review and possibly revise, 'I had better first do the difficult ones on Joyce and Donne – both I should think will end up as merely long articles in books of collected articles, but perhaps the Donne, as so many angles to it have been cropping up, could make a short book to itself.'[5]

It is a great pleasure to acknowledge the help I have received during the preparation of this volume. First and foremost, as in editing *The Royal Beasts* and *Argufying*, I must thank Hetta Empson for entrusting me with the task, for her unintrusive faith, and for her unstinting hospitality in Hampstead (where I am also cheered by the fellowship of John Henry Jones). Rodney Dennis, Curator of Manuscripts, is always a welcoming and most witty host during my visits to the Houghton Library, Harvard University; and Elizabeth A. Falsey, who has undertaken the staggering job of cataloguing the Empson Papers, is unfailingly resourceful in helping me to get at the multitudinous bits and pieces I need. For their advice and information in various capacities I am indebted to Professor Sir Frank Kermode, Dr Barbara Ozieblo, Dr David B. Pirie, Dr Theodore Redpath, Professor Christopher Ricks, Professor Mark Roberts, and Mr Colin A. Ronan. Finally, for their bottomless patience and professionalism (and their surprising friendliness) I offer thanks to Anne McDermid, my agent at Curtis Brown, and to Kevin Taylor of Cambridge University Press.

I am immensely grateful to the British Academy for the award of a Research Readership which enabled me to make happy progress both with this volume and with a biography of Empson; and to the Research Fund of the University of Sheffield for timely financial assistance.

John Haffenden
University of Sheffield

Sources and acknowledgements

'Donne and the Rhetorical Tradition' was first published in *The Kenyon Review*, 11, Autumn 1949. Copyright 1949 by Kenyon College. Reprinted with permission. 'Donne the Space Man' was first published in *The Kenyon Review*, 19, Summer 1957. Copyright 1957 by Kenyon College. Reprinted with permission. 'Donne in the New Edition' first appeared in the *Critical Quarterly*, 8, 1966, and is reprinted by permission of *Critical Quarterly*. 'Rescuing Donne' was first published in *Just So Much Honor: Essays Commemorating the Four-Hundredth Anniversary of the Birth of John Donne*, edited by Peter Amadeus Fiore; University Park, PA: The Pennsylvania State University Press, 1972, pp. 95–148. Copyright 1972 by the Pennsylvania State University. Reproduced by permission of the publisher. I am grateful to Professor Sir Frank Kermode for supplying me with an offprint of 'Rescuing Donne' with emendations in Empson's hand: I have incorporated in this edition the few small alterations and corrections that Empson desired. There is one essay I have chosen not to include here – '"There Is No Penance Due to Innocence"', Empson's review of *John Donne: Life, Mind and Art* by John Carey (*The New York Review of Books*, 28:19, 3 December 1981, pp. 42–50) – not because I feel it necessary to protect the innocent, though it is an angry essay (John Carey clearly needs no such protection), but because the largest part of the critical debate it covers, especially the discussion of Donne's 'Elegy XIX', is fully rehearsed in 'Rescuing Donne'; even though there is bound to be a degree of reiteration in a collection such as this, to insist on downright repetitiousness seems beyond the call of editorial duty.

The other essays – specifically 'Donne's foresight', 'Copernicanism and the censor', 'Thomas Digges his infinite universe', 'Godwin's voyage to the Moon', and 'Appendix on Galileo' – are taken from Empson's own typescript drafts. All of these latter pieces

post-date 'Rescuing Donne' (1972), and indeed it is apparent that
Empson had been working on draft after draft of them throughout
the last decade of his life; there is some evidence, for example, to
suggest that 'Copernicanism and the censor' dates from about 1982.
The pieces on Godwin and Galileo were provided with titles by
Empson himself; other titles are editorial. As John Henry Jones found
to his anguish when editing *Faustus and the Censor*, Empson always
wrote numerous drafts of his books and essays: it was, for him, a
matter of both principle and experience that an essay should be
kneaded into readability by being urged through the typewriter as
many times as necessary – sometimes a dozen or more times – until
he was satisfied it had achieved the careless ease that was characteristic of his best prose. In the case of the first three of these
previously unpublished essays, and the 'Appendix on Galileo', it has
been a fairly straightforward matter to determine the most developed
state of the typescript. 'Godwin's Voyage to the Moon' was a serious
challenge, however, since there are some five or six (it is even difficult
to be quite sure) typescript drafts – hundreds of pages of top copies
and carbons – in varying states of revision; but I feel reasonably
confident, after tackling the big job of collation, that the text in this
volume represents the most advanced state of the essay. As far as
Empson was concerned, all of these essays were trial pieces; I believe
they demonstrate that his intellectual pep went undiminished to the
end. Occasionally – very occasionally – I have had to synthesise a
sentence or a phrase, but the words are 100 per cent Empson.

Professor Sir Frank Kermode has generously given permission for
me to quote extracts from his letters to William Empson. Extracts
from the letters of the late Dame Helen Gardner are published by
kind permission of Katherine Duncan-Jones.

In editing both published and unpublished essays, I have been
mindful of Empson's protestation, in a letter to the *New Statesman* (5
June 1955), that 'the bits of my prose which Mr Vallins blamed in
Good English had been written with particular care, chiefly to avoid
misunderstanding in the reader, and...I thought the complaints
against them wrong-headed'. As far as style goes, therefore, I have
tried to limit myself to correcting infrequent misspellings and to
normalising or supplying some points of punctuation for the sake of
clarity. Other silent emendations have been of a usual copy-editing
order. But I am also conscious that Empson is famous for being able

to quote vast amounts of poetry from memory, and equally famous for misquoting (poetry and prose) in his published works. 'I am very bad at correcting proofs of my own writing', he wrote in a letter to the *Hudson Review* in Autumn 1966,

always seeing what I meant to write and considering whether it should be improved, and in my first book I foolishly imitated Hazlitt in what seemed a civilised practice, making incidental quotations as I remembered them, which was sufficient for the purpose. The effect of the combination was that a close study of an odd bit of punctuation in a poem would sometimes appear with the punctuation wrong, and nearby there were evidently careless quotations. My paragraph would make nonsense until the punctuation was put right, and I struggled to do this as soon as possible, but my opponents were already saying that I had cheated; I had misquoted the text in order to make it fit my interpretation, they said, and they have continued to do so. Now... almost any other form of our mortal frailty would then have tempted me more.

Accordingly, I have attempted to check the majority of the quotations, both poetry and prose, in this volume, though I cannot claim to have been comprehensive (some of them I just could not locate). I can only hope against hope not to have introduced misquotations, and more importantly not to have harmed any of Empson's interpretations and their supportive evidence.

Quotations from Donne's poetry have normally been collated with the standard text edited by Herbert J. C. Grierson, *The Poems of John Donne* (Oxford: Clarendon Press, 1912). Although Empson always favoured the Grierson text, he was casual about orthography and often modernised the titles of poems (e.g. 'The Ecstasy' rather than 'The Extasie'): I have not felt it necessary to regularise Empson's usage in respect of titles, except for just a few occasions where an uncorrected citation could be confusing.

One other matter needs a word or two of explanation. While Empson himself rarely supplied details of sources and references, I have chosen to furnish quite a full apparatus of annotations, together with additional references; and some of these annotations extend to works of criticism that have been published in the years since Empson's death in 1984. My reason for supplying such references is not just to equip Empson's essays with the patina of pedantic scholarship; it is because Empson committed himself for more than fifty years to putting forward deeply felt and long-deliberated arguments about Donne, his poetry, and his world, and I am sure he would hate to think that his essays were being gathered together merely for the sake of the historical–critical record. These studies were vital to him, so I have provided annotations with a view to setting the essays in the widest possible context of the living debate about Donne; to show how the argument goes on – and Empson's continuing centrality to it.

Introduction

I think one major and much needed reform is now in progress,
a decisive break away, if it can be pressed hard enough, from the
iron rule of the T. S. Eliot men. It is the recognition that people
held a great variety of religious or philosophical opinions in the
sixteenth and seventeenth centuries, though they were cautious
about printing it; instead of all having to agree with T. S. Eliot,
because they knew no other.

from the introduction to Empson's unpublished Clark Lectures, 1974

'No man really likes being promoted to the class of Licensed
Buffoons', wrote William Empson in 1966, at a time when he was
given cause to reflect on his own critical reputation, 'but it has been
an important post in England since the time of Jaques, I suppose, let
alone Bernard Shaw.'[1] Empson's status as a Licensed Buffoon has
recently been rehearsed, or rather ironically celebrated, by John
Carey, Merton Professor of English Literature at the University of
Oxford, in a review of Frank Kermode's *An Appetite for Poetry*.
Empson, Carey writes,

was pugnacious, irascible and dogmatic – a rottweiler to Kermode's
pekinese. Far from sharing Kermode's courteous hospitality to divergent
viewpoints, he thought he was right, and that anyone who disagreed with
him was detestable and base. In fact, he was persistently wrong, indeed
crack-brained, on some issues, as Kermode shows. He believed all his life
that John Donne was interested in space travel, and in the theological
problems of extra-terrestrial life-forms, and he once assured Kermode that
Donne's 'The Good Morrow' took place on the planet Venus. But even in
these loopy seizures Empson compelled attention because he passionately
believed in himself.[2]

Given such a stalemate – Carey's humorous allegation that
Empson was wrong when he thought he was right – I propose in this
introduction to review and evaluate Empson's extensive writings on

Donne, which appeared over a period of no less than half a century, from 1930 to 1981, and to seek to understand why – during the last 30 years – they have been patronised as *divertissements*, more or less irrelevant to the proper business of Donne scholarship.

Certainly the first point to be stressed is that, as John Carey admits, Empson's arguments from Donne's poetry – specifically the love-poetry – were consistent from first to last. 'Practically all [Donne's] good poems', Empson maintained, are concerned with enunciating a secret freedom from church and state; far from being the fruits of waggishness, or 'typically capricious and inconstant' (to use Carey's phrase about Donne),[3] they are seriously sceptical, rebellious, and indeed revolutionary. Looking back in 1974, Empson remarked:

It was not a new idea in 1935 that the love-poetry of Donne claims a defiant independence for the air of lovers, especially by setting them to colonise some planet made habitable by Copernicus. A campaign to exterminate the idea was then in progress, using very little reasoned argument, and its success has naturally made the poems seem pretty trivial to a later generation.[4]

He was referring to his earliest sustained presentation of the theory, 'Double plots' (1935), in which he argued that the Renaissance cultivated a 'desire to make the individual more independent than Christianity allowed', and that 'one did not want to submit to the inquisition of a central divine authority even at best...' The Copernican hypothesis, soon to be proved by scientific discovery, allowed an escape-route for the dissident.

The idea that you can get right away to America, that human affairs are not organised round one certainly right authority (e.g. the Pope) is directly compared to the new idea that there are other worlds like this one, so that the inhabitants of each can live in their own way. These notions carry a considerable weight of implication, because they lead at once to a doubt either of the justice or the uniqueness of Christ.[5]

If the Logos is at once 'the underlying Reason of the universe and... the Christ who had saved man', to describe any other human being as fulfilling that dual role is to deny the singular revelation of Christ as creator and redeemer. Crashaw did as much in 'The Weeper' when he described Mary Magdalene as 'a sort of rival Christ': 'It is she now who underlies the order of nature... Since her tears are both the essential stars and the essential dew (and so on) they reconcile earth and heaven, they perform the function of the sacrificed god... The Protestants were clearly right in calling this version of the invocation of saints heretical, because it destroys the uniqueness of Christ...' So too, Empson went on, in

'The First Anniversarie' Donne gives an enormous picture of the complete decay of the universe, and this is caused by the death of a girl of no importance whom Donne had never seen. Ben Jonson said 'if it had been written to the Virgin, it would have been something' but only Christ would be enough; only his removal from the world would explain the destruction foretold by astronomers. The only way to make the poem sensible is to accept Elizabeth Drury as the Logos.[6]

What all this adds up to, by Empson's reckoning, is a version of pastoral, whereby the poet – necessarily standing at a remove, 'because an artist never is at one with any public' (*Pastoral*, p. 14) – salutes the worth of individual conscience over institutionalised rule. Jonson was astute to think the *Anniversaries* 'profane and full of Blasphemies';[7] but as far as Empson was concerned, that heresy was creditable and indeed heroic: 'Blasphemy was a serious accusation, and we need not suppose that [Donne] expressed his deepest feeling in defending himself against it.'

In 'On Metaphysical Poetry' (*Scrutiny*, 2:13, December 1933), James Smith, a Cambridge friend of Empson's, ventured to define the essence of metaphysical verse in these terms: 'verse properly called metaphysical is that to which the impulse is given by an over-whelming concern with metaphysical problems; with problems either deriving from, or closely resembling in the nature of their difficulty, the problem of the Many and the One.' As old as Plato, the problem of the Many and the One includes these examples, he noted: 'At times the individual has fought against, and depended upon, its fellow individual, much as multiplicity unity; or the individual has fought against the universal; or against the universe, or against God.'[8] Empson agreed with Smith's essay, which he thought 'excellent'; adding only: 'The supreme example of the problem of the One and the Many was given by the Logos who was an individual man.'[9]

Empson worked outside the current of Anglo-American criticism for most of the 1930s and 1940s, teaching first in Japan and then in China; so that the message he carried to his Far Eastern students, as in these unpublished notes linking the strategy of Donne's poetry to the political appropriation of Petrarchism by the Elizabethan court, reiterated what he took to be the orthodox view of the 'deeply sceptical and inquisitive' character of Donne's mind – albeit that Donne may have 'felt the drama of scepticism rather than any rational necessity for it':

The assertion that somebody *is* the whole world, or that their death will destroy the whole world, is always coming up in Donne's work... It is an ancient belief that the king or emperor has a magical effect on the country he rules; if there are floods and disasters, that proves he is insincere. In a sense he *is* everything, because he is magically connected to everything. In Donne's time this line of thought, partly because recovered from the classics, had been revived in a remarkable degree about Queen Elizabeth. 'The divine right of kings' is not a medieval idea, but one taken up by the family of Tudor, and in England this kind of poetry was first written about the queen. But the metaphysical idea, that the person is everything just as whiteness is all white things, makes a different connection. Christ is the logos in theology, that is, he is the underlying reason which keeps the universe obeying its laws, and he was also an individual man. And by his death he altered the conditions of the whole world. So what Donne says about his heroines was seriously believed about Christ. He is stealing fire from the two most sacred sources, royalty and religion, and the effect is to say with insolent force that he cares about nothing but the love-affair that he describes.[10]

James Smith had fully concurred in 1933: 'To Donne the most important things that exist are himself and his mistress, the most important relation between them the everyday one of love.'[11] Just so, Empson wrote about 'Donne and his imitators': 'they really are metaphysical. They believe (though not all solemnly) that a love-affair is the fundamental means of understanding the world, or that the real purpose of building any system of knowledge is to understand love. If this is so, it is natural to bring your whole world-view into a love-poem.'

By Empson's reckoning, the damage was done to 'traditional' critical readings such as his own by the reactionary forces of the Christian religion, with T. S. Eliot as its literary high priest. In 1931 Eliot made the unsupported assertion, 'Donne was, I insist, no sceptic';[12] and in due order Allen Tate (among other critics) bowed to the new wisdom. In 1611, Donne had balefully discerned in 'The First Anniversarie' that the 'new Philosophy calls all in doubt'; but following Eliot's lead Tate chose to observe in his review of *A Garland for John Donne* (the volume in which Eliot's 'killer' of an essay appeared) that Donne's interest in the new cosmologists, Copernicus and Kepler, took the straightforward form of 'an anxiety about the physical limits of consciousness and the bearing of that question on the scholastic conception of body and soul, which Donne presents in the terminology of St Thomas. Donne knew nothing of a scientific age, or of the later open conflict between the two world-views, science and religion.'[13] Empson felt justified in scorning what he termed Tate's 'elegant mufflement'. Christian critics celebrate the Creator, he said, and yet they deny that a seventeenth-century poet could have felt staggered by the soul-provoking news about the true disposition of the cosmos He created. Empson enjoyed pointing up the ironically heretical implications of Tate's false position:

Well come now, this bit of hush-up naturally excites an impulse to hush-up this awful bit of hush-up too, as it happened to be an awful gaffe our old pal [Tate] made. Donne invented this conflict at the same time as the Roman Inquisition, but apart from the high terrible example of Donne it has been rare among English poets; it is a gross slander to pretend that they all despise the works of their Creator and the discoveries of the divine plan achieved during their lifetime.[14]

Empson first had to fight for this ground after the war, in 'Donne and the Rhetorical Tradition' (1949), where he argued that 'the final point' of the arcane research of Rosemond Tuve's *Elizabethan and Metaphysical Imagery*, as applied to Donne, 'turns out to be that he did not at all mean the kind of thing a modern critic admires him for, because Donne thought he was only applying the rules of rhetoric in a particularly rigorous and stringent manner.'[15] As he understood Rosemond Tuve, he explained,

she treats the Donne line of talk that the idealised woman is a world, or that the two happy lovers are a world, as a straightforward use of the trope *amplificatio*. That is, in effect, it is like Pope in the 'Pastorals', saying 'Where'er you walk, cool gales will fan the glade./Trees, where you sit, will crowd into shade.' I do not mean that the Pope lines are flat; the nostalgia of their frank untruth is almost heartbreaking; but still the thing is meant to be untrue; it is a trope. I do not think you get anywhere with Donne unless you realise that he felt something different about his repeated metaphor of the separate world; it only stood for a subtle kind of truth, a metaphysical one if you like, and in a way it pretended to be a trope; but it stood for something so real that he could brood over it again and again ... But [Miss Tuve] says that the astronomical images in Donne are 'dialectical counters in a war of wits', and she has a firm footnote denying that 'what we like to think of as the peculiar character of metaphysical imagery' has among its causes 'the disturbed *Weltanschauung* which accompanied the acceptance of the Copernican world-picture'.... I think it is obvious that his separate planet... was connected with Copernicus; and I notice that Miss Tuve gives no reason for thinking otherwise. She merely finds it natural, as she is classifying tropes, to assume that they are all fairly similar standard objects, rather like spare parts of machinery...

I deny, then, that Donne is simply 'using' a well-known trope, the standard howling hyperbole of the Counter-Reformation, when he identifies any person or pair of persons he chooses to praise with the Logos; because he regularly throws in the idea forbidden to Catholics of a separate planet, out of reach of the Pope, and this inherently lifts the old trope into a new intellectual air.

Thus Empson highlights in Donne's poetry this recurrent nexus: the syncretism of 'the metaphor of the separate planet', derived from the contemporary debate about astronomy or cosmology, with 'the trope based on the Logos', meaning that one might escape the sanctions of Christian dogma. Yet the generality of criticism in post-war years has tended to share Tuve's view that the astronomical metaphors in Donne are 'dialectical counters in a war of wits'; that he is at best brilliantly outrageous but hardly dissentient in any seriously sustained way. Frank Kermode, for example, proposed that Donne's 'commonest device' was to depend 'heavily upon dialectical sleight-of-hand, arriving at the point of wit by subtle syllogistic misdirections... making a new and striking point by a syllogism concealing a logical error'. The poet 'exercised his wit on the theme of sexual love, and... was inclined to do this in a "naturalist" way'.[16] To state only so much is to rest content with the bluff masculinity of Donne; let us delight in his audacious wit and look no further. Empson believed that Donne's celebrations of love amounted to a defiant doctrine, challenging canon law and received morality; as he wrote to Kermode: 'you take for granted that Donne does not mean what he says'.

'I entirely agree that Donne must have been felt as a shock', Kermode replied, 'and all the part of Miss Tuve's book which says he wasn't is not only wrong but easily shown to be so. Some of this shock is a matter of being a little risqué in theological matters, certainly'. However, he went on, Donne 'always uses' the new-philosophy argument 'exactly as he uses alchemy, angelology and all the rest of it, as providing useful illustration'.[17] But surely, to call Donne's imagery 'illustrative' is to mitigate the shock of the poetry. James Smith made the appropriate deduction more than twenty years earlier: 'If Donne merely plays ducks and drakes with metaphysics, we may as well abandon our investigation'.[18] For his part, Empson sought to credit Donne with being purposefully provocative, slicing through convention, with his imagery not incidental but integrative.

The early Elegy XIX, 'To his Mistris Going to Bed', which Kermode was quite right to call 'magnificently erotic',[19] became for Empson a crucial measure of Donne's outrageousness. Spoken by a naked man, already abed, to a woman who is classily dressed in 'wyerie Coronet', gown and 'spangled breastplate', the poem hurries her to bed – hustles her, if you will – with a blend of exaltation and rapt encouragement. 'Off with that girdle, like heavens Zone glittering/ But a far fairer world incompassing.' As she doffs successive garments and accessories, the poet hymns her:

> Now off with those shooes, and then safely tread
> In this loves hallow'd temple, this soft bed.
> In such white robes, heaven's Angels us'd to be
> Receavd by men; Thou Angel bringst with thee
> A heaven like Mahomets Paradise; and though
> Ill spirits walk in white, we easly know,
> By this these Angels from an evil sprite,
> Those set our hairs, but these our flesh upright.
>   Licence my roaving hands, and let them go,
> Before, behind, between, above, below.
> O my America! my new-found-land,
> My kingdome, safliest when with one man man'd,
> My Myne of precious stones, My Emperie,
> How blest am I in this discovering thee!
> To enter in these bonds, is to be free ..

And finally, to extol the virtue of shared nakedness, he claims that women:

>   are mystick books, which only wee
> (Whom their imputed grace will dignifie)
> Must see reveal'd. Then since that I may know,
> As liberally as to a Midwife shew
> Thy selfe; cast all, yea this white lynnen hence.
> There is no pennance due to innocence.
>   To teach thee, I am naked first: Why then
> What needst thou have more covering than a man.

Sex, says the poem, is not what the churchmen say, it is not sinful but pure; there is no need to mortify ourselves. At least, that proposition

is what the text of 1669 (the first to print the poem), as enshrined by
Sir Herbert Grierson, says; it is the *textus receptus* which Charles Coffin
could celebrate in 1937 as needing 'no apology for treating love,
unattenuated and unrefined by spiritual encumbrances, in a robust
and downright manner. The refreshing realism is saved from being
objectionable – though perhaps not sufficiently for those who always
regard Donne in ecclesiastical perspective – by the native vigor of the
poet.'[20] Empson thought it needed no apology for the vigour with
which it confuted conventionality, its resolute heterodoxy. But the
lovely line 46, 'There is no pennance due to innocence', is a textual
crux; other manuscripts, arguably more authoritative, read variously
'There is no pennance, much less innocence' and 'Here is no
pennance, much less innocence' – both of which reverse the meaning
of the line, as Empson maintained, by scoffingly acknowledging the
speaker's impenitent guilt. The wooer's expressions of urgent wonder
turn into the rake's profession of bad faith. Grierson printed 'There
is no pennance due to innocence', from the edition of 1669, on the
grounds that it represented 'a softening of the original to make it
compatible with the suggestion that the poem could be read as an
epithalamium'.[21] Empson favoured that reading, but certainly not
for its softening properties: 'we need not give much weight to [the]
charitable idea that Donne wrote the poem for his own marriage', he
suggested.[22] The reason why the woman addressed and undressed is
innocent, he argued, 'is that she is the Noble Savage, like Adam and
Eve before the Fall (they are indeed the type case of lovers on a
separate planet); she is America, where they are free as Nature made
them, and not corrupted, as we are, by "late law". Sweet the line
may well be called, but it was meant to take effect as a culminating
bit of defiant heresy.' When determining a copy-text in this case, he
thought, a key question is obvious: 'what was the origin of *due to*? It
cannot be an unmeaning slip; it reverses the whole point of the line,
wittily.'

Frank Kermode admires the poem for what Saintsbury termed its
'frank naturalism'; for cocking a snook at morality, but not for
transgressing it in a deliberative way. 'I take this poem', he told
Empson, 'as being of the sort that does habitually say, "let's have no
more of all that cant about 'honour', 'innocence' etc." "You
certainly aren't penitent; thank god you're not 'innocent'"; so off
with that white linen."'[23] In short, for Kermode, the speaker vaunts
his guiltiness, and expressly bows to conventionality through the very

act of reckoning with it in such a form. Empson constantly pressed the point that the poem must be honourably heretical, or else it is obscene and – if you follow the logic of its argument – directly insults the woman who is otherwise exhorted to share a free act of love; 'why is it essential', he challenged Kermode to explain,

> to suppose that the young Donne was not heretical, however much he appears to be? In other cases, the Christian critics are quite happy to say that an author had very wrong ideas till he was converted, but in the case of Donne they have somehow decided to twist both the text and the biography so as to pretend he never was ... Of course, I should agree that the convention of wit-writing made it safer for Donne to write like this ... and maybe he did alter the line in the elegy himself later in life, to remove the only bit which has to be regarded as heretical if taken seriously. But this let-out process gives no reason for supposing that he can't really have entertained the ideas which he expressed.[24]

In a series of essays, published in 1957, 1966, 1972 and 1981, he returned to Elegy XIX as a touchstone of critical taste and judgment; perhaps most convincingly in an essay-review of Helen Gardner's edition of *The Elegies and The Songs and Sonnets*:

> All through the poem, the lady is encouraged to undress by being told it is the right thing to do, for very exalted reasons ... [and] most of the comparisons are celestial: she is a better world, and her girdle is the Milky Way; she is one of Mahomet's angels, or a sacred or magical text, only to be read by men dignified through her 'imputed grace' (the Calvinist doctrine here implies an awestruck sense of unworthiness). There is a steady rise in these exhilarated claims, and he calls her 'innocent' when he gets to the top. Donne is fond of arguing his way through an apparently indefensible case, and his logic is habitually sustained; he would think it shame to collapse and confess himself guilty ... at the climax of a speech for the defence. Or is he supposed to be telling the lady how much he despises her? The crucial moment of seduction seems the most unpractical time he could choose.
>
> Indeed, a more general question imposes itself: 'Why is this not simply a dirty poem, please?' I think it becomes very dirty if you make the poem jab his contempt into the lady at the crisis of the scene of love, thus proving that all his earlier flattery of her must be interpreted as jeering.

In conclusion, he averred, the poem 'is defiant, and that is why it is not dirty; it is a challenge ... It is only our modern orthodox young Donne who has to be made to express a specific sense of sin even while writing a love-poem.'

Nonetheless, it can be maintained, Donne's elegies are in any case only ingenious variations on subjects out of Ovid's *Amores*: displays of sheer cynical wit, or what J. B. Leishman termed 'discourses upon a broomstick',[25] outrageous in the degree to which they are impudent. Leishman classified Elegy XIX as a 'dramatic' elegy, smoothly witty and frankly suggestive *à la* Ovid, as opposed to certain others which might be considered in some way (speciously) logical or argumentative (p. 76). Yet few critics deny that Donne's elegies are much more than pastiches of Ovid's mode of sexual provocation; and Elegy XIX makes little sense at all unless it prosecutes a logical argument. One might also claim that the line 'Here is no pennance, much less innocence' is merely a superb example of apodosis, a rhetorical clincher that turns the argument on its head. Even so, the line still seems more like a sneering inversion, the crowing of a cad, than the thrillingly subversive 'There is no pennance due to innocence', which proposes a radically progressive principle.

J. B. Leishman enters a further caveat, however, which is to say that we must 'resist the temptation to regard such poems as autobiographical, or to infer from them anything about Donne's own conduct, morals and opinions' (p. 58). To that warning one must again reply: Donne was not just mimicking Ovid, he was reworking his model, reinventing the material, and we serve him ill to evade his individual meaning.[26] Indeed, it is a staggering irony that Empson's long campaign to prove the courageously heretical character of Donne's poetry, and to defend the poet from pietistic detractors, gains all the more point when you contrast his high-minded version with the portrait of the poet that John Carey presents in *John Donne: Life, Mind and Art* (1981). A number of Empson's readers (including Kermode) have judged that his account of Donne's style of mind and poetry is obsessively wayward; that he is at best describing himself in the image of Donne. John Carey's Donne, let it be said, is obnoxious. Donne's poetry is impelled by egotism, which is its 'consuming force', says Carey;[27] Donne is best understood as a shame-faced recusant, driven by a lust for power; his art is the art of ambition, seething with self-regard and relentlessly on the make. The poems, which Carey seems scarcely to like at all (apart from 'The Progresse of the Soule', which he considers a neglected masterpiece), prove it. The *Songs and Sonnets* are 'largely about the instability of the self', and riddled with symptoms of apostasy: 'the love poems', he writes, 'are a veil for religious perturbations'.[28] Most likely taking his cue from Helen Gardner, who says that in the early poems 'one is aware of the dominance of the masculine partner who, if his mistress denies him

what he wants, bullies or abuses her',[29] Carey describes Elegy XIX
as a sadistic poem, exemplifying the 'almost pathological imperious-
ness' of Donne's 'urge to impose power'; it expresses 'a wish to insult,
humiliate and punish'.[30] (Carey is not alone in offering such an
extreme reading; more recently, Thomas Docherty has absurdly
called the poem a study in 'auto-eroticism, masturbation', with the
woman having 'no value in the poem'.)[31] Not surprisingly, Empson
believed that his own account of the poet and the poetry – however
outlandish it seemed to some readers – rescued the work from such
'sordid and mean-minded' imputations. Whereas Empson compliments the poet's libertarianism, 'panting, bug-eyed' Carey commits
a libel.[32] On the one hand, the poem is defiant and unabashedly sexy;
on the other, indecent and punitive. So much depends, therefore – as
Empson urged for 30 years – on the viciousness of the variant line
'Here is no pennance, much less innocence'. But for that line, he
argued, readings like Carey's would be confounded:

the whole point of all the previous arguments has been to imply that the
action will be innocent... Donne is tenacious of an argument in a poem, and
would not rat on it... Still, if the girl is a prostitute, as Dame Helen
[Gardner] appears to tell us in an allusive footnote, there is nothing to rat
on; both the characters are only pretending, and it is a comfort to them not
to have to bother with holy scruples.

Thus, on Dame Helen's view, the poem is deflated but still good humored.
On Carey's view, the man seduces an innocent girl by arguments purporting
to prove that yielding will not be sinful, and then triumphs over her, at the
very moment of penetration, by telling her she will go to hell for it. This is
sadistic pornography, a very evil thing which Carey is right to be indignant
about, but it has emerged from his own mind.[33]

(In case we suspect that Empson is simply answering one libel with
another in such remarks, Carey's point of view may be judged from
just two sentences in his book: 'We are careful to talk, nowadays, as
if we believed that the male ought to respect the female's individuality. Donne is above such hypocrisies, and states, with
measured resonance, his lethal hunger.')[34]

Curiously, Empson and Carey come close to agreement on one
central point of argument, when they seek to explain the covert
meaning of what Carey calls the poet's 'transmutation' of 'private
love into something of global significance' (p. 124). But whereas
Carey sees this recurrent feature of the love poems as stemming from

a process of compulsive substitution – Donne displacing the reality of his religious agitations on to 'the relatively innocuous department of sexual ethics' (p. 38) – Empson hails a campaign of exalted defiance, with the poet 'erecting personal love into a rival to Christianity'. This is the issue on which Carey high-handedly rated Empson for indulging in persistently 'crack-brained' notions, which he characterised as the belief that Donne 'was interested in space travel, and in the theological problems of extra-terrestrial life-forms'. To clear up that last matter first: Empson never said that Donne was interested in 'extra-terrestrial life-forms' *per se*, only as the metaphorical and metaphysical opportunity that he took to vindicate his claims for love. The idea of love as 'a mystery or cult' (as another editor, Theodore Redpath, calls it)[35] comes up very directly, for instance, in a number of poems including 'A Valediction: forbidding mourning' (which Donne may well have written just before a trip to France in 1611):

> So let us melt, and make no noise,
>   No teare-floods, nor sigh-tempests move;
> T'were prophanation of our joyes
>   To tell the layetie our love.

Even Helen Gardner granted thus much: 'The superb *égoisme à deux* of these poems... their stress on secrecy and insistence on the esoteric nature of love – a religion of which Donne and his mistress are the only saints... – make these poems a quintessence of the romantic conception of passionate love as the *summum bonum*.'[36] Likewise, 'A Valediction: of the booke' makes what Empson termed the 'astonishing' claim that these lovers' letters will teach posterity everything it needs to know:

> This Booke, as long-liv'd as the elements,
>   Or as the worlds forme, this all-graved tome
>   In cypher writ, or new made Idiome,
> Wee for loves clergie only'are instruments:
>   When this booke is made thus,
>   Should againe the ravenous
>   Vandals and Goths inundate us,
>   Learning were safe; in this our Universe
> Schooles might learne Sciences, Spheares Musick,
>   Angels Verse.
>
> Here Loves Divines, (since all Divinity
>   Is love or wonder) may finde all they seeke...

Yet when Helen Gardner, in her edition, commented (p. 194) – 'Since "university" was frequently used for "universe" at this period, I assume that Donne regards the words as interchangeable' – Empson wittily pointed up the heterodoxy of Donne's position with this response: 'Only at Oxford would a don take for granted that the university teaches the angels how to sing before God.' Donne's outlook in the poem 'really does believe in the religion of love', he pressed on. 'But it cannot believe in the uniqueness of the historical Jesus, since any man (or married couple) aware of the truth may be called on to act as messiah, as in America or on the planet Mars, and may do it well enough.' (He nailed Allen Tate's 'lie' – 'The logical argument of "A Valediction: forbidding mourning" is a Christian commonplace' – with the riposte: 'it is a universal, and for that matter pagan, commonplace...')[37]

It is a measure of Gardner's resistance to any heretical hidden agenda that she refused to countenance a staring impiety in another poem, 'The Relic', where the poet says that, in a future age of 'mis-devotion', 'Thou shalt be a Mary Magdalene, and I/ A something else thereby.' Quite a few readers feel sure that Donne must mean 'a Jesus Christ'; but Helen Gardner would never suffer the notion: 'It has been suggested that Donne intended that his bone would be thought to be a bone of Christ and this has been supported by the revival of the hoary *canard* that Luther said that Christ and Mary Magdalene were lovers. But however sunk in "mis-devotion" an age was it would surely be aware that the grave of Christ contained no relics other than his grave-clothes.'[38] Theodore Redpath exercises a long footnote on the line, deciding in favour of the 'very bold sense... that people in that age of "mis-devotion" will take Donne's bone for one of Christ's'.[39] But even he, though sympathetic to Empson's arguments, failed to comprehend the more subtle and radically different point that Empson posed in 'Donne the Space Man':

It has been objected that Jesus left no bone behind him on earth, and indeed this clearly made Donne safer; no doubt he himself would be ready with this objection if challenged. But '*a* Jesus Christ' would be logically a very different entity from the one Jesus, and the point I am trying to make all along is that this kind of poetry continually uses the idea that the attributes of the Christ can be applied to others.

Gardner expostulated to a draft of Empson's essay: 'Need you give currency to this notion of Mr. Redpath's[?] Surely even in the most wildly superstitious countries "a bone" dug up could not be taken as a relic of Christ, who left only grave-clothes in the tomb. The only physical relics ever referred to are the holy foreskin!'[40] Empson patiently explained: 'the central idea I am imputing to Donne is that there can be many incarnations, so the belief that Jesus left no bones on earth would not affect Donne's possible status as founder of a new religion... By the way, I really did think years ago that this meaning was taken for granted; I certainly didn't learn it from Redpath's edition.'[41] She replied, with mounting indignation, 'I cannot see how you can believe that a bone with a love token round it could possibly be taken in the most deeply superstitious region... for a bone of Christ. And if this meaning were "taken for granted" many years ago I think it only proves what extraordinary notions people can cherish.'[42] And he returned yet again, still placidly: 'I am puzzled you do not see that "*a* Jesus Christ" would be inherently different from "Jesus Christ"'.[43]

In truth, the exchange is profoundly puzzling, for it reveals the imaginative limitations of Helen Gardner's literal-mindedness. From the outset, in her first letter (19 October 1956), she had misapprehended the radical burden of Empson's article: 'your main attitude towards Donne & his poetry I sympathize with very strongly,' she wrote, immediately after informing him that she had given a talk – 'to an Anglican & Orthodox group' – which included quotations showing 'Donne conceiving, as you suggest, possibilities of salvation in Jesus Christ beyond a Church & beyond where the Gospel is preached'.[44] One would think that Empson had made himself perfectly explicit in 'Donne the Space Man', as in this observation: 'Theologically, the most reckless of Donne's poems are those in which he presents himself as... the founder of a religion, the Christ of all future reckless lovers.'

Donne put the idea of space travel – as a corollary of the post-Copernican discovery of a possible plurality of inhabited worlds – to the service of 'denying the uniqueness of Jesus', Empson maintained. 'In our time no less than in Donne's', he wrote, 'to believe that there are rational creatures on other planets is very hard to reconcile with the belief that Salvation is only through Christ... One might suppose, to preserve God's justice, that Christ repeats his sacrifice in all worlds... but this already denies uniqueness to Jesus, and must in some thorough way qualify the identity of the man with the divine

Person.' Probably the only space-writer to have handled this 'real problem', he reckoned, was

the Anglican C. S. Lewis; rather brilliantly in *Out of the Silent Planet* (1938), where we find that our Earth alone required the Incarnation because it had fallen in a unique degree into the power of the Devil; but in the sequel *Voyage to Venus* (1943) we gather that all future rational creatures will have to evolve in the image of Man, throughout all galaxies, as a technical result of the Incarnation; and this feels too parochial even to be a pleasant fantasy.

Respectfully, he submitted a copy of 'Donne the Space Man' to C. S. Lewis, who reassured him, 'there's nothing in either of your two references to me which I object to', and went on with an attractive grace:

I can't say I have so far seen any connection with journies to other planets in any of the passages you deal with. That may be the obtuseness of a sick man. Also, you and I clearly have opposite qualities. You seem to me liable to see in all poetry things that aren't there; and I no doubt seem to you constantly blind to what is. Both are probably right. Perhaps if we were rolled into one we'd make a quite decent critic... or wd. the result be deadlock and *aphasia*?

But at least, unlike Helen Gardner, Lewis had taken the large point of the piece, and acknowledged its significance: 'If you are right', he conceded, 'it will be most important'.[45] Clearly he had no doubt of the implications of Empson's argument that 'The young Donne, to judge from his poems, believed that every planet could have its Incarnation, and believed this with delight, because it automatically liberated an independent conscience from any earthly religious authority.'

To see into the heart of the matter of Donne's love-poetry, Empson thus felt certain, a critic must arbitrate between two judgments. For the first, C. M. Coffin is representative: 'It would be idle to say that Donne's love poems are within the range of doctrinally conceived orthodoxy.'[46] The other position is taken by M. F. Moloney, who argues that Donne's interest in the new science, 'particularly in the new astronomy, was rather a popular and poetic interest whereby he caught up new ideas, toyed with them, wove them into the fabric of his poetry, but at no time saw in them a challenge to the stability of traditional Christianity.'[47] Empson saw that no one could balance those books: Donne's unorthodoxy may be appreciated only if you allow for the full seriousness of his interest in the new science. Frank

Kermode told Empson, with reference to the explosive charge of 'The Relic', 'I entirely agree about "a something else thereby", finding it strange that there has been so much hesitation over it. Donne's mind worked theologically, he was all out to be *épatant*...'; although he went on: 'However, the "something else thereby" is in my view only an example of the sort of thing liable to happen, not an example of a substantial and persistent doctrine of Donne's.'[48] If there were still any doubt about where he stood, Kermode stated in a further letter: 'Donne makes precise use of doctrines for the truth of which, outside the poem, he does not vouch.'[49] In other words, for Kermode, Donne is the impresario of insincerity.

According to Empson, the truth stood to the contrary. Donne held genuine advanced views, he spoke up for 'liberation and enlightenment'. 'I think he was an earnest young man all the time he was working on his love poems', he remarked to Kermode in conversation, 'instead of being a flibberty-gibbet as T. S. Eliot said... [T]he more you regard him as serious... I mean as having a basis of conviction behind what he says... even if talking in a riddle-like manner, I think that makes the poetry better.'[50] J. B. Leishman, who sought to discredit the idea that Donne should be seen as metaphysical in any true sense, is yet surprised, not to say unnerved, when he approaches that key group of poems – including 'The Good-Morrow', 'The Sun Rising', 'The Canonization', 'A Valediction: forbidding mourning', 'A Nocturnal' and 'The Dream' – which are obviously 'more serious, more impassioned, more tender' than so much else that he considers 'merely witty'. This group expresses 'the recurring theme of the all-sufficiency of two lovers and the recurring image that together they form one world'. The poet's 'idea', he finds (with an unmistakable air of being fully taken aback), 'that he and his beloved are a world in and for themselves' is 'quite foreign to Ovid'.[51] ('What can Ovid prove then?' Empson aptly chafed in his notebook.)[52] Again and again, with bug-eyed astonishment, Leishman discovers that this theme in Donne is discomfortingly serious and single-minded. His pioneering wonder is apparent, for example, in this remark: 'These continual assertions that he and she are a world, are *the* world, are an epitome of everything, are not merely hyperbolical.' How very inconvenient, is his obvious reaction; but what to say about it all? One can sense the relief, just a few pages later, when he decides to turn turtle from the orbit of Donne's 'private world' – 'this element of extremism, of untranscendental extremism', as he terms it – with the remark that 'this digression ... is leading us into rather deep waters.'[53]

   Empson waded in where others teetered: he was eager for the liberating extremism of Donne's new world. The motif of the separate planet 'leaps at you', he believed, in 'The Good-Morrow', a poem on which he rested his case. I need quote only the last two stanzas (of three), including a small variant that Empson favoured:

> And now good morrow to our waking soules,
> Which watch not one another out of feare;
> For love, all love of other sights controules,
> And makes one little roome, an every where,
> Let sea-discoverers to new worlds have gone,
> Let Maps to other, worlds on worlds have showne,
> Let us possesse one world, each hath one, and is one.

> My face in thine eye, thine in mine appeares,
> And true plaine hearts doe in the faces rest,
> Where can we finde two better hemispheares
> Without sharpe North, without declining West?
> What ever dyes, was not mixt equally;
> If our two loves be one, or, thou and I
> Love so alike, that none doe slacken, none can die.

Empson's argument runs as follows: 'The world of the lovers, with its two "hemispheares", is one of the planets recently implied by Copernicus to be habitable; and the two lovers, jointly, have become the Intelligence or angel which pushes it round. There is a point in all this (which the editor [Helen Gardner] ignores), as in calling the lady of "Elegy XIX" his America; he is beyond the claims of church and state. The slow line tolling out "one" has the awe of a space-landing ...' (There is a small textual crux in line 14, where the great majority of manuscripts, including all manuscripts of Groups II and III, reject "Let us possesse one world" in favour of "our world", though it makes no material difference to Empson's interpretation. Theodore Redpath persuasively suggests that "our" has even more intimacy than the sonorous "one" that Empson preferred.) But where is the evidence for the stunning suggestion that Donne posits an independent dispensation for the lovers on a separate planet? It is manifest in these lines:

> Let sea-discoverers to new worlds have gone,
> Let Maps to other, worlds on worlds have showne,
> Let us possesse one world ...

'The point of "worlds *on* worlds",' Empson explained, surely correctly, 'is that you can get one planet lying behind another, further away';[54] in other words, the imaginative *mise-en-scène* is extra-terrestrial, in the realm of other habitable worlds. But do other critics go along with Empson? Clay Hunt, after worrying the evidence in *Donne's Poetry* (1954), concludes that Donne had in view only the New World of America; to which Empson responded, most acutely: 'Why are they both in the plural then? What does the line about maps add to the line about discoverers...?' Theodore Redpath offers the cautious gloss that 'worlds' might be either '"continents", or "worlds" in a sense which would include celestial bodies'; though he had earlier expressed the view that Empson's interpretation of the 'worlds' here was probably correct.[55] Most significantly, Helen Gardner does not comment at all on the phrase 'worlds on worlds'; she allows only that the 'maps' are 'probably "maps" of the heavens showing new spheres' (p. 198), and refers us to a note on the subject of 'new spheres' (in her edition of the *Divine Poems*), which explains that the Jesuit mathematician Christopher Clavius (in his revised Commentary on Sacrobosco's *De Sphaera* published in 1607) at-tempted to preserve the old Christianised astronomical system, the immutable firmament, by inventing an eleventh sphere of fixed stars to explain the 'fourth motion' observed by Copernicus (originally there were just eight spheres; but Ptolemy had already added a ninth, the Primum Mobile, and Alphonsus of Castile proposed a tenth): it was all a vain ruse to 'save appearances' and so reject the outrageous conception of a heliocentric universe. Helen Gardner is most reluctant to accept that Donne, even as late as 1610, might actually be referring to Galileo's discoveries, which 'powerfully supported the Copernican hypothesis' (as she cannot refuse to acknowledge);[56] and thus – coming full circle at last – we understand that she dismisses the very idea of Empson's interpretation with respect to this poem, 'The Good-Morrow', which might have been written some years earlier still.

Helen Gardner has to track a long way away from the line that Donne indubitably wrote in 'The Good-Morrow' – 'Let Maps to other, worlds on worlds have shown' – in order to explain it away by reference to a sonnet that the poet would write when he turned parson. In that sonnet, which begins 'I am a little world made cunningly', Donne bewails the fact that he has betrayed his body and soul into 'black sinne' and proceeds to an invocation, which Carey rightly terms 'a vast gesture of despair'.[57] This is the end of the octet and the beginning of the sestet:

> You which beyond that heaven which was most high
> Have found new sphears, and of new lands can write,
> Powre new seas in mine eyes, that so I might
> Drowne my world with my weeping earnestly,
> Or wash it, if it must be drown'd no more:
> But oh it must be burnt...

Helen Gardner, who shies away from the likelihood that Donne – in calling upon 'new sphears' and 'new lands' – is referring 'to the newly revealed immensity, and possibly to the infinity, of the universe', summons Alphonsus and Clavius to justify her tame suggestion 'that he is calling on discoverers generally: astronomers who find new spheres and explorers who find new lands'.[58] Her account makes Donne tidily conservative, not a man who is given to grasping the breathtaking implications of an infinite universe. 'I take it', wrote Empson in 1957, 'that the converted Donne first reflected on his old idea of the separate planet, as an escape from the Christian Hell, and then wrote the poem specifically to renounce this heresy'; and earlier still, in 1949, when he put a gloss on the poem so penetrating and illuminating that no critic can better it: 'I think the remorseful hope of atonement with God is crossed with a shrinking hunger for annihilation and escape from God. Both of them are dominated by the image of the separate planet.' Later on, in a commentary he supplied to Frank Kermode, he added the sorry sardonic observation, 'it's a wonderfully thrifty use of his old material, to make the metaphor itself testify against his earlier uses of it'.[59] None of those acute comments were written merely to rally Gardner, for they develop his earliest discussion of the poem, in *Some Versions of Pastoral* (1935), where he had also perceived, very relevantly: '*Drowning* the world *no more* brings us back to Noah and an entirely pre-Copernican heaven.'[60] *Pace* Helen Gardner's evasion of the likelihood that Donne would be thinking of an infinite universe, and implicitly of plural worlds, when he featured 'new sphears' and 'new lands' in the sonnet 'I am a little world made cunningly', Empson noted that in *Ignatius his Conclave* (most probably written the very same year, 1610) Donne had specified 'the moone... the planets, and other starrs, which are also thought to be worlds', and so stressed this judicious deduction: 'the opposition makes plain that *world* means "*inhabited* star".' Furthermore, 'one would suppose, following the ordinary procedure of a linguist, that Donne meant the same thing for example by "a globe, yea world" in the "Valediction, Of Weeping".' As to Carey's contemptuous misrepresentation of Empson's argument – 'he believed all his life that John Donne was interested in... the theological problems of extra-terrestrial life-forms, and he once assured Kermode that Donne's "The Good-Morrow" took place on the planet Venus' – Empson has never left any room for doubt that what is being described is 'a continual metaphor' (*Pastoral*, p. 76). He told Frank Kermode, 'I think that living on another planet is an extremely powerful symbol for the claim of the lovers to have independent rights';[61] and elsewhere that in 'The Good-Morrow' Donne 'doesn't want to *discuss* space-travel; he is only comparing it to the situation of the lovers'.[62]

In any event, as well as introducing 'worlds on worlds' on top of the 'new worlds' lately discovered by seafarers, Donne goes on to ask in 'The Good-Morrow',

> Where can we finde two better hemispheares,
> Without sharp North, without declining West?
> Whatever dyes, was not mix'd equally;
> If our two loves be one, or, thou and I
> Love so alike, that none doe slacken, none can die.

'It was a regular thing', Empson explained, 'to have a pair of globes, for the earth and the stars; the young ladies in Oscar Wilde's plays are still being taught "the use of the globes", very properly... What Donne praises, in contrast to both these globes, is one made by combining the hemispheres of an eyeball from himself and an eyeball from his mistress, and he remarks with truth that this hasn't the usual properties of either of the public globes.'[63] It is practically ungainsayable that Donne makes a truly astonishing claim which sins against the fixed cosmology of current Christian dogma. The world constituted by the two hemispheres of the lovers – 'our world' – is 'better' than both the 'new worlds' of the Americas and the 'worlds on worlds' of the Christianised Ptolemaic scheme. It is undeclining and incorruptible, or – in Leishman's good phrase – 'indestructible because irreducible';[64] in Empson's terms, the lovers have in effect (so much more explicitly than implicitly) colonised a planet beyond the sovereignty of church or state. Theodore Redpath, seeming almost to hold his breath as he finds himself abetting this heresy, which he terms 'the bolder hypothesis', reaches exactly the same conclusion: 'if "none" in "none do slacken" refers to the lovers', he writes,

then 'none' in 'none can die' must surely most probably [*sic*] also refer to the lovers? Now, in that case, what the final lines of the poem will be saying is that if the lovers' love be actually a complete unity, *or* they love so similarly that neither of them slackens off in relation to the other's love, then the *lovers* will never die, i.e. they will achieve immortality. That would certainly give a strong meaning to the final lines...'[65]

Verbum sapienti sat est. Not unexpectedly, Helen Gardner's commentary as usual provides an inverse index to the real presence of the poet's happy heresy: here she cannot wriggle out of agreeing with Empson's and Redpath's interpretation, but clings to Donne's 'If' as if to hold his head above deep water: 'Conditional clauses must always suggest an element of doubt.'[66] 'The Good-Morrow' figures among the group of poems that she classifies, rather shiftily (that is, for want of a better word), as 'philosophic'; but she goes on to propose, flagrantly insulting the poet, that we need not imagine he means what he says: 'I do not intend by this to suggest that they were written to expound a philosophy of love.'[67]

If Donne does make use of the defiant implications of the new astronomy, as Empson insists, there are two consequential questions to be addressed. The first is a question of dating: was it only after about 1604, and so after his ruinous marriage to Ann More, that he learned enough of the scientific facts (as most critics seem to think) to exploit their implications in the challenging form of these poems? Second, if that is the case, and if the poems (or at least Empson's interpretation of them) collapse into inconsequentiality unless they are founded upon empirical science rather than speculation, is Donne speaking of his wife in the love-poems or merely imagining an all-consuming love?[68]

The two questions go together; and the received answers commonly lead to some extraordinary slurs on the poet. John Carey works to demonstrate the good case that 'we can discard the notion that the sexually promiscuous Donne who prowls through the elegies and the more wayward of the love lyrics was a figment of his imagination' (p. 73); even though he seems to forget that on an earlier page of his book he has described the love poems in general as comprising a 'fantasy world' (p. 38). He claims for Donne's marriage, honourably and impressively, 'Donne's fidelity to Ann was absolute: when he had her, he wanted no other woman' (p. 73). But then, in the pages immediately following, he crushes any suggestion of sentimentality *vis-à-vis* the couple's life together: 'The world-obliterating ardour of the love poems ("She'is all States, and all Princes, I,/ Nothing else is") does not correspond to the realities of Donne's married life. Or rather, it corresponds to them if at all, in no simple way. To proclaim the all-sufficiency of the woman for whom he had sacrificed his career may have been the defiant response with which Donne's imagination faced worldly disaster. And it may have been made more defiant by the realisation that she did not, after all, mean everything to him' (p. 75). In short, the love poems are fantastic concoctions; and again, either Donne does not mean what he says or – even if he is imagining a sincere and unexampled state of love – his wife is about the last person he would have in mind. Empson agreed with just part of Carey's conjecture, that the love poems may in some sense have been 'the defiant response with which Donne's imagination faced worldly disaster' (p. 75), when he wrote in 1957 that Donne 'was keenly, if sardonically, interested in the theology of the separate planet – from fairly early, though he did not come to feel he was actually planted on one till he realised the full effects of his runaway marriage'. For the rest, he was disgusted, because Carey's argument requires the critic not merely to disparage Ann Donne (on the basis of negligible evidence) as unequal to her husband's gifts – she could inspire his love, it seems, but not the poetry – but also to depict Donne as self-aggrandising, frustrated and insincere, a worldling who boasts of a fabulous love but entirely without conviction. In 1608, seven years into his recklessly passionate marriage, Donne would pen this letter:

I write from the fireside in my parler, and in the noise of three gamesome children, and by the side of her whom, because I have translated into such a wretched fortune, I must labour to disguise that from her by all honest devices, as giving her my company and discourse; therefore I steal from her all the time which I give this letter, and it is therefore that I take so short a list... But if I melt into a melancholy whilst I write, I shall be taken in the manner; and I sit by one too tender towards these impressions.[69]

Trawling for proof that Donne's 'dissatisfaction is discernible', Carey quotes only the first part of the letter and comments with stupefying bluntness (p. 74): 'Actually staying in the same room as his wife was, we gather from this, scarcely more than a benign duty.' (J. B.

Leishman felt nothing of Carey's vulgar assurance when he commented on the same passage, 'Tenderness, yes, but tenderness, one
might be tempted to think, more dutiful than spontaneous, though
just how right or how wrong one would be I cannot really decide.')[70]
Empson's gloss is altogether more humane: 'we know that [Donne]
felt compunction at having reduced Ann to such misery...[and]
what crops up in the surviving letters, repeatedly, is this honourable
sense of compunction.' In a later letter, dating from 1614, Donne
would write of his wife, 'So much company, therefore, as I am, she
shall not want; and we had not one another at so cheap a rate as that
we should ever be weary of one another'[71] – on which Empson's
comment seems plumb perfect: 'No convention made him talk like
this.' Empson believed it an urgent duty to stand up for Donne
against his denigrators.

   Presumably Carey's account of the poet and these poems took its
cue from Helen Gardner, who determined in 1965: 'I do not doubt
that there is a connexion between Donne's love for Ann More and the
appearance of this theme in his poetry... But the poems themselves,
even the most idealistic, are too far from the reality we know of for us
to speak of them as written to Ann More, or even about her.' She
continued:

It is a lover and his mistress, not a husband and wife, who prefer to be blest
'here on earth' rather than to share with others the full bliss of heaven, who

> dye and rise the same, and prove
> Mysterious by this love;

and tell the sun that his duty is done by warming them and that the bed they
lie in is his centre.[72]

There is in fact precious little evidence to sustain such a conjecture,
only her own critical desire to prove that Donne's poetry is positively
infused with Italian Neoplatonism in the early years of his marriage.
Yet the casuistical poem she cites last in that passage, 'The Sun
Rising' – which includes the staggering assertion 'She'is all States,
and all Princes I,/ Nothing else is;/ Princes doe but play us...' – can
just as well be designated as a prime example of 'inverted platonism',
which Empson boldly called 'the only bit of metaphysics in
Metaphysical Poetry'. Empson accounted for Donne's nigh-heretical
originality like this:

When Donne, presenting himself as an unsanctified lover, implies that such
couples have exactly the same right to an inherent autonomy as Christ and

his Church, so that religious language can be used to make claims for them, he has at least the air of meaning something much more direct and startling. All he has done, you may protest, is compare love to religion, a trope which could not have the faintest novelty; it is probably as old as mankind and anyway had obvious sources in Plato and the Troubadours. But he somehow manages to put the equation the other way round; instead of dignifying the individual by comparison to the public institution, he treats the institution as only a pallid imitation of the individual.

Judging by what she falsely calls 'objective criteria' – (i) 'the kind of relation between a man and a woman that they assume'; and (ii) 'metrical form' – Helen Gardner groups all the poems I have discussed in the years of the poet's married life.[73] They must have been written, she believes, at a time when Donne really got cracking on 'recondite reading', that is between 1602 and 1614 (to which Empson responded acutely, 'what does she think the earlier Donne was busy at?'). Her tendentious and crypto-biographical classification thus licenses Carey's biographical aspersions. (Although Carey apparently jibs at her speculative specifics when he says of the *Songs and Sonnets* that 'there is not a single poem to which a precise date, about which all scholars agree, can be given', his inferences otherwise follow her scheme.)[74] If those poems were indeed written after his marriage, and yet none of them to his wife, and if no adultery took place, they must be 'the product of an intense life of fantasy,' as Empson put it. Being convinced that to force such a shape on Donne's career simply invited critics to attribute base attitudes to Donne the man – they make him 'sulk and insult his wife' – Empson riposted: 'Professor Gardner does not realise what a strain it would be to elaborate and write up a series of hallucinatory erotic day-dreams, unsupported by any theory or framework, and entirely without self-approval.' For that generous reason at least, if for no other, he believed, 'about a dozen of the poems in her "Songs and Sonnets II" ought to be put back into "I", the group written before marriage, to avoid maligning the poet and allow an intelligible development of his character'.

However, saving Donne from a displeasing appearance as a husband can not be accomplished if the chronological parameters tell against it; and this brings back into blurry focus the question of the theology of plural worlds. If Donne was innocent of any extra-marital love-affair and yet did not write in homage to his wife, is it possible some of the poems that apotheosise love – specifically those that exploit the defiantly 'pastoral' device of linking 'the trope based on the Logos' with 'the metaphor of the separate planet' – were written before his marriage in January 1601, perhaps even in the 1590s? Predictably, John Carey, citing selective evidence, scoffs at the notion that Copernican astronomy may have spoken to the poet in any special way. Donne was indifferent to the truth or otherwise of the new theories: 'He wanted to feel free to entertain or dismiss them, and to play them off against his existing patterns of thought, as mood or occasion prompted... Ideas to him were plastic... Given human-kind's imperfect faculties, all science was, on his reckoning, science fiction anyway, and he used it as a bargain basement' (pp. 249–50). Likewise Frank Kermode: 'It would be very unlike [Donne] to be much affected by the new philosophy.'[75] Helen Gardner, in designing her edition of the *Songs and Sonnets*, admitted that she chose to stress 'literary' rather than 'philosophical and theological sources' – so wilfully marginalising the metaphysics.[76] But what was the state of play of scientific discovery during Donne's early life? How deep did his knowledge run? And might he have speculated while the astronomers still searched?

Copernicus, of course, could not prove anything. He put forward a mathematical theory which just happened to crab the Aristotelian metaphysical system that had long been assimilated to Christian ecclesiasticism; he was certainly no heretic. *De Revolutionibus Orbium Coelestium* (1543) did not deeply disturb the churchmen. As for empirical science: in 1572, when Donne was born, the Danish astronomer Tycho Brahe observed a 'new star' (it was visible in England too), a miracle which bid fair to undermine the shapely old order of immutable heavenly bodies, though it fizzled out of sight within two years (as he predicted it would); but then his pupil Johannes Kepler discovered two more new stars, in 1602 and 1604 (also visible in England), as he reported in detail in *De Stella Nova* (1606) – a copy of which he sent to James I (who showed a keen interest in the heavens and later invited Kepler to become Astronomer Royal) – as well as the elliptical movement of the planets (*De Motibus Stellae Martis*, 1609); and Galileo trumped the field with the discoveries he published in *Sidereus Nuncius* in 1610. Just as soon as Galileo's work appeared, Sir Henry Wotton, Donne's close friend and correspondent, despatched a copy to King James; he may even have sent another copy post-haste to Donne, who instantly made use

of it – first in *Conclave Ignati* (*Ignatius his Conclave*), which was entered
in the Stationer's Register on 24 January 1611, and then in *An
Anatomie of the World*. Among other amazing matters, Galileo had
located a number of new stars; he knew what the Milky Way was all
about; and he had seen by means of his 'cannons' that the physical
characteristics of the moon, with its astounding asperities that
disproved the long-unquestioned idea of the perfection of the
quintessence of extra-terrestrial matter, looked not unlike those of the
earth: it had turned out, as Carey choicely puts it, to be 'knobbly'
– or, as Sir William Lower described to Thomas Harriot what he had
seen through his 'perspective Cylinder' in the winter of 1610, 'like a
tarte that my Cooke made me the last Weeke – here a vaine of bright
stuff, and there of darke, and so confusedlie all over'.[77]

Students of Donne know full well that he kept abreast of the
writings of Kepler and Galileo. His eager interest in astronomy is
evident, for example, in *Biathanatos* (possibly written by 1612, though
not published till 1648), where he engrosses *De Stella Nova* so as to
sneeze at 'Aristotles followers' – those 'Schollers [who] stubbornly
maintain his Proposition still, though by many experiences of new
Stars, the reason which moved Aristotle seems now to be utterly
defeated'. References to cosmological transformation occur frequently in his works of this time – *circa* 1610–14 – most notably
including the stellar journey of Elizabeth Drury who 'baits not at the
Moone, nor cares to trie/ Whether in that new world, men live, and
die' ('The Second Anniversarie', ll. 195–6); as well as in the satirical
Ignatius his Conclave, where it is proposed that Loyola should be sent to
found a *Lunatique Church* in the moon (Kepler quite seriously believed
that the moon might be inhabitable): Donne's tract is replete with
the very latest astronomical learning. In sum, no one can possibly
doubt that Donne was up with the stars and star-gazers.

In the 1930s, however, several scholars rehearsed the evidence of
Donne's attention to the new philosophy; unfortunately for the
purposes of Empson's thesis, the consensus of their findings goes to
show that Donne seemed more depressed then exhilarated by the
'new astronomy', that he writhed back and forth between Aristotle
and Copernicus, and that he was disturbed above all by the 'Decay
of Nature' (as in 'The First Anniversarie'). Marjorie Nicolson, in
'The "New Astronomy" and English Literary Imagination' (1935),
finds that the *Songs and Sonnets*, 'the majority of which critics agree
were written before the turn of the century, contain no astronomical

figures of speech, no reflection upon astronomical conceptions.' It was only after 1604 (Kepler), and more especially for a while after 1610 (Galileo), that Donne entertained what Nicolson styles 'cosmic reflection' – and then in a state of despondency followed by resistance and rejection. He was excited to learn about the brave new world and brilliant new heavens, but loth to assent to their philosophical implications. The novelty of the new astronomy became for him merely 'another source for figures of speech, another vehicle for his restless imagination'. Empson took heart from this passage in her essay:

The idea of a plurality of worlds, which Donne had suggested in his earlier poetry, was indeed for a churchman a dangerous tenet, even, as it came to be called, the 'new heresy'. The condemnation of [Giordano] Bruno had listed that belief as one of the chief charges brought against him; and many orthodox Protestants, as well as Catholics, felt that such a conception struck at the roots of the Christian idea of Christ, who died to save *this* world.[78]

Empson seems to have presumed that the phrase 'which Donne had suggested in his earlier poetry' referred to the love-lyrics of the 1590s, but he had hopefully misread the context of the words; in fact, what Nicolson stresses is that Donne caught up the idea of plural worlds only in the period between 1604 and 1614. Ironically, if Empson had realised his misapprehension, he might have found comfort in a comment by Helen Gardner in her letter of 19 October 1956: 'Prof. Nicolson's arguments from the text are ludicrous. She has no notion of the textual problems of Donne's poems.' (Empson Papers). Indeed, Professor Nicolson does rather facilely advise that we should read the poetry 'thoughtfully, with due attention to chronology', even though we have almost no idea whatever of the chronological orders of the *Songs and Sonnets*.[79]

   Dr C. M. Coffin, in *John Donne and the New Philosophy* (1937), produced the most thoroughgoing study to date of Donne's interest in the new science, though it is weaker as literary criticism; and he too declares that in the poems written around the time of *Ignatius his Conclave* (1610–12):

Donne has become neither the advocate of the new nor the stubborn disciple of the old ... [W]e see the imagery springing from the doctrine of the moving earth intermingled with figures of the fixed center and the spheres of Ptolemy ... With the exception of the two *Anniversaries* these poems cannot be said in any way to be directly concerned with the problems raised by the new philosophy. They disclose an appreciation of the Copernican doctrine enriched by the facile contrast it receives in the presence of allusions to the old.[80]

Perhaps the most that can be said, he concludes, is that 'Donne's studies of the discoveries made by Galileo's glass' provided 'an effective means for the adornment of compliment and tribute'[81] – very much as Frank Kermode would have it. All the same, C. M. Coffin puts forward at least one important counter-argument against those who underrate Donne's respect for astronomical science. Kermode suggests that Donne 'jeers' when he brings up the new discoveries in *Ignatius*, citing the passage which introduces the name of '*Keppler*, who (as himselfe testifies of himselfe) *ever since* Tycho Braches *death hath received it into his care, that no new thing should be done in heaven without his knowledge*'.[82] Yet he stops short of quoting the next sentence, which is more sanguine than scornful: 'For by the law, *Prevention* must take place; and therefore what they have found and discovered first, I am content they speake and utter first.' In addition, Coffin's thorough analysis of Donne's pamphlet argues most persuasively that what Donne utters *in propria persona* 'concerning the new philosophy ... is expressed with tolerance, even with sympathy. At no time does he ever flatly deny its truth.'[83] When Donne drops into hell and discovers 'a certaine Mathematician', he is surprised when the figure turns out to be none other than Copernicus, since he 'had never heard ill of his life, and therefore might wonder to find him there'. Coffin identifies the key to the encounter:[84]

In the words that follow, Donne absolves the new philosophy from heresy and confesses his admiration for its doctrines, for it is a perversity ascribed to the papists rather than fate or merit that has brought Copernicus thither:

yet when I remembered, that the Papists have extended the name, and the punishment of Heresie, almost to everything, and that as yet I used *Gregories* and *Bedes* spectacles, by which one saw Origen, who deserved so well of the *Christian Church, burning in Hell*, I doubted no longer, but assured my selfe that it was Copernicus which I saw.

In the debate which follows, no one can see why Copernicus should have been consigned to hell, let alone figure as a top denizen, a rival to the infamous Ignatius – who even remarks to Copernicus, 'those opinions of yours may very well be true'. Despite John Carey's depreciative comment – 'This nonchalant acceptance of the Copernican theory contrasts strikingly with Donne's glum account, in *The*

First Anniversarie, of the universal perplexity and doubt to which it has contributed ("new Philosophy cals all in doubt"), though the two passages were written within a few months of each other'[85] – it is surely of primary significance, as Coffin shows, that in his presentation of Copernicus Donne is obviously 'deferent' to the last.[86]

In the years between 1604 and 1614, the received wisdom maintains, Donne flittered or floundered. Unable to settle for Aristotelian metaphysics *or* Neoplatonic mysticism *or* the disturbing implications of a reconstituted cosmos, his work seems torn by self-contradiction. John Carey takes the view that this situation was fortunate, for it provoked the poet's creativity: 'Renaissance scepticism was a poetic advantage to Donne... because it made all fact infinitely flexible, and so emancipated the imagination... When he writes about love his scepticism has a liberating and deepening effect.'[87] Yet both *Ignatius his Conclave* and 'The First Anniversarie' were written to meet specific occasions, to suit different peculiar audiences. 'We can select neither as Donne's "real" response' to the new science.[88] While still hoping for worldly advancement and so cultivating rich patrons, Donne had already set to work for what Carey aptly calls 'the Anglican propaganda machine'; and in due course he was virtually obliged, by King James I himself, to take Holy Orders in January 1615. It would be a wonder if he had not felt riven between Ptolemaic cosmology and the new world order. Moreover, Empson observed, it would be difficult to 'deny that he was very capable of casuistry'. Thus Empson hazards: 'Probably he had come to accept the half-way theory of Tycho Brahe, which could be said to hold the field on the existing evidence; but there was nothing definite in that to disprove life on other planets, once you had got the idea into your head.' (Tycho Brahe, who discovered the fleeting new star in 1572, was one of the most assiduous astronomers of the late sixteenth century. Though an admirer of Copernicus' hypothesis, he did not think it physically demonstrable and in 1588 published his own diagram of the universe, a spherical version of the Copernican system which retained the centrality of a stationary earth with the moon, sun and fixed stars revolving round it. His hybrid or 'half-way theory', as Empson calls, it , has been described by J. L. E. Dreyer as 'a stepping-stone from the Ptolemaic to the Copernican system.')[89] However, by the same token that we cannot know Donne's deep beliefs about the revolutionary astronomy in the period after 1604, let alone after 1610 – when he was on the brink of middle age and presently had to pummel himself into the mould of Anglican respectability – it is impossible to disprove Empson's argument that he could have taken the idea of plural worlds into his head at a much earlier stage, even during the 1590s. Those critics who have investigated Donne's concern with the 'new Philosophy, that denies a settlednesse... but makes the Earth to move in that place, where we thought the Sunne had moved' (as he would put it in a sermon of 1626)[90] presume that he became excited and dispirited, turn and turn about, only after he got to know the evidence published by Kepler and Galileo. But that is the fallacy of literalism. It remains eminently possible that in an earlier year this notoriously sceptical poet was less shaken than stirred by the new science, and needed little more than speculation to seek to defy received religious and secular authority in a poem like 'The Good-Morrow'. Once he had made 'the obvious deduction from Copernicus', he could have 'toyed with it recklessly in his early poems'. Most likely, Empson further suggested, 'he took it seriously as a poet; and this doesn't at all mean taking it as a fancy, but concentrating on what the human consequences would be if it were true – treating it like a theologian, you might well say, though not like a scientist'.

Like minds were not far to seek. Empson's unpublished draft writings include this pertinent passage (which is expanded in the unfinished essay entitled 'Donne's Foresight'):

It is often said that Donne wrote the poems largely for an audience of clever ambitious young men of his own age, so it is relevant to consider Nicholas Hill (1570–1610), who was for a time secretary to the Earl of Oxford and had some relations with the wizard Earl of Northumberland, who sponsored Donne's marriage; Ben Jonson wrote an ugly dirty poem against him, stuffed with hatred of all original thought [epigram 134], so he must have been known to Donne. He was a Copernican and believed the planets to be inhabited, also that the soul is composed of tenuous matter, like the angels. He became a Catholic without abandoning these beliefs, and his *Philosophia Epicurea* (1601) was published in Paris; a second edition was thought worth bringing out nine years after his death. He remarked that the other planets must have day and night, like the earth, or the people on the sunny side would cook; perhaps Milton vaguely remembered this when he illogically gave day and night to Heaven. My opponents maintain that Donne took no interest in the consequences of the new astronomy till everyone else did, when Galileo reported his observations through the telescope (1609), so that his apparent earlier references to the subject are delusions; but even the earliest of them might well be inspired by Hill.[91]

Our picture of Hill has been greatly enhanced in the period since Empson's death by Hugh Trevor-Roper's essay 'Nicholas Hill, the English Atomist', which must surely rank as a minor classic of literary detection. Among other matters, Trevor-Roper establishes that Hill could not in fact have been steward of the Earl of Oxford, but that he was almost certainly patronised by the Earl of Northumberland at Syon House in the 1590s (and would thence have come into the orbit of Sir Walter Ralegh). With respect to Donne's probable prompt knowledge of heliocentric theory, and of the postulate of plural worlds, it is useful to have it confirmed that Hill wrote one other, unpublished, work – it was in line with the 'principles' of Giordano Bruno, said Robert Hues (who knew Hill) – with the tantalising title *De Infinitate et Aeternitate Mundi* (the title comes down to us by way of John Aubrey). But what Empson seems not to have known – there is a fair excuse for this particular gap in his knowledge – is that Donne indeed owned a copy of *Philosophia Epicurea* (it was Jonson's copy, which Jonson must have shoved over to him) and was fully familiar with its contents. During the period 1603–11, and probably in the earlier years of that period, Donne penned a little satirical work in Latin entitled *Catalogus Librorum Aulicorum*, a Rabelaisian *jeu d'esprit* apeing real authors by attributing to them the titles of mock works.[92] '"The first book in the list"', as Trevor-Roper notes, is '"How to distinguish sex and hermaphroditism in atoms"', by Nicholas Hill, Englishman, together with a companion work by the same author on the anatomy and midwifery of such atoms.' However, while Trevor-Roper infers from Donne's jest, and from Jonson's contempt, 'that, for over thirty years after its publication, the work of Nicholas Hill was apparently unnoticed in England except in the ribald conversation of poets in the Mermaid Tavern',[93] equally it might be argued that even as Donne took the mickey out of Hill he took good note of his 509 obscure propositions on the infinite universe and its plural worlds. Nonetheless, *pace* Trevor-Roper, Hill may have been 'the only known English disciple of the great Italian heretic' Bruno, but he was not 'the first Englishman to advance the theory of a plurality of worlds':[94] that distinction belongs to Thomas Digges. We will need to come back to Hill, and Bruno, and Digges.

Furthermore, in the next paragraph of his draft essay, Empson touched upon another work that could have been a major source of inspiration for the young Donne – if only a manuscript copy had been to hand while he was still in his twenties:

The posthumous *Man in the Moone : or a discourse of a Voyage thither by Domingo Gonsales, The Speedy Messenger*, by Francis Godwin, would have to be an important influence if it was available early enough. Godwin was born in 1562, and the *DNB* thinks he wrote this very good adventure story while a student; he took his M.A. in 1584, the year after Bruno had visited Oxford 'talking loudly', and the child Donne would arrive only a few years later. Mr Grant McColley has argued (*Modern Philology* 1937) that the story must be late; I agree that if early it must have had a few modern details added after 1601, but this would be likely to happen.

In fact, those words adumbrate a substantial, exceptionally convincing essay on *The Man in the Moone*: Empson's piece not only goes very far to demonstrate that an early draft of Godwin's spry story must have been written by the turn of the seventeenth century, it is also the outstanding analysis to date of a sadly neglected classic of science fiction.

The reason why Donne's advanced ideas would need to be disguised in the poetry is well known: in the 1590s, progressive thinkers were still subject to persecution. As John Carey reminds his readers, 'Donne was born into a terror, and formed by it.'[95]

Indeed, it seems almost beyond danger of dispute – as Empson was the first to suggest in the draft essays I have entitled 'Copernicanism and the Censor' and 'Thomas Digges His Infinite Universe' – that successive editions of an amazingly progressive work by one of the foremost English astronomers of the Elizabethan age were impaired by state censorship. In 1576 (when Donne was just four), Thomas Digges took the occasion of printing a new edition of a *Prognostication euerlastinge of righte good effecte...* (first published in 1553) by his deceased father Leonard, to append to it a treatise entitled *A Perfit Description of the Caelestiall Orbes, according to the most aunciente doctrine of the Pythagoreans, latelye reuiued by Copernicus and by Geometricall Demonstrations approued.* This seemingly unassuming quarto was the very first English work 'to advance the idea of an infinite universe as a corollary to the Copernican system';[96] and it proved to be most popular, going through at least six more editions by 1605; though it was almost unknown outside England, for it was written not in Latin but in the vernacular. A diagram Thomas Digges published with the treatise makes it patently clear that his account of the cosmos outreached the pale of the Ptolemaic system. 'This orbe of starres fixed infinitely vp extendeth hit self in altitude sphericallye,' pronounces the legend.[97] Thus the excellent question that occurred to Empson was: given that the very capable and honest young Digges was active in astronomical researches, why did he not introduce any more advanced scientific information into the later editions of his *Perfit Description*, which 'was clearly intended by Digges as a sort of stop-gap until he could publish a far more important work he was writing'?[98] Why did he never bring the work up to date? It is a signal fact that each one of the later editions – 1578, 1583 (colophon 1584), 1585, 1592, 1596 and 1605 – was printed anew in its entirety. Francis R. Johnson and Sanford V. Larkey, who rediscovered Digges' publication in the Huntington Library in 1934, make this much abundantly clear too: 'Although we know none of the details of Digges' astronomical investigations after 1573, we may be certain that he continued his work in astronomy, for we have, not only his promise to do so in the *Alae*, but also his reference in 1579 to his not yet completed 'Commentaries vpon the Reuolutions of Copernicus' and the 'late *Obseruations*' upon which that work was grounded.'[99] It was not as if he could have sneaked into his own work yet more boggling bulletins under cover of his eminent father's safe old *Prognostication euerlastinge*, even though the *Perfit Description* was not as a rule listed as a separate title. Anthony à Wood, in his *Historia et Antiquitates Universitatis Oxoniensis*, 'notes the 1592 *Prognostication* under Leonard Digges' name, adding to the entry the words, "Cui subnectitur Orbium Copernicanarum accurata descriptio."' And there are other contemporary citations which would have alerted the licensing authorities to this Trojan treatise even if they had not troubled themselves to study the copy for each new edition in the first place. Andrew Maunsell, to cite just one example, 'when he came to enter the 1592 edition of the *Prognostication euerlastinge* in his catalogue in 1595, recorded also the full title of Thomas Digges' *A Perfit Description of the Caelestiall Orbes*.'[100]

Thus Empson's suspicion that the censor must have curtailed Digges' plans for further publications in support of Copernicanism looks strongly grounded. Johnson and Larkey, albeit unwittingly (censorship does not cross their minds), lend credence to Empson's case with these remarks:

We may justly regret that Digges was forced to lay aside his astronomical studies and never completed his 'Commentaries vpon the Reuolutions of Copernicus,' for that work might very well have anticipated by a quarter of a century several of the discoveries made by Kepler and Galileo. Such high expectations for this work are not unwarranted, for Digges' book on the new star that appeared in Cassiopeia in 1572, which he published in 1573 under the title of *Alae seu Scalae Mathematicae*, was, next to Tycho Brahe's, the ablest work on the phenomenon.[101]

Colin A. Ronan, in his presidential address to the British Astronomical Association in 1991, has demonstrated beyond any reasonable doubt that the reflecting telescope, in a truly practical form, was in fact invented in England by Leonard Digges, probably sometime between 1540 and 1559. Thomas Digges, who set about to promote his father's achievement, first described the characteristics of the reflector in a work invariably known by its short title, *Pantometria*, in 1571. (This invention was presently confirmed in a report by William Bourne to Lord Burghley, *c.* 1580.) The worrying fact, however, is that Thomas Digges wrote in his *Pantometria*, 'But of these conclusions I minde not here more to intreate, having at large in a volume by it selfe opened the miraculous effects of perspective glasses', and then altogether (or so it seems) failed to deliver that more enlightening work. Like Empson, Ronan believes that the censor must have slapped an embargo on any further publication; but unlike Empson, he thinks censorship was put into operation for military reasons – the Elizabethan version of a D-notice – to stop news of an invention that could descry objects at a great distance, such as a hostile armada, from reaching the Spanish. Thus the only certain evidence to prove that Thomas ever examined the heavens through a reflecting telescope – by which he was led to the concept of an infinite universe – is the diagram published in the *Perfit Description* of 1576.[102] All the same, since the authorities did allow Digges to publish and republish his popular text, with its tell-tale diagram, Empson's argument that the censor must in fact have been wary of letting him print further observations to prove the case for Copernicanism seems to be quite as sound as Colin Ronan's argument from state security.

In any event, John Donne would assuredly have been conversant with the star-gazing work of Digges, and with the full significance of his 'Perfit Description' of an infinite universe – the diagram with its complementary prose commentary – long before Galileo shook the faith of Catholic Europe.

The fate of Giordano Bruno the Nolan (as he styled himself) must have stunned Donne. In 1600 he was burned alive by the Roman Inquisition, after being incarcerated and cross-questioned for nearly

eight years. Bruno's major offence 'seems to have been his astronomical conceptions, whether because they were not in accord with
the Scriptures, or also because they presented grave religious
consequences'; and, according to a reliable reconstruction made by
Émile Namer in 1966, the eight heretical propositions of which he
stood accused in 1599 included 'the doctrine of the infinite universe
and innumerable worlds, which opposed the idea of a creation in
time'.[103] Rejecting orthodox dogma, including the fiction of a finite
universe and an anthropocentric teleology – the notion that the
universe is ordained for humankind – Bruno the brilliant heresiarch
wrote of a world soul, a divinity both transcendent and immanent,
sensitive and intellectual. He conceived of the innumerable habitable
worlds of an infinite cosmos in terms of a kind of universal pantheism.
(The idea of inhabited other worlds actually derives from Anaximander and Democritus, and from the mystic Nicholas of Cusa.)[104]
'If then spirit, soul, life, is in all things, and to a varying extent filleth
all matter, it must assuredly be the true act and true form of all
things', Bruno wrote; and also: 'the divine essence which is all in all,
filleth all...'[105] This infinite open universe is a function of the *potenza
infinita*, the *potenza divina*.[106] However, since only a finite universe can
be believed to be created – by a God who stands behind or beyond or
above his handiwork (perhaps even paring his fingernails) – Bruno's
largely speculative vision of an infinite and intelligible system, and a
God in nature, blasphemed against Christian doctrine. (Tycho
Brahe, the true practical astronomer, disdained him with a snide
pun: 'Nullannus nullus et nihil'.)[107] 'A Brunian man', writes a
Brunian advocate, Antoinette Mann Paterson,

can no longer look up in the heavens to the heavenly father who, having
made the whole cosmos just for him, now watched over him and directed his
steps. This was very damaging to the makers of ethical standards who
received their guidance by 'direct revelation' from this good father, since
Bruno had, in effect, cut off the nonempirical source of ethical rules and
regulations by denying that heaven and earth were different places.[108]

There can be no doubt at all that Donne knew of Bruno's work and
reputation. As Empson wrote in 1966, Bruno 'was the leading
exponent of the plurality of worlds, and the eight years of his
imprisonment *incommunicado*...had recently begun when Donne
wrote "Satire II" [which W. Milgate, in the Oxford edition of the
Satires, dates 1594–5]. When the storm broke, over Galileo, Donne

had already changed sides, retreating in despair from the interplanetary spaces; but he of all men cannot have been ignorant of the
issues earlier.' Born into a Catholic family of famous ancestry, and
with close kin who were martyred, Donne grew up 'doubtful as
between all sects' and 'became an adviser to Anglican officials on
theological controversy while still uncommitted'. He would assuredly
know all about the plural worlds of an infinite universe, as Empson
believed; and indeed, 'To assume he never thought of [the
interplanetary spaces] makes his career much less coherent.' As
Empson mentioned too, Bruno visited England in 1583–5 (just before
Donne matriculated at Oxford), and was cultivated by Sir Walter
Ralegh and Sir Fulke Greville. He gained a small notoriety at Oxford
when he attempted to expound his ideas and fell into a disputation
with the dons; the débâcle was recorded with ripe prejudice by
George Abbott, a future Archbishop of Canterbury, and a fellow of
Balliol College, in *The Reasons which Doctour Hill Hath Brought, for the
Upholding of Papistry* (1604): 'he vndertooke among very many other
matters to set on foote the opinion of Copernicus, that the earth did
goe round, and the heavens did stand still; whereas in truth it was his
own head which rather did run round, & his braines did not stand
still'.[109] The episode is parodied in Robert Greene's *Friar Bacon and
Friar Bungay* (*c.* 1587). In his *Cena delle Ceneri*, published just a few
months later, Bruno got his own back, with interest (the dons were
dullards and Copernicus was right, he raged), though the scandal he
aroused with that work obliged him to seek shelter from assault.[110]
Later on, in *De gli eroici furori* (*Of Heroic Passions*), a tartly polemical
and putatively misogynistic commentary on a number of 'sonneti'
written by himself (only English ladies escaped the contempt of
Bruno's anti-Petrarchism, since he had contracted an apparently
sincere case of Elizabetholatry: 'quell' unica Diana', he lauded the
Queen), Bruno rebuked another friend, Sir Philip Sidney, for
squandering his talents in writing love-sonnets instead of applying
himself to higher devotions.[111]

Sir Walter Ralegh became the patron of a loose circle of scientists,
mathematicians and philosophers which sometime included Christopher Marlowe and the free-thinking, forthright Henry Percy, Ninth
Earl of Northumberland (1564–1632) – who chanced to marry in
1594 Dorothy Devereux, sister of Penelope, Lady Rich, the 'Stella' of
Sidney's sonnets – as well as the most accomplished English mathematician and scientist of the day, Thomas Harriot (1560–1620).

George Chapman, in his eulogistic poem *Shadow of Night* (1594), which Marlowe is quite likely to have seen in manuscript before his death in June 1593, invoked Ralegh and Harriot as 'soul-loved friends'; Northumberland he dubbed 'deep-searching'. However, in 1594 (nearly two years after Ralegh's disgrace and imprisonment), 'Sir Walter Rawleys Schoole of Atheisme', as this group of natural philosophers had been styled in a vehement religious tract by the Jesuit Robert Parsons, was investigated for heresy by an ecclesiastical commission appointed by the Privy Council; and the stigma – the suspicion that these academicians dabbled in dangerous arts – stuck hard.[112] (Parsons called Harriot a 'coniurer', the 'Master' of the school. Certainly Harriot was known to the philosopher–magician John Dee, who referred to him as 'Amici mei'.) Even if it were to be proven that Donne had no actual connection with the 'Schoole', he would surely have known of their researches through popular report. Most notably, there is little doubt that Shakespeare penned *Love's Labour's Lost* (1593–4), which Empson considered 'painfully cliquish',[113] as in part a satire on Ralegh and his associates; John Dover Wilson even argued that Harriot was the original of Holofernes, though it seems far more likely that Shakespeare's 'schoolmaster' is a composite portrait of Bruno, Harriot, Chapman, and other members of the 'schoole of night'.[114] (Ted Hughes has recently, by way of his readings in Mircea Eliade and Frances Yates, caught up with the key idea that 'the supreme inner illumination that manifests itself so fully in Shakespeare' may have been informed by the syncretic philosophy of Hermetic Occult Neoplatonism, as put about by Bruno, although the 'crucial facts seem to have disappeared, almost as if selectively eliminated'. Hughes reasonably ventures: 'Since Shakespeare's patron, Southampton, was the best friend of the Earl of Essex, who married Sidney's widow and inherited Sidney's social world, it seems more than likely that Shakespeare was familiar with the ideas of both Bruno and Dee. The aristocratic society behind *Love's Labour's Lost*...was certainly preoccupied with Occult Neoplatonism, which at that time – circa 1593 – was reaching the peak of its fashion in contemporary England.')[115]

Thomas Harriot, who may well have been impious – if not a deist, as John Aubrey's gossip would have us believe[116] – must have been a 'schoolmaster' in every sense: he was almost certainly the focal point of an informal scientific circle. From 1591 he was retained as a pensioner of the Earl of Northumberland at Syon, where he pursued his brilliant, ramifying and largely unpublished researches.[117] But suspicion bit at his heels, and during Sir Walter Ralegh's trial in 1603 he was comminated by the Lord Chief Justice as an 'atheist' and a 'devill' (Marlowe was reported to have smeared him by alleging 'that Moyses was but a Jugler, and that one Heriots, being Sir Walter Raleigh's man, can do more than he'):[118] it was a 'soul-searing experience' which seems to have crushed Harriot for several months.[119] After the Gunpowder Plot in 1605 Harriot was charged to answer to an interrogatory written out by no less a personage than James I himself.

Donne's only known contact with the 'Schoole' is curious and still unexplained. In February 1601, soon after his secret marriage to Ann (a minor of sixteen years), Northumberland acted as an intermediary with his unsuspecting and presently irate father-in-law, Sir George More.[120] Just how Donne came to be so well acquainted with the so-called 'Wizard Earl' is not known: it may be that Northumberland, a great patron of the arts, had simply volunteered to intercede in the case of an improvident and luckless poet, and that they were introduced by a third party. As secretary to Sir Thomas Egerton, Lord Keeper of the Great Seal, and with living quarters in York House, Donne had access to many notable and influential figures (possibly including Sir Francis Bacon); and in any case, he had gained his position by way of becoming fast friends with Egerton's son (also Thomas) during the Azores expedition of 1597 under Essex and Ralegh; and so it is not impossible that Ralegh himself introduced him to a wider acquaintance with minds as immoderately thirsty as his own.[121]

Another piece of evidence, published by Marjorie Nicolson in 1940, did hold out (for a brief while at least) the chance that Donne even knew Harriot himself. When devising *Conclave Ignati* in 1610, as R. C. Bald was willing to acknowledge in *John Donne: A Life* (the standard biography), Donne must have put himself in debt to

Kepler's most recent work, his *Somnium*, for even the framework of the cosmic voyage and the fiction of the moon as a habitable region. At least, Kepler himself thought so years later when he came across *Conclave Ignati* and read it. Yet the *Somnium* was not published until after Donne's death...and the problem arises of how Donne could have seen it. The most natural link between Donne and Kepler would have been the mathematician Thomas Hariot...a frequent visitor to the Tower of London, where the Earl [Northumberland] was deep in his alchemical studies and

Raleigh was busying himself with the composition of the *History of the World*... It is thus not unlikely that Donne was in touch with the two famous prisoners in the Tower during these years, and that he was also acquainted with Hariot, the trusted friend of both.[122]

If only things were quite so simple. In fact Edward Rosen, in his authoritative edition of Kepler's work, had already ruled out the chance that Donne might have seen a copy of the *Somnium* by 24 January 1611, when *Conclave Ignati* was entered in the Stationers' Register: Kepler himself recorded that it was only in 1611 that a first copy of his fictive work 'was taken from Prague' (where he was then living).[123] Notwithstanding, it is not unimaginable that Kepler had got the date wrong; after all, the text of the *Somnium*, with the addition of its innumerable notes, was not published for donkeys' years – not till 1634 – and it was none other than Kepler who surmised the influence of his own work upon *Conclave Ignati*; and anyway Kepler in 1610 may have told a friend in some detail about his conception of a space-spree, and that gossip may then have posted the plot to England. (In fact, Kepler had been in direct touch with Thomas Harriot for four years, since October 1606: who better to regale with his very latest, deliciously lunatic tale?)

However, what is more telling in Professor Nicolson's paper, 'Kepler, the *Somnium*, and John Donne', is her argument apropos the structure of *Conclave Ignati*, which is to say that even though 'Donne's first words clearly suggest that he is writing a cosmic voyage', the body of the work fails to match up to that exordium. Donne announces that he experienced an '*Extasie*' which gave him 'liberty to wander through all places, and to survey and reckon all the roomes, and all the volumes of the heavens, and to comprehend the situation, the dimensions, the nature, the people, and the policy, both of the swimming Ilands, the *Planets*, and all those which are fixed in the firmament.' Marjorie Nicolson comments, acutely, 'Surely this is a complete outline of a cosmic voyage; yet the device is entirely neglected in the work itself'; and thus she deduces that Donne must have drafted the bulk of *Ignatius* only very shortly before he came across Kepler's nifty notion, and that shortage of time or the printer alone prevented him from refashioning the entire scheme of his satire as a cosmic voyage.

Donne therefore contented himself with the mere addition of a new introduction and conclusion in which he deliberately adopted the double device of dream and cosmic voyage used by Kepler in the *Somnium*, with the result that the *Conclave of Ignatius* has continued to puzzle critics who have recognised the inconsistency of the two different forms used by Donne, but who have found no satisfactory explanation for the lack of artistic unity in the finished work... Falling into the hands of the English poet and satirist, the first modern scientific cosmic voyage, written on the continent, caught the imagination of the English poet, who at least suggested, if he did not finally produce, the first modern cosmic voyage in England.[124]

Nicolson's fetching guess would make just as much sense if Donne never actually read a copy of the *Somnium* but only got wind of it at the last minute before delivering *Conclave Ignati* to the printer. Of course it may equally well have been the case that a certain religious scruple held Donne back from recasting *Conclave Ignati* in the shape of a space story; but it must be significant – as Empson (who does not appear to have noted Nicolson's article) observed in 'Donne the Space Man' in 1957 – that Donne allows, albeit out of the mouth of Lucifer, that 'other *stars*... are also thought to be worlds'. In any event, it is still very possible that Donne was in touch with Harriot by 1610, and that he was excited by hearing of Kepler's unpublished manuscript; even the scrupulous Bald declares that Donne would have felt ardent to read the *Somnium*. Carey's case that Donne 'remained a sceptical conservative' in astronomy, and Kermode's statement that it 'would be very unlike him to be much affected by the new philosophy', both look less secure: they exaggerate Donne's superficialism. By contrast, Empson's argument that Donne at first took heartily to the idea of limitless space seems altogether more tenable.

There is no corroborative evidence to prove that Donne knew Harriot before 1610, but he certainly did know the Earl of Northumberland by 1601; moreover, as I have noted, Northumberland acted in his behalf on a highly sensitive personal mission. Thus it seems improbable to think that he was not in touch with the ideas of Ralegh's 'Schoole' – particularly those of Harriot – throughout the decade, and maybe since the 1590s. As Empson insisted, such a chronology would make his career more coherent, especially if some of the audacious love-poems actually date from the earlier period.[125] Peter J. French, in his biography of the magus John Dee (1972), had no doubt that Donne would have featured, with Dee, Harriot, Marlowe, and Ralegh, in the Syon House group that gathered around Sir Henry Percy (it is vital to note too that Dee had himself been the patron and friend, possibly even the guardian, of the first

English proponent of the heliocentric theory, the young Thomas Digges, who esteemed Dee as his 'mathematical father': if Donne did know Dee, he might have had the opportunity to enjoy a close encounter with Digges); so too, among others, R. H. Kargon (albeit in deference to Edmund Gosse) in *Atomism in England from Hariot to Newton* (1966), and Saverio Ricci in a recent analysis of Bruno and the 'Northumberland Circle'.[126] Even John Carey, in an 'Afterword 1990' to the new edition of *John Donne*, quietly acknowledges that Harriot was Donne's 'friend' (p. 272). At all events, Thomas Harriot himself was in touch with Johannes Kepler by 1606, and they went on to exchange information about the advancement of science. Kepler is known to have addressed his correspondent, in an otherwise restrained and formal letter, as 'Hariote celeberrime'.[127] Both Kepler and Harriot (who favoured the heliocentric world order) rejected the idea of an infinite cosmos, but both accepted the conception of infinitely numerous worlds, a plurality of inhabited globes or planets, within our solar system. Harriot is reported to have said, at some time before June 1610, 'that in that huge space between the stars and Saturn, there remain ever fixed infinite numbers [of stars].'[128] Kepler, likewise staying within the bounds of the Copernican scheme, strove in his *De Stella Nova* (1606) to trash the idea that there might be an immeasurable number of worlds in the 'Spheare of the starres'; but significantly, as Professor Grant McColley argued, Kepler was principally 'objecting to [the] association of the heliocentric system with the theological problem of the nature of God and the infinite inhabited systems of Bruno'.[129] All the same, Kepler and Harriot (and Tycho Brahe too) acceded to the first stage, the conception of plural inhabitable worlds.

However, the certain reason why both astronomers had to worry about the idea of an infinite cosmos is because Giordano Bruno had predicated it, and proselytised for it. No scientist could afford to ignore the conception of a cosmography which threatened to repudiate the theology of a created universe. Kepler referred in 1606 to 'infelix ille Jordanus Brunus'; and Harriot's undated papers include a pregnant citation, which was brought to notice only in 1933: 'Nolanus, de immenso et mundis.'[130] Frances Yates, writing in 1936, accepted the suggestion that this marginal jotting read 'Nolanus de immenso et mundi' and that Harriot had thus confused the titles of two of Bruno's works, *De Immenso* and the Italian dialogue *De l'Infinito Universo et Mondi*. But in point of fact, as Hilary Gatti has demonstrated only of late, Harriot was specifically referring to the last of the three great Latin poems that Bruno published in Frankfurt in 1591, *De Innumerabilibus, Immenso, et Infigurabili, seu de Universo et Mundis* (usually known as *De Immenso*). This seemingly innocuous correction is radical and excitingly important, as Gatti explains, for the reason that *De Immenso*

offers us Bruno's final vision of the immense, the unbounded universe. It also contains ... the theory of the comets, which Bruno used as a fundamental argument against the immutability of the heavens; and the theory of the movement of the sun round its own axis. In some of these pages Bruno reached, through philosophical argument, intuitions which would later be developed scientifically by Galileo. It is then of the greatest interest to note that this work (and only this) is specifically mentioned by title in the writings of the Northumberland group.[131]

But Harriot not only adverted to Bruno, he also drew extensively on his work. Daniel Massa, in an article on Bruno's influence in seventeenth-century England (1977), is the first to publish this additional direct reference by Harriot (British Library Add. MSS. 6785, f. 310ᵛ): 'Interpretatio NOLANI De Motu. Elementares propositiones. T. Tempus/S. Spatium/G. Gran.' It has also been established of recent years that another document in the British Library, a treatise headed 'De infinitis progressionibus' (Add. MSS. 6782, ff. 362–74), is by Harriot; written in his own hand, it must have been put together by 1603. Massa explains the engrossing significance of those two citations, which again draw on *De Immenso* (and *De Minimo*, published the same year, 1591):

For both Hariot and Bruno, atomism is directly linked to the two infinites, minimum and maximum, in a parallel anti-Aristotelian framework. In his section 'De Infinitis' Hariot discusses the coincidence of minimum and maximum in the same manner as Bruno. Bruno had argued for an infinite universe composed of matter that could be split only to the *minimum*, the monad or atom that constitutes the basic indivisible of Hariot. Hariot adopted Bruno's views.[132]

Furthermore, Nicholas Hill, in the first edition alone of his *Philosophia Epicurea* (1601) – which (as pointed out above) Empson judged to have been a most likely influence on Donne's thoughts about superlunary life – likewise stipulated 'Nolanus' in a marginal note listing those philosophers, including Nicholas of Cusa and Copernicus, who had inspired the heliocentric theory.[133] Massa argues that *Philosophia Epicurea* is in fact saturated with none other than the self-same texts that absorbed Harriot at much the same time, Bruno's *De Immenso* and *De Minimo*. Saverio Ricci too stresses Hill's fulsome reliance on Bruno – 'tanto che la *Philosophia Epicurea* diventa di sovente una *Philosophia Nolani*'. Indeed, after citing a persuasive set of parallel passages, Ricci quite reasonably concludes that

la convergenza più significativa e diretta tra Hill e Bruno si verifica sulla questione delle dimensioni dell'universo. Hill accoglie la teorie dell'universo infinito e della pluralità dei mondi formulata nel *De Immenso* (che egli avrebbe potuto leggere nella biblioteca di Percy), la cui dimostrazione si fonda sul principio dell'effetto adeguato alla causa, vale a dire sull'idea che alla potenza infinita di Dio deve necessariamente corrispondere una creazione infinita.[134]

In reliable confirmation of such deductions, there is the evidence of Robert Hues (quondam pensioner of the Earl of Northumberland), who testified from personal knowledge that Hill 'professed himself a disciple of Jordanus Brunus'.[135] Moreover, on top of the compelling evidence of those citations, and following an early lead by Grant McColley, Ricci shows that William Gilbert (d. 1603) – author of the majestic and hugely influential study *De Magnete* (1600), which Hill also read while framing his *Philosophia Epicurea* – had likewise put himself in debt to *De Immenso* in his own final, posthumous work *De Mundo nostro Sublunari Philosophia Nova* (Amsterdam, 1651).[136] According to a scrupulous recent exponent of Gilbert's work, 'There are good reasons to think that Gilbert ... believed in the heliocentric universe.' Thus it should come as no surprise to us to learn that Gilbert in *De Mundo* appropriated from Thomas Digges' 1576 diagram of the cosmos the representation of the fixed stars in an unlimited, heliocentric universe.[137] To sum up, once we bring together all the now accredited references to *De Immenso* – by Northumberland, Harriot, Hill, and Gilbert – one can only deduce that this particular work by Bruno enjoyed an extraordinary vogue in England during the decade following its publication in 1591. If Donne edged even in the slightest degree into the Northumberland circle during the period, he could not have avoided being set to con his Bruno – and certainly before his marriage in 1601. And so maybe Donne himself did read *De Immenso* (1591) – in which Bruno had incidentally described a colourful journey to the moon – before making up his *Conclave Ignati*; and only then came to feel, just as he was about to launch it into the world, that deletion is the better part of discretion? At all events, as Arthur O. Lovejoy astutely maintained in *The Great Chain of Being* (1936), 'it is Giordano Bruno who must be regarded as the principal representative of the doctrine of the decentralized, infinite, and infinitely populous universe; for he not only preached it throughout Western Europe with the fervor of an evangelist, but also first gave a thorough statement of the grounds on which it was to gain acceptance from the general public.'[138]

Thus – even if Donne had no personal access (through Northumberland or Harriot) to the researches of Ralegh's academicians, and so to their lucubrations on other worlds – it is surely impossible that he should not have come face to face with the notorious Nolan's world-shaking views, even in the years of his green manhood. Furthermore, three of Bruno's amazing cosmological dialogues, notably including the so-called 'ultra-Copernican' *De la Causa, Principio e Uno* (*Of the Cause, the Beginning and the One*) and *De l'Infinito Universo e Mondi* (*On the infinite universe and the plurality of worlds*), though written in Italian and issued with a Venetian imprint, were in fact penned and first published in London in 1584 – not so much from fear of censorship, so Bruno later claimed, as 'because the publisher advised him that they would sell better with a foreign imprint'.[139] The young Donne must have devoured them with considerable interest.

In 1936, a year after completing *Some Versions of Pastoral*, Empson wrote a review of *A Study of Love's Labour's Lost* by Frances A. Yates, who was one of the first historians to seek to sort out the pieces of the 'School of Night'; and he ended up by identifying the ineluctable bond between Bruno's heresy and the defiance in Donne's poetry – an insight that became the central theme of the later essays:

It seems a very odd muddle that the new astronomy should be connected with pantheism; her explanation is that Pythagoras had said the earth moved (though not round the sun), and this was a convenient appeal to the ancients, so a Copernican tended to swallow him whole. But the theological point is quite definite. The final eight questions on which Bruno died rather than retract are not known, but in the recorded trial at Venice he is clearly connecting his belief in the infinity of worlds with his doubt of the divinity of Christ, and in the trial of Galileo we have the straight question – 'did Christ die for the inhabitants of other worlds?' If there are many worlds, either Christianity is intolerably unjust or Christ went to all of them; if there are many Christs there may be a bit of Christ in everybody, and you can write as Donne did about Elizabeth Drury. People seem to have agreed that it was a foolish error of the Inquisition to make a fuss about Copernicus. It might, I think, as plausibly be maintained that the Copernican view really does involve pantheism, and that the questions he unwittingly put to the church have never been answered.[140]

Arthur O. Lovejoy, writing in the same year, palely concedes that the theory of the plurality of inhabited worlds 'tended to raise difficulties' for Christian dogmatics, most especially in connexion with the

drama of the Incarnation and Redemption [which] had seemed manifestly to presuppose a single inhabited world... Were we, as Thomas Paine afterwards asked, 'to suppose that every world in the boundless creation had an Eve, an apple, a serpent, and a Redeemer?' Had the Second Person of the Trinity been incarnate on innumerable planets in turn, or was ours the only portion of the universe in which moral agents had any need of redemption?[141]

There can be little doubt that Donne comprehended the problem, for in the (grammatically defective) first paragraph of his verse letter 'To the Countesse of Huntington', beginning 'That unripe side of earth' (which was probably written by 1605), he wonders most pointedly about the peoples lately discovered in the Americas in terms of their being 'Depriv'd of that free state which they were in,/ And wanting the reward, yet beare the sinne.' Empson commented in 'Donne the Space Man': 'The main thought in the background here, or so it seems obvious to me, is the mystery of how such an arrangement, though essential to Christian dogma, can be reconciled with belief in the justice of God. Indeed it is possible that the reason why the previous lines were cut is that they expressed the same idea more alarmingly... but the passage at least proves that the theological difficulty was knocking about in his mind.' Wesley Milgate, in his edition of the Verse Letters (which came out ten years after Empson's piece), conjectured 'that the poem began with the thought that people who do not know the Countess and who live outside the range of her "influence" are like those remote, uncivilized men who live in the uncultivated ("unripe") half of the earth only now coming into our knowledge'.[142] Such a gloss, it is relevant to note, comes very close to the construction that Empson put upon 'The First Anniversarie', for it could well be the case that Donne had at first proposed ('more alarmingly') to treat the Countess of Huntington – like Elizabeth Drury, and like the lovers in the lyrics – as assuming the status of the Logos, as another model of the Christ; which would explain why Donne may have cut the opening lines of the poem, when he came to feel (as Empson put it) 'anxious to appear theologically correct'.

Lovejoy, while acknowledging that the theory of a plurality of worlds is incompatible with the doctrine of the Atonement, remarks merely, 'These difficulties were recognized at least by the early seventeenth century, but they do not appear to have been regarded by the theologians of the time as very serious'; and he proceeds to cite texts dating from 1622 and 1638 which arguably demonstrate that the church had come to terms with this momentous issue.[143] But it will not do: churchmen were assuredly angered and consternated by the new philosophy up to the time of Galileo. Clavius, the Aristotelian-Jesuit astronomer whom Helen Gardner adduces to disinfect Donne, attacked Copernicus as late as 1607. Earlier still, in *Initia Doctrinæ Physicæ* (1567), Philip Melanchthon, *Preceptor Germaniae* – 'one of the founders of the new Protestant University of Wittenberg, the university where Hamlet was lurking when his father was murdered, if you remember', noted Empson[144] – indicted the infinity–plurality doctrine. Grant McColley paraphrases what he calls Melanchthon's 'most vital argument':

there is but one Son of God, our Lord Jesus Christ, who was sent into the world, was dead, and was resurrected. He did not appear in other worlds, nor was He dead and resurrected there. Nor is it to be thought that if there are many worlds, something not to be imagined, that Christ was often dead and resurrected. Nor should it be considered that in any other world, without the sacrifice of the Son of God, men could be brought to eternal life. As Melanchthon reasons, to accept a plurality of worlds is to deny or to make a travesty of the Atonement.[145]

In sum, given Donne's up-to-the-minute fascination with the emerging new astronomy, and his known predisposition to affront authority, it is far from impossible to believe that he took advantage in his poetry of the potent philosophical implications of the Copernican revolution – not only to snub church and state, but to aver the autogeny and supreme value of human love – as when proclaiming in 'The Good-Morrow' that the lovers are 'two better hemispheares' and imperishable. That poem says that 'worlds on worlds *have showne*', which might suggest that it could not have been written before Galileo's *Sidereus Nuncius* had actually disclosed a welter of new stars; but the measure of its implied heresy may be reckoned retrospectively from a sermon Donne gave on 26 April 1625: 'The fulnesse, the compasse, the two *Hemispheres* of Heaven, are often designed to us, in these two names, *Joy* and *Glory*: if the *Crosse* of Christ, the *Death* of Christ, present us both these, how neare doth it bring, how fully doth it deliver Heaven it self to us in this life?' Critics often cite Donne the divine to prove that he always pooh-poohed the problems of the new philosophy, just as Helen Gardner did when she quoted to Empson this extract from *Fifty Sermons* (1649): 'There are an infinite number of stars more than we can distinguish, and so, by God's Grace, there may be an infinite number of souls saved, more than those of whose salvation we discern the ways and means.'[146] And yet that late passage is still allowing the conception of plural worlds, and admitting that God alone knows how He will save those to whom the Gospel has never been preached. As Empson commented in an unpublished draft letter, 'I would never impugn the desperate sincerity of Donne when becoming a parson; he had gradually induced himself, and the poems hint at it, to renounce the larger view of the world which had been his heresy.'[147] Both Marjorie Nicolson and Grant McColley cite a portion of the following passage from *Devotions upon Emergent Occasions* (written 1623):

Men that inhere upon *Nature* only, are so far from thinking, that there is scarce anything *singular* in this world, as that they will scarce thinke, that this world it selfe is *singular*, but that every *Planet*, and every *Starre*, is another *world* like this: They finde reason to conceive, not onely a *pluralitie* in every *Species* in the world, but a *pluralitie* of *worlds*; so that the abhorrers of *Solitude*, are not solitary; for *God*, and *Nature*, and *Reason* concurre against it.[148]

Nicolson thinks that the passage shows Donne playing with the idea of plural worlds, without side; McColley that he is making an adverse pronouncement. Both are plainly wrong, for the whole thrust of Donne's argument is directed against singularity and solitude and in favour of plurality – 'all *plurall things*' – even by analogy with '*God* himself' who accommodates 'a plurality of persons'. It is surely significant too that in none of the sermons in which Donne adverts to the idea of plural worlds does he disavow the discoveries of astronomical science.

'Anyone conversant with Donne's work', wrote C. M. Coffin, 'will readily appreciate how consistently his revolutionary temperament is implied and how frequently specific statement of his unorthodoxy is made... Perhaps it is most easily sensed in *Songs and Sonets*.'[149] So far from having to sense anything in the poetry, Empson took it as a truth universally acknowledged – at least when he was young – that the young Donne was an advanced thinker who 'held broad and enlightened views on church and state, that he was influenced by the recent great scientific discoveries, and that he used the theme of freedom in love partly as a vehicle for these ideas to show what the ideological and sociological effects of Paracelsus and Copernicus would turn out to be'. Indeed, he was genuinely amazed that he had to battle for his position in later years. But Donne was not in the least interested in actually colonising the planet Venus, a place liberated from law and dogma, Empson had to explain; any such notions would be 'pretty flimsy'. Far more central to the love-poems, he argued in the 1960s and 1970s, is the idea that

Donne and his woman are teachers in a school, or founders of a religion; they are founding the real religion of love, whereas Christianity, which had usurped that name, was busying itself with burning Christians alive [as in the case of Bruno]. I cannot believe that this line of talk was considered trivial or flippant... What has become startlingly clear in the last ten or twenty years is that the suppressed popular religion of those times was exactly like that of many young people today; California Buddhism, as one might say now, or The Wisdom of the East as people said a hundred years ago, meaning exactly the same doctrines as the Radical Reformers held in the sixteenth century, and were persecuted for. They were ignorant and poor, and they persistently said they got their opinions from Plato. They denied that Jesus was God, except so far as any man might become God if he achieved the divine vision.

Empson even tried to persuade himself that Donne's position on this crucial score ran close to that of 'the discreditable Family of Love', an enthusiastic sect founded in the 1540s by one Hendrick Niclaes ('Henry Nicholas'), a Westphalian visionary who maintained – according to the sniffy account of J. L. Mosheim (*An Ecclesiastical History*, 1806) – 'that he had a commission from heaven, to teach men that the essence of religion consisted in the feelings of *divine love*'.[150] 'Begoddedness' was the word. As Empson explained, the Family of Love believed 'that Christ was merely a state of mind...[and] that any man may become Christ, because Christ is only a condition of being, rather like an avatar of Vishnu or a reincarnation of the Buddha; just as the lady has a Real Presence in every one of her reflections upon Donne's tears – just as there could be a Martian Christ, as real as the human one'; and, one might add, just like the function of 'the trope based on the Logos' as Empson had described it in *Some Versions of Pastoral* in 1935. Mosheim bewails, 'The principles of this sect were afterwards propagated in England,

and produced no small confusion...' – until Queen Elizabeth issued a proclamation against the Familists in 1580 (James I likewise proscribed them in 1606). Nigel Smith helpfully highlights the news that the Family of Love had been an organised sect in several English cities since the 1550s, and that 'English Familists continued to exist into the early seventeenth century'; wherefore 'the idea of the Family of Love exercised a considerable hold over the popular and literary imagination for most of the century. The most famous examples are Jonson's and Middleton's inaccurate portrayals of Familism as sexually licentious but the obsession has been shown to be far more extensive.'[151] Empson did well, more than thirty years ago, to spot the likeness between the heresy of Hendrick Niclaes and Donne's progressive thought. (It is relevant to note that John Dee, whom Donne would have met in the Northumberland circle, 'may have gleaned some of his religious ideas' from the Family of Love.)[152] However, if Donne did cast about for parallels to his revolutionary sentiment, he need have looked no further than to the intuitive pronouncements of Bruno, who 'believed the *law of love* and that it sprang from God, which is the Father of All, that it was in harmony with nature, and that by love we may be transformed into something of his likeness'. A. M. Paterson has urged the idea that Bruno's idea of 'trans-identiating with all of the life of the cosmos' favourably 'reminds us of the Zen and the Buddhist and the Indian philosophies which frankly recognized the cosmic side of the human personality'[153] – a suggestion which may licence Empson's fancy that Donne might have claimed kin with the illuministic Niclaes. All the same, it is doubtful that Donne had in mind anything so programmatic as the Family of Love. 'I do not say that Donne *was* a Familist ... that would be much out of his line', Empson conceded to Frank Kermode; 'but that he and his intended readers were very well aware of these alarming people, though one might get into trouble for printing about them. I am ready to agree that all these dangerous references were jokes, or at least he would have claimed they were if accused of blasphemy; but why did the joke seem so piercing or alarming, or somehow true?'[154]

Hints of blasphemy are patently prevalent in Donne's poetry, if readers are prepared to see them. 'That love is a private religion, no less august than the public sects, was a thing he regularly argued in verse', Empson maintained. 'It was a matter of believing too much,

not of being a "sceptic"...' In particular, he argued, 'The Dream'
bodies forth a blasphemy which is altogether more piercing than the
'splendid' jest that Helen Gardner would have it; its heresy would fit
the Family of Love. After reading Empson's interpretation of this
perfectly structured poem, John Sparrow (who had edited *Devotions
upon Emergent Occasions* while still a schoolboy) wrote in 1972: 'Your
bull's eye – and Leishman is also a victim here – is *The Dream*...
where I am sure you are right.'[155]

> Dear love, for nothing lesse then thee
> Would I have broke this happy dreame,
>   It was a theame
> For reason, much too strong for phantasie,
> Therefore thou wakd'st me wisely; yet
> My Dreame thou brok'st not, but continued'st it,
> Thou art so truth, that thoughts of thee suffice,
> To make dreames truths; and fables histories;
> Enter these arms, for since thou thoughtst it best,
> Not to dreame all my dreame, let's act the rest.
>
> As lightning, or a Tapers light,
> Thine eyes, and not thy noise wak'd mee;
>   Yet I thought thee
> (For thou lovest truth) an Angell, at first sight,
> But when I saw thou sawest my heart,
> And knew'st my thoughts, beyond an Angels art,
> When thou knew'st what I dreamt, when thou knew'st when
> Excesse of joy would wake me, and cam'st then,
> I doe confesse, I could not chuse but bee
> Prophane, to thinke thee any thing but thee.
>
> Comming and staying show'd thee, thee,
> But rising makes me doubt, that now,
>   Thou art not thou.
> That love is weake, where feare's as strong as hee;
> 'Tis not all spirit, pure, and brave,
> If mixture it of *Feare, Shame, Honor*, have.
> Perchance as torches which must ready bee,
> Men light and put out, so thou deal'st with mee,
> Thou cam'st to kindle, goest to come; Then I
> Will dreame that hope againe, but else would die.

Curiously enough, although J. B. Leishman compliments the poem
as 'dramatically convincing...an absolutely consecutive and continuous piece of argument from the first line to the last', he yet
decides that the situation is probably 'all dream...purely dramatic

and imaginary' (*The Monarch of Wit*, p. 187). John Carey, stabbing a line out of context ('My Dreame thou brok'st not, but continued'st it') declares that 'waking and sleeping life are not distinguished but superimposed: girl blends into dream, dream into girl' (*John Donne*, p. 269) – which might be well said about Keats' 'The Eve of St Agnes' but is inapplicable here. The poet tells the woman directly that he broke off his dream when she woke him; none the less, since the dream was 'too strong for phantasie', it is much to the good: she will fulfil his dream, make it real, in person. After all, a love-dream that is 'too strong for phantasie' is on the brink of becoming a wet dream ('Excesse of joy would wake me'), which would be a pity. What do these critics suppose is happening between the frank aplomb at the end of the first stanza – 'Enter these arms...let's act the rest' – and line 1 of the third stanza, 'Comming and staying show'd thee, thee', where the syntax must mean that she has proved to be a phenomenon and not a figment of his imagination? The poet knows he has not been dreaming of an apparition, for he has had palpable proof of her presence. Thereafter, but only on getting up in the morning ('rising') – it has clearly been a night of stolen love, and she has left him early – he starts to doubt the evidence of his senses; but he is reassured to think she will come back at nightfall. Her absence will serve to stimulate his passion anew, which is the purpose he imputes to her; and meanwhile he will 'dreame that hope againe' (the 'happy dreame' of line 2, that he is making love with her). If she does not return, however, he 'would die' because his redoubled hopes will be laid waste. But the poem culminates in self-reproach: he begins to fear that after a night of such glorious love, such a blessing, she may not come back again; but it is an unworthy thought, a false apprehension, reflecting badly on the poet himself (he properly chides himself as 'weake', l. 24) for evincing a momentary loss of faith in her supernal qualities.

Helen Gardner places the poem in a group of four which she calls 'persuasions to a mistress to yield or arguments against honour'.[156] Since 'The Dream' is clearly not an argument against honour, this must mean that she thinks of it as a persuasion to a mistress to yield – an interpretation which flies so wide of the mark as to seem absolutely bizarre. Elsewhere she construes it as an example of the way in which Donne transforms the 'old Petrarchan theme of the love-dream... by the brilliant stroke of bringing the lady herself into the room just as the dream reaches its climax of joy; and for the

sadness of waking there is substituted disappointment in actuality
and a return to the pleasures of dreaming'. In the notes to her edition
she reiterates, 'Donne has transformed a stock Renaissance theme,
that of the dream in which the lover enjoys what his mistress denies
him waking, by treating it dramatically.'[157] *Dramatic* does duty, just
as it does for Leishman, for saying that the whole situation is anyway
imaginary, the wish-fulfilment of an erotic dream. But her reading
runs quite contrary to the words on the page: at no point does the
poet suggest either that he is disappointed with the 'actuality' of the
event or that he prefers dreaming; he has misgivings only when the
woman leaves him. Irked by Gardner's 'grossly false' account,
Empson took time to spell out the obvious: '*Comming* to his bed at just
the right time showed her to be omniscient, like God, and *staying* was
another action worthy of her divine nature; *rising* explains that while
staying she got into bed. There is no hint of disappointment so far; it
only appears when she goes away again... Rather than accept a life
of mere fantasy, he would kill himself.' Theodore Redpath takes
equal pains to note that one of the key features of Donne's originality
here – as against the old habit of oneiric self-abuse in medieval Latin
poetry and the Petrarchan tradition – is that he makes 'the girl
appear in reality just when his sexual excitement had reached a high
pitch in his dream.'[158] It is difficult to explain Gardner's reading,
which seems to scant every item of Donne's adulation of the woman
in the middle stanza, except on the basis of her aversion to the claims
the poet presents. And such seems to be the case: Gardner calls the
'climax' of that stanza a 'fine hyperbole', and we note the restrained,
reluctant epithet. Donne's overstatement is so excessive, in other
words, that she cannot believe him to be serious in dubbing the
woman divine: the poem must be a fantasy. Whatever the case, it is
worth remembering that Donne may not have titled the poem at all.

There are three textual cruces in the poem which reward an
excursion – even though the plethora of manuscript evidence is
infernally complicated, with a wealth of memorial corruption, scribal
error and 'contamination'. Furthermore, as Gardner points out, no
manuscript collection contains 'solely the *Elegies* or solely the *Songs
and Sonnets*'.[159] Thus Gardner's work involved a formidable business
of collating *variae lectiones* from twenty-eight manuscripts, which she
classified into five groups (IV is just one manuscript, the Westmore-
land, written in the hand of Donne's friend Rowland Woodward,
and includes only one of the *Songs and Sonnets*). For the purposes of

constructing a text of the *Songs and Sonnets*, and so correcting where necessary the first (posthumous) edition of 1633, she determined, only Groups I, II and III – with a little support from their friends – had real value; with the proviso that 'the Group III manuscripts are further from Donne's papers than the manuscripts of Groups I and II'. The relations of Groups I and II in particular allow for the construction of *stemmata*. She observed in conclusion: 'Since the first edition was based on the manuscripts of Groups I and II [and] since in many cases it is impossible on grounds of intrinsic merit to make any choice between the readings when Group III reads against Groups I and II ... I have retained the reading of the edition when it has the support of Groups I and II and been content to record the reading of Group III as a variant.'[160]

This amount of information may lead us readily to the first crux of 'The Dream', which figures in the couplet (ll. 7–8):

> Thou art so truth, that thoughts of thee suffice
> To make dreames truths; and fables histories

Whereas Grierson printed 'Thou art so truth', as in the first edition, Helen Gardner opts for 'so true', which is endorsed only by Group III and a medley of manuscripts from Group V which she otherwise (elsewhere) finds grossly contaminated or 'sophisticated'. Yet 'so truth' has the support of Groups I and II, so that one would expect the editor's own rule to apply. Her self-exculpation runs as follows: 'In spite of Grierson's defence of "so truth" as the more difficult reading and his quotation from Aquinas to support the interpretation that Donne is equating the lady with God who is truth itself, I find "so truth" a very forced expression and the repetition of "truth ... truth" unpleasing to the ear. Also, to impute divinity to the lady at this point is to spoil the fine audacious climax by anticipation.'[161] Theodore Redpath, in his second edition of *The Songs and Sonets*, agrees to print 'so true', adding the comment that he has 'searched in vain for a parallel use of "so" to qualify a noun'.[162] (I have put to Dr Redpath the notion that 'so' could mean 'thus' or 'accordingly' – which would require the unproblematical introduction of a full period in the previous line, or else the grammar goes awry – and he comments: 'I am tempted by the possibility that "so" could mean "in such a way". However, the possibility of catching "truth" from line 8 seems almost a probability.')[163] Empson's commentary does away with all mumbling objections: '"truth – truth" is [would be] ugly, but the slight vowel change with the plural makes *truths* all right ... *So truth* has strong support from Groups I and II, and the objection that the expression is "forced" seems merely a resistance to the thought which it expresses.'

Helen Gardner jibs again at the next crux, in line 14, where again Groups I and II agree in reading

> Yet I thought thee
> (Thou lov'st truth) but an Angell, at first sight

and she prints – this time agreeing with Grierson in retaining the reading of *1633* – '(For thou lov'st truth) an Angell'. She concedes that, by itself, the reading of Groups I and II makes 'a wittier line, the poet apologizing for having thought her merely an angel. But, taken with the following line which begins with "But", "but an Angell" is awkward; and taken with the whole stanza it makes the point too soon and spoils the fine hyperbole of the close.'[164] Redpath thinks Gardner's argument from the 'buts' a weak one; 'but an Angell', he feels, is not only more witty but intriguing.[165] The point here, as nobody can deny, is that the poet believes that the lady is only an angel until he realises that she can read his thoughts (l. 16), which is a gift reserved only to God (*apud* Aquinas, angels are not mind-readers). Empson finds the *1633*-Grierson–Gardner line 'a pointless variant', for the sure-footed reason that Donne is driving an argument through the poem: an argument which Dame Helen either mistakes or misrepresents.

But the third crux is surely decisive, since it locks the logic tight. In lines 19–20 Helen Gardner prints

> I doe confesse, it could not chuse but bee
> Prophane, to thinke thee anything but thee.

Her version thus matches neither *1633*, which provides 'I must confesse', nor the manuscripts of I, II and III – most of which read 'prophaness'. She is prepared to be inconsistent (as a textual editor) in rejecting 'prophaness' – 'in spite of its high manuscript authority' – she explains, because she cannot believe that Donne wrote such 'a hopelessly unmetrical line'.[166] (Both J. C. Maxwell and F. W. Bateson, it should be said, saw no reason to deny the line on grounds of prosody; nor does Redpath.)[167] At all events, the reading of *1633* is agreed to be eclectic by most specialist critics; and some sort of bowdlerisation of Donne's original looks to be very evident. As Dr

Redpath gratifyingly explains, two distinct readings therefore seem to have been current before *1633*.[168] One is supported by Groups I and II and some other manuscripts:

> I doe confesse, it could not chuse but be
> Prophanesse, to think thee any thing but thee.

The other has a mixed bag of supporters, mostly from the ranks of Group V:

> I doe confesse, I could not chuse but be
> Prophane, to think thee any thing but thee.

Dame Helen glosses her mutated version of the lines in this fashion: 'Like the Deity she [the lady] cannot be defined or described: she is only she.' '*Like* the Deity', not '*As* the Deity': the clear inference to be drawn is that Dame Helen prefers to soften the brunt of the blasphemy. Donne is allowed to liken the lady to God only in terms of her being incomparable and ineffable. To think that she is really God, or even better than God, would be profane: Donne is thus given to confess that it would profane God to believe the lady to be anything other than herself.

Yet, as Empson was the first to see, the poet has already identified the lady as God, since she shows the ability to read his mind; and therefore he must mean something more superbly nefarious at the end of the stanza, and not to signal a loss of nerve or shamefacedness. 'Donne says it would be profane to call the lady anything but herself', wrote Empson in 'Donne in the New Edition', 'and as she is plainly not the Christian God he means she is something better – the cooing repetition of *thee* makes clear that *she* would be profaned, not God ... the poem though literally blasphemous does not insinuate any active and influential heresy'; and again in 'Rescuing Donne': 'the poet apologises to the lady for mistaking her for God (as Petrarchan poets do) because he realises now that, since she is better than God, she was insulted by the comparison'. As John Sparrow said, a 'bull's-eye'.

Empson felt that, 'though it is all right to be eclectic, one should not jump from one version to another, as the Gardner text does for *profane*, within one sentence'. Mark Roberts went a good deal further, arguing in a powerful review of the Gardner text:

What is unacceptable is the attempt to have it both ways, the erection of all this 'scientific' apparatus as a cover for unregulated eclecticism, the pretence of principle when the only consistent principle is personal taste. It may be that the best way to edit Donne is to rely on one's literary judgment and select the readings that please one most. I doubt it, but this is at least a possible attitude.[169]

Empson, more indulgent on that score, limited himself to recording his distrust of Gardner's aesthetic and ideological taste: 'I think that she has arrived at a wrong belief about the poet on non-literary grounds, and that this vitiates a number of her conclusions; but, of course, she did right to form an opinion.' Moreover, he judged, 'An editor, I think, should not print a text censored by the author when under duress, or after having changed his beliefs so much as to be out of sympathy with it. The poem should appear as when geared up to its highest expressiveness and force.' Accordingly he constructed this account of what may have happened in the case of 'The Dream':

> All Group v report him saying 'I do confess, I could not choose but be/ Profane, to think thee anything but thee'; and when, in all manuscripts except the Group v ones, he is made to say '*it* could not choose.../ *Profaneness*', it is plain that the poet himself got cold feet, and inserted a useless precaution. No one else would have thought that this tiny indirection would be enough to make him safe; and therefore the Group v manuscripts must be reporting his first version.

In general, he preferred the readings of Group v; and throughout 'Donne in the new Edition' and 'Rescuing Donne' argued hectically, on occasion fancifully, that they preserved the poet's thrillingly iniquitous first locutions.

Professor Roberts, in his review of Gardner, propounds a strong case for believing that whereas Groups i and ii – the manuscripts Gardner invariably favours – both represent revised texts (dating from about 1614 and 1625 respectively), and so have less authority, 'Group iii MSS. are likely to give a somewhat tarnished, but possibly accurate, image of Donne's original version of a poem.'[170] He points out too the irony of Gardner's inconsistency: when editing the *Divine Poems* she proposed (pp. lxxvii–lxxviii) that Group iii manuscripts often preserved the readings of Donne's original versions, but then she refused to let them hold the same reliable primary status in respect of the *Songs and Sonnets*. She argued in her latter edition,

> I see no evidence for any revision in the majority of the *Songs and Sonnets*. There is no particular reason why Donne should have wished to revise them. The *Satires* and the *Divine Poems* are a different matter... A man on the verge of ordination [i.e. in 1614] might well wish to make alterations in poems

written some years before when he was a layman. There is no evidence that Donne regarded the *Elegies* and *Songs and Sonets* as poems likely to advance his career.

Yet there are obvious exceptions to that sweeping slender judgment, as she has to allow when she constructs a mish-mash of 'The Dream'. Theodore Redpath seems little impressed by Gardner's grand assertions, for – like Mark Roberts – he argued in 1983 that it is 'quite possible' that the Group III manuscripts of the *Songs and Sonnets* represent the earliest versions; in addition, 'it would seem likely that all other extant manuscript collections…derive from manuscript material outside the tradition of both Groups [I and II], and *in circulation before 1614*'.[171] His statement therefore includes the Group v manuscripts that Empson laboured to extol for their heretical boldness. Indeed, Dr Redpath's commentary on 'The Dream' goes far to vindicate Empson's acuity: 'I would guess that Professor Empson was quite possibly right in suggesting that Donne altered the lines when revising the poem, so as not to confess that he might be profane. If Professor Gardner is right in thinking that Group I MSS descend from a revised text of 1614, just before Donne's ordination, Professor Empson's suggestion would seem to have a fair degree of probability.'[172]

Furthermore, what neither Empson nor (presumably) Roberts realised when reviewing Helen Gardner's edition of the *Songs and Sonnets* – solely because she omitted to mention it in her apparatus – is that the Group v manuscripts of 'The Dream' are not alone in reading 'Prophane'. Gardner observes that the *consensus* of Groups I, II and III (which she would usually find irresistible) reads 'Prophaness', unlike *1633* which reads 'Prophane'. Most perplexingly, however, even while rejecting 'Prophaness' on the grounds that Donne could not have spoiled the 'splendid' rhythmic run of his own stanza, she adds: 'I do not doubt that "Prophane" is a correction made in the copy for *1633* and do not regard its appearance in manuscripts outside the main groups as argument for its authenticity.'[173] In other words, even here she insists upon dismissing the evidence of Group v manuscripts, which offer 'Prophane', because they are inauthentic ('the editor's apparatus refuses to admit any authority for reading *profane*,' as Empson put it); rather than heed their degeneracy, she will trust her own ear for metrical beauty – which also just happens to yield up 'Prophane'. Theodore Redpath is yet the first scholar to reveal that two Group III manuscripts,

Luttrell and O'Flaherty (*sigla*: *Lut* and *O'F*) – two out of the four manuscripts in that Group – also support Group v in reading 'Prophane'. *O'F*, which Gardner calls an 'edited' copy of *Lut*, was '*possibly corrected twice, from* Profane *to* Profanesse *and back again*,' he helpfully notes;[174] which might even allow for the possibility that its reading was first brought into line with Groups I and II, but that a shrewd scribe recognised the contamination and reinstated the author's original. Moreover, if Theodore Redpath is right in his conjecture – following Wesley Milgate's analysis of the *Satires* – that Group III manuscripts and the majority of the manuscripts in Gardner's category v (*A25, JC, D17, Cy, O, P, S,* and *K*) do represent the earliest versions of the *Songs and Sonnets*, it would seem at least possible that the same argument might apply to the *Elegies*. In addition to *Lut* and *O'F* from Group III, the following manuscripts from Group v support the reading 'Prophane' in the 'The Dream': *HK2, A25, Cy, P, B,* and *S*. Turning back to Elegy XIX, 'To His Mistress Going to Bed', we discover a teasing concurrence: the line that Empson battled to vindicate, 'There is no pennance due to innocence', is supported both by *JC, Cy, O, P, B,* and *S* from Group v and by the same separatist duo from Group III, *Lut* and its offspring *O'F*. This striking coincidence may or may not give aid to Empson's mighty argument – *vis-à-vis* 'To His Mistress Going to Bed' – against the massed ranks of Frank Kermode, John Carey, and other critics, but it might give one pause before bowing to Dame Helen's determinative decree: 'I cannot regard the variant as anything but scribal in origin.'[175]

'Why will nobody believe a word I say about Donne?' Empson asked in 1973. 'The argument about the Songs and Sonnets looks to me so clear, and it does not get refuted, only treated with silent passive depression; maybe all right as a joke against Helen Gardner is the most they will say.'[176] Christopher Ricks, who sent him words of praise for 'Rescuing Donne' in 1972, received a mild reproof in reply: 'Even you will not say it is right, or even sensible, but you allow me to be serious. The only other recipient who has answered at all is [Graham] Hough, who says it is a complete waste of time to tease the old woman, though everyone knows she is often silly.'[177] In an earlier year, before Empson began to assail Gardner's misconstructions, John Crowe Ransom accepted 'Donne the Space Man' for the *Kenyon Review* (1957) with this comment: 'I don't think

[Donne] could be magnificent without the burden of thought which you attribute to him.'[178] Just four months before Ransom's letter, it is interesting to know, Helen Gardner had written to Empson: 'I am now editing the Love Poems: Elegies and Songs and Sonnets and would that I *had* any evidence for dating them';[179] between then (15 September 1956) and the issue of her edition in 1965, she had managed to construct what one critic has called 'an absolute pyramid of speculation' about the dating and grouping of those poems, much of it based on the 'biographical inferences' she otherwise professed to find 'unsound': 'it is opinion', wrote A. L. French, 'and should be clearly recognised as opinion'.[180]

For his part, Empson had no training at all as a bibliographer, so that his critiques are normally based on deep-seated aesthetic and ideological convictions, not to say prepossessions; but at least he did not fall into the error of applying print assumptions to a poet who, unlike Ben Jonson, was fiercely jealous of his manuscripts. Like Herbert Grierson, and indeed directly because of Grierson, Empson was deeply attached to the text of *1633*, as if an authorial imprimatur lay at the back of that first edition. But whereas Grierson allowed his aesthetic judgements to get the better of bibliographical objectives, Empson did instinctively focus his attention on a manuscript mentality and try to meet the case with a likely story of manuscript transmission. However, while Empson aimed to free the poet from the dual strait-jacket of stemmata and sanctimoniousness, scoffing at Gardner's editorial methods and critical findings, another scholar has recently oppugned the idea that sensible readers must otherwise bow to Gardner's unassailable authority. In 1984, the year of Empson's death, Ted-Larry Pebworth argued that although Gardner and Milgate, in their respective editions, had been 'somewhat more accurate than Grierson', they still 'shared and even built upon their predecessor's anachronistic assumption of an authorially stabilized text.' Without even adequately showing that the old text needed to be revised in the first place, Gardner followed Grierson 'in ordering the manuscripts hierarchically according to their general agreements with the printed texts'; and yet she studied and reported far fewer manuscripts than were known to exist (in the case of *The Elegies and Songs and Sonnets*, just 43 out of more than 100 extant 'manuscript artifacts'), and her principal device was to substitute 'the Groups I and II manuscripts for the 1633 edition as preserving between them authorially set texts'. The grave fallacy of her practice of 'treating manuscripts of composite origins as if they had single origins' can be demonstrated from the case of British Library MS Lansdowne 740 (*L74*), which Gardner and Milgate feature as a member of Group II. In truth, 'the volume contains paper having eleven different watermarks and ... its contents were entered by at least twelve people over a period of more than a century. Specifically, its fifty Donne poems were copied in at least two hands on paper with four different watermarks.' All in all, Gardner's 'monolithic view' of the manuscript groups is extravagantly specious; she built penthouses onto castles in air, as Pebworth puts it:

Gardner's elaborate stemmata, supposing the existence of numerous unverified compilations, are constructed in order to account for the fact that the existing evidence does not support her conclusions. Rather than allowing the documentary evidence to dictate her theories of transmission, Gardner allows her preconceived theory of transmission to dictate the supposition of nonexistent manuscripts.

To give Gardner her due, all of her theories of textual transmission are posited merely as suppositions. But she and Milgate nevertheless work from the assumption that her theories are facts... Moreover, Gardner and Milgate, like Grierson, print only selected variants from those relatively few manuscripts consulted; and those that they do report are presented in such a cryptic, often misleading fashion that it is virtually impossible to reconstruct from them the readings of any given manuscript.

Thus Pebworth's argument totally endorses Empson's damning complaint. 'In treating the groups as monoliths, and in most cases not even reporting individual readings that deviate from the majority, Gardner and Milgate obscure what may well be telling steps in the textual histories of individual poems.'[181] It is high time to look again at Empson's critique.

Certainly, by the 1960s, Empson won a reputation for putting the cat among the pietists – most notably in *Milton's God* (1961) – but he was far from wishing simply to debunk Gardner when he fought to rescue Donne: he was fully in earnest in loathing the latterday picture of the poet and his poetry. On one point only did they agree, when Empson maintained, 'the estimate of probability turns on one's view of the interests, and the character, of the poet himself'; and Gardner: 'You may pay your money and take your choice. Neither Grierson, nor Professor Empson, nor I can claim to "prove" scientifically anything at all.'[182] Empson stated his case in 1967, when he wrote that his interpretation of John Donne had 'never been refuted, only swept out of fashion. Broadly, I think he meant what he said, and had experienced what he described. Surely, the onus of proof lies with the denier – who says that Donne never experienced mutual love, but cooked up fantasies about it, from his reading of pious and theoretical authors, while neglecting his wife.'[183] The onus of proof is still in the same court, with the advocates of a miserably domesticated Donne. Say, why did an anonymous versifier, writing soon after Donne's death, hail him as 'The late Copernicus in Poetrie'?[184]

John Haffenden

CHAPTER I

Donne and the rhetorical tradition

I can't offer any new view of Donne, that is, my opinions however
unacceptable have appeared in book form already; but I have been
reading some of the recent learned works about the Elizabethan
rhetoric teaching and its influence on the poets, and I feel something
needs to be said about them. I shall mainly be concerned with Miss
Rosemond Tuve's massive study *Elizabethan and Metaphysical Imagery*.
I also read *William Shakespeare's Small Latine and Lesse Greeke* by T. W.
Baldwin (2 vols.; Urbana, Ill.: 1944) and *Shakespeare's Use of the Arts
of Language* by Sister Miriam Joseph (comforting things to have in
bed with one while the guns fired over Peking) and such is the extent
of my erudition on the matter.

   Of course, in a broad way, these authors are quite right; the
rhetoric training did have a great effect on any poet who had been
through it, and even the assertively unlearned Shakespeare (the case
seems pretty well proved) had been through it all in his grammar
school. All the same, the new research does not seem much use in
detail. The only important Shakespeare crux I can find Mr Baldwin
trying to clear up is Hamlet's 'Fix a comma twixt our amities'. He
speaks triumphantly about this, and really does I think explain how
it came to be written; and yet the only moral seems to be that
Shakespeare's training led him for once into writing a bad line – bad
now and bad then (maybe as an attempt to make Hamlet a bit of a
university pedant it went over with the first audiences tolerably). In
general, I feel that the recent enthusiasts for the rhetoric training
don't show enough respect for the united verdict of three centuries
(with which Shakespeare concurred before his time – the main
evidence that he had the training comes from his jokes against it) that
the whole structure was footling, that 'all a rhetorician's rules / Serve
only but to name his tools.' So far as it all made the boy practise
inventing tropes it did give a sort of professional ease in handling

them, which no doubt improved both the poet and his audience. But the final use of the learned research, when Miss Tuve applies it to a man like Donne, turns out to be that he did not mean at all the kind of thing a modern critic admires him for, because Donne thought he was only applying the rules of rhetoric in a particularly vigorous and stringent manner. Of course I don't deny that some modern critics may have misread him. But it seems to me that she is cutting out one of the major themes of Donne's poems, and telling us that it was only put in by our own ignorance and self-indulgence.

The chief technical question raised by Miss Tuve, it seems to me, is how far the meanings of words in such poetry are meant to be narrowed. She sometimes goes very far, as when saying (p. 132) that in *catachresis* 'Only the prick of the point of connection is to be felt, whereas in synecdoche what is unmentioned is meant to be half-glimpsed ... [I]t is clear, when one reads whole poems rather than culled images, that the poets expect the reader to shear off irrelevant suggestions with a keenness approaching their own.' *Irrelevant* begs the previous question, which is whether the prick of more than one point may be relevant, as surely it may. Thus, in Donne's comparison of the separating lovers to the pair of compasses, she says (see p. 214), some modern readers think there is a 'self-protective irony' because compasses are low and inherently 'unimaginative' objects employed by school children; but this is a misreading; Donne does not express a 'tortured confusion'. I am rather hampered by not having read any critic who takes this view of the compasses. But surely the reality, the solidity, the usefulness, and the intellectual uses of the compasses, their reliability in a situation where native intuition cannot guess the answer unaided, are all relevant to the comparison. The series of 'pricks' from detailed points at which the comparison fits are a delightful grace, but they can be thrown aside in the last line, 'And makes me end where I begun' – the final point in drawing the circle is where the pencil began, but not also the centre, whereas Donne means he will return to his wife. What he chiefly wants to imply by the comparison is that his argument about true love is not a fanciful convention, such as he has laughed at in earlier poems, but something practical which he has proved in experience. No doubt Miss Tuve might answer that this is an *allegoria* not a *catachresis*, but it has always been considered a specially 'violent' image, and that seems to be her criterion for *catachresis*. If you can switch round the technical terms however you like I do not see how they can ever decide anything.

Earlier in the book, however, she has emphasised very strongly the wealth of possible meanings in a metaphor. In a *translation* (such as 'Another Antony / In her strong toil of grace') the figure furnishes many meanings, she says, not under the control of the poet 'except as he reins them in with the tiny threads of the co-operating words. All tropes give the reader his head in this fashion' (p. 100). Thirty pages later she has managed to jerk back the reader's head in a savage bearing-rein or martingale, obviously weakening the powers of this poor horse, and I cannot see how she has done it. Nor indeed do I know why his head was ever loose. I think it is true to say that she can never quote her rhetoricians as specifically admitting that a metaphor may have more than one point of likeness; she is reduced to claiming that the Elizabethans 'could hardly fail to know it'. The Ramists, apparently, recognised that a metaphor could have more than one logical function, but that is not the same thing. If the rhetoricians did not even say this much it seems clear that the poets had to go beyond them even to do what Miss Tuve approves.

The licence allowed to Cleopatra's 'toil of grace' is not extended to Hamlet, and here I think Miss Tuve is overplaying her hand. Many people would be prepared to read Donne in a narrower manner, but when the same argument is used on Shakespeare they will have more of a shock. There is a footnote (p. 293) about the lines:

> Or to take arms against a sea of troubles
> And by opposing end them.

If you have been properly trained in rhetoric, she says in effect, and are thereby able to pick out the logical essential in a metaphor and drop the irrelevant, you will be spared from the romantic idea of fighting the waves and also from the absurdity of thinking you could win; that is, the *sea* here is a metaphor intended to be forgotten at once, which does not affect the phrases either before or after. I do not understand why she thinks this an attractive offer. The Arden edition, which happens to be the nearest, tells me of four authorities who report that 'the Celts, Gauls, and Cimbri exhibited their intrepidity by armed combats with the sea', and says where Shakespeare could have read about them in English. (Anyway there is Xerxes as well as the northern legends.) However, it goes on, the word *sea* is anyway a stock metaphor for a battlefield, fitting *slings and arrows*, so on either count the eighteenth-century critics were wrong in wanting to emend it. Even the narrower half of this very sensible note, written by the despised Dowden, goes beyond Miss Tuve, who thinks that our only business with *sea* is ' the logical task of abstracting "vastness, recurrence of numberless units"'. No doubt few listeners in the theatre have much time for taking arms against the sea, as the speech is rattled off; but the overtone of this idea is just what is wanted. Hamlet already feels that it is hopeless to fight his situation, so the idea of a possible surprising success needs to be excluded from a phrase which otherwise sounds hopeful in a heroic manner; also he feels that to act as if fighting the waves (a traditional idea even if remote) would have a certain splendour and might therefore lead to peace – the idea of *ending* the waves of course is not absurd because it means they stop attacking you when you drown. In a case like this, surely, the ordinary reader is entitled to ask, like the Caliph in *Hassan,* for 'one reason, one small and subtle reason' *why* he must be ordered to regard this passage as so much duller than it appears. Miss Tuve is content to report the findings of taste; her phrase is 'I cannot believe that many Renaissance readers would have been troubled by...' What she is really doing, I fancy, is going back to the eighteenth-century, not the sixteenth; she is trying to give Theobald what he wanted without the embarrassment of having to emend the text.

The argument is not really different, I think, when it is applied to more strained and less good authors. For example (p. 187) 'Marston's first image below would be the opposite of efficacious if the *gulf* remained long enough to swallow up the *cormorant*':

To everlasting *Oblivion*

Thou mighty gulfe, insatiat cormorant,
Deride me not, though I seeme petulant
To fall into thy chops...

'The vaguely sensuous epithet for *gulf* allows it, too, to have *chops.*' Actually *gulf* had a regular meaning 'space into which prey is swallowed', best recalled nowadays through 'maw and gulf, / Of the ravined salt-sea shark' in *Macbeth,* but not as strained as you might think from that one use; the OED has quite flat uses like the wicked wolf who had taken many sheep into his gulf (Spenser). Miss Tuve seems to take for granted that the word means, as nowadays, 'great empty space below one, into which one might fall', but the primary English use is about the sea, though the root is cognate with 'gulp'; various uses including the modern one arise toward the end of the sixteenth century, but I should fancy 'whirlpool' or maelstrom (as more directly connected with a bay of the sea) was what Marston would take as the head meaning in this rather blank context. Anyway the idea that the word has only one meaning, most of which must be abandoned before you arrive at the cormorant, seems to me ill-informed. Nor can I see that *mighty* as an epithet for a chasm has the peculiar merit of being 'vaguely sensuous' in so high a degree as to let it have jaws; at least I suppose I can, but that would mean reading it like Victorian poetry; what Miss Tuve is doing here is just what she blames other people for. Surely the process is quite simple; the word has two senses, of which the first is non-living to mark the inhumanity of Oblivion (a whirlpool I think, but a chasm if you prefer); then the poet wants to personify this abstraction rather more, so he moves over to the sense 'gullet', and this is attached to the cormorant without any strain. The cormorant has the jaws; its gullet need have no jaws; and its own gullet is not likely to swallow it. In general, I think, what seems to us a strained metaphor in these authors was supposed to be mediated by a double meaning (replaced in 'the *sea* of troubles' by a stock metaphor). I am rather surprised that Miss Tuve never even envisages this possibility.

There is a similar puzzle when she sets out to illustrate the difference between seventeenth-century poets and modern ones. The first lines of Yeats' 'Byzantium' are quoted as a case where 'we explore irrelevances and delight in ambiguous suggestions', a thing which the reader of Donne should avoid doing.

> The *unpurged images of day* recede;
> The *Emperor's drunken soldiery* are abed;
> *Night resonance* recedes, night-walkers' song
> After great cathedral going...

The italics are Miss Tuve's, and she says that Renaissance writers

might easily have used such details, but they would not have been metaphorical; if part of an *allegoria*, either the similitudes would have had the public character of symbol, or some indication would assist the reader to enjoy clearly perceived relatedness and such suggestions as fell in therewith. (p. 127)

All this baffles me completely. Yeats has told us in 'Sailing to Byzantium' that he is going there, and explains what he expects of it; the second poem, written a few years later, describes (very properly) the disillusion of the spiritual tourist when he has arrived. The lines are simple description; part of an allegory of course, but not metaphor at all. We do not need to hunt about in Yeats' prose writings to learn what Byzantium 'meant to' him; it can hardly help meaning what it meant to Yeats. It survived the Dark Ages of Europe and maintained a splendid other-worldly art throughout them; any mystical old poet could have wanted to withdraw there from our coming troubles. But when Yeats gets there he finds an ordinary Fascist type of state, gross, brutal, and violent. The memories of what he saw there during the day in Byzantium have to fade before his vision of ghostly and eternal perfection, the thing he came there to see, can arise again in his mind. Such is the meaning of the first two lines, wonderfully compact; then 'night's resonance recedes' is a direct sensuous description of the unexpected calm of the night, and how far an echo will carry in it; well may a ghost appear. There is no question of metaphor in all this. I have to suspect that Miss Tuve simply doesn't know what the lines are about.

A good deal therefore seems to depend, in Miss Tuve's account of the Metaphysicals, on her technical term *catachresis*; they often use this figure, and in this figure it is assumed that extra meanings are cut out. I am not sure that this is her line of argument, but at least it would be a real one. The figure is said to be the same as *abusio*, is described as 'violent metaphor', and is claimed as 'What modern criticism calls the "radical" or the "dissonant" or the "conical" image' (p. 130), which do not sound identical in any case. Apparently one seventeenth-century rhetorician, [John] Hoskins, actually did say that it was 'more desperate than a metaphor'. I am quite ignorant about this, but Sister Miriam Joseph's book is obviously a careful summary of the rather confused uses of these technical terms, and her picture of *catachresis* is quite different. There are three distinct accounts of the term, listed in her index; the second specifically defines *catachresis* as 'verbs and adjectives employed in a transferred sense' (whereas ordinary metaphors are nouns); the third defines it exactly like metaphor and gives examples which are all verbs or adjectives; the first is Sister Miriam's attempt to reconcile the other two. I gather that some rhetoricians toyed with the idea of generalising the term, but that the idea itself was a thoroughly tidy and pedantic one, making a distinction about grammar, not about whether you were 'radical' or whether you had to cut out all but the prick of the point of connection. As to Hoskins, no doubt he thought it a bit 'desperate' to use a verb as a metaphor at all. As to *abusio*, Sister Miriam does not list the term, and Miss Tuve does not quote anyone actually using it as a term of praise. I suspect that they did not. Except of course as one might say 'one of the most brilliant things in the style of Henry James is his decisive use of *the vulgarism*. How *artificial*, to a truly refined reader, his use of *the vulgarism* will always appear.' This critical remark strikes me as true and yet as a silly way to talk about the style of Henry James. In any case, it is far from what we were looking for, that is, that people were *taught* to cut out all the meaning except the prick of the point from the specific trope *catachresis*.

However the only possible objection to the exercise of analysing Donne's rhetoric is that it tends to 'explain things away', and I must now try to show that that happens. As I understand her, she treats the Donne line of talk that the idealised woman is a world, or that the two happy lovers are a world, as a straightforward use of the trope *amplificatio*. That is, in effect, it is like Pope in the 'Pastorals', saying 'Where'er you walk, cool gales will fan the glade. / Trees, where you sit, will crowd into a shade.' I do not mean that the Pope lines are flat; the nostalgia of their frank untruth is almost heartbreaking; but still the thing is meant to be untrue; it is a trope. I do not think you get anywhere with Donne unless you realise that he felt something different about his repeated metaphor of the separate world; it only stood for a subtle kind of truth, a metaphysical one if you like, and in a way it pretended to be only a trope; but it stood for something so real that he could brood over it again and again. The question is one of truth, or rather truth-feelings, and Miss Tuve ought not to be eager to disagree here, because one of her main points is that seventeenth-century poets believed it was their business as poets to display general truths. But she says that the astronomical images in Donne are 'dialectical counters in a war of wits', and she has a firm footnote denying that 'what we like to think of as the peculiar character of metaphysical imagery' has among its causes 'the disturbed *Weltanschauung* which accompanied the acceptance of the Copernican world-picture' (p. 198). I agree that the poets who imitated Donne do not seem to have caught from him any of this line of interest, but in the young Donne I believe it was fundamental. I think it is obvious that his separate planet, which comes in one form or another into practically all his good poems, was connected with Copernicus; and I notice that Miss Tuve gives no reason for thinking otherwise. She merely finds it natural, as she is classifying tropes, to assume that they are all fairly similar standard objects, rather like spare parts of machinery.

She seems a little embarrassed by Jonson's remark that the 'Anniversaries' were blasphemous, and has to explain that educated readers knew they were only a standard trope. 'Jonson mistook his amplification of a universal for a description of an exception... Renaissance images of this sort... ask us to look, through particulars, at the blinding light of significances or essences' (p. 149). Donne is praised for answering that 'he described the Idea of a Woman and not as she was'.[1] and we are given other phrases such as 'imitating not the particular but the simple idea clothed in its own beauties'. But it doesn't seem likely that Jonson wouldn't know what every educated reader knew, and in any case I shouldn't have thought that it *is* part of the idea of a woman that her death is making the sun fall onto the earth, 'being weary with his reeling thus'. The only saving grace of the 'Anniversaries', granting that poor Elizabeth Drury had nothing to do with it, and that the whole thing seems in rather bad taste however much he needed the money, was that Donne really did feel things were breaking up. Blasphemy was a serious accusation, and we need not suppose that he expressed his deepest feeling in defending himself against it. I feel the two poems really are a bit blasphemous, somehow; perhaps from assuming that anybody can be treated as the Logos, perhaps from feeling that things can break up so completely not through any act of God but through a failure of the spirit of man. In any case, it seems to me that Jonson's criticism was a penetrating one, and it is tedious to be assured that they were only talking about rhetorical rules.

Owing to Donne's complete control of the rhetorical instrument, says Miss Tuve, it is particularly 'illegitimate' in his case 'to fit out his poems with overtones which diverge ambiguously from his apparent meaning and which are only to be traced in the connotations of his image-terms'. It seems to me, on the contrary, that much of the haunting quality of Donne comes from writing about a total situation, without realising quite how much of it he was getting into his language or even what all his cross-currents of feeling about it were; he broods like a thundercloud, as well as flashing like one. I have tried to show this in detail in two previous books of mine, and will give page references in case anyone cares to look them up; assuming, you understand, that this is the kind of criticism of Donne that Miss Tuve disapproves. In 'A Valediction, of weeping' (my *Ambiguity*, pp. 139–45) I think there is an idea that the lovers will be unfaithful when they are separated, an idea which adds to the extremity of grief but is much opposed to the absolutism of the kind of love which seems to be presented; and in the Holy Sonnet 'I am a little world made cunningly' (my *Pastoral*, pp. 74–8) I think the remorseful hope of atonement with God is crossed with a shrinking hunger for annihilation and escape from God. Both of them are dominated by the image of the separate planet, and the point is not so much what 'connotations' this 'image-term' *might* have to a self-indulgent reader as what connotations it actually does have in its repeated uses by Donne. At least, I hope I made this clear about the religious poem, where a definite argument is needed. In the 'Valediction' I think my approach to the poem is simply the natural one; after all it begins

> Let me powre forth
> My teares before thy face, whil'st I stay here

and the whole reason for this, unflinchingly elaborated, is that they will become 'nothing' when they are apart. The planet metaphor is not needed at the start but serves to drive home the awful isolation of the human creature; he can't be blamed if he tries to get along with what his planet provides him; once the lovers are separated they are absolutely separated. Of course, a critic must then go on to argue that other metaphors in the poem fit in with what he puts forward as its central theme, but to do this is merely to show that they 'observe decorum', in Miss Tuve's language. I am not sure whether she would consider this an adequate defence. If she objected that the emotion or attitude of the poet cannot be complex, merely because he argues so much, I think she would ignore the whole tone of his better poems:

> Till thy teares mixt with mine doe overflow
> This world, by waters sent from thee, my heaven dissolved so.

'These broken pieces of grammar which may be fitted together in so many ways are lost phrases jerked out whilst sobbing', I said in my piece about it, and no doubt that way of putting the thing underrates the control which the poet never loses, but it still seems to me more lifelike than the way Miss Tuve talks. No doubt she could turn round and say that my ignorant modernistic conception of rhetoric is a false one, and that a really well-trained Ramist would think of the conscious disorder in these cries of pain as a triumph of the true art.

I should applaud her if she said that, but I do not see that it would leave anything surviving of her attacks on the critics who have tried to strike out phrases about the metaphysical style. Of course my particular interpretations might still be wrong, but she would have lost her main line of defence.

Poor Mr Eliot, not to mention minor figures, comes in for a good deal of teasing for having said that Donne felt his thoughts, or did not suffer from the peculiar separation between intellect and emotion which arose later. It was a time when 'the intellect was at the tips of the senses' and so on. Admittedly these are literary phrases, therefore a kind of pot shot at the real point, but they seem to me good ones. As Miss Tuve spends a great many pages in claiming that the old rhetoricians firmly avoided ever making the separation in view, it seems clear that she agrees with the point Eliot was making. However, I can understand that she might not feel quite easy about saying so. What she does succeed in showing about the dear old pedants whom she praises is that they rode serenely over a number of baffling gulfs lying in the path of a writer, which later thought has been forced to examine; she can never (so far as I can see) quote them as saying anything helpful about these gulfs – they seem sensible only because they seem like children, and any actual writer then as now had to jump over the gulfs by his own muscles. One can heartily agree with her that the innocence of the rhetorical training saved it from giving false answers to the problems facing a writer; but she cannot combine this with claiming that the rhetoricians gave definite answers which the writers must have acted on.

All the same, she offers two definite points of difference between seventeenth-century poets and Romantic or modern ones; the later ones believed in Expressing their Personality and thereby Exploring the Unconscious, and you misread the early ones if you suppose these ideas present. The second is different from the first, because your personality is expected to be worth attention but you are vaguely assumed to have the same unconscious as everybody else. The reason is a practical one; if you can't explain what seems to you a good line, and still decide to print it, you are trusting that the reader has the same feelings as yourself. The two halves of the puzzle inherently go together; there would be no point in publishing lines which are *only* good because they express your (unique) personality unless the public had some (underground) means of knowing what they had expressed. The puzzle is real, but that is only to say that it had always existed; the Romantics only drew attention to it. (In the same way, if the Freudian theory is true, writers previous to Freud ought to illustrate it; the idea that it is unhistorical to suppose that Hamlet illustrates it merely takes for granted that it is not true.) I don't deny that there is a certain lack of self-consciousness about seventeenth-century writers even when they are writing about themselves, even when like George Herbert they treat the reader with a certain reserve. The reason why 'Ah, my dear God, though I am clean forgot, / Let me not love thee, if I love thee not' ['Affliction (i)', 65–6] is not fussy in spite of its baffling ambiguity is that he thought of it as an effective appeal to the heart of God (as it might have been to a loved woman – 'Give me more love or more disdain'); it is not primarily a display of his own complex state of mind to an interested reader. Cases where the difference is important are rather rare, but I should think this is one. While Miss Tuve is blaming the modern critics for ignoring the difference, it seems to me, she gets very near saying that a poet trained in rhetoric must be read only for his surface intention. These poets had also heard (if they needed to hear of it) of the ancient doctrine that a poet when inspired might say more than he knew. Her ideas about the simplicity of Donne's purpose in a love-poem sound to me hard to distinguish from the objections of Dryden, saying that Donne perplexed the minds of the fair sex when he would have been more sensibly employed in moving their passions.

In short, I think it has a steadying effect if you contrast Donne with Pope, instead of letting Miss Tuve drive home the contrast that she supposes between Donne and Yeats. Pope apparently did feel that he ought not to publish a line unless he could explain why it was good at every point. Miss Tuve in effect asks us to believe that Donne felt the same; a particularly odd idea about Donne, who took for granted that none of his good poems could be published in his lifetime at all, and was ashamed because he had to publish the 'Anniversaries'. The more usual view is that authors before and after the Dryden–Johnson period were alike in an important point of practice; they would stick to a line merely because it felt good, not necessarily because they were equipped to defend it. This must be true in the main about the Elizabethans, or Shakespeare could not have happened. The unconscious was therefore let in, though the unformulated rules about just where it could be let in were very different from the Victorian ones. In comparison with this practical matter, the question about whether you express your personality does not seem to me important. Any tolerable author knows that the way to express your personality is in the course of expressing something else, which you care about and want other people to care about. Donne obviously does express a striking personality in a pungent and concentrated manner; T. S. Eliot indeed suspected him of being too keen on it to write good sermons.[2] It is hard to believe that he was wholly unconscious of the process, merely because he had been taught rhetoric; and Miss Tuve herself insists that the rhetoricians did not get in a writer's way. However I do not feel that these questions, though they have to be recognised, are really the important ones.

The important ones seem clear if you have to lecture about him to students who find him a novelty (by the way, I get an impression that the young feel him much more remote now than the young did twenty years ago, and I wish they didn't). You get a series of assertions such as that the individual praised is the Logos of the virtues he or she typifies, he or she is the abstract idea Beauty or Virtue itself, and therefore constitutes the reality of those qualities in any person who possesses them. The lovers who are a separate planet get part of their dignity from this process, because they epitomise the actual world and are partly its Logos; this is what equips them to be a complete planet. Now first, as Miss Tuve emphasises, one has to recognise the rhetorical method; the student has to agree that it is linguistically tolerable for a poet to talk in this extraordinary way. But that is only part of the necessary fuss of exegesis; the second stage is the important one, when he has to decide 'What is the point of it? Is it silly?' I do not think it is much help, except as a kind of soother to a student, to point out like Miss Tuve that the allegory of Spenser is at bottom toying with the same fundamental ideas. The point about Donne is that he makes the absurdity of the ideas hit the reader with such force.

The contemporary Spaniards, I understand, were using these ideas as starkly as Donne, who knew Spanish and was brought up as a Catholic; he read Spanish mystics as a boy at Oxford. There seems no doubt that he learned his main rhetorical trick from Spain. (The motto on his youthful portrait is in Spanish, and Spain was still the great danger to England; it must have been rather like a modern Englishman or American displaying a motto in Russian.)[3] But the Spaniards used these tropes, in a certain sense, like Pope; they did treat them as a device of rhetoric. True about Christ, this kind of assertion could be used by a Catholic poet in a Catholic country as a well-known and supremely magnificent formula of praise, and yet not be blasphemous because it was clearly recognised as a trope. However this account is too simple; the Catholics, as the Protestants put it, worshipped saints; that is, when they used the formula about a saint not a king (or when the English Crashaw used it about a saint) there was supposed to be a queer but not at all embarrassing kind of truth in it. Contrariwise the Protestants tended to feel that man should meet God unobstructed and were not keen to use the paradoxes of godhead even on Christ himself when regarded as man. Miss Tuve I should expect is making an important point when she says that the Metaphysicals used Ramist rhetoric or logic, and that this was felt as interesting because it went with being Protestant (Ramus was a Protestant martyr). One can quite see Donne feeling that the Protestant treatment gave an extra gaiety to his defiantly Catholic but startlingly displaced trope. In any case, when his imported line of paradox first hit London, it meant something a great deal odder than it had done in Spain. I think it seemed nearly as strange as it does to a reader nowadays (and if so Miss Tuve's account is misleading). Donne too, of course, in spite of the Catholic upbringing, felt the strain of the thing, and made use of it. No doubt the trick satisfied the violence of his temperament; he really did feel that the rest of the world was dissolved by the passion of the moment. But the idea of generalising the doctrine of the Logos also fascinated him because he had a deeply sceptical and inquisitive mind, even if one that felt the drama of scepticism rather than any rational necessity for it. Miss Tuve suggests that we read these ideas back into Donne; so far from that, I think that by sticking to the surviving texts we tend rather to underrate the scepticism of the 1590s, which could not get printed. The tavern talk, it seems probable, was full of brash atheism, suggested for one thing by the repeated changes of official religion; full of what comes down to us in the accusations claiming to report the talk of Marlowe. These are not particularly 'like' Marlowe, but he probably said them as well as a lot of other people; the only point of reporting them was that they served to classify him as a well-known wicked type. It is odd to find, for instance, that the great work of Hooker, so much revered by later Anglicans, could be published only by Government influence; no publisher would take it on its merits because they knew nobody would buy it

except the Government side. The first readers of Donne in manuscript, it seems clear, were quite ready to pick up the sceptical
implications.

They were driven home by his other standard trope, indeed the
two together are required if the new idea is to be given its full force
and generality. Donne incessantly clashed the rhetorical claim that
some individual or pair of individuals was the Logos against the new
ideas of Copernicus, in the only form which made them a practical
danger to theology – the idea that there is life on other planets, to
which presumably Christ has not gone. We are often told that Galileo
was condemned merely because he made man unimportant, no
longer at the centre of the universe; this is unfair to his accusers, and
I suspect it has been a disingenuous way of avoiding the real difficulty
he raised. Man could easily be made trivial as half of the paradox that
he was also supreme. The career of Bruno makes the position clearer;
one of the main points in his condemnation was that he believed in a
plurality of worlds. If there are more worlds than one they cannot all
be under the control of one Pope; if Copernicus says that the earth
behaves like the planets we are faced with the problem of how the
inhabitants of other planets can achieve salvation. Of course your
own planet, in that age of discovery, raised the same problem very
sharply; wherever one's ship beached one found innocent islanders or
civilized Chinese or what not. But it could be said that they all might
have heard of Christ, and ought to be under the Pope; about the
inhabitants of Mars no such argument could be used. The separate
planet stood for freedom. Milton, for example, was being particularly
Protestant when he put in his epic, though he was shifty about
astronomy, lines like 'Stored in each orb perhaps with some that
live'. But he could not have gone on to discuss their relation to the
Redeemer; the problem was a real one to both sects; the point was
that it was sharper for the Catholics, since they were committed to a
single living authority as well as a single Christ, and the Protestants
tended to ride out of the difficulty (so far as they admitted it) by
treating it as one that hurt the Catholics more.

I deny, then, that Donne is simply 'using' a well-known trope, the
standard howling hyperbole of the Counter-Reformation, when he
identifies any person or pair of persons he chooses to praise with the
Logos; because he regularly throws in the idea forbidden to Catholics
of a separate planet, out of reach of the Pope, and this inherently lifts
the old trope into a new intellectual air. For one thing, on the new

planet, having got there by recognising a mystery, you can thumb your nose at the old earth and express your personality or your unconscious desires. You might even be thumbing your nose at industrious persons who can't understand what you mean because they know the rules of the rhetoricians.

CHAPTER 2

Donne the space man

Why then should witlesse man so much misweene
That nothing is, but that which he hath seene?
What if within the Moones faire shining spheare?
What if in every other starre unseene
Of other worldes he happily should heare?
He wonder would much more: yet such to some appeare.
(Proem to Book II, *The Faerie Queene*)

Present-day writers on Donne, I have recently come to realise, have
never heard of a belief about him which, twenty or thirty years ago,
I thought was being taken for granted. I can't believe I invented it;
it was part of the atmosphere in which I grew up as an undergraduate
at Cambridge. Nor, so far as I can gather, has it been refuted (though
there are two old magazine articles, regularly listed in footnotes,
which I have looked up and will discuss); I fancy the detailed
evidence for it did not get collected because that seemed unnecessary.
I myself, being concerned with verbal analysis, thought I could take
this part of Donne's mind as already known; and all the more, of
course, when I was imitating it in my own poems, which I did with
earnest conviction. The current of fashion or endeavour has now
changed its direction, and a patient effort to put the case for the older
view seems timely. The text of the poems, I think, gives strong
evidence, but perhaps only in a literary way; that is, the poetry
becomes better, both more imaginative and more coherent, if the
hints implying this opinion are allowed the weight due to a consistent
use. I must begin by trying to state the position as a whole.

Donne, then, from a fairly early age, was interested in getting to
another planet much as the kids are nowadays; he brought the idea
into practically all his best love-poems, with the sentiment which it
still carries of adventurous freedom. But it meant a lot more to him

than that; coming soon after Copernicus and Bruno, it meant not being a Christian – on one specific point only, that of denying the uniqueness of Jesus. Maybe the young Donne would have denied that this denial put him outside Christianity; as would the young Coleridge for example, who arrived at it by a different route; but they both knew they had to be cautious about expressing it. In our present trend of opinion, as I understand, to impute this belief to the young Donne will be felt to show a lack of sense of history, to involve a kind of self-indulgence, and to be a personal insult to the greater preacher. I shall be trying to meet these objections, but had better say at once that I think the belief makes one much more convinced of the sincerity of his eventual conversion, and does much to clear the various accusations which have recently been made against his character.

No reasonable man, I readily agree, would want space travel as such; because he wants to know, in any proposal for travel, whether he would go farther and fare worse. A son of my own at about the age of twelve, keen on space travel like the rest of them, saw the goat having kids and was enough impressed to say 'It's better than space travel.' It is indeed absolutely or metaphysically better, because it is coming out of the nowhere into here; and I was so pleased to see the human mind beginning its work that I felt as much impressed as he had done at seeing the birth of the kids. One does not particularly want, then, to have Donne keen on space travel unless he had a serious reason for it.

One needs first, I think, to see that the theological dilemma is real. In our time no less than in Donne's, to believe that there are rational creatures on other planets is very hard to reconcile with the belief that salvation is only through Christ; they and their descendants appear to have been excluded from salvation; by the very scheme of God, indefinitely and perhaps for ever. One might suppose, to preserve God's justice, that Christ repeats his sacrifice in all worlds (the curious phrase in two of the creeds, 'begotten before all worlds', must have acquired a certain resonance in Donne's time), but this already denies uniqueness to Jesus, and must in some thorough way qualify the identity of the man with the divine person. It becomes natural to envisage frequent partial or occasional incarnations on this earth; and I understand that the young Coleridge, though boldly, was following a tradition of Platonic theorisers:

Finally, on such a view might not Christ be the world as revealed to human knowledge – a kind of common sensorium, the idea of the whole that modifies all our thoughts? And might not numerical identity be an exclusive property of phenomena so that he who puts on the likeness of Christ becomes Christ? Hooker alludes to the idea as a well-known one in the preface to the *Ecclesiastical Policy*: 'When they of the family of love have it once in their heads that Christ doth not signify any one person, but a quality whereof many are partakers...how plainly do they imagine that the Scripture everywhere speaketh in the favour of that sect.'

The present state of scientific theory (if I may fill in the picture) almost forces us to believe in life on other planets, though the reason is different from the traditional 'Great Chain of Being' so magnificently expounded by Lovejoy. Our solar system probably has no other rational inhabitants at present (if Mars has irrigation canals the builders are probably long extinct), and probably few other stars in our galaxy have habitable planets; though I gather that recent theories have tended to increase the number, and no theorist thinks the sun likely to be the only one. But there are thousands of millions of other galaxies (if not an infinite number, which I still hope can be avoided) and that decides the probability; it makes the mind revolt at any doctrine which positively requires our earth to have the only rational inhabitants. Believers in the Great Chain thought that God would be sure to fill the universe with all possible life, whereas most theorists now regard the universe as inherently capable of producing life but only through a staggering application of the laws of probability. It is thus likely to be rare; regarding stellar and biological evolution as a continuous process, you would expect fewer stars to produce life than acorns to produce oaks. But this picture gives us even less excuse than the earlier one for regarding ourselves as unique. We may feel that there is less practical danger of meeting such creatures, but not that any theoretical problem about their existence has been removed.

The problem of God's justice to men had of course long been familiar; it seemed so agonising to Dante that he raised it in Paradise (Canto xix) saying that on earth it had long caused his mind famine; the reply seems to me only to dramatise the mystery. An Indian is already the example of a man deprived of the Redeemer. But the European maritime expansion made it hit the attention of Christians much more; the number and variety of people found to be living out of reach of the Gospel, many of them not noticeably worse than

Christians, came as a shock; especially to Protestant late-comers like the English, who were rather in the business of saying the Spaniards treated the natives very wickedly (to be fair to the Spaniards, they ran into the wickedest civilisation built on human sacrifice then surviving). To make the problem absolute, by supposing intelligent life on other planets, gave therefore a frightful cutting edge to a problem already felt as painful. The question of such life seems to get little attention till late in the seventeenth-century, either in England or France, but critics cannot merely assert that it was invisible to Donne; and on the other hand Lovejoy in *The Great Chain of Being* treats it as stale, and adduces philosophers discussing it ever since Plato, but one may suspect his philosophers were such high-flying characters that they did not much affect ordinary opinion. Also a good deal of censorship may be expected. It became almost traditional to say that Copernicanism was at first resisted because it removed Man from the centre of the universe, a blow to his pride; but the centre was considered the lowest-class place, and any debasement of Man was only half of the paradox that he was also made in the image of God. I suspect that this story was often told as a deliberate evasion of the real problem. The only space-writer I know of who has handled it is the Anglican C. S. Lewis; rather brilliantly in *Out of the Silent Planet* (1938), where we find that our Earth alone required the incarnation because it had fallen in a unique degree into the power of the Devil; but in the sequel *Voyage to Venus* (1943) we gather that all future rational creatures will have to evolve in the image of Man, throughout all galaxies, as a technical result of the Incarnation; and this feels too parochial even to be a pleasant fantasy. When we study a man in the past grappling with a problem to which we have learned the answer we find it hard to put ourselves in his position; but surely a modern Christian knows no more about this than Donne or Bruno, and has no occasion for contempt. The young Donne, to judge from his poems, believed that every planet could have its Incarnation, and believed this with delight, because it automatically liberated an independent conscience from any earthly religious authority.

The police state which uses torture to impose a doctrine was very familiar in the sixteenth-century (though this may come as a surprise to anyone who has adopted Christianity as an escape from Communism); and when we first find Donne discussing such matters, in the rightly praised 'Satire III', usually dated about 1594, when he was twenty-two or -three, the whole climax of the argument is against all popes or princes who do this wicked thing. The poem seems often to get regarded as a commonplace bit of Anglican liberalism, but it was not usual, or safe, then, and the licensers still doubted whether to publish the Satires after his death. The last two burnings alive for heresy in England were in 1611. In 1593 a group of anti-Puritan laws had been passed making any attack on the ecclesiastical settlement a criminal offense punishable by banishment or death, and a Henry Barrow had been executed for having formed a sect; also Donne's younger brother had died in jail that year for having harboured a priest.

The poem apparently is using the courage of the maritime adventurers simply to argue that we should be as brave in fighting the Devil; but, considering the emphasis at the end on how much danger the seeker of the true religion may have from earthly power, they seem somehow also to give inherent argument for freedom of conscience. The poem expects heathen philosophers to be prominent in Heaven. There is nothing about the argument from planets, but the poet was clearly in a frame of mind ready to take that up with the necessary earnestness. The first hint of playing at it, as a poetical trope, comes I think in 'Elegy XIX', usually dated a year or two later.

A reader may suspect that problems about the inhabitants of other planets had simply not occurred to anybody in the period. But one man did write about such things; it was Bruno, who was *incommunicado* under the Inquisition from 1592 till 1600, while Donne grew from say 20 to 28; he was then burned alive at Rome. We have an account of his first deposition because he was arrested at Venice, where the Inquisition was more decent in the sense of less secretive; he was pathetically confident, but he at once confessed, or rather claimed as the real subject for discussion, that he did believe in the plurality of worlds. Eight years later (or so we are told in a gossiping letter) this belief figured in the bucketful of accusations which were read out before he was burnt alive. Such was presumably why James Joyce so greatly admired The Nolan, as he esoterically called Bruno; it seems worth pointing out, now that critics are so busy explaining that Joyce was an orthodox Catholic. However, it is not claimed that Bruno invented this belief. Mr F. R. Johnson in his *Astronomical Thought in Renaissance England*, Baltimore: The Johns Hopkins Press, 1937, found that the English Thomas Digges had already in 1576, for a re-edition of his father's book on Copernicus, sponsored an infinite universe and a plurality of worlds. Bruno was staying in England from 1583 to 1585, and the Digges book was given two of its many reprints during that brief time. Maybe Digges was considered a crank (he appears as a prominent citizen in Leslie Hotson's *I, William Shakespeare*), but the book went on selling; at worst his position would be like the present one of Mr Robert Graves, whose views on mythology are not prominent in universities but are in the Penguin series. Bruno's friends, such as Sidney, were interested in the book, says Mr Johnson, and he suspects that the visit suggested the plurality of worlds to poor Bruno, who did not start the fatal process of writing about it till afterwards. There is a reason why the English should feel comparatively free here. Protestant leaders on the Continent had at once called Copernicanism absurd because it contradicted the Bible (e.g. Psalm 93: 'the world also is stablished, that it cannot be moved') but seem to have thought it too absurd to require organised persecution; whereas Rome, taking the matter slowly and seeing it as a whole, eventually decided to stamp out belief in inhabitants of worlds out of reach of the Pope. But the Church of England, being a *via media*, had neither nailed its flag to a unique authority, the Pope in Council, nor to a unique text which had to be interpreted rigidly – if one is allowed to interpret the Bible in the light of church tradition, it seems fair to interpret astronomical texts in the light of their purpose; thus the Anglicans could afford to treat the matter casually. At bottom, one would think, they too had a problem about the status of the Redeemer on other planets, but as time went on they found they were content to allow it to be more disturbing to both their opponents than to themselves. This rather accidental position probably had a decisive effect, because anything else would have made Newton impossible; but at the time it seems chiefly to have caused silence – people who were aware of the question felt both that it might be dangerous and also that it did not impose itself as one which positively ought to be raised. The Church of England has a good later record on such matters, but at the time Donne could not have known which way it would go; he might even have thought, as some critics have supposed, that the Catholics were being more liberal about it than the Protestants; but, even so, this would only give an extra twist to the gay defiance of his style.

No other poet of the time, I have to admit, betrays this excitement about the topic; not even the imitators of Donne. I quite understand that this makes scholars unwilling to recognise the topic in Donne either; indeed, anyone who has had to supervise a university thesis on 'The Literary Effects of Copernicus' in the period will have been driven to conclude he had surprisingly little. But it is intelligible that Donne should be alone here. In the first place, he would know all about it; he became an adviser to Anglican officials on theological controversy while still uncommitted – 'an independent and dis-obliged man', as he described himself to the king's favourite; and it is agreed that he read Kepler's book about a *nova* in 1606 and Galileo's about his discoveries through the telescope in 1610, as soon as they came out, which presumes that he was interested in the subject beforehand. Also, he was brought up as one of a spreading Catholic family, with martyrs, though himself doubtful as between all sects; to get himself martyred merely to please his relations would be ridiculous, but he would think it dishonourable merely to join the safer and more rewarding sect. He needed to be allowed to recognise the variety of the world, and the Anglicans were the most likely to let him do so; though it is hard to pin the matter down, as by saying that they recognised the validity of other orders, or the possibility of salvation for members of sects without orders; indeed, Donne while uncommitted might well doubt whether that church would come to recognise its own nature firmly enough. Just how much conformity was required in a secular career is a confusing question, and one which his cast of mind would make very subtle. It is from this background that he was keenly, even if sardonically, interested in the theology of the separate planet – from fairly early, though he did not come to feel he was actually planted on one till he realised the full effects of his runaway marriage. By the time he took Anglican Orders I imagine he was thankful to get back from the interplanetary spaces, which are inherently lonely and ill-provided. I don't deny that he was very capable of casuistry – his sense of honour would work in unexpected ways; but at least he had joined the only church which could admit the existence of his interplanetary spaces. To assume he never thought of them makes his career much less coherent.

Perhaps I should add a bit of biography, not to address this article only to specialists. Born in 1571 rather than 1572, Donne after spending his inheritance on seeing the world got a job as personal secretary to Sir Thomas Egerton, then Keeper of the Great Seal and eventually Lord Chancellor, but lost it in 1601 by secretly marrying the niece who was acting as hostess of the grand house. He couldn't have been certain when he did this that it would break his career, because it wouldn't have done if the father hadn't behaved foolishly; the father first insisted on having Donne sacked and then found he had better try to have him reinstated, which Egerton refused on the very English ground that the fuss about the matter had been sufficiently ridiculous already. Donne then had a long period of grizzling in poverty, gradually killing his wife by giving her a child every year (she died in 1617), but becoming famous in the right circles as an expert on theology in all known languages. King James sensibly enough refused to give him any job unless he became a parson, this being what he was obviously good at, and at last, the year before his patron Sir Robert Drury died, when the money position for his family was becoming hopeless, he consented to become one, early in 1615, and was at once recognised as an overwhelming preacher; though one whom Mr T. S. Eliot has reasonably suspected of using his personality too much.[1] These flat remarks are not at all meant to accuse him of insincerity in taking Anglican Orders, though he never denied a certain feeling of desperation about it; I am much more inclined to accept the view that he was one of the few men who constructed the intellectual platform from which later Anglicans felt able to behave moderately and well.

There was another factor which made the separate planet much less prominent, in the first impact of Donne's love-poetry upon the clever ruling-class young men who saw it in manuscript; and I must first deal with that. The hero or mistress praised by a poem was habitually treated as the incarnation of some virtue, by a tacit analogy to the universal Logos who was also a man. My reader may well attack me from the rear, and say that, though there was indeed some question of blasphemy about the earlier Donne, as we happen to hear from Ben Jonson,[2] it was nothing to do with a separate planet. Of course I agree that without this convention Donne's tricks could not have been introduced, but I maintain that he made the convention itself feel startingly different; he had a shock impact, at the time, so it is no use for a modern scholar to say that if you only learn the convention you will find the poetry quite placid. It seems to have been a matter of introducing into Protestant England the grand Counter-Reformation style of compliment which the young Donne had acquired from his reading in Spanish (the motto on the first painting of him is in Spanish);[3] the Catholics, or so the Protestants said, worshipped saints, and they somehow felt it wasn't blasphemous to treat an individual in poetry as an incarnation, whereas the

Protestants felt it was very bold – as Donne wanted them to do, though he left doubt about just how bold his full meaning was.

You might say that Donne is at bottom only using the same basic trope as Spenser; why then should poor Donne be picked out as provocatively skirting the edge of blasphemy? When Spenser [in *The Faerie Queene*, Book V] takes the character Arthegall both as the eternal principle of Justice itself and as Lord Grey, whom he praises for suppressing Ireland by sword, rack, and fire, he is treating an individual man as a kind of incarnation, on the analogy of Christ, and you might reasonably feel that the result is blasphemous. But both the abstract idea and the contemporary person are merely tied on to a character in an invented story, as extra bits of interest, and the reader may invent others if he prefers. When Donne, presenting himself as an unsanctified lover, implies that such couples have exactly the same right to an inherent autonomy as Christ and his church, so that religious language can be used to make claims for them, he has at least an air of meaning something much more direct and startling. All he has done, you may protest, is compare love to religion, a trope which could not have the faintest novelty; it is probably as old as mankind, and anyway had obvious sources in Plato and the Troubadours. But he somehow manages to put the equation the other way round; instead of dignifying the individual by comparison to the public institution, he treats the institution as only a pallid imitation of the individual. All the imaginative structures which men have built to control themselves are only derived from these simple intimate basic relations, and the apparently fantastic compliment is no more than brutal fact.

> She'is all States, and all Princes, I,
>   Nothing else is.
> Princes doe but play us; compar'd to this,
> All honor's mimique; All wealth alchimie.
>
> ('The Sunne Rising', 21–4)

He leaves out the corresponding epigram about religion, but he could not be unconscious that it was possible. To a poet who was trying to express all that, at a time when it was much too dangerous to express plainly, the metaphor of the separate planet would clearly be a technical help.[4] But it is not as necessary to Donne as the trope based on the Logos, which he is using, in one form or another, all the time.

Theologically the most reckless of Donne's poems are those in which he presents himself as a martyr to love and thereby the founder of a religion, the Christ of all future reckless lovers (it is personally inoffensive, though the self-pity is real enough, once you realise it is meant to be general – anybody can become a Christ in this way); and here he can't easily present himself as on a separate planet, because he has to be within reach of his eventual worshippers. No doubt 'The Canonization' and 'The Funeral' would seem too remote to be alarming, and even in 'The Relic' he only supposes it is in a time of 'misdevotion' that, if a gravedigger turns up

A bracelet of bright haire about the bone

(her haire and his bone), these objects will be worshipped as relics;

Thou shalt be a Mary Magdalen, and I
A something else thereby...

Still, I was glad to see that the recent edition by Mr Redpath of the *Songs and Sonets* (1956) is at last willing to envisage that 'A Jesus Christ' is what the poet ostentatiously holds back from saying.[5]. It has been objected that Jesus left no bone behind him on earth, and indeed this clearly made Donne safer; no doubt he himself would be ready with the objection if challenged. But 'a Jesus Christ' would be logically a very different entity from the one Jesus, and the point I am trying to make all along is that this kind of poetry continually uses the idea that the attributes of the Christ can be applied to others. The advocates of St John, who was presumably John Donne's patron saint, neither produce a suitable anecdote nor make the line scan. The first readers of the manuscript seem to have thought of the more obvious meaning, however much Donne denied it even to them. One would think the process must have been dangerous; at any rate it carries to the limit the convention of comparing the hero in view to Christ.

This formula, I think, clears up a slight scandal created in the great days of the Donne revival by M. Pierre Legouis (*Donne The Craftsman*, Paris: Henri Didier, 1928, pp. 61–70), which the English-speakers have tended to ignore as the view of a cynical Frenchman. He argued that 'The Extasy' is a drama of seduction; that is, we are meant to laugh at the woman who is deceived by its apparent idealism. He quoted a passage from a near-contemporary French comedy in which a similar argument has this effect, and what convinced him that Donne meant the same was that both passages introduce a spectator. In Donne he is hypothetical, but Donne insists that he would 'part far purer than he came', and ends the poem:

> Let him still marke us, he shall see
>   Small change, when we'are to bodies gone.

As to the idea that the heroine of the poem was Donne's wife, went on M. Legouis,

The mere choice of a bank of violets for the scene of this incident, not to mention the presence of a spectator, even one 'by love refined'... renders it both unlikely and undesirable that married love should be the theme of *The Extasie*. Yet one must own that Payne's supposition provides the best, and perhaps the only, way of clearing the hero from the charge of hypocrisy, by making him a considerate bridegroom.[6]

Also he tied up his parallels with Donne's background of Spanish Catholicism: 'In all these characters the influence of the worse sort of Spanish Jesuits appears very clearly.'[7] I think indeed there is no way out of this position except to realise that Donne as usual is being very challenging, and uses the indecency by ordinary standards of welcoming a spectator to drive home the fantastic character of his claim. He is making human love the reality of which the love for God is the shadow; logically then it deserves ceremony, and as the founder of a new cult he needs to train his disciples. He believes what he says about love, indeed he feels that its truth is almost recognised by poetical convention, but he is gleefully concerned to show that the belief is more startling than the convention recognises. I think this puts his intentions on a decent footing.[8]

Mr Marius Bewley in the *Kenyon Review* for Autumn 1952 gave an unpleasant picture of the Donne of the *Anniversaries* as cheating the sorrowing father who paid for them; the secret Catholic used them to express loathing for his Protestant environment.[9] Surely, if Donne had chosen to go abroad and announce himself as a Catholic, he could have had more money without such nastiness. It is more natural to suppose that he believed what he says in the poems – that the unified world-picture of Catholicism had broken up. No doubt he didn't want people to realise what his method could also imply – that any individual, such as poor Elizabeth Drury, might now be conceived as having the same claims as Christ; this is the only obvious thing Ben Jonson can have meant by calling the poems blasphemous, and Donne had to deny it, but his answer was at worst a very remote kind of cheating. The promise to write such a poem yearly for a money grant had already put him into a rather embarrassing relation with Sir Robert Drury, and his mind though tortuous was sensitive; I don't believe he was capable of cheating about it in the way Mr Bewley supposes. Apart from various references to life on other planets, the passage that everybody has quoted goes on to explain his meaning, that the unified world-view has broken up into isolated individuals (they could be 'economic men', or atoms obeying laws in the void):

> 'Tis all in peeces, all cohaerence gone;
> All just supply, and all Relation:
> Prince, Subject, Father, Sonne, are things forgot,
> For every man alone thinkes he hath got
> To be a Phoenix, and that then can bee
> None of that kinde, of which he is, but hee.
> This is the worlds condition now, and now
> She that should all parts to reunion bow,
> She that had all Magnetique force alone…
>
> ('An Anatomy of the World: The First Anniversary', 213–20)

Her father had expected her to marry King James' eldest son, whose own death was considered at the time a national disaster, and quite probably did produce the eventual Civil War. Donne therefore wasn't exactly writing about nothing for pay, as critics tend to presume. But he had become enough of a ruling class or responsible character to see the objection to a state of affairs at which his earlier poetry had simply rejoiced; there had been a time when he was very thankful to be merely an atom or a planet.

Mr M. F. Moloney, in a study from the Catholic point of view (*John Donne, His Flight from Mediaevalism*, 1944), gives a detailed argument that Donne in later life was rather irritated and suspicious at the claims of Christian mystics, and deduces that he never had any mystical experience himself. But there is another half of the religious world which believes in the Absolute rather than the personal God, and the ecstasy which Donne records in his secular love-poetry is a matter of being in contact with That. For one thing, the ideal love as he conceives it ought to be the melting of two personalities into one. The position is Asiatic rather than Christian, and no doubt he felt very unsupported in it except by the temporary exhilaration of a splendid paradox. All the same, this idea of dissolving into the godhead, rather than seeing God, continues to crop up in his religious writing after conversion. When he begins the great 'Hymne to God my God, in my sicknesse' with:

> Since I am comming to that Holy roome,
>   Where, with thy Quire of Saints for evermore,
> I shall be made thy Musique...

it seems natural to suppose that he hardly expects a personal immortality. Mr Clay Hunt (*Donne's Poetry*, 1954), whose very lively and intelligent book I am now to attack at various points, explains that the phrase

implies a specific mystical doctrine which, because of its paradoxical character, seems to have appealed particularly to Donne's speculative imagination. According to this doctrine the individual soul is absorbed after death into the joys of heaven, but at the same time it retains its identity and can contemplate those joys as a spectator. Donne refers to this concept a number of times.[10]

That seems a good case of having it both ways. I am pretty ignorant about all this, but see no reason to doubt the account given by Aldous Huxley in *The Perennial Philosophy*, that absorption into the Absolute was recurrent among Christian mystics but a good deal frowned on by the official churches. Certainly one must not think it was unheard-of except in the East; you could hardly get more of it than in the peroration of Sir Thomas Browne:

And if any have been so happy as truly to know Christian annihilation, ecstasies, exolution, liquefaction, transformation, the kiss of the spouse, gustation of God, and ingression into the divine shadow, they have already had an handsome anticipation of Heaven; the glory of the world is surely over, and the earth in ashes unto them.

That is very unlike Milton, for example, who seems to decide in *Lycidas* that God would give him a lot of praise in Heaven, as a first-class author, even for the books he hadn't written. Mr Moloney, as I understand, would limit mysticism by definition to a direct relation with a personal God; whereas the later Donne, retaining contact with his past, took the opposite idea as far as he could without falling back into heresy. Such for example must be the background of the end of Holy Sonnet IX, which a recent coolly theological critic has found paltry:

> That thou remember them, some claime as debt,
> I thinke it mercy, if thou wilt forget.

The idea does then 'fit the separate planet' and so forth. Also it fits the universalising of the idea of Christ, by making individuality less important.

Mr Hunt makes a graver accusation against Donne for the religiosity of the poems written while he was unregenerate. He says for example about 'The Canonization' (in which Donne pretends that posterity will worship him as a saint of true love):

That self-defensive poem about John Donne's renunciation of worldly values, which, as I have argued, must have derived from his inclination to feel a certain private righteousness as he brooded on the suffering which he had incurred by his marriage, is the most clearly Catholic in its imaginative pattern of all of his major love poems. (pp. 172–3)

It was particularly unpleasant of Donne to call himself a martyr, because the broad fact was that he had ratted on the family duty of becoming one. He had, says Mr Hunt, 'the disposition, in moments of depression, to imagine a martyrdom for himself, and to think of himself at those times as a Catholic at odds with the World' (p. 175). This line of thought suits those who believe he was always a secret Catholic, even when he became an Anglican parson for money. How readily one can imagine this shifty character, and with what intense disgust. Surely it is much more probable, as well as more agreeable, to expect that he didn't feel committed to either sect, and saw no reason to give either of them an excuse to burn him alive. He remarked for example of Rome, Wittenberg, and Geneva (*Letters*, p. 29): '[T]hey are all virtuall beams of one Sun, and wheresoever they find clay hearts, they harden them, and moulder them into dust'; this strikes me as more strongly felt than the balancing clause 'and they entender and mollifie waxen'. However, I agree that 1611 is remarkably late for the process to be still going on so firmly in the mind of Donne; little as he liked having to print the *Anniversaries*, I think he must have been hardened by then into feeling that the process was an imaginative convention, not a heresy; indeed, no one could seriously accuse him of believing that poor Elizabeth Drury was the Logos. His chief new cosmological opinion, as is made clear in *All Coherence Gone* by Victor Harris (Chicago: University of Chicago Press, 1949), is that the universe was decaying, an idea he had only played with before, and indeed played at refuting in his *Paradoxes*; he seems to have remained sure of it from now on. However, if I am accused as is now usual of 'undergraduate atheism' or some such phrase for raising the doubt, meaning that it is absurdly unhistorical, I must answer that there was a good deal of undergraduate atheism knocking about the London of the 1590s; as we learn from the accusations claiming to report the talk of Marlowe, which don't sound much like Marlowe but must have served to classify him as a well-known wicked type. It was a natural result of hope and verbal expansiveness after the fierce changes in the official religion, and a historian who refuses to believe in it merely because nobody dared leave any documents about it can be deceived by any police state. As to the use of Catholic imagery in 'The Canonization', its basic conceit could only be applied to the one sect which did 'worship saints', and surely its only sectarian effect is a satire on that one. Maybe even the Anglicans at the time, when these matters were much less clear-cut than we now suppose, would be liable to call it blasphemous too. If you realise that Donne was showing a good deal of perky courage, as well as a secret largeness of mind, I think this particular libel against him becomes an easy one to reject.

However, it is connected in the mind of Mr Hunt with a more general suspicion that there is something sickly about the mind of Donne. He makes a charmingly real-life approach to 'The Canonization', and tries to say what he can in favour of the poem (p. 86):

the sainthood conceit and the general identification of love with religious experience ... are intended to imply a serious philosophic statement. Donne commits himself, at least in part, to the logical implications of his central religious metaphor, and, in a sense, the analogy is actually meant as a conceptual proposition. The poem says, in effect, that, fantastic as this analogy may seem, it may contain elements of truth beneath its surface improbability.

But he has to conclude, with firm honesty, that the poem does not really come off; the last stanza is not strong enough for the basic claim (p. 87):

[E]ven in that final stanza there are still suggestions of slick cleverness in Donne's elaboration of the sainthood conceit, so that some loose ends of levity and wit-for-wit's-sake are left dangling at the end of the poem.

He doesn't say which bits, but I think he came to the right conclusion, granting to start with that he didn't realise how big the claim was meant to be. If the private religion of Donne's love has *exactly as much* claim to 'contain elements of truth beneath its surface improbability' as the official religion which it parodies, fully equipped with rack, boot, thumbscrew, and slow fire, then you can see some point in having the later congregation pray to Donne 'send us back the reality which we have lost.' There is an agreeable stirring of the Old Adam in Mr Hunt when he confronts the belief that each act of sex shortens a man's life a day, a belief, he says, that must have given Donne many uneasy moments, and he is probably right in connecting it with the quaint self-importance of a sexual pun in 'The Canonization':

> Wee dye and rise the same, and prove
> Mysterious by this love. [26–7]

Except the corn die in the ground, said St Paul rather oddly, it cannot sprout; and Mr Hunt makes some penetrating remarks (p. 85):

The mystery of the love is that the lovers are spiritualized through the bodily 'death' of sexual intercourse...The lovers are certainly destroying themselves physically. But their willingness so to mortify the flesh, Donne suggests, stands as evidence of their essential contempt for all material things.

That is, the quaint medical theory gives a moral weight. But surely, Mr Hunt has himself inserted the thought about 'spiritualizing'; Donne merely says that they rise 'the same'. Other reflections could be made about the familiar mysteries of renewal and regeneration; there was presumably a rich backgroud to the bit of folk-lore taken over by St Paul, and Donne recalls what it really meant ('containing some elements of truth') while firmly ignoring what St Paul said it meant. Unless you take the intention to be so very firm and brave, here as in many other cases, it really does seem, as so many critics have felt, to be in rather bad taste. I need to try to present the thing in human terms; you might hear a top-grade lawyer (and that is more or less what Donne was in the field of theology) talk like this in his unbuttoned moments – 'well, of course, the whole thing's become so frightfully technical, you'd think one twitch could send it completely haywire, but that's actually how it works' – and you wouldn't deduce from such talk that he was at all bad at his profession, nor yet at all likely to cheat at it. This I think is the basic mood which became something much more passionate and searching in the great love-poems. Their mystical doctrine was always a tight-rope walk, a challenge to skill and courage, and after all it never pretended to offer any hope, only an assurance that people who called him wrong were themselves wrong.

The idea of man as a microcosm, goes on Mr Hunt, searching more deeply for the point where he feels there must be something sickly about Donne, was a commonplace to the seventeenth-century, but (pp. 176–7) 'Donne's inclination to attitudes of withdrawn eccentricity' made him use it as 'a philosophic validation of withdrawal and introversion'.

This is the conclusion which Donne derives from the concept in 'The Good-Morrow,' 'The Canonization,' and 'The Sun Rising,' and it obviously lurks behind 'A Valediction: Forbidding Mourning' as well: one is a world in oneself, and to oneself, and in that private world one can find all that other men desire; in fact – and here Donne wrests from the doctrine of the microcosm an implication which it did not normally carry – the private world of oneself is a *better* world than the world which ordinary men know.

I thought perhaps it was American of Mr Hunt to feel you're mad if you aren't a good mixer, but it turned out that the English Mr J. B. Leishman (*The Monarch of Wit*, 1951) had previously felt the same. What people have disliked about Donne, he recalls with full historical detail (p. 220), is 'a renunciation of the world, not in favour of otherworldliness, but in favour of a kind of private world,' and

Such an isolation, such a detachment from all the ordinary concerns of life, as left a man able to feel reality, to feel that he was completely alive, only in and through his relationship with his wife would have seemed to Johnson something not far removed from insanity.

This at least admits he had a woman with him in his Paradise; Mr Hunt's complaint, oddly enough, would only fit the religious poems, written when Donne was a prominent public figure. The process of judgment that we critics have gone through in such a case, is more complex than we have to remember in summing up; we would not say that any mystic is mad, being an introvert, nor even that Blake was mad because both mystical and devoted to his wife; but we feel that the younger Donne of the love-poems hasn't somehow a reasonable claim to be sane though an introvert. Or rather, I would feel that, and would agree with Mr Hunt, if I did not feel that the idea of the separate planet, and the explorer spirit that goes with it, make a decisive difference to 'tone'. Besides, they may have corresponded to a truth; as a free-lance consultant on theological controversy, Donne though poor had rather the status of an intellectual buccaneer. One might suspect, to be sure, that he was less conscious of the psychological dangers of introversion than we have had to learn to be; as is commonly said, his period more or less invented the individualism of the private world – consider Montaigne. But no one doubts that he went on trying to get hold of money for his family from the outer world, by means of his own line of thought, which was on matters of general public concern (it is the refusal to do that which excites moral indignation against introverts); worldly and unscrupulous he has been considered, but not soft as well. In any case, the extreme intellectual interest of the idea of the separate planet seems to have been what first attracted him, before he realised its convenience as an expression of his temperament or his misfortunes. Hence this essay may now at last arrive at its topic, and I am sorry to have been so frightfully long in getting there; it is merely because I felt there were so many prejudices in the way.

If you start at the first poem in the book [i.e. Grierson, *The Poems of John Donne*, 1912], 'The Good-Morrow', the separate planet surely leaps at you from the page. I have to argue with modern exegetists, not for the pleasure of nagging, but to understand what resistance needs to be overcome; I can claim to have selected a distinguished opponent in Mr Hunt. It does not occur to him that any such idea is present; and I think two rather opposed presumptions are working together in his mind to shut it out. He feels that Donne was being rather neurotic (whereas space travel would feel boyish) but also that Donne was at any rate being high-minded, that is, backing spirit against matter (but Donne often tries to get out of this dichotomy).

> If ever any beauty I did see,
> Which I desired, and got, t'was but a dreame of thee.
>
> And now good morrow to our waking soules,
> Which watch not one another out of feare;
> For love, all love of other sights controules,
> And makes one little roome, an every where.
> Let sea-discoverers to new worlds have gone,
> Let Maps to other, worlds on worlds have showne,
> Let us possesse one world, each hath one, and is one.
>
> My face in thine eye, thine in mine appeares,
> And true plaine hearts doe in the faces rest,
> Where can we finde two better hemispheares,
> Without sharpe North, without declining West?
> What ever dyes, was not mixt equally;
> If our two loves be one, or, thou and I
> Love so alike, that none doe slacken, none can die.   [6–21]

'Donne is playing in this line [12] on two meanings of the word "world"', begins a footnote by Mr Hunt, encouragingly (pp. 227–8), but, after some rather complicated evidence that the Old World was given that name, he deduces that the only New World in view was America. Why are they both in the plural then? What does the line about maps add to the line about discoverers – how could people put new continents on the map without discovering them? (It is true that they did, but a joke about bogus discoveries here would only weaken the rhetorical effect.) It was a regular thing for a long while to have a pair of globes, for the earth and the stars; the young ladies in Oscar Wilde's plays are still being taught 'the use of the globes', very properly. Donne found it a natural turn of rhetoric to move from one to the other within a couplet, as in a bad poem to the Countess of Bedford:

> We'have added to the world Virginia, 'and sent
> Two new starres lately to the firmament.
>
> ('To the Countesse of Bedford', 67–8)

But Mr Hunt fully recognises the existence of the star-globe; he only wants to exclude it from this couplet. Discoverers, he thinks, are low people, symbolising restless promiscuity, so they can't be paired with looking at a star-map, which is a spiritual thing. But it would never have occurred to Donne that you couldn't have discoveries in the stars. What Donne praises, in contrast to both globes, is one made by combining the hemispheres of an eyeball from himself and an eyeball from his mistress, and he remarks with truth that this hasn't the usual properties of either of the public globes, for example 'sharp north' where the lines of longitude come to a point (of course these would be marked out for measurement on the star-globe too). I do not have to deny that the imaginative effect is rich; you could feel with wonder that our own earth is being improved by the discovery of the New World – it is getting to know itself better, as the pair of lovers are; but this rather refined thought would not get in the way of the insistent thought about the stars.

Incidentally, Mr Hunt remarks that the line

> Let us possesse one world, each hath one, and is one

is very ugly in sound; this I think merely comes from not wanting to feel its drama. The sound requires it to be said slowly, with religious awe, as each party sinks into the eye of the other; it is a space-landing. Then there is a pause for realisation, and the next verse begins in a hushed voice but with a curiously practical tone: 'You know, there's a lot of evidence; we really are on a separate planet.' It is never much use talking about a sound-effect unless you know what it is meant to illustrate.

The reason for the curious resistance of Mr Hunt, I think, becomes clearer when he goes on to compare this passage to the middle of the 'Valediction: forbidding mourning', where the topic requires Donne to say that their love is refined enough to outlast a separation:

The basic concept behind these lines is that of the contrast between the two different substances of which the earth and the heavenly spheres are composed: between matter, the heterogeneous substance of the earth, which belongs to the category of 'things visible' and is gross, mutable, and mortal; and the fifth essence, the homogeneous substance of the spheres, which belongs to the category of 'things invisible' and is pure, stable, and eternal. (p. 65)

He deduces that in 'The Good-Morrow' (pp. 65, 67)

The world of their love is, in other words, like a celestial sphere … [T]heir love for one another has enabled the two lovers to discover at last their 'sphere,' their natural and proper mode of existence in the ordered scheme of the cosmos.

I hope the reader realises, what I didn't at first myself, that these spheres are Ptolemaic spheres, an imaginary series concentric with the earth, finally ten in number, most of them only concerned to carry one planet, or the sun or moon (the sphere of the fixed stars seems not to be meant). Thus the picture is now said to be invisible, whereas in the poem they are fascinated by seeing each other's eyes. It is true that in the 'Valediction', where the situation required it, Donne said that such refined lovers 'care less' to miss each other's bodies; but even this implies that they still care; and he goes on at once to the material analogies of the beaten gold and the compasses. Invariability (which is required for the eternity of the lovers in the last lines of 'The Good-Morrow', already quoted) was imputed to visible heavenly bodies, not only to Ptolemaic spheres; that was why it was such a shocking bit of luck to have two large *novae* in the crucial period. They were considered to prove that the heavens were corruptible. Besides, it is the whole point of a microcosm to be small;

it is cosy to have your own island, cave, house in a tree; this ancient sentiment is one of the reasons why the kids like space travel. Surely to make Donne say that his 'proper sphere' is the whole globe of heaven is to make him disagreeably smug, which he does not deserve. Here, as so very often, a critic who sets out to be highminded, even though in a sympathetic manner, only succeeds in looking unusually low-minded.

However, Mr Hunt draws attention to an important point. Instead of simply backing Copernicus, Donne gets a kind of lock-grip on his reader by arguing from both Ptolemy and Copernicus at once (pp. 189–91). According to Ptolemy, the planets are more or less in heaven, and matter there is much better-class than matter here. Copernicus merely showed that it was convenient for calculation to treat the earth as one of the planets (with various learned qualifications), but the obvious deduction was that life on other planets is simply like it is here. Matter is very refined on Donne's secret planet, as in Ptolemy, and this allowed him to treat his refined lovers as still material; but without Copernicus their position in the universe would not have seemed plausible. It is a charming arrangement, but it gives us no reason to suppose that he meant by his love something purely spiritual. Nor does it imply that he positively disbelieved in life on other planets; in his last poem, according to Mr Hunt, he reverted to medieval geography (pp. 104–5), but this doesn't prove that he disbelieved in the Red Indians.

A rather thrilling confusion about 'spirit', I think, crops up when Mr Hunt examines 'Elegy XIX', the one where a woman is undressing and Donne calls her 'O my America! my new-found-land'. Otherwise Mr Hunt is extremely good on the poem; I confess I had vaguely assumed, as no doubt most readers do, that the tropes are 'merely emotive', whereas they tell us a good deal about Donne's attitude to theology. The poem is probably Donne's first approach to his separate planet, no doubt a rather unconscious one; he liked to make unwonted use of any convention, and this particular path was to open into a grand view:

> Off with that girdle, like heavens Zone glittering,
> But a far fairer world incompassing.   [5–6]

Certainly, he need only mean 'Your body is more beautiful than *this* world, which is encompassed by stars as your body by that belt'; but the later lines drive home that she is a New World, and here astronomy is in view, so I expect she was starting to become a planet in his own mind. I set out to quote Mr Hunt on 'spirit' (pp. 21–2, 30):

[If the body is] mere evanescent 'clothing' for the eternal reality of the spirit, the Mystic Ecstasy might be thought of as an experience in which the soul divested itself of its temporal clothes and went naked to immediate contact with God ... Donne's irreverent allusions to spiritual love and to the Beatific Vision in the climactic section of a poem celebrating the pleasures of purely physical sex could be intended only as ridicule of the school of Platonic Love ... [The lines] present the whole-hearted acceptance of a sensual satisfaction as an act which entails taking up a philosophic option, which forces one to embrace philosophic materialism and to reject completely the doctrines of philosophic idealism – to reject, in fact, the fundamental doctrines of Christianity.

I agree that the poem feels heterodox; I hope the precedent given by Mr Hunt will save me from being thought tendentious there. But I think it is very wrong to suppose that the effect is mere jeering. Surely the first fact about the poem is the surprise we feel at its having such a high moral tone. Donne, indeed, loved to argue his way out of a fix with defiant brilliance; but this temperament often goes with a certain self-righteousness, and here he feels genuinely exalted. Nor is the picture unlifelike, especially if, as seems likely, it recalls the first sexual success of a strictly-brought-up young man; furthermore, one who doubts the value of the strictness and has felt a certain shame at submitting to it. He feels proud, he feels liberated, he feels purified (the effects of unsatisfied desire excite disgust, so that release from them can excite a keen sense of purity). What have any of these feelings to do with 'materialism'? What can be meant by calling the pleasure 'purely physical'? I wouldn't have thought, to begin with, that philosophical idealism was the fundamental doctrine of Christianity, let alone that an adherent of it can never accept pleasure. My English Composition class in Peking, their eyes all shining with asceticism and idealism, would habitually write down sentences like 'The Russians are very good because they are so material, and the Americans are very wicked because they are so material.' When I objected to this they readily agreed it was against the rules and said, 'But how do you say it in English then?' The word 'spirit' in the *Faustus* of Marlowe regularly refers to devils (as in 'Thou art a spirit: God cannot pity thee'). To revere the dichotomy between matter and spirit leads to hopeless confusion when reading Donne, because

though he too is badgered by it he keeps playing tricks with it, feeling
that it ought to be transcended. What is more, though I presume he
knew they were tricks, he did not think of them as such completely
wild tricks as the hardening of our intellectual outlook makes us do
now. As Grierson pointed out long ago in his notes to 'The Extasy',
Donne continued to expound in sermons the then decent, though one
might think Lucretian, belief that spirit is a subtle kind of matter
[Grierson, II, p. 45]:

The spirits in a man, which are the thin and active part of the blood, and so
are of a kind of middle nature, between soul and body, those spirits are able
to doe, and they doe the office, to unite and apply the faculties of the soul to
the organs of the body, and so there is a man.

I am pretty ignorant about Paracelsus, who was the latest thing in
medicine at the time and the second major influence (say the recent
thinkers) on Donne's mind after Copernicus, but one of his main
points was the mystery of the self-healing powers of the body ('dying
and rising the same'), which obviously did need attention. To take
the simplest case, it is an astounding thing, once you think of it like
that, that a broken bone heals of its own accord; and yet the spirit
that does this isn't exactly sensible – a reasoning man has got to tie
the splint right, or the bone doesn't have a chance to heal properly.
You ought to learn to collaborate with spirits, but not respect them
too much.

   Almost at the end of the poem, Mr Hunt rejects the printed version
–

> cast all, yea, this white lynnen hence,
> There is no pennance due to innocence.

– and gives instead the version of most manuscripts:

> Here is no pennance, much less innocence.

The other reading of the line [he says] makes the poem go startling pure and
sweet at this point, and for no intrinsic reason that I can see. Grierson agrees
that the version which I give was probably the original form of the line and
suggests a plausible explanation of Donne's having softened it up later: a
marginal note in one of the manuscripts (which gives the sweeter version of
the line) indicates that Donne may have revised the poem to use as an
epithalamion, possibly as his own. (p. 214 note 39)

This is the Bridgewater manuscript, of which Grierson does not speak
highly [Grierson, II, pp. xcix-c], and we need not give much weight

to its charitable idea that Donne wrote the poem for his own marriage. But I understand that this reading deserves weight on another ground, though I don't know the manuscripts myself. (The Bridgewater manuscript is in the Huntington Library.) It is thought probable that the other manuscripts which give Grierson's reading derive from the Bridgewater; now this poem, and the comment on it, are added to the Bridgewater in a different handwriting. A copyist often makes random mistakes, as I would myself if I had to write out the whole text of Donne. But if a man adds one poem to a collection he is presumably interested in it; and if after giving a variant line he adds a note whose point wholly depends on this change (because Donne could not have wanted to say that his bride was not innocent) then he must have known what he was doing. He might have been organising a pious lie, but this would be rather absurd with so many other manuscripts to check him. It seems more likely that the line had been bowdlerised into the other form, confessing that the pleasure was not innocent, or simply made to talk sense by some critic who could not see the point of the original; also the poem was often omitted from a collection of the poems as too indecent. The man who added the poem to the Bridgewater manuscript knew the original version, which he gave, and had invented a theory which made it good and sensible; this he added in a note, to justify his including the poem. I think this is the only plausible explanation; because, if you realise the central interest of Donne about such matters, you find the version with less authority (Grierson's or 'the sweeter' or the Bridgewater version) so very much the better one. Even if Donne wrote it later himself, he was only giving the poem a more direct thrust. The reason why she is innocent is that she is the Noble Savage, like Adam and Eve before the Fall (they indeed are the type case of lovers on a separate planet); she is America, where they are free as Nature made them, and not corrupted, as we are, by 'late law' ('The Relic', l. 30). Sweet the line may well be called, but it was meant to take effect as a culminating bit of defiant heresy.

It may seem improbable that Donne would be thinking about the Noble Savage, being himself an extremely urban, not to say socially climbing, character. But he put in for the job of Secretary to the Virginia Colony, or so we are told in a gossiping letter of February 1609 (e.g. *Donne's Prose*, E. M. Simpson, 1924). King James could not directly have kept him from being employed by a 'private company', as he could from being Ambassador to Venice and suchlike things which poor Donne went on applying for; but Delaware, perhaps realising that the assignment was a tricky one, did not appoint till he got to Jamestown; where he chose the future historian of the colony, William Strachey, who had arrived one month before with other survivors of the Bermuda wreck used in *The Tempest*. The whole colony insisted on piling onto the boats and trying to get home, but on the way out they met Delaware's supply fleet and said they would turn back and have another go; thus making the first successful English colony. It is rather hard to envisage Donne in this touch-and-go set-up, but I doubt if he would have been sent home after two years, as Strachey was; the job would have saved him from having to dramatise his conflicts as a famous preacher. You would be thinking of him now as a very different literary figure.[11] The Red Indians crop up carrying their theological weight, presumably a bit later, in the second Letter to the Countess of Huntingdon:

> That unripe side of earth, that heavy clime
> That give us man up now, like *Adams* time
> Before he ate; mans shape, that would yet bee
> (Knew they not it, and fear'd beasts companie)
> So naked at this day, as though man there
> From Paradise so great a distance were,
> As yet the newes could not arrived bee
> Of *Adams* tasting the forbidden tree;
> Depriv'd of that free state which they were in,
> And wanting the reward, yet beare the sinne.   [1–10]

The main thought in the background here, or so it seems obvious to me, is the mystery of how such an arrangement, though essential to Christian dogma, can be reconciled with belief in the justice of God. Indeed it is possible that the reason why the previous lines were cut is that they expressed the same idea more alarmingly; the surviving version begins where my quotation does, making it the only poem by Donne which has quite evidently been cut. On the other hand, the recipient may well have treated it casually enough to lose the first page. It is a bad poem which he probably churned out as a tedious duty, hoping to get some bills paid for his wife, and he might seem anxious to appear theologically correct; but the passage at least proves that the theological difficulty was knocking about in his mind.

I must now try to follow up Donne's use of the word 'sphere', because the belief that he meant a Ptolemaic sphere instead of a separate planet has appeared as a possible escape from my thesis. You might reasonably say that Donne uses words strictly, and after so much reading in astronomy would always give *sphere* the technical meaning of 'Ptolemaic sphere'. The answer is that he usually does do that, and does not use the word directly to mean a separate planet. In 'The Good-Morrow' we only get the combined form 'hemisphere', which, though actually older in the English language for the star-map, had then come into regular use for the earth-map; as one would expect, from the progress of geography, but I checked it in the OED. Thus the problem does not arise in the case Mr Hunt selected; also, when you do get the word *sphere* with the meaning 'Ptolemaic sphere', the context will often imply the planet.

We had better go straight to 'The Extasy', presumably Donne's biggest attempt at expressing his doctrine of love. Here the soul of each lover gets used as the matter which the soul of the other in-forms, but then this process makes one new soul, using both their souls as the matter, indeed the two atoms, which it in-forms. After this extremity of refinement, the poem at once says that their literal bodies should embark on the act of sex, because

> ...Wee are
> The intelligences, they the spheare. (51–2)

Here we have a profound textual crux, but it is commonly agreed that Grierson was right when he rejected the reading of all editions in favour of the reading of all manuscripts; what he rejected was the plural *spheares*, which apart from not rhyming throws away the whole claim that this couple has achieved identity. It has been pointed out, in favour of the reading 'spheares', that Donne seems habitually confused about the degree of identity asserted, or rather never quite loses touch with the facts of life, and even here has used plurals only just before: 'Our bodies why doe wee forebeare?/They are ours, though they are not wee, Wee are...' (50–1), Yes, but the previous verse began 'Wee then, who are this new soule, know', and the poem has now to make its startling leap from the ideal to the practical; it is essential, as a matter of rhetoric, to tide over the shock by repeating the paradox about numbers. A critic who resists recognising the paradox at all should remember that, though used in a challenging way, it was not in the least 'far-fetched'; it derives from the remark of Adam, described in the chapter-heading of Genesis 2 as 'marriage instituted' and optional in the Anglican Marriage Service, that man and wife shall be one flesh.

If then we accept the reading 'spheare' in the singular, it becomes evident that the two lovers are together on a separate planet; because a normal Ptolemaic sphere only carried one planet, or perhaps one sun or one moon. It was driven round by an angel, or 'intelligence', which could only be supposed to take its seat at the glowing point where the business of the sphere was manifested. In the poem the punning word 'intelligences' has always been in the plural, which does seem poetically right, but the meaning has to be that the one soul formed out of the two lovers is the angel which keeps in motion this Ptolemaic sphere. And we may observe against Mr Hunt that the sphere consists of their actual bodies, not of anything more refined.

Trying to implement my own linguistic theory, I would say that Donne started writing by giving the word *sphere* no meaning but 'Ptolemaic sphere' (though of course the basic geometrical sense of the Greek word was in regular English use), but that his successful uses of the word made it increasingly suggest to him 'planets' as a secondary meaning. The technical meaning appears alone, for example, and is made unusually beautiful, in 'Loves Growth':

> If, as in water stir'd more circles bee
> Produc'd by one, love such additions take,
> Those like so many spheares, but one heaven make,
> For, they are all concentrique unto thee.   (21–4)

The context is about trees blossoming in the spring-time, and he is probably thinking of the rings on a sawn tree-trunk, which number its years. But even here, as usual, in the lines immediately preceding, he has thought of the planets as somehow likeable just *because* they are not enormous like the celestial spheres (of course, on the other hand, he is quite willing to say that his separate planet is larger than our earth, but our earth is in any case tiny):

> And yet no greater, but more eminent,
>   Love by the spring is growne;
>   As, in the firmament,
> Starres by the Sunne are not inlarg'd, but showne.
> Gentle love deeds, as blossomes on a bough,
> From loves awakened root do bud out now.   (15–20)

Mr Redpath endorses a rather baffling note by Grierson to the effect that the stars appear larger at dawn.[12] I had always thought Donne simply means that the planets are seen by light reflected from the sun

– just as the moon obviously is, because of its phases. The proof of this belief did not come till Galileo in the autumn of 1610 saw Venus as a half-moon through his telescope, too late for his decisive publication of that year [*Siderius Nuncius*]; and probably any critic would put this rather boyishly fleshly poem by Donne a good deal earlier. But it had been an argument against the new astronomy that the planets do not have phases like the moon; that is why the phases of Venus were so important as soon as they were discovered. They would not have phases if they were balls of fire ('purer' than the moon); but a man like Donne, who wanted them to be like the earth, and to colonise them with a pair of lovers, would want them not to be balls of fire. On the other hand [Arthur O.] Lovejoy in *The Great Chain of Being* refers to an opinion of Kepler published in 1627 that the sphere of the fixed stars acted as a protective cover, reflecting back the heat and light of the sun, and on this view it is clearly the fixed stars, not the planets, which are lit by the sun; they behave like cat's-eyes on a motor road. I had the problem put up to Mr Charles Singer, a major expert in the history of science, and he felt sure, as I had hoped, that the lines of Donne can only refer to the belief that the planets are seen by light reflected from the sun.[13] An idea that the diffused light from nebulae may be reflected light is older, but not the cat's-eye fancy about distinguishable fixed stars. This fits the symbolism of the poem; the sun in the springtime is the returning force of nature and fertility, and without 'sensual' desires the lovers could not show their love to one another; just as even Platonic lovers, if they had not the use of their 'senses', could not know one another to be present. The interpretation seems not to fit the poem because it leaves out the idea of change, of improvement at the dawn or the spring-time; but the logical jump is rather typical of Donne, and the human meaning is that he always loved her (like the sun) though his bodily desires were variable. Donne has no subtle observation of nature like 'black as ash-buds in March', except possibly in 'The Calme', and could not have got away from the obvious fact about the stars that they disappear at the dawn; though it was very sympathetic of Grierson to prove that they get larger by a quotation from *The First Men in the Moon*. Well then, I think Donne set out to use his Ptolemaic sphere purely in this case but could not help bringing in planets. Indeed I think he increasingly came to feel (in love-poems) that the metaphor of the Ptolemaic sphere needed to be moderated by the metaphor of the planet; but here he is halfway through the development.

He had completed it by the time he wrote the splendid 'Valediction: of weeping':

> O more then Moone,
> Draw not up seas to drowne me in thy spheare.   (19–20)

Here we have another problem about the history of science, very properly raised by Professor J. Isaacs, who remarked that Donne seemed to be anticipating the tidal theory of Newton. Kepler, always a wild thinker, proposed a theory that the moon attracted the sea and thus caused the tides, in a publication of 1609 [*Astronomia Nova*]; this was jeered at by Galileo in his great 1610 book, because Galileo regarded action at a distance as too metaphysical for science – he proposed instead what may be called a sloshing theory, due to the rotation of the earth. Now here a critic would not mind putting the poem later than the controversy, but I was certain that the English sailors already had opinions about the tides, and I am pleased to be able to report that Mr Singer rejected this bit of dating with a hint of contempt.[14] The magical idea which Kepler was brave enough to support was merely the truth which a practising sailor had long had to learn; and Donne had sailed on the Essex Expeditions. As a poet he was very free from intellectual snobbery about his authorities.

Being more powerful than the actual moon, she might be able to raise tides as high as the moon's Ptolemaic sphere; hence *in thy spheare* means 'while I am still in your presence saying goodbye'. But, though this sphere is undoubtedly the chief sense of the word in this tremendous line, I think the trope feels too strained unless you are allowed, illogically, to think of her as ruling a globe, such as the moon, which has its own tides on its own surface. This apparently irrelevant idea has been a good deal thrust on us by the poem already; it has driven home that, just as any ball can be made into a map of the world (when the poet wrote 'quickly' he probably idealised the clumsy process, and thought of two hollow hemispherical printing clamps), so any tear of his with her reflection on it will take rank as a planet. Or rather, he first says that this tear will become 'All', a microcosm, but then he says it will 'a globe, yea world, by that impression grow'. The basic idea of the microcosm, as I should perhaps have recalled earlier, was that each man somehow reflects the whole world, obviously in his rational mind so far as he understands the world (and this in itself is an astonishing thought; it joined on to the problem about infinitesimal numbers), but also even where he doesn't understand the world (which was somehow an even more astonishing thought, and important to Paracelsus) because of the mysteries of his nature. Here we see Donne, as often, first taking this idea for granted; then throwing in on top of it an idea that the whole earth is only a microcosm too, just as a man is, because it is only one of the globes in the universe, and you would find on Mars analogues to everything on earth. Such is the regular effect of the metaphor treating their love as a separate planet. The surprise here is that instead of as usual making them secure from the world, it makes them pathetically vulnerable; once the lovers are separated they are absolutely separated, so great is the isolation of these starry habitations; high though their love is, it cannot reasonably be expected to be a faithful love – once they are on different planets they become 'nothing'. Even while they are still together the splendid arrangement is precarious, as when one of her tears falls onto one of his tears and destroys the shape which had made it a minifying reflector of her face. What gives the poem such depth is that it throws away the boast against the common world, or the joke from impudent plausibility of pretending to boast, which he usually extracts from this metaphor, though the metaphor still makes their love appear celestially valuable. I now think I made the wrong deduction from the 'irony' in the poem, long ago in my book *Ambiguity*; that is, I was right about the details of the text which make irony possible, but it is directed against his own previous extravagant use of the metaphor, not against the woman now in view; so that she may have been his wife. At any rate, if you are at all interested in the poem, I do not see how you can deny that it involves a separate planet. He does, to be sure, while sobbing, call her his 'heaven', but it would be quaint to deduce that he thought of her only as a star-map.

There may be a more interesting or general linguistic point about the word 'world' than about the word 'sphere'. To Donne and his first readers, I think, it meant a large *inhabited* area; that is, they wouldn't have called America the New World unless they had found Red Indians there, though we feel now they might have called it that anyway. The OED behaves rather unusually in stating that the etymological meaning is 'age' or 'the life of man', though of course this doesn't decide the exact flavour of the word in Donne's period. I can offer a clear case of Donne's own use of the word from *Ignatius His Conclave* (1611):

the moon, of whose hills woods and cities Galileo the Florentine hath thoroughly instructed himself, the planets, and other stars which are also thought to be worlds...

Here the opposition makes plain that *world* means '*inhabited star*', and presumably Donne was only following his long settled habits; but it is conceivable that the publication of Galileo in 1610, which Donne was making use of at once, had somehow altered his feeling for the word. Whether he wrote first in English or Latin might be an interesting point. An opponent may find subtle evidence, but till it is brought one would suppose, following the ordinary procedure of a linguist, that Donne meant the same thing for example by 'a globe, yea world' in the 'Valediction: of weeping'.

In Holy Sonnet V I should think *spheare* has become an ambiguity:

> I am a little world made cunningly
> Of Elements, and an Angelike sprighte,
> But black sinne hath betraid to endlesse night
> My worlds both parts, and (oh) both parts must die.
> You which beyond that heaven which was most high
> Have found new sphears, and of new lands can write,
> Powre new seas in my eyes, that so I might
> Drowne my world with my weeping earnestly,
> Or wash it, if it must be drown'd no more:
> But oh it must be burnt! alas the fire...

and so on, ending with a prayer for the fire 'which doth in eating heale'. (By the way, here again the intelligence which propels a Ptolemaic sphere lives at the planet which the sphere carries round). I take it that the converted Donne first reflected on his old idea of the separate planet, as an escape from the Christian Hell, and then wrote the poem specifically to renounce this heresy.

At any rate, the astronomy throughout the octet is otherwise completely pointless. Such was what I meant in my book *Pastoral* (p. 74), but I left the idea of renunciation rather obscure, perhaps vaguely supposing Donne's unconsciousness to be at work, and then I deduced, or so a reader might well think, that the separate planet also gets hinted at in the love-poems. I can easily see now (living in another world) that this was very unconvincing to an opponent; if you didn't find the separate planet prominent in the earlier poems you would hardly expect it in this one. All the same, I had a skeleton of argument behind me when I put the case the wrong way up. This sonnet is agreed to be fairly late – Grierson dates it after 1617. Now

Donne was undoubtedly familiar with separate planets by 1611, because of the reference I have just quoted. As I would put it, the row about astronomy which he had foreseen was now happening. What my opponent has to argue is that Donne isn't really familiar with the idea in earlier poems, but only appears to be, by accident; and I think that the spectacle in this poem, of Donne renouncing his old heresy, makes my opponent's theory even yet more improbable (because he has to make this poem meaningless too, as well as the earlier ones). For that matter, most of the later sayings of Donne still famous are also a renunciation of separateness; as in 'No man is an *Iland*, intire of it selfe; every man is a peece of the *Continent*, a part of the *maine*', or 'never send to know for whom the *bell* tolls; It tolls for *thee*'.[15] However, I still think that when Donne wrote this poem there was another near-heresy knocking about in his mind, which he was not completely renouncing; he would prefer, very understandably, to melt into the godhead rather than meet God face to face.

There is a small textual point here which looks like (perhaps unconscious) censorship somewhere. Naturally there were a lot of manuscript copies, for a famous poet who refused to publish during his life-time, and the editors of the first edition (1633) had some trouble with the licensing authorities, who began by objecting to all the *Satires* and four of the *Elegies*. The poems added in the second edition (1635), such as this one, were presumably simply found in another manuscript, but it is also natural to think that a certain amount of care in selection had happened earlier, when a man had a manuscript made for him, and no doubt paid for it. In this poem Grierson printed the plural *lands*, evidently rightly, but with the support of only one manuscript. All previous editions, and the only three other manuscripts which include the poem (all others omit it) give the singular *land*. Now of course copyists have a natural tendency to random error, but the textual history here looks as if the poem had been viewed with a vague anxiety. The singular *land*, stubbornly preferred by all but one manuscript, tends to discourage the idea of life in stars; if Donne was thinking of the planets as newly found to be habitable, or indeed of the two *novae* themselves as habitable, he could hardly avoid the plural. Given the singular *land*, however, a reader determined to exclude land from the heavens could envisage two groups of discoverers, the first group saving appearances for the old astronomy by adding further Ptolemaic spheres, the second group finding land in America; it would be very strained grammar, but Donne does strain his grammar. Whereas if he calls the stars 'lands' he is bound to imply that they are habitable. Not to bother further about the copyists, it seems clear anyhow that the poet used *sphere* as an ambiguity, starting with 'Ptolemaic sphere' and going on to 'nova', with the idea of habitable planets also open in the next clause about 'lands', so as to include either view of the controversy. However, I imagine the process was almost automatic – Donne was not trying to be tricky but to sum up the background of the controversy, in one way not wanting to alarm the reader or be too definite about his old heresy, in another way writing shorthand for himself or God and not much worrying about the reader. Thus the choice of words would be rapid and unbothered; by this time he had had a lot of practice in making such references.

One should try to keep his whole mind in view, though the results are bound to be uncertain. I had better give a bit of prose from the later mind of Donne. We have him using astronomy for a comparison in a letter to Sir Henry Goodyer, believed to have been written in April 1615, soon after his ordination:

And I think that as Copernicus in the mathematics hath carried each further up, from the stupid centre; and yet not honoured it, nor advantaged it, because for the necessity of appearances it hath carried Heaven so much higher from it; so the Roman profession seems to exhale, and refine our wills from earthly dregs and lees more than the Reformed, and so seems to bring us nearer to Heaven; but then that carries Heaven further from us, by making us pass so many courts, and offices of saints in this life, in all our petitions, and lying in a powerful prison in the next, during the pleasure, not of him to whom we go, and who must be our judge, but of them from whom we came, who know not our case.

There are various points of interest here. Mr Moloney remarks charitably that Donne might be excused for getting his Catholic doctrine wrong after such a lapse of time, and continues to argue that Donne never in his heart broke with Catholicism; the passage, he says (*John Donne, His Flight from Mediaevalism*, p. 41), 'represents a secession from the traditional faith inspired not by the fiery insistence that Rome had been false to her trust, but simply by the wishful feeling that perhaps a less intransigent faith would serve'. I think this view comes from not realising the sickened loathing which this doctrine commonly inspired among Protestants. The picture called up is of a soul in the torment of Purgatory still having to worry about human politics, wondering whether the church might yet be induced to allow the releasing prayers of persons on earth to get attended to by God. That is, you can never get away from the Papacy, because it has made a deal with God, as between two governors of slave states, that God will imprison any soul whom the Papacy accuses, however unjustly. Historians commonly say that the explosion of the Reformation was touched off by an extra use of this doctrine to pay for the building of St Peter's, which is designed to make man feel tiny and has marching enormous all round its inside walls the text used to justify the doctrine – 'whatsoever thou shalt bind on earth shall be bound in heaven'. Such was what the Protestants thought blasphemous, and in public Donne would have to concur; he of all men could not be ignorant of the disputed interpretations of the doctrine. The way it crops up in his mind for this private letter, though expressed with a rather touching moderation, does not suggest to me that he was a secret Catholic. At least, it would make him very dislikeable if he was; it would be so laboriously tricky. On my theory, we are free from suspecting this unpleasantness; we see Donne's mind rather casually echoing the whole association of thought which he had expressed so splendidly in his love-poetry. Grierson [*The Poems of John Donne*, pp. 235–6] thought that the reason why all editors suppressed Holy Sonnet XVIII ['Show me deare Christ, thy spouse'], till it was at last published by Gosse, was that they were shocked at finding him write as if still doubtful about Rome. No doubt the editors did find his mind alarming; but he is merely expressing a logical readiness to reconsider the question, and the habitual direction of his enthusiasm comes out when he asks of the True Church

> Dwells she with us, or like adventuring knights
> First travaile we to seeke and then make love?

which makes even Malory a bit of a space man. Donne's mind is rather hard to make sense of, because it is so invincibly balanced, or simply legal; it cannot help seeing all the alternatives as if in a chess-game; but that inherently made it demand a fair amount of latitude.

I should agree however that there is one point where the modern sceptic is liable to become unhistorical in thinking of Donne as a sceptic. Donne is not tacitly or half-consciously opposed to the whole cult of human sacrifices as such, whereas this strand of feeling had become prominent in the Church of England by the end of the seventeenth century. It is an old joke against the Church of England,

and I think also a truth greatly to its honour, that it became determined to keep Christianity at bay: 'You aren't going to be let burn each other alive any more, not in the parish of the Vicar of Bray, anyhow'; and no wonder that that song, though it seems to be jeering at a low-minded man, conveys a triumphant justification of him. Many people feel nowadays, and I among them, that Christianity in its origin, unlike the other major religions of the secondary civilisations, disastrously failed to cut itself off from the Neolithic craving for human sacrifice; this might seem a recent line of thought, but it only reinforces a moral sentiment which is already old. Even so, it is not as old as Donne, and would anyhow be foreign to his temperament. Of course Donne makes a kind of joke when the lover or husband describes himself as a sacrificial victim, suited to be the founder of a cult, but the joke is not against the reality of sacrifice; so far as it is doctrinal at all, it is against the Christian claim to uniqueness. He probably did not regard it as a metaphor to write

> Whilst yet to prove,
> I thought there was some Deitie in love

and would have agreed, and seriously felt, however heretical about what could count as a sin, that sin being an obstacle to union with the divine demanded expiation. In his return to Christianity he insisted upon retaining the status of victim, as in the mysteriously splendid line, ''Cause I did suffer I must suffer paine.'[16] This may be one of the things which have led so many critics to dislike his temperament, but it is a consistent intellectual position. He is still, for example, maintaining that sacrifice is not exclusive to Christianity in the religious poem 'The Crosse', written as a Christian; here again you might argue that he was only using a standard Counter-Reformation style, and didn't really mean the implications of his use of it, but the more natural reading is that he had contrived to alter what the style implied. He says that he could not be robbed of the Cross, because the loss of it (or, presumably, never to have been allowed to hear of it, like the Red Indians or the inhabitants of other planets) would itself be another cross. The cross indeed is inherent in the geometry of the universe, and this is bound to make it seem independent of a particular event on earth:

> All the Globes frame, and spheares, is nothing else
> But the Meridians crossing Parallels.   (23–4)

where *spheares* could mean 'sphere's' or 'spheres'', but there is little occasion for decking out every Ptolemaic sphere with this network, so I should think *Globes* means 'the earth-map's' and *spheares* means 'the star-map's'; though there is nothing to prevent it from meaning 'all other planets'' either. Surely a man returning to Christianity in this frame of mind could only enter a sect which claimed a certain localism, and did not claim to control all the universe and the courts of Heaven.

Going back to the bit of prose from a letter, it seems worth pointing out that Donne is very well-informed. The argument that Copernicanism puts Heaven further off gets a ringing line in 'Holy Sonnet V', already quoted; in the love-poems, presumably, it had been a background implication that if you got onto a separate planet you were safer from the Christian God as well as from the Pope. This argument had already been used by Aristotle, who rejected the movement of the earth round the sun on the specific ground that, since the fixed stars had no parallax, it made them improbably far away. There wasn't enough technical skill to observe parallax in even one fixed star till about the middle of the nineteenth century. However, the real objection for the human mind was not this lack of evidence, but that, till you had reached the idea that the fixed stars were like the sun, there was no intellectual satisfaction to be got in exchange for thinking them so far away. Donne had not invented this, so he was not cheating about Copernicus, any more than about the Pope (that is, he was not hiding a secret conviction); like other people at the time, he had no adequate grounds for not preferring the half-way theory of Tycho Brahe. At least, that seems to be the way the argument developed, and I know of no references to the contrary; also it explains how they could believe the *novae* to be inhabited, which seems to us very absurd; but Lovejoy in *The Great Chain* firmly treats the belief in other solar systems, not merely in other inhabited planets, as traditional among philosophers and indeed as what Bruno meant by 'the plurality of worlds'. Lovejoy, however, points out that Tycho, Kepler, and Galileo rejected the belief, and here we seem to have a definite case where the scientists, let alone the poets, were unaffected by the mystical philosophers; no astronomer deduced from Bruno's infinite universe the correct conclusion that the fixed stars must be like the sun.

We may observe finally that Donne is still thinking of Rome as somehow responsible for Copernicus, which seems to us a trick; he

had done it in the love-poems chiefly by the style, by using the grand
Counter-Reformation trope and making it mean something different; but the effect is definite enough to have made some people
expect he thought Rome more liberal about the matter than the
Protestants. However, what he assumes is true in a way; Copernicus
after all was on the committee which made our present calendar,
which the Protestant English for many generations after Donne
ridiculously refused to employ. Donne would no doubt think of this
as one of the points where Rome and Copernicus undoubtedly
deserved credit. His prose style, however tiresome, has the merit that
every side of a question keeps getting hinted at; and I think the whole
balance of his state of opinion is made luminously clear even in the
short bit quoted.

I feel I should apologise for so much 'background material', but
with Donne it seems to be mainly doubt about the background which
makes a critic reject the arguments from the text of the poems. It is
high time to return and try to be useful about the details of that. 'Aire
and Angels' is a difficult poem; probably it has done more than any
other to make the unspecialised reader think Donne rather a cad, and
there has been a recent move, discussed in Mr Redpath's edition, to
make its grammar call women purer than men instead of men purer
than women.[17] The reason why one gets this uneasiness is that the
final epigram seems to conflict with the story told by the poem, let
alone with the tone of it. The beginning is:

> Twice or thrice I had loved thee,
>   Before I knew thy face or name;
> So in a voice, so in a shapelesse flame,
> *Angells* affect us oft, and worship'd bee;
>   Still when, to where thou wert, I came,
> Some lovely glorious nothing I did see.

But after that, he argues for four more lines, it became the proper
thing to descend to bodies, and the verse ends:

> And therefore what thou wert, and who,
>   I bade Love aske, and now
> That it assume thy body, I allow,
> And fixe it selfe in thy lip, eye, and brow.

This is both magnificent and lifelike; he is describing what Stendhal
called 'crystallisation'. The second and final verse, which feels much
flatter, begins by claiming that in the process he has just described, as

quoted, he was trying to 'ballast' his love, make the boat steadier by weighing it down with more matter, but then he found that too much matter would sink the boat (that is, the metaphor says that a balanced arrangement about matter is necessary even for high forms of life); but then the poem seems to end with a resentful sneer against loved women:

> ...nor in nothing, nor in things
> Extreme, and scatt'ring bright, can love inhere;
>   Then, as an Angell, face, and wings
> Of aire, not pure as it, yet pure doth weare,
>   So thy love may be my loves spheare;
>   Just such disparitie
> As is twixt Air and Angells puritie,
> 'Twixt womens love, and mens will ever bee.

Not a brutal sneer; indeed some critics find the poem tender and more serious than usual – Donne has managed to break out, they feel, from over-exalting or debasing women throughout one poem, and achieved a more balanced attitude. I think that the poem does deserve this kind of praise (such a critic has got the intended tone of the poem right) but also that the critic does not deserve to say it till he has seen the point of the poem. On the face of the thing, if a man with the habits of the young Donne is trying to achieve a balanced attitude about the inferiority of women, their impurity is not a sensible item for him to pick out.

One needs to get the story of the poem clear. It goes through as many stages as a novel, and for most of the time she is the angel, not Donne. He first imagined her repeatedly – she is the ideal required by his nature – then when he saw her in public he fell into trance; afterwards he managed to get acquainted, and then her face became Love in person, a process like the Incarnation of Christ – the word *assume* makes a vague theological comparison. The whole of this first verse would appear standard to Chaucer, and naturally Donne wanted to add on something up-to-date. Between the two verses we are to assume he gets to bed with her; nothing else gives any point to the dramatic drop in the exalted tone, and at any rate this saves him from being self-righteous about his purity. After becoming accustomed to her body he still regards it as somehow unearthly, like an angel's. But he gets an uneasy feeling that he mustn't be overwhelmed by its brilliance, because he needs to protect his other interests; it may well occur to the reader, though it doesn't to the poet, that she too might want him to earn money, or in simpler times bring meat to the cave. After this change, his peace of mind still depends on being certain she loves him back, so that he can have her body when he does need it, on emerging from his reading, hunting or what not. Such is the peculiar sense in which he now incarnates his love not in her body but purely in her love, and feels an instinctive assurance that this process gives him steadiness to handle the world. It seems to me important to point out that the thoughts of Donne about love, so far from being over-subtle, were already real in the Stone Age. The anecdote cannot be called cynical; an ancient truth about the relations of men and women is recognised and glorified. All the same, the more you feel the story to be true, the more you feel Donne was cheating if he ended the poem by claiming he had proved men to be purer than women. To begin with, the poem has told us nothing whatever about the reactions of the lady. Chivalry he was by way of revolting against, but not logic and justice; and it is a plausible view that he wrote the second verse long after the first, in a disillusioned frame of mind, but even so he must be interpreted as making one poem, unless the poem is simply to be called bad.

The explanation I think has to be that he is making his joke, or his grand poetical conceit, not against the woman he loves but against 'purity', that is against the suggestion carried by this word that the best kind of love requires sexual abstinence. I gather I am likely to meet resistance here, but I do not quite know what. Surely he often did do this in poems, both seriously and wittily, and felt he had proved it in experience; such is the point where you might call him Renaissance rather than Medieval, if you were trying to make sense of those terms. Perhaps this is why Professor C. S. Lewis has accused him of want of delicacy, calling Rosalind as a witness, and implying that Donne when trying to be profound about the relations of soul and body only succeeded in being coarser about them than less fussy authors. It is true that Donne when trying to be courtly often seems very much a member of the professional classes, but I am not sure that a sensible lawyer on either side would bring Rosalind into the witness-box; she would not back Lewis if he quoted the Fathers of the Church, and was not above making fairly complicated jokes herself. But Donne's poetical arguments from absurdity were drawn from learned theories now remote, and one may hope that the joke in this poem seemed better than it does now. The great dictionary is not much help, as the meanings required for alchemy and angelology were so specialised; but under 'I. Physical: unmixed...' it has a good subhead 'c. Spotless, stainless, transparent', with a quotation of 1481, 'the moon is not so pure that the sun may shine through her as another star'. (It also distinguishes chastity from both moral and ceremonial defilement.) A critic should step back, I think, and reflect that the theme of 'Aire and Angels' was very fundamental to the developing sciences, however inadequately treated in the poem; chemistry depended on techniques for handling gases, beginning with distillation (the 'limbeck' so prominent in Donne), especially as a means of getting substances 'unmixed', and the gradual realisation of the nature of the different 'airs' went through much viewing of them as 'essences' (principles with their inherent virtue in a concentrated form) and 'spirits' (wind-and-breath by derivation, as was equally well known to Swift in the *Tale of A Tub*). The theories were applied to astronomy, but they were chiefly concerned with drugs for medicine; a man's fate may depend on the stars, but there is always a time in his life when he feels it depends on the doctor, and the doctor had to be an alchemist as well as an astrologer.

I am not sure how much this background needs to be read into the poem, but I think it lets one get into better proportion the argument that he meant to say women's love is purer than men's, and not men's purer than women's. The argument is surprisingly strong, and I should think Donne was conscious of putting in the details it relies on; but one cannot say that this was the single meaning he wanted for his final epigram. It would be so much against not only common opinion but the theories he was arguing from that it would need saying much more clearly, a point he would appreciate. The centre of the argument making him praise women is that *it* in 'not pure as it', among the lines last quoted, must refer to 'air before being condensed by the angel to make himself a visible body', therefore to the woman; not to the angel, who at this stage of the poem has become the man. To call an angel 'it' really is peculiar; I am told that it is unique in Donne, and anyhow would strike the first readers as a frank devaluation of this angel. However, you can see how Donne happened upon this piece of grammar; he has already called his love 'it', though it is the child of his soul, and called his visions a nothing, and called her body 'things'. Secondly, if 'purity' can mean 'transparency', a view which is at any rate supported by the great dictionary, then 'air before it is condensed by the angel' is patently purer than the angel as a visible object. Then the next line 'So thy

love may be my loves spheare' is consistent in making the angel (and
the man) the more solid body, because he becomes the planet moving
on the Ptolemaic sphere of the woman. There is no need to disagree
with Mr Hunt that the Ptolemaic sphere was considered purer than
the planet moving upon it. Mr Hugh Sykes Davies, who has been
arguing for making the poem call women purer, or rather call their
love 'less involved in the need for physical expression', regards
the *spheare* as diagrammatic rather than astronomical;[18] but Mr
W. A. M. Murray tells me that Paracelsus made 'the sphere' mean
the body when regarded as uninfluenced by its own animal spirits,
therefore as helplessly material; and this seems hard to combine with
Mr Davies' view. It may well be that the contrast of the Paracelsian
meaning comes into many of Donne's uses of the word *spheare*; all I
can say is that it would have to make a profound contradiction or
joke. There seems no doubt, after surveying the uses in the poems,
that Donne regularly gave the word the astronomical meaning, even
if other meanings came in.

But then again, granting the astronomical meaning for *spheare*, a
reader may turn round and recall that 'an intelligence' was what
ruled a Ptolemaic sphere, and the pure creature used the planet only
as its country house. Yes indeed, that is the joke. These spirits also
had the names of pagan gods, such as Mars or Venus, who did not
pretend to be purer than the ether. Meanwhile the actual use found
by theorists for these spirits was merely to drive the celestial sphere
round at constant speed, so that they may properly be regarded as a
high-grade derivative of petroleum suitable to aeroplane engines –
the modern pun would be tiresome if it did not come to us directly
from the theoretical confusion which Donne was satirising. We had
better go back again to 'The Extasy' for Donne's view of the relations
of soul to matter:

> On man heavens influence workes not so,
>   But that it first imprints the ayre,
> Soe soule into the soule may flow,
>   Though it to body first repaire.   (57–60)

Surely this looks as if he himself felt, as a modern reader must do, that
there was something very interesting to say about the relations of Air
and Angels if only one could manage to say it. Grierson's note here (II,
p. 44) shows that Donne had backing from Du Bartas, therefore
presumably from a lot of other books he was reading, for the belief

that air was pretty full of 'virtue', as one would suppose since it is very nearly what 'spirit' means; air need not show up at all badly against a minor angel, if you are interested in confusing the modes of being.

It seems to me clear that Donne was half guying the theories and half imaginatively enjoying them, even if I have got the details wrong. What a modern reader feels to be more immediately serious, before accepting the magic of the wit or poetry, is a simpler or more sociological matter; what Donne really did think about women, and how he behaved to them. Living as we do after change in the legal position of women, we would like to know more about his actual habits; apart from his minor poems jeering at women, the complete silence of his adored wife cannot but leave on us an impression of patient suffering. It might seem a plausible view that his habitual contempt for women merely broke out at the end of this love-poem, so that even for a reader at the time he spoilt this poem by finishing on a platitude – that is, the end always felt bad, but now feels worse. I do not think this a likely piece of clumsiness for the mind of Donne. 'The Extasy' denies all 'disparitie' between the sexes, because the lovers become one soul, and the modern reader whether male or female tends to find this extremity an implausible one; but it does not strike us as treating women with a contempt for which we are now too far advanced. It seems fair to point out that he made less of a mess of his marriage than Coleridge did. The hostess of the palace of the Keeper of the Great Seal did behave splendidly under the terrible privations of life on a separate planet, whereas the girl Coleridge thought natural enough for the banks of the Susquehanna would probably not have turned out well even if he had collected his group to go there. The mind of Donne was much cluttered with learned authorities who called women inferior to men, but to say that they were wrong was equally fixed in his mind as his first gambit when describing his reception in high society. Of course he would also sometimes write satire against women, but what he seriously believed about them, I should expect, and I think normal opinion still agrees with him, was that women though not inferior to men have a deep 'disparitie' from men.

It therefore seems worth pointing out that this disparity is all that the end of the poem asserts; the words do not literally say either that women are less pure than men or that men are less pure than women. The phrase *not pure as it, yet pure*, if you take *as* to mean 'like', positively labours to avoid comparison and means 'they are pure in different ways'; also it strikes me that this reading has a period flavour, so that it was more likely then than now. In the same way *Aire and Angells puritie*, with no apostrophe for the possessive, could easily mean 'the kind of purity in air and the kind of purity in angels'; indeed the *1669* editor, or the copyist he was following, probably felt that this needed making clearer when he changed *Aire* to 'Airs', and the change is still more needed now. Donne, no doubt, rather enjoyed ending with something that looked harsh if misunderstood, and I imagine that this is a fairly early poem, but he would not intend to be misunderstood radically. The whole poem has described a 'disparitie' between the loves of men and women, and seems to me to do that with massive truth; surely it is only fair to the poet to allow his final epigram to mean 'such is the disparity'.

However, it would be no good for me to present the poem as simple, thus claiming to outwit both the opposed groups of critics. I must not say that their problem is a mere mistake, because Donne neither intended to call women purer than men nor men purer than women. What he meant to do, when he added a second verse to his first splendid one, was to say something very teasing about purity. What has become too obscure is not the problem but the answer. I think he meant the reader first to accept the final epigram as a platitude in favour of men, then revolt against this view and realise that it might be in favour of women, then realise that the only truth told is about an actual unlikeness between the sexes. Surely, Donne was expected to be clever, by the first readers of these poems in manuscript whom he actually wished to please; it is not stretching the historical possibility to suppose that the second verse is meant to be clever. Indeed, there could be no point in arranging the words so as to make possible the present disagreement among critics except to make evident confusion of the conception of 'purity'. I do not pretend that my view makes the end of the poem very good (rather few jokes are eternal, and probably no technical ones) but it does save you from having to regard the end of the poem as bleakly meanminded.

The separate planet is only in the background of the great 'Nocturnall', but the tone of the poem is greatly improved if you recognise it there. I was convinced of this by a recent exegetist, Mr Richard Sleight, who very honestly reports that the word 'world' in the poem means more than he knows. At least, he says, 'Most readers

would probably agree that the word has some such unifying effect as
has been described; the reasons for the effect are not so easy to find':
I do not think he claims to find them in his later remarks, and if he
did I would think him wrong. He argues that Donne implies his own
'reintegration' or recovery from grief even while pretending to
describe his grief as absolute; in the line about alchemy 'Donne is
tilting at the alchemists and at himself taking himself too seriously',
and at the end '[h]e does not definitely commit himself to the
harmony of death nor the dialectic of living' – but surely the end of
the poem says he will prepare to join her in death. Mr Sleight feels 'it
is unsatisfactory to believe that grief, however severe, is eternal except
in Romantic poetry', and this I find rather bloodless. (Or perhaps it
is one of the emotional confusions promulgated by neo-classicism.) I
think he is right in feeling there is something to say about the tone but
fails to nail it down.[19]

The word comes into each of the first three verses; in the first for
the ordinary world, now at midwinter; in the second the spring will
be a 'new world', because Donne cannot conceive of a recovery from
this winter, and indeed speaks as if already outside mundane
experience; in the third we find that Donne and his mistress till she
died were a world to themselves, as if on a separate planet. However,
this idea seems chiefly remembered from previous poems, and I
would not go as far as Mr Redpath, whose note makes it the meaning
of the grammar:

> Oft a flood
> Have wee two wept, and so
> Drownd the whole world, us two; oft did we grow
> To be two Chaosses, when we did show
> Care to ought else; and often absences
> Withdrew our soules, and made us carcasses. (22–7)

He takes *us two* as in apposition to *the whole world*,[20] and no doubt this
idea is what needs suggesting to the reader in a footnote, but the idea
can only be a secondary one because the alternative grammar is too
colloquial to be ignored – 'and wept enough tears, just us two, to
make another Flood'. If we were expected to forget the hyperbole,
and explain it completely away as only meaning a separate planet,
there would be no point in using the trope here, where it has a rather
special point. When first used, probably in the remote past, the trope
was meant to have a kind of dramatic truth as the kind of nonsense
that a person could only believe when half mad with pain. Donne

now uses it almost playfully, so as to put the real solemnity further on:
'How unhappy we used to think we were, when we were ruining
ourselves for love; but looking back now, when she is dead, it seems
to me we were having tremendous fun. For one thing, we felt so
important, because nothing was real except our feelings for each
other; but now I feel entirely unimportant – I am as if no world had
ever been created.' Surely this is the only human basis for saying he
has become the elixir of the first nothing (l. 29); he used to have a
separate planet, and now it is as if it had never been. We need not
doubt the mood of despair, but it is much sweetened by the glee with
which he looks back on their bold love, so that he can give assurance
to the next crop of lovers; and the fierce cosiness of the idea of the
independent planet is I think a main source of this warmth.

There is a similar casualness about the hyperbole in 'A Valediction: forbidding mourning', where I had best begin by recalling
a controversy.

> Moving of th'earth brings harmes and feares,
>   Men reckon what it did and meant,
> But trepidation of the spheares,
>   Though greater farre, is innocent. (9–12)

Mr C. M. Coffin, in his *John Donne and the New Philosophy* (1937), took
this as a reference to Copernicus (p. 98): 'Of the new astronomy, the
"moving of the earth" is the most radical principle; of the old, the
"trepidation of the spheres" is the motion of greatest complexity',
and 'Donne does not deny the truth of either doctrine – if he did the
whole point of the argument would be wasted and futile.' As time
went on, this case became rather a victory for the new rigour, in its
campaign to make poetry as dull as possible; Mr W. K. Wimsatt in
his essay 'The Intentional Fallacy' (first published 1946) proved that
the line refers to an earthquake.[21] This would do actual *harm*, at a
point of time, and afterwards (hence the past tense) men would
reckon the damage and invent a superstitious *meaning*, none of which
applies literally to the new astronomy. Mr Wimsatt gave a qualifying
sentence before the bang of his final one, but I expect he felt that only
made the bang stronger (*The Verbal Icon*, p. 14):

Perhaps a knowledge of Donne's interest in the new science may add
another shade of meaning, an overtone to the stanza in question, though to
say even this runs against the words. To make the geocentric and heliocentric
antithesis the core of the metaphor is to disregard the English language, to
prefer private evidence to public, external to internal.

The way that *private* goes with *external* is rather subtle; I remember a fellow lodger who was very cross because he found his razor had been used – a man's face, he said, is the most private part of his body. I agree that the earthquake is the chief meaning, but that is no reason to deny that Donne, when he first tasted his line and found it good, was conscious of a secondary meaning which he rather hoped to insinuate. The effect of giving the phrase both meanings is to say, 'And also the sudden introduction of the idea that there may be life on other planets has affected the Churches like an earthquake.' At this remove, the phrases can apply tidily to Copernicanism; the threat to the churches' absolutism, Donne can mean, has frightened them and tempted them to persecution. It is what I call an equation, and of Type III (in *The Structure of Complex Words*); in the mind of Donne, the major sense of 'moving of the earth' is the Copernican one, but the sense demanded by the immediate context is the earthquake, indeed this is also what the reader is likely to take as the major sense, and yet Donne thinks of Copernicanism as the subject of his equation, the part that comes first in the sentence expounding it. That is, the Copernicanism, and not the earthquake, is the one you are expected to understand better after the two have been compared. This Type tends to express a fixed belief of the speaker but to be resisted by the hearer, or only absorbed unconsciously; which seems to fit here. Of course, this theorising only claims to show that the case is normal, not to prove that the extra meaning occurred to Donne; but we have some reason to expect so from the verse immediately before:

> So let us melt, and make no noise,
>   No tcarc-floods, nor sigh tempests move,
> T'were prophanation of our joyes
>   To tell the layetie our love. (5–8)

The second half takes for granted that they are a separate religion, as usual, but the first half, though less obviously, regards them as on a separate planet. It would be tiresome to use these conventional hyperboles, while the tone treats them as commonplace, without a moderating idea that the floods and tempests are only rightly so called within the private world of the lovers. She is tenderly exhorted to be patient, but he is rather prepared to laugh at her if she makes a fuss; the effect is cosy. This situation regularly suggested to him his secret planet, so naturally a Copernican idea came into his mind for the next verse; but he did not much want it for this poem, so he thrust it down to a secondary meaning. If you dislike my claiming to know so much, I have to answer that I think it absurd, and very harmful, to have a critical theory, like Mr Wimsatt's, that a reader must not try to follow an author's mind.

In all this, I am not sure how far I am arguing for an opinion as if it were new when in fact it is accepted, or was accepted till quite recently. I was rather puzzled on looking up the article by Marjorie Nicolson, 'The "New Astronomy" and English Literary Imagination' (*Studies in Philology* 32, 1935), so often given in footnotes. She seems at first strongly opposed to my thesis, maintaining that Donne only wrote about new astronomy during a short period after 1604, when Kepler discovered the second Nova (the first had been in 1572) and the pressure of controversy and discovery became hot; all the references to astronomy in the *Songs and Sonnets* are 'purely conventional', she says, giving as her example the one already considered about the sun 'showing' the stars ['Loves Growth']; though she does not say what it means.[22] But then at the end she remarks casually:[23]

But only occasionally in the *Sermons* does Donne venture upon the more philosophical connotations of the Galilean discoveries. The idea of a plurality of worlds, which Donne had suggested in his earlier poetry, was indeed for a churchman a dangerous tenet, even, as it came to be called, the 'new heresy'. The condemnation of Bruno had listed that belief as one of the chief charges brought against him; and many orthodox Protestants, as well as Catholics, felt that such a conception struck at the roots of the Christian idea of the sacrifice of Christ, who died to save *this* world.

'Which Donne had suggested in his earlier poetry' – she seems to take it for granted, and merely feel that this general deduction from Copernicus doesn't count as a technical bit of astronomy. It counted for a good deal as part of the poems.

I also looked up 'Kidnapping Donne' by Merritt Y. Hughes (*Essays in Criticism*, Second Series, California University Press, 1934), the other warning reference regularly given in footnotes;[24] this is harder to deal with, because it works by suggestion and general assertion. The title, as you expect, means that various people up to 1934 had been trying to kidnap the young Donne by presenting him as a freethinker, whereas Mr Hughes speaks of his 'essentially Catholic mind'.[25] But I think it is the Catholics who deserve this reproach, and the case has something of the real horror of kidnapping, because they are likely to damage him so much that he is no use to them when they have got him. To suit their purpose, he has to be a sordid cheat. You might think it about as bad for me to make him nurse a special heresy, but that wouldn't involve his honour as one of a Catholic family, and Catholics will agree that it could more easily be renounced or digested before devoting himself to the Anglican Church. I do not need to deny that he spoke vaguely against Copernicanism in later life (no case is offered of his doing it decisively). When he says in sermons, for instance, that it is more wonderful to have the sun go round the earth all the time than to have it stand still once for Joshua, he is merely illustrating a general truth, equally sound whichever way round they go; it need not be called 'good evidence that the new theory never disturbed the bottoms of his mind that his emotions were deeply involved in the old cosmic scheme'.[26] Mr Hughes is more convincing when he takes an almost opposite position, and says that Donne habitually regarded the new theory as 'a potential of evil' (p. 45); maybe he did feel that with part of his mind, whether the bottoms or not; it doesn't prove he didn't think the portent important, or couldn't have toyed with it recklessly in his early poems. Mr Hughes agrees that Donne thought the universe was decaying, because the heavens had been shown to be variable (to expect the end of the world was of course quite orthodox); he quotes some lines from the third Letter to the Countess of Bedford, where Donne is saying the world is hopelessly bad compared to her (she is Virtue in person, l. 25, and a separate world, l. 87):

> As new Philosophy arrests the Sunne,
>   And bids the passive earth about it runne,
> So we have dull'd our minde, it hath no ends;
>   Onely the bodie's busy, and pretends;
> As dead low earth eclipses and controules
>   The quick high Moone: so doth the body, Soules.   (37–42)

'That way, for him, lay madness', says Mr Hughes (p. 46). I have quoted three more lines than he did to show that Donne does not imply disbelief in the new philosophy; presumably Donne believed in this explanation for eclipses of the moon, so if anything he implies that he also believes the theory which would lead to madness. Probably he came to accept the half-way theory of Tycho Brahe, which could be said to hold the field on the existing evidence; but there was nothing definite in that to disprove life on other planets, once you had got the idea into your head. The other arguments in the article seem to me to work mainly by suggestion, as when we are told (p. 48) –

The *Songs* and *Elegies* show no trace of the scientific and metaphysical skepticism which was penetrating England from Italy at the close of the sixteenth century...

The strategy here seems to be to allow everybody else to be a sceptic so long as the one case in view is kept pure. Even if we had heard more about this scepticism in the period, which I am far from denying, it is hard to see how such evidence could prove that Donne did not hold a simple positive belief in life on other worlds.

In spite of his consistent interest Donne never took natural science seriously; from first to last his attitude resembled that of Nicholas of Cusa in the *De Docta Ignorantia*. His contempt for adepts of natural philosophy can hardly be distinguished from contempt for natural philosophy itself. (p. 51)

Thus, in the *Problems and Paradoxes*, he spoke of 'Physitians contemplating nature [who], finding many abstruse things subject to the search of Reason, thinks [*sic*] therefore that all is so.' Now, this quotation was presumably selected by Mr Hughes to prove Donne's contempt; and it is remarkably weak evidence for contempt.[27] Compare the hysterical attacks written by Pope and Swift on adepts of natural philosophy. As to Nicholas of Cusa, I have no need to deny that, for a man so well-read as Donne, the traditional philosophic attitude to such questions as that of life on other planets would give a firm support, a feeling of security, when (rather with another part of his mind) he accepted the obvious deduction from Copernicanism. But that is no reason to deny that he did accept it; all it shows is that he had ways of getting out of it, and I daresay he used them when he decided he had better get out of it. This is no argument against the direct literary evidence in the love-poems that at an earlier time he had accepted it. As to 'taking it seriously', he took it seriously as a poet; and this doesn't at all mean taking it as a fancy, but concentrating on what the human consequences would be if it were true – treating it like a theologian, you might well say, though not like a scientist.

There is a rather splendid bit of strategy in Mr Hughes when he warmly praises 'Satire III' (p. 52):

His defence of liberty of conscience against the principle *cuius regio eius religio* deserves to be even better known that it is...

Now, the principle *cuius regio eius religio*, though not intellectually impressive, was an attempt to stop burning people alive; it said 'let the Reformation lie as it has fallen; let us agree on co-existence, the way we are now'. I do not see how a single word of Donne's poem could be twisted into an attack on this clumsy attempt at moderation, as apart from an attack on religious persecution in general. Donne is simply against burning people alive for their religious convictions, and Mr Hughes has managed to praise him for it in a form of words which really means that Donne, with the warm approval of Mr Hughes, wanted to burn people alive a great deal more. I really think this case ought to be enough to clear the minds of those humble literary students like myself who often see a footnote referring us to a rather inaccessible article called 'Kidnapping Donne' and feel, Oh well, what seems to me obvious must have been all disproved in some awfully specialist way.

I ought finally to admit that the idea of the private planet has at least once crossed the mind of the more recent critical world. It occurred to Mr Leishman (1951), who naturally felt he was making a discovery. Grierson had suggested that the 'Nocturnall' might well have been written to Donne's wife, because the third stanza speaks a stronger language than that of Petrarchan adoration; Mr Leishman adds:

What, though, so far as I am aware, neither Grierson nor any other commentator has noticed is the remarkable similarity between the image, or 'conceit', in this stanza and the one in that fiendishly ingenious poem *A Valediction: of weeping*...It is natural, and, I think, legitimate to assume that this poem, like several others in which he speaks of her and of himself as forming two hemispheres, or one perfect world, was written out of his experience of marriage...[28]

He deduces (pp. 176–7) that the 'Nocturnall' was written in Paris on the night of the 13th December 1611, Donne was there with the Drury family, and anxious about his wife's coming child-birth (Isaak Walton says he knew by telepathy that not the wife but the child was dead, and so it was, but one can well believe there was a certain amount of confusion). As a young man I snatched at any chance to hear wisdom drop from Mr T. S. Eliot, and he once remarked that the test of a true poet is that he writes about experiences before they have happened to him; I felt I had once passed this test, though I forget now in which poem. The doctrine makes one very doubtful of any dating of poems by internal evidence, and I should think it might be true of Donne. Otherwise the dating seems to me very plausible, and I ought to applaud Mr Leishman here, not grumble at him. It is a most curious thing, but it is true, that a critic can decide whether a passage is 'Petrarchan' or not without really knowing what it means. But still, the only definite reason for supposing that Donne refers to a separate planet in the 'Nocturnall' is that he does it so often in other poems, sometimes obviously, but often so vaguely that we are only sure of it because the poem becomes better if we recognise it; whereas Mr Leishman seems to regard the process with chill distaste, and merely to classify together, for purposes of dating, those cases of it which are particularly hard to ignore. I am much inclined to agree that Donne wrote these poems to his wife, because that makes them so much more practical for his actual situation at the time; but I can't help agreeing here just for once with the anti-biography critics that the point is rather unimportant, compared to realising what the poems mean and deciding whether you find them beautiful after doing so.

CHAPTER 3

Donne in the new edition

I

The points which I hope to establish against Professor Gardner's account of Donne's love-poems (*The Elegies and The Songs and Sonnets*, ed. Helen Gardner, Oxford: Clarendon Press, 1965), in text and dating, may not seem very important; but to accept her ruling is to let an old controversy go by default. The current view has been taken for granted often enough, indeed for much too long, but only now is it consolidated by a claim to scientific proof; and the proof needs to be recognised as radically inadequate.

In the twenties, when I was young, it was a usual assumption among critics that Donne was somehow an advanced thinker, or at any rate an interesting one, who cast an independent eye on both church and state. Thus F. W. Payne said in his book on Donne (1926):

His correct interpretation of the effects of the dark beginnings of our modern science places him on a level with Mr H. G. Wells for piercing insight.[1]

Everyone in the Eng. Lit. business under forty is deliciously outraged on hearing this sentence, but I still think that these authors both did have piercing insight. It was fair to get tired of critics like Payne because they did not say what Donne had seen, but Donne's use of astronomy gives a definite example. Professor Marjorie Nicolson could still say as late as 1935 (*Studies in Philology*):[2]

The idea of a plurality of worlds, which Donne had suggested in his earlier poetry, was indeed for a churchman a dangerous tenet, even, as it came to be called, the 'new heresy'.

As soon as Copernicus' book came out, Melanchthon said that it implied inhabitants of other worlds, and that this was incompatible with Christianity.[3] Either the Father had been totally unjust to the Martians, or Christ was crucified on Mars too; indeed, on all inhabited planets, so that his identity in any one appearance became precarious – a theologian could be driven near to the position of the discreditable Family of Love, that Christ was merely a state of mind which any convert could achieve. Donne as an expert on theology would have to know about this. When he colonises such a planet with a pair of lovers, outlaws apparently from their own society, he automatically frees them from the rival jurisdictions of Queen Elizabeth and the Pope. His verse claims the rights of natural freedom for his love-affairs before his marriage, and the marriage cost him his job, so he talks in the same way (rather confusingly for an editor) about both of them. It has been said that as an ex-Catholic he had none of the Puritan worries about Copernicus, and could display the broadmindedness of Rome; but the disappearance of Bruno would have to be a rumour of the coming storm. He was the leading exponent of the plurality of worlds, and the eight years of his imprisonment *incommunicado* before being burnt alive at Rome had recently begun when Donne wrote 'Satire III'. When the storm broke, over Galileo, Donne had already changed sides, retreating in despair from the interplanetary spaces; but he of all men cannot have been ignorant of the issues earlier.

A *Garland for John Donne* (1931) seems to have been the book which released the revolt against the way the twenties had praised him. T. S. Eliot said: 'Donne was, I insist, no sceptic: it is only that he is interested in and amused by ideas in themselves'[4] – in short, he was a tedious fribble, who did not mean anything he said, unless it was a pious formula. This made a total change of direction in the flood of critical comment, though I cannot find that any serious evidence was offered for it at any stage. Students in essays about Donne are to this day copying out the very unhelpful remarks about him by Eliot, such as that he felt his thoughts because he came before the Dissociation of Sensibility, or (later) that he didn't because he came after it.[5] The function of these manœuvres was to distract attention from what Donne actually did think. Still, to do T. S. Eliot justice, he would not have been mainly concerned with hiding a heresy; as a poet deriving from the French Symbolists, he considered it very low-class to think in poetry at all, let alone argue; so he showed great nerve in praising a school of poets who argued all the time, and felt he was only charitable in saying one need not attend to it. The effects on Donne have been very bad; a grimly dismal change it seems to me, from the days when I was imitating him in my own verse with love and wonder.

I may be told that a man who is ignorant of bibliography has no right to speak about the text; but it strikes me that bibliographers have become much too secure in this immunity or extraterritorial right. In a recent book on Milton I recalled, quite incidentally, the traditional suspicion that he had foisted Pamela's Prayer into the *Eikon Basilike*, and more than one critic rebuked me for not knowing that this story had been in Madan's *New Bibliography of the Eikon* (1950). It did not take special knowledge to explode Madan's argument on this point, in my second edition, only attention to the evidence that he himself provided; what was remarkable was that, apparently, no one had done it before, in the fifteen years since he had published. He, I should think, was doing a bit of lawless chivalry, 'defending the memory' of the poet even at the cost of distorting the scheme of dates. The method of Professor Gardner is inherently likely to build up delusion. Good readings are those attested by good manuscripts, and good manuscripts must be given most weight; these are the ones which on the whole give good readings, being in a good tradition. But 'good' readings may easily come to mean, for Professor Gardner, those which she has been brought up to prefer. In general, the technique carries means of protection against the fallacy; but it is doubtful whether they are adequate in the present case.

This technique, for establishing lines of descent among a group of manuscripts, was invented to deal with the manuscripts which are our sources for classical literature. The copyists, often monks, were unlikely to know any other source of the text than the one they copied, or any tradition about what it ought to contain; they were separated from their brother copyists and the author by immense gulfs. So far from that, the copies of Donne were made during or just after his adult lifetime, all for one leisured talkative group of people, in easy contact with one another, and probably with the author (at least up to 1614, when he was calling in texts for an edition; Gosse, II. 68). Herbert J. C. Grierson, who did the basic classification of the Donne manuscripts for his great edition of 1912, writes about the labour amusingly but with some care to retain his dignity (vol. II. p. cxi); he is rather surprised that the technique worked as well as it did, though the affair was so like Gulliver in Lilliput. But then, he was prepared to believe that some apparently erratic manuscripts record the poet's first draft, whereas Professor Gardner claims (in general) to refute this possibility. If her reasons are adequate, they are not presented adequately in the book.

Her edition of the *Divine Poems* (1952) had four groups of manuscripts; the first deriving from the collection Donne himself made in 1614, in which he then probably made some changes; the second compiled from Donne's own papers some time after 1623; and the fourth the single manuscript '*W*', made by Donne's friend Rowland Woodward at various dates. The manuscripts of the third group, she said, are not all descended from one text, but 'agree in preserving' a slightly different text (*Divine Poems*, p. lxix). She then suggested (p. lxxvi) that they were assembled, without contact with the author, from copies of poems which he occasionally made for his friends, but this she no longer believes (*The Elegies*, pp. lxxxi–lxxxii). Further manuscripts have been collated for the present edition of the love-poems, and a new class V has been made, of inferior manuscripts, which includes several (*B*, *K*, *S*) cast out from her old class III. We are told, in general, that they were found to give 'erratic' readings for the love-poems. The surviving four manuscripts in Group III are all (p. lxxiv) what Professor Gardner calls 'edited' manuscripts, using the quotation mark because she thinks a copyist ought not to do the work of an editor:

The writer of *Lut* was aware of textual difficulties. From time to time he sets an alternative reading in the margin and at times he has corrected his text. I suspect that at other times he has adopted a reading from his second manuscript... (p. lxxiii)

so that his text is 'contaminated' with the text of Group II. But surely it is a good thing that these later copyists acted like editors; such work does not deserve the traditional rude word. What one would like to have, as well as an apparatus listing these preferences, would be some estimate of their purpose; do the 'editors' seem interested in getting the first or the last version written by the poet, the smoothest or the roughest line, or what? To upbraid them for contamination is only to admit that the classical technique no longer fits the case.[6]

II

The most important crux is an early one, in 'Elegy XIX' ('To his Mistris Going to Bed'). Just before the end of the poem, the standard text [i.e. Grierson] reads:

> Then since that I may know;
> As liberally, as to a Midwife, shew
> Thy self: cast all, yea, this white lynnen hence.
> There is no pennance due to innocence. (43–6)

But Professor Gardner prints:

> Here is no pennance, much lesse innocence.

I agree that the lady was probably the wife of a rich citizen; hence the jewelled hair-net and the chiming watch; but the editor seems to regard this as sufficient proof that the love can't have been called innocent. Literary criticism here has won its way back to the childlike prosiness of Bentley's emendations to *Paradise Lost*. All through the poem, the lady is encouraged to undress by being told it is the right thing to do, for very exalted reasons – hidden no doubt from the gross senses of conventional persons. At the most triumphant moment she becomes America, where men are even now 'like *Adams* time / Before he ate' (as a later poem tells us);[7] eminently a place where 'nature, injured by late law, sets free'[8] the desires of lovers. But most of the comparisons are celestial; she is a better world, and her girdle is the Milky Way; she is one of Mahomet's angels, or a sacred or magical text, only to be read by men dignified through her 'imputed grace' (the Calvinist doctrine here implies an awestruck sense of unworthiness). There is a steady rise in these exhilarated claims, and he calls her 'innocent' when he gets to the top. Donne is fond of arguing his way through an apparently indefensible case, and his logic is habitually sustained; he would think shame to collapse and confess himself guilty, with a simpering presumption of forgiveness, at the climax of a speech for the defence. Or is he supposed to be telling the lady how much he despises her? The crucial moment of a seduction seems the most unpractical time he could choose.

Indeed, a more general question imposes itself: 'Why is this not simply a dirty poem, please?' I think it becomes very dirty if you make the poet jab his contempt into the lady at the crisis of the scene of love, thus proving that all his earlier flattery of her must be interpreted as jeering. A whole generation has been brought up to believe that 'bitter irony' is the most poetical of the tones (Poe said melancholy was that); so they are proud to find it in all the most appreciated bits of literature, ruining them every time; and this is supposed to make them 'orthodox'. The chief benefit from reading imaginative literature is to make you realise that different people

have held extremely different moral beliefs; the chief effect of the
'scholarly' approach, saying perhaps 'a typical example of the
naturalist convention, copied directly from Ovid', is to save you the
trouble. Poets, when they are writing well, usually believe what they
say; though as a rule they also realise that certain other people would
say the opposite very firmly. In short, this poem is defiant, and that
is why it is not dirty; it is a challenge to someone, perhaps to the
fanatic tutors from whom Donne had recently escaped. You may call
such an epigram a joke if you wish, but it is a kind of joke which often
drives the man who makes it to accept as a duty some bold and
painful course. This tone of defiance was the easiest aspect of Donne
to recognise and imitate. Most of the Cavalier poets would
occasionally rally the parsons in a parody of theological language –
because they were so dashing, which meant highminded, ready to
daff the world aside for love. It is only our modern orthodox young
Donne who has to be made to express a specific sense of sin even while
writing a love-poem.

Such is the reason why I dislike the Gardner line; but I well
understand that we must submit to reality, and accept the authority
of the manuscripts. On looking at the apparatus and notes of the
edition, however, one finds that, of the three variants for the line, the
Gardner choice has the least manuscript authority. Of course, she
may still be right, but it is a case for reasoning; one needs to decide
how the curious structure of the three alternatives can have arisen. I
have become convinced, rather unwillingly, that Donne bowdlerised
the line himself. This was probably done in 1614, when he was much
frightened at being ordered by his criminal patron [Somerset] to
print his verse, immediately before he took orders. The line would
sound like a doctrinal heresy, even if it wasn't one; and the pious
would object to that, far more strongly than to a poem which could
be read as a dirty joke. But then, surely the proposed edition could
have left this one out. Perhaps he made the change twenty years
earlier, when some climbing and worldly young friend saw no point
in the romantic climax, and wanted the poem to be a dirty joke,
exactly as the pious would. The new line would seem to Donne
tolerable as an irony; indeed, it might echo the terrible irony on
innocent at the end of 'The Apparition'; he would not need to feel he
was knuckling under. He boasted of being careless about his poems;

he would say 'All right, I'll turn it round for you', and merely write in two words above two erased words, giving the line:

> There is no pennance much less innocence.

– 'much less the bad kind of thing which *they* call innocence'. In a way, the poem is free to use either line, because it presumes a disagreement, with the poet denying what the pious assert. But he would be deluding himself if he thought of this excuse for his weakening, because most readers were now free to interpret the poem in a way which he did not intend – or had not intended.

Also, this abrupt bowdlerisation spoilt the picture. In the old line, *There is* introduced a general proposition; now it makes the speaker point at the lady from far off, whereas the previous line says 'cast... *this* white lynnen hence', making him close enough to fumble at it. Wise collators therefore arrived at the line approved by Professor Gardner:

> *Here is* no pennance, much lesse innocence.

We may now examine the textual situation. The poem was not printed till 1669, perhaps being thought too indecent till the Restoration, and was then, says Professor Gardner (p. 130),

printed from a manuscript related to *Cy, O, P,* but having some poor readings of its own and others in common with inferior manuscripts such as *B*.

These are all group V manuscripts, and give our standard reading *due to*; it also occurs in two of the Group III manuscripts, half of them. The other two give the Gardner reading, and so does one group V manuscript (whereas six group V manuscripts give our standard reading). Overwhelming authority, however, is enjoyed by the third version:

> There is no pennance much less innocence.

which is given by Groups I, II and IV. Professor Gardner of course is right to reject this line, because it is bad. As she agrees that Donne made changes in at least two of the poems ('The Curse' and 'The Good-Morrow') she needs a good reason for saying that he made none here, where it would provide an obvious explanation. She says:

The agreement of groups I, II and III (less *Lut. O'F*) with *W* establishes 'much lesse' as the true reading, and I cannot regard the variant as anything but scribal in origin. (p. 133)

This is very mystifying. One assumes that 'the variant' must be *due to*, as that is the alternative to 'much less', but it was pointed out to me that the variant needs to be *There*. Putting *there* for 'here' could indeed be scribal in origin, in the sense of a slip which meant nothing to the scribe; but then, what was the origin of *due to*? It cannot be an unmeaning slip; it reverses the whole point of the line, wittily. And yet its grammar depends upon a previous accident, the change to *there*. Whereas, if you allow the process to go the other way round, there is no dependence upon accident and everyone behaves in character. The autograph of the poem, with its autograph correction, survived to be copied; no other source need be presumed. The loyal groups accepted the correction, but the more independent copyists who were the source of group V kept to the original text, still visible underneath (the purpose of such corrections would be very plain). Afterwards, the clumsy line left by the impatient botching of the author was put right in some of the 'edited' texts of Group III.

The editor's rejection of this possibility is somehow connected with the manuscript *W*, the sole member of group III (her p. lxxii):

The fact that groups I and II and *W* witness, with minor individual aberrations, to the same text of the Elegies rules out, in my opinion, the possibility that some of the variants in other manuscripts represent Donne's earlier versions. Everything points to the first section of *W* being an early collection.

It gives no poems later than 1598. Still, as it includes none of the *Songs and Sonnets*, that degree of purity was not hard to attain. If I were convinced by the editor's conclusion, it would only make me believe that Donne bowdlerised the line early (because a friend jibbed at it, maybe while Donne happened to be in a mood of resentment against women; perhaps soon after the love-affair recorded in the *Elegies* which ended in writing 'The Apparition'). Still, as we now learn that *W* is in Woodward's own handwriting, his degree of intimacy with the poet needs to be considered. He was about Donne's age, but there is no evidence of contact between them till Donne writes a verse letter, during his seclusion after his marriage, which refuses in a snubbing high-minded manner to let Woodward see any more of his poems. It begins 'Like one who'in her third widdowhood'; like her, his Muse now 'affects...a chaste fallownesse':

> Since shee to few, yet to too many'hath showne
> How love-song weeds, and Satyrique thornes are growne
> Where seeds of better Arts, were early sown. (4–6)

'Manure thy selfe then...And with vaine outward things be no more mov'd' (34–5). It is possible that Woodward had already copied the *Elegies*, which seem to have become available as a group, whereas the *Songs and Sonnets* had not been; in any case, Donne continued to refuse him the *Songs and Sonnets*, and would clearly want him to have a bowdlerised copy of the *Elegies*. The only argument I can find for calling his copy early is that he headed some verse letters to [Henry] Wotton 'To Mr H.W.' not 'To Sir H.W.'. Wotton was knighted when made ambassador to Venice in 1604, and Woodward was there in 1605 as a member of his staff; so he could not make the mistake in ignorance. But, if he were allowed to copy an old text (with bowdlerisations written onto it), he would retain 'To Mr H.W.' as of historical interest, dating the poem before 1605, though he would loyally accept any later alterations by the poet.[9] Professor Gardner must have further arguments about *W* up her sleeve, but I do not see how they can prove what she claims.

There is an entertaining detail about manuscript *B*, the Bridgewater manuscript, made for the son [John] of the Egerton with whose niece Donne eloped. 'Elegy XIX' is added in another handwriting, with a note: 'why may a man not write his owne Epithalamion if he can doe it so modestly'. This man had probably invented the theory that the poem was written for the marriage, expecting it to interest Lord Ellesmere (Ann was his first cousin); but no one suggests that he invented the line on which his theory depends. Professor Gardner, as already quoted, expresses contempt for the first printed version of the poem by saying it has some poor readings 'in common with inferior manuscripts such as *B*'; but, whatever reason she has for condemning *B* as a whole, it can give no reason for presuming that this addition by another hand has the same faults; she merely seems irritated by anything to do with *B*.[10] The flavour of this kind of argufying clings to a reader's palate all through her book.

In her apparatus for the poem itself, there are twelve variants for which *B* is quoted, apart from a handwriting contraction, and only one of them weakens the meaning. She judges *B* wrong in all but two cases; as a matter of literary preference (and she appears to blame the manuscript for 'trivial variations and patent errors'), I consider it right in all but three. For example, the poem begins:

> Come, Madam, come; all rest my powers defie,
> Until I labour, I in labour lie.
> The foe oft-times having the foe in sight,
> Is tir'd with standing though he never fight.

The editor reads '*they* never fight', following her usual loyal manuscripts, which direct our attention to the numerous army rather than the one male organ. Trivial no doubt, but a bowdlerisation rather than a patent error; though we need hardly call on the poet himself to invent it.

I was distressed by a change in 'The Good-Morrow', though it is slight, because the text of *1633* and Grierson is so beautiful. Anyway, the example gives us an interesting glimpse of Donne improving his poems.

> Let sea-discoverers to new lands have gone,
> Let Maps to other, worlds on worlds have showne,
> Let us possesse one world, each hath one, and is one.
>
> My face in thine eye, thine in mine appeares,
> And true plaine hearts doe in the faces rest...   (12–16)

'Possesse *our* world' reads Professor Gardner, and her note (p. 198–9) expresses a conviction that this is more fitting to the thought:

I do not doubt that the reading of *1633* ('one world') reproduces an error in Group I. The 'world' of each is the other. Since they are 'one' they possess one world which is 'ours', but there are also four worlds, since each 'hath one and is one'...

She has some skill, it will be observed, in imitating Donne at his worst, when he is struggling to obscure the obvious; but he is not doing that in the present case. The world of the lovers, with its two 'hemispheares', is one of the planets recently implied by Copernicus to be habitable; and the two lovers, jointly, have become the Intelligence or angel which pushes it round. There is a point in all this (which the editor ignores), as in calling the lady of 'Elegy XIX' his America; he is beyond the claims of church and state. The slow line tolling out 'one' has the awe of a space-landing, and then they begin muttering to one another; 'There's evidence for it; we really are on a planet of our own.' No wonder she remarks, of this and other variants in the poem: 'It is difficult to argue for the superiority of either version.'

However, she does spare the text from destruction at four other similar points, which she accepts as later improvements by the author; and she here (p. 197) points out that different copyists might derive both versions from the same piece of paper.[11] 'Sucked on childish pleasures, sillily' became our familiar *country pleasures, childishly*, 'slumbered' and 'fitter hemispheares' become *snorted* and *better*; and *or, thou and I | Love so alike, that none doe slacken, none can die*, at the end, was a correction from:

> Whatever dies, was not mixed equally.
> If our two loves be one, both thou and I
> Love just alike in all; none of these loves can die.   (19–21)

The poet thus removed a rather baffling picture. In our usual version, it is easy to accept *none* as envisaging two lovers only; the grammar for it should be 'neither', but the metre requires shortness. The earlier draft, by saying 'all', seems to insist upon many loves; are we to see the couple surrounded by fluttering Cupids, in the farm they have established on the planet Venus? Or are they already the teachers of a school, evangels of a religion of lovers? The poem seems unfinished, whereas the revision aims at leaving no loose ends. At any rate, this change leaves no doubt about their unity, and the change to *one world* has the same effect; it is thus inherently likely to have been made at the same time.

The next question is why Professor Gardner left it out. All five improvements are found in the Group I manuscripts, but *one world* is not also found in the 'allied but independent' manuscript *H40*. Group I manuscripts are all derived from one lost copy of a lost autograph text, and *H40* from another lost copy of it, thus 'providing a check'. But no reason is given why *H40* or its lost original is better, less likely to make a mistake here, than the lost original of Group I (on p. lxvi, *H40* is admitted to contain errors). After a brief expression of certainty, Professor Gardner gives literary or philosophical support for her choice; probably she felt too that the line as it has always been printed is needlessly harsh and strained. An editor, when the chances are even, should choose the reading which seems better; but such a choice cannot claim the grim authority of a scientific law.

A small variant in the 'Valediction: of weeping' seems to me to raise large issues. The tears of Donne, so long as he weeps in the presence of the lady, are valuable because they carry a tiny reflection of her:

> For thus they bee
> Pregnant of thee;
> Fruits of much griefe they are, emblemes of more,
> When a teare falls, that thou falst which it bore,
> So thou and I are nothing then, when on a divers shore. (5–9)

With authority from Groups I and II, the editor changes *thou falst* to 'thou falls'; in her note, after admitting that *falst* occurs in Group III (apparently the whole of Group III, and the Group V manuscripts *Cy*, *O*, *P*, *B*), she says: 'I regard it as an obvious correction of what might easily be taken to be a false concord' (p. 196). The meaning is 'That image of you, which was on the tear, falls with it', and 'the basic conceit is that an image reflected in a tear is an emblem of death by drowning'. But any copyist, one would think, and certainly the editorial ones of Group III, would understand as much of the poem as the Professor does in these two sentences. Besides, a pedant correcting the grammar would surely complete the process and put 'that thou falst *whom*'; *that thou falst which* is not over-simple but a grammatical paradox, such as the Professor is determined to shoo out of her text. She is doing what Theobald did to Shakespeare, altering the text to make a duller and simpler kind of poetry; and no wonder she can claim authority from the more decorous copyists; they too would want less strain in the grammar and a less harsh rhythm.

Previously, the separate planet in Donne's love-poetry (this tear is said to 'grow' into a 'world', and the second verse is about making a globe map) had been used to argue the safety and independence of the lovers who had reached it; but now he sees another aspect of space-travel – if they become separated, the gulfs between them are absolute. He sees her with a terrible clarity falling away from him on her tiny planet; such is the immediate effect, not needing interpretation from previous poems. The point of *thou falst* is to say 'It really is you'.

I may be told that he could not become confused in this way and that the phrase is not an 'immediate effect' but a 'forced expression'. It is easier to appreciate, certainly, if you recognise in it an important element in Donne's thought, which was what made him attend to the little reflections on the tears in the first place. This is the only bit of metaphysics in Metaphysical Poetry, and has been reasonably described as 'inverted platonism'. The style is commonly used to praise a ruler or saint or mistress, who is told 'You are in person the Platonic Idea of Justice, Virtue, Beauty' or whatever quality is being praised; and a memory of the chief example of this line of thought was in easy reach: 'You are like Jesus, who was the Logos as well as being an individual man, and this gives you magical power, as it did him' (at any rate, magical powers are usually deduced, as the poem goes on). Surely, unless you realise that this was what he meant about Elizabeth Drury, the 'Anniversaries' are just raw nonsense. The trick became conventional later, a thing a court poet could do as easily as 'make a leg' (the easiness is part of the charm of *Ask me no more where Jove bestows*), but the first readers of Donne seem to have felt it as liable to be dangerous, whether as Roman Catholic (an importation of the magnificent flattery of Spain) or as Radical-Reformist. The Family of Love believed that any man may become Christ, because Christ is only a condition of being, rather like an avatar of Vishnu or a reincarnation of the Buddha; just as the lady has a real presence in every one of her reflections upon Donne's tears – just as there could be a Martian Christ, as real as the human one. *The Everlasting Gospel* by A. L. Morton (1958) is a convenient short account of these sects. The reason why I have to appeal to Indian religion to make their ideas intelligible is that they were expunged from our tradition, mainly during Donne's life-time, in blood and fire. Such ideas are of course not prominent in this example, but they are a permanent background to his use of this characteristic trope, and important to him as well as familiar, so that he could write *thou falst* without the fancy seeming a trivial one.

The same point of difference, without any textual crux, appears in a note (p. 222) on two lines of 'The Relic':

> Thou shalt be a Mary Magdalen, and I
> A something else thereby.

It has been suggested that Donne intended that his bone would be thought to be a bone of Christ...But however sunk in 'mis-devotion' an age was it would surely be aware that the grave of Christ contained no relics other than his grave-clothes.

Professor Gardner would do better to inform herself about the beliefs of the fanatics of Donne's time. The grammatical form 'a Jesus

Christ' presumes a doctrine of messiahship which does not limit the field to the historical Jesus, and this idea was thoroughly familiar, though shocking. Donne of course is not presenting himself as a member of a fanatic sect, but as a martyr of True Love (a private thing); he supposes, as often elsewhere in his love-poems, that he will be worshipped as a saint when the world has grown sick of the religion of torture-worship, then hard at work burning people alive. Instead, the editor presumes that his bone is to be ascribed to one of the men who had enjoyed the Magdalene while she was unregenerate; but why should the pious adore, and expect miracles from, this mere cause of sin? The collapse of rational explanation makes it evident that the editor is fighting a rearguard action here. Maybe the poem was only an exercise in flattery; but it uses the resources of his rhetoric in a specially vehement and transparent form.

The argument from the meaning (over *thou falst*) is what seems to me decisive, and I would be tempted to argue, as Professor Gardner does, that the copyists who oppose my reading are just being stupid. The case does not look like a bowdlerisation. And yet the lay-out of the manuscripts for *no pennance due to* and *thou falst* is almost the same; both are supported by the group V manuscripts *Cy, O, P, B*, and *thou falst* by all the group III manuscripts, instead of only half. I had no idea of choosing such a recurrence, looking only for cases where the edition spoiled a beautiful poem. Then I found that the editor in her Preface (p. vii) and more thoroughly in her Introduction (pp. lxxvii, lxxxii) claims to have defeated *Cy, O, P* by discovering *HK2*. They derive from it, she finds, and it is only a copy of a group II manuscript, adding random errors, so her research 'enables us to dismiss as degenerate some of the manuscripts that Grierson thought contained early readings' (p. vii).

Well, in the two cases I happened to choose, *HK2* is undoubtedly not the source of our standard text; it does not include 'Elegy XIX', and votes with Professor Gardner over *thou falst*. Grierson may still be wrong, but the argument as printed does not refute him in these cases. The group of manuscripts is found not to have only one source, and this, I suggest, is inherently likely for Donne manuscripts.

It looks then, from the parallel, as if Donne himself made the change to 'thou falls', and he would only do it for reasons of private conscience, to renounce his earlier heresies; he could not fear scandal from so faint a hint. He was a man capable of this rather extravagant scrupulosity; but, to provide evidence, a more external case of censorship is wanted. Some variants in 'The Dream' make the point amusingly clear. The lady entered the bedroom while Donne was dreaming about her, and this showed a divine omniscience. The text should be:

> My Dreame thou brok'st not, but continued'st it,
> Thou art so truth, that thoughts of thee suffice,
> To make dreames truths; and fables histories...
>   Yet I thought thee
> (Thou lovest truth) but an Angell, at first sight,
> But when I saw thou sawest my heart,
> And knew'st my thoughts, beyond an Angels art...
> I doe confesse, I could not chuse but bee
> Prophane, to thinke thee any thing but thee.

Professor Gardner prints 'so true' against strong authority, and comments (p. 209):

In spite of Grierson's defence of 'so truth' as the more difficult reading and his quotation from Aquinas to support the interpretation that Donne is equating the lady with God who is truth itself, I find 'so truth' a very forced expression and the repetition of 'truth... truth' unpleasing to the ear. Also, to impute divinity to the lady at this point is to spoil the fine audacious climax by anticipation.

'Truth–truth' is ugly, but the slight vowel-change with the plural makes *truths* all right, and this has fair support from Groups II and III. The corrected text may well have been hard to read. *So truth* has strong support from Groups I and II, and the objection that the expression is 'forced' seems merely a resistance to the thought which it expresses. Donne says it would be profane to call the lady anything but herself, and as she is plainly not the Christian God he means she is something better – the cooing repetition of *thee* makes clear that *she* would be profaned, not God. Plainly this climax is not spoiled by ascribing to her one of the attributes of the deity beforehand. The editor then retains the pointless variant '(For thou lov'st truth) an Angell' (printed in *1633*, and one of the few cases where Grierson was wrong in accepting that edition) on the grounds that the repeated *but* is ugly, and that this line too would spoil 'the fine hyperbole of the close'. But logic is so prominent in Donne's verse that repeating a word with another meaning does not hurt, and here the first *but* means 'only' ('you won't mind my saying – I thought you were only a housemaid'). Professor Gardner's apparatus is very capricious, as she forewarns us (p. xciv); here she will not let us know whether any manuscripts support the reading she prefers, though she lists the strong support for the one with a point to it which she rejects. Nor does Grierson tell us, so I am free to hope that Donne never wrote the line they print; but, if he did, the good line is his second thought. The parody of theology in *so truth* would also have to be a second thought, as 'true' is given by all manuscripts except some of Groups I and II.

On the other hand, second thoughts evidently told Donne that he must not 'confess he was profane'; that might give stupid people a handle. So he altered the lines to:

> I must confesse, it could not chuse but bee
> Prophaness, to thinke thee any thing but thee.

Professor Gardner claims merit for printing *prophane*, like all previous editions, in the teeth of Groups I and II. As 'prophaness' gives 'a hopelessly unmetrical line', she must 'prefer the charge of inconsistency to that of being deaf to the music of Donne's verse'. I don't find the extra syllable very trying, but it does need explanation. Donne, it seems clear, after changing the second 'I' into 'it', felt that thorough grammar required the abstract noun as well. Here again the editor's apparatus refuses to admit any authority for reading *prophane*, but there is an admission in a note (p. 210):

I do not doubt that 'Prophane' is a correction made in the copy for *1633* and do not regard its appearance in manuscripts outside the main groups as argument for its authenticity.

We can discover who they were. In the previous line, 'I' is given as the reading of *Cy, P, B* and so on, the usual gang of sordid contaminators; and we may be sure they read *prophane* as well, because otherwise they would give the absurd form 'I could not chuse but bee / Prophaness'. As usual, they are giving the text as it was before it was bowdlerised, and the editor does not choose to let us know that she is for once agreeing with them. She makes no attempt to explain what had happened to the manuscripts here; and I do not see how there could be any explanation except the one she rejects. The variants for the sentence about *prophane* would alone be strong evidence for thinking that *Cy, O, P* sometimes preserve for us the uncorrected text; adding *pennance due* and *thou falst*, this theory has enough evidence to 'hold the field', that is, be accepted till some better explanation is found. It is not enough for Professor Gardner to tell us she despises *Cy*, *O*, *P*; as A. E. Housman said, in an article on textual criticism, 'action with a motive is more probable than action without a motive'.[12]

It is, however, very odd to find Donne gearing up the blasphemy in one paragraph and toning it down in the next. This poem is evidently early, and to say that he did not even keep copies of his poems might be only his grand manner; he probably mulled over them, and made small changes, every few years up to 1614. Even so, he did not remove *so truth* when removing 'I...prophane'. But then, to call a lady 'divine' in a poem was standard, and this poem merely does it thoroughly; he might even claim, if he had to defend himself, that he was rebuking such talk by a parody of it; and the poem though literally blasphemous does not insinuate any active and influential heresy. But in confessing himself profane he laid himself open to a stupid retort, and a man who had started accusing him might look round for better ammunition.

Professor Gardner could answer that, in most of these cases, I have in effect agreed that her text is the right one, as it gives the final decision of the author. The point could be taken further; many readers would have agreed with her if she had printed 'so true' as the *better* version, and accused the later version *so truth* of bad taste. An editor, I think, should not print a text censored by the author when under duress, or after having changed his beliefs so much as to be out of sympathy with it. The poem should appear as when geared up to its highest expressiveness and force; so I would print the corrected *so truth* and the uncorrected *prophane*. But, though it is all right to be eclectic, one should not jump from one version to another, as the Gardner text does for *prophane* within one sentence. In all these cases, though her information is very interesting, it does not give her enough reason to spoil the established text, which was well prepared for by collators who 'edited'.

III

I am now to consider the dating of the poems in the new edition; here again the difference is not numerically large. The editor divides the *Songs and Sonnets* into I and II, with exactly 27 poems in each group, and says that the second group were all written after Donne's marriage in December 1601. My view is that about ten of the second group need to be put back (of course, more of them may in fact be early). None of the first group needs bringing forward. A rule of interpretation is more likely to affect the public image of the poet, though perhaps it is widespread already; Professor Gardner insists that none of Donne's poems were written to his wife, so that practically all the poems in group II are about love-affairs with other women. However, no adultery took place (at least, I am told that this is what her Introduction means); the poems are the product of an intense life of fantasy. Until Donne's marriage threw him out of work, the editor decides (pp. lviii–lix), he had not much time for reading, but during the two and a half years at Pyrton, from 1602 to 1605, he read authors who held Neoplatonic or philosophic views on love, and he illustrated them in verse with imaginary situations. He is praised (p. xxx) for having 'imagined and given supreme expression to the bliss of fulfilment' in mutual love, with the firm implication that he never achieved it. This theory makes Donne a feebler kind of man than he was, and also makes him treat his wife very badly, so it encourages a thorough misreading of the poems.

The editor has a serious bit of evidence, and she naturally puts it at the start of the General Introduction (pp. xvii–xviii):

The poems that Donne wrote on this theme of mutual love are charged with such a tone of conviction and expressed with such a naked and natural force of language that it is commonly assumed that they must directly reflect an actual experience of such a rapturous discovery of a new heaven and a new earth in love; and many critics have taken them as celebrating his love for Ann More and their reckless marriage. But Donne himself has warned us against making any such simple equation between the truth of the imagination and the truth of experience. Writing to Sir Robert Carr in 1625, in apology for the feebleness of his poem on the death of Hamilton and the reward of the blessed in heaven, he said: 'You know my uttermost when it was best, and even then I did best when I had least truth for my subjects.'

Carr was a Scots courtier, five or six years younger than Donne, and the first letters to him seem to date from 1610; Donne treats him with reverence as a go-between in the struggle for employment (Gosse, *The Life and Letters of John Donne*, I, 238). Later, probably in 1619, he gives this patron a copy of his treatise on suicide, and admits having promised to send him 'the poems' – which is not at all likely to mean the *Songs and Sonnets*. Donne is within six years of his death when he writes the brief but earnest note of 1625, saying he would rather have travelled with the corpse to Scotland and preached a funeral sermon there; his last known attention to his love-poems had occurred ten years before. He may have come to agree with Ben Jonson, and considered poems like 'The Calme' and 'The Flea' his highest flights. He must have been long accustomed to use the traditional escape for poets, 'The truest poetry is the most feigning', let alone that for gentlemen, 'She never loved me back really.' But these were not even relevant here. Just after Carr began to notice him he published the two 'Anniversaries', about a girl he had never met; his other elegies and verse-letters would be the main part of his verse known in court circles; and an elegy is what is in prospect. Professor Gardner behaves as if she is wringing a new doctrine out of a sacred text; she can hardly think that Donne meant Carr to interpret this letter, at the time, as saying: 'You know my most intimate poems of mutual love, written long before we had met, and they were best when I didn't really love the girl, though I was pretending to.' Even if this were possible, he would still be saying he had had a subject, and not only a day-dream. The sentence cannot be made to do what the editor wants of it.

She makes a concession, writing on the theme of 'mutual love' (p. xxviii):

I do not doubt that there is a connexion between Donne's love for Ann More and the appearance of his theme in his poetry, and that we can see reflected in these poems Donne's situation in the years that followed his marriage. But the poems themselves, even the most idealistic, are too far from the reality we know of for us to speak of them as written to Ann More, or even about her. The bond they celebrate is not the bond of marriage.

It was humiliating to be thrown out of employment, and housed by the charity of his wife's cousin; no doubt he would grizzle, while keeping up his law and planning his come-back; day-dreams about torturing her father with the equipment in the Tower, which he commanded, would seem natural enough. Donne had become 'a disobliged man', as he said later to the king's favourite. Instead, we must envisage him huddled up behind the locked door of the study, too poor to get out of earshot of the squalling brats but wrapped in a dream of being still a rich adulterer. One of the poems which the editor ascribes to this time ('Love's Growth') says:

> Love's not so pure, and abstract, as they use
> To say, which have no Mistresse but their Muse. (11-12)

Surely he would have found writing this, under such circumstances, intolerably humiliating? Gosse gave the same date to this poem, but he assumed that the wife would be flattered to be called a mistress; no sin-haunted libertine could do that, in the mind of Professor Gardner. Dimly realising maybe that her picture is a strange one, she recalls that art is a mystery (p. xxi):

If Shakespeare's imagination could give life at the same time to a Mercutio and a Romeo, to an Iago and an Othello, why should we think it impossible for Donne to turn from the mood of 'Love's Growth' to the mood of 'Love's Alchemy'?

Well, in the first place, because he wasn't writing a play. She rightly emphasises that his work feels like direct experience, it has 'dramatic intensity' (p. xix), 'a tone of conviction, an accent of truth' (p. xx). I agree that this effect is not got by literal truth, but it depends on living in the world described – wishing your lie was true, instead of the similar but less smart thing which has just happened. It needs to be fresh; and it requires, not great leisure but a mind free to concentrate itself upon such matters, briefly. A man hardly could write like that when he had just been exasperatingly wronged, and was in consequence too poor even to buy the clothes necessary for paying visits and seeking his fortune. One can indeed imagine an aesthete who would settle down thankfully after a runaway marriage, while digging his cabbage patch maybe, to construct good poetry out of the insights which city life had afforded him; but Donne always rigidly refused to allow this kind of importance to his poetry. Professor Gardner does not realise what a strain it would be to elaborate and write up a series of hallucinatory erotic day-dreams, unsupported by any theory or framework, and entirely without self-approval – Donne must have been lying out of shame when he wrote the pious letter to Woodward, saying that his Muse was in a chaste fallowness. And why should this course be a temptation? Sex, after all, was the one thing he wasn't starved of just then, and didn't need to imagine. There is a ready explanation, however, if he wrote the 'Farewell to Love' at this time. It tells us never to bother about women, because a man gets bored with a woman as soon as he has enjoyed her; surely his wife would not believe that this was merely part of an erotic survey? We must suppose, if we accept the editor's dating, that he married for ambition, and turned nasty when he was disappointed.

But we know that he felt compunction at having reduced Ann to such misery. He could fairly have said it was the fault of her father, who had unreasonably insisted on throwing the husband out of employment; but what crops up in the surviving letters, repeatedly, is this honourable sense of compunction. He says in 1608 (Gosse, *The Life and Letters*, I, 214):

I write from the fireside in my parlour, and in the noise of three gamesome children, and by the side of her, whom because I have translated into a wretched fortune, I must labour to disguise that from her by all honest devices, as giving her my company and discourse; therefore I steal from her all the time which I give this letter, and it is therefore that I take so short a list...But if I melt into a melancholy whilst I write, I shall be taken in the manner; and I sit by one too tender towards these impressions.

In 1614, refusing to pay a visit because it would leave his wife alone with the children, he is still saying (Gosse, *The Life and Letters*, II, 48):

So much company as I am, therefore, she shall not want; and we had not one another at so cheap a rate, as that we should ever be weary of one another.

No convention made him talk like this.

The editor of course has a reason for her account of the biography; she wants the poet's head to be practically empty till he is converted to Neoplatonism. During the leisure after his marriage he is to discover Leone Ebreo, who had published in 1535, and use his ideas for day-dreams. But the main claim of Donne's early poetry, which must have been recognised as he founded a school of satirists, was to revolt against the platonising then current and let in the fresh air of realism. Of course he knew about the things he excluded; you might as well say he didn't know classical mythology. Later (though before the turn of the century, I think) he took to 'inverted platonism', but this was very different from copying out the simplicities of Ebreo, whom he would consider out of date when he began his career. It is by the easy device of ascribing all poems which make thoughtful reflections about love, however boyish, to this late date that Professor Gardner builds up her striking picture.

And then again, what does she think the earlier Donne was busy at? A young man can canter through an inheritance and yet find himself confronted by many hours when he might just as well be reading a book; and the editor gives us no reason to doubt what

Donne said himself, that he had from his youth a hydroptic desire for knowledge. No doubt Egerton kept him fairly busy, but he was secretary for less than three years. Besides, the editor does not ascribe the increased thoughtfulness in the poet wholly to the leisured reading after his marriage; a change had already begun when he wrote 'The Progress of the Soul'. This has a dedication dated August 1601; his marriage was in that December, and as Egerton's secretary he had been seeing the Essex conspiracy at close hand. The unfinished poem seems to me to have little to do with either, and I expect it was abandoned as soon as public affairs became exciting. Later, while having to decide about his love for Ann, he tried to resume the poem as a way of calming himself, but found he could only manage a dedication. To date the dedication of an unfinished poem is in any case a fidgety thing to do, and cannot be relied on for the date of the main writing. Professor Gardner says (p. lviii):

The man who wrote this poem had intellectual interests very different from those of the author of the *Satires* and the *Elegies*. He had been reading more curious authors than Horace, Ovid, and Martial. I find it hard to believe that a man whose mind was filled with these concerns and who had set himself so ambitious a task as this poem launches out on was, at the same time, writing love-lyrics.

Might it not also be hard to believe that he was seducing his employer's niece? To abduct the hostess of the palace of the Keeper of the Great Seal may properly, indeed, be called ambitious, but to assist the operation by writing her a love-lyric could hardly be out of keeping. The conviction that he could never have written a poem to his wife, because a libertine despises marriage, becomes almost splendid here. It seems to be merely a result of assuming that Donne was like Baudelaire and Valéry.

The 'Valediction: forbidding Mourning', says Professor Gardner (p. xxix), cannot have been written to his wife before going to France with Sir Robert Drury in 1611; because it forbids mourning:

> T'were prophanation of our joyes
> To tell the layetie our love.   (7–8)

'This is not an argument to use to a wife, who has no need to hide her grief at her husband's absence.' An outraged footnote continues:

When we consider the circumstances in which Donne left his wife in 1611, to face alone the last weary months of pregnancy and her eighth labour, it seems impossible to accept Walton's statement, first made in 1675, that 'A Valediction: forbidding mourning' was written on this occasion.

I hope this means that Professor Gardner will give us a biography of the poet; the sentence as it stands is hardly more than a threat that she has ammunition in reserve. The story as usually told is that Donne asked his wife's permission, which she only granted because they depended on the allowance from this patron; so then she went and stayed with relations in the Isle of Wight. Some of her relations were rich and grand, so we may hope she had a pleasant holiday. I should warmly agree that he was a bad husband to give his wife so many children, if this is what is at the back of the editor's mind; but the idea seems to have been unknown at the time, and besides, Donne was becoming more under the influence of the church throughout his married life; we may be sure that the clergy would have denounced any relief for child-birth, then as later. Donne says nothing in verse about his children because he found them merely a nuisance, but this didn't keep him from being devoted to his wife; I expect Blake and D. H. Lawrence would have felt the same, if they had not been spared. That love is a private religion, no less august than the public sects, was a thing he regularly argued in verse, and he might assume it here. But the idea that the gentry keep a stiff upper lip, and do not expose themselves to being comforted by people they despise, was in easy reach. He tells her not to cry because it weakens her and is bad for her, but what he says also calls out her reserves of pride – both in her lost grandeur and her renunciation of it for love. Yet no explanation would suffice. What is likeable in Professor Gardner's book, not found in the set-piece of praise for the great love poet in her Introduction, spurts out in hot jets of contempt for this twisting cad; they emerge from many an unlooked-for cranny. Peering into the darkness behind the façade, I think I make out another figure looming beside the vast shade of Oscar Wilde – can it be Mrs Pankhurst? A man does not need to be an aesthete, she would clearly agree, before he can be a pig to women.

I would not deny that the later poems to his wife are darkened by the slow approach to capitulation. He seems to have become genuinely afraid of the new philosophy, as no other English poet did, and this helped to pull him down. That he would have to turn parson, as the king would allow him no other employment, became increasingly clear – and to do it with honour or without shame would require tearing himself to pieces in public, for the sermons which T. S. Eliot intelligibly found vulgar;[13] also it would amount to a separation from his wife. This is plain from the beastly sonnet he wrote on her death ['Since she whome I lovd, hath payd her last debt', *Divine Poems*, p. 14], begging God not to be jealous any more as he has stopped loving her. I am glad that Professor Gardner adopted the punctuation of the [Roger E.] Bennett edition (*The Complete Poems of John Donne*, Chicago, 1942):

> But why should I begg more love, when as thou
> Dost wooe my soule, for hers offring all thine.   (9–10)

He goes on: 'Even now that I have given up her love to win yours, you are still jealous if I so much as love a saint.' He no longer expected to meet her in the next world: 'when we shall go to them, whether we shall know them or no, we dispute';[14] and he finally broke his promise to be buried with her, choosing St Paul's. No wonder he had fought like a cat to avoid having to dedicate himself to this disgusting God.

While explaining that he could not have written poems to his wife, the editor reports him quoting from St Jerome, in a sermon, that there is nothing more disgusting than for a man to love his wife like a woman he commits adultery with (the running translation by Donne softens the Latin into 'not a more uncomely, a poorer thing, than to love a Wife like a Mistresse'). 'Cf.' says the editor, grimly presuming that he thought the same when he wrote the poems (p. xxix). But this is unfair to Donne. He accepted the cynicism of Christianity about love, along with all the rest of its horrors, because he could not otherwise feed his wife and children. We have few more striking martyrs to domesticity. The simpering egotistic nastiness of Jerome and Baudelaire, the familiar alliance of the devotee and the debauchee, was entirely foreign to his mind.

This darkening of the sky probably explains the great 'Nocturnall'. I accept the view that he wrote the poem in France in 1611, thinking that his wife had died in childbirth (as it is about the shortest day, commonly called St Lucy's Day, and has quite enough concentration, there is no need to drag in a woman called Lucy). Then all the details are real; he may well look back on their first struggles together as a time of great happiness, absurdly mistaken for suffering, before he began being gradually distilled into increasing degrees of privation. But now the rest of his life must be preparation for the next world; if she is dead, there is nothing to keep him out of the church any longer, and (though the thought is not fit for verse) money will have to be got hold of for all those children. His language at the climax entertains an obscure hope that they may be together in Heaven; perhaps his last attempt to reconcile the two claims.

Such then are the large questions at issue when one tries to decide on the dates of the poems. Professor Gardner has made a study of the metres for the purpose, reporting for example 'there are no "philosophic" poems...in the stanzas that are made up of a combination of decasyllabic with octosyllabic lines' (p. lvi). Even if the poet did prefer a type of stanza for a type of poem, that would not prove that all such poems were written together; it would rather suggest the contrary. I agree that there is a type of love-poem to another woman which would seem all right to his wife and to the world she lived in – the poem bemoaning a great lady's refusal to go to bed with him, for which she might toss him some gold. Trying to get his wife's bills paid in this way would produce a Platonic poem; but such a poem, boasting of the continence of the lovers, might have been written quite early, as a stage in the wooing of an alderman's wife; it is not a secure means of dating. The main reliance has therefore to be upon historical detail, and I think that very few of the arguments are even plausible.

'The Sunne Rising' says:

> Goe tell Court-huntsman, that the King will ride... (7)

James' taste for hunting became a recognised inconvenience, so there would be some point in laughing at it here. Professor Praz was the first to say so; without answering Gosse, who had said that Henry IV of France was just as probable. The young Donne was well aware of foreign courts, and most kings found hunting an escape from deskwork. I expect this poem was written to his wife, not long after they got to Pyrford, and therefore before the death of Elizabeth; but to have it written earlier to another woman would do no harm. There is a nice case in 'A Valediction: of the booke', which says that a woman wrote Homer. This idea, say the notes, was hard to get at before Lipsius mentioned it in Latin (Antwerp 1602), though extant in Greek (Rome, *c.* 1550; Basle, *c.* 1560). Surely the poet knew plenty of dons who would give him titbits like that. The poem is likely to address his wife, as it boasts that the pair have gone through a long struggle. It is not very good, but the deduction from the wild piece of learning can be accepted.

We now arrive at the 'Farewell to Love', which tells us that a man becomes bored with a woman as soon as he has been to bed with her.

> ...from late fair
> His highness sitting in a golden Chaire,
>   Is not less cared for after three dayes
>   By children, then the thing which lovers so
>   Blindly admire, and with such worship wooe...   (11–15)

Professor Gardner (p. 213) quotes a learned authority on gingerbread fairings, who lets out that he has never seen a moulding of a monarch on a throne, and that mouldings usually represented nursery-rhyme or otherwise legendary figures; but then he rallies sufficiently to testify that a representation of a reigning monarch might sometimes possibly have occurred. No one can object that the evidence here is forced, but the result is forced; the poem is firmly printed among the 'philosophic' ones written after marriage. And now the editor can put 'Love's Alchemy' there as well, because the two poems, she remarks, are 'alike'. I sometimes feel baffled by this criterion, but here I can agree; in each poem one finds a rather nasty brash boyishness.

'The Undertaking' (apparently claiming chastity as well as secrecy for a love-affair) has to be in the after-marriage group because it mentions *specular stone*. The notes (p. 180) explain that Donne could have got the legendary information about this from a work by an Italian author first published in 1599, and that he did read this work because he names the man in *Ignatius his Conclave* (1611); but that he could have got everything he says in the poem out of Pliny's *Natural History*, and indeed must have done (some people say) because he confuses two stones mentioned in consecutive passages there.

In 'The Primrose' the poet sees a lot of the flowers on a hill, and says:

> ...their forme, and their infinitie
> Make a terrestriall Galaxie,
>   As the small starres doe in the sky:
> I walke to finde a true Love...   (5–8)

He means a flower which would bring good luck because it had an even number of petals, but he proceeds to consider the kind of woman he wants, fitting in a series of arch stock insults against women, who appear to be an almost unknown enemy nation; at the end, he becomes practically incoherent with artfulness or spite or something. One needs three periods to classify these poems; the third after marriage, as in the editor's II, the second after he has at least enough acquaintance with a mistress to afford companionship in intrigue, though he may denounce her, and the first to contain this kind of thing. I suppose he has only yet achieved prostitutes, and hopes to hide it by pretending to despise the great ladies who have yielded to him. For her date, Professor Gardner quotes (pp. 219–20) an argument that no one knew the Milky Way to be made of stars until Galileo printed [in *Siderius Nuncius*] what he had learned from his telescope (1610); she also refers us to *Batman Upon Bartholeme* (1582). *Batman* is a sturdy compact handbook of popular science, and it says that even Aristotle already knew that the Milky Way is made of tiny stars. None the less, the editor 'incline[s] to think' that there is 'a topical reference here'. She feels obliged to think this because it has been a recent fashion to say that Donne only became interested in astronomy for a brief time after Galileo's publication; but he is already using technical astronomical terms in the *Elegies*. '[O]n the principle of Occam's razor', continues the editor (p. 257), the poem must have been written in 1613, together with 'Good Friday' (the one poem crudely boyish, the other sadly beaten down), because this is the only date when Donne is known to have visited Montgomery Castle. We may be sure Donne went to the Castle as soon as he could get invited, Occam or no, but he couldn't have gone before 1599, too late for such a poem (p. 253). The story that the poem was written about the primroses at Montgomery Castle appears in the second edition; it is a rather sweet piece of toadyism, calculated to please everyone, but not at all liable to be true.

'The Anniversarie' says *Two graves must hide thine and my coarse* which presumes that the lovers cannot marry; and it begins by saying that *All Kings, and all their favorites* are older by a year now than when the lovers first met. The notes comment (p. 199):

When read with 'The Sun Rising' and 'The Canonization' this poem seems likely to have been written, as they were, when James was on the throne. It breathes the same scorn for the Court from which Donne was an exile.

Surely he was already quite capable of scorning courts in the *Satires*; this poem is a standard member of my second group. 'The Canonization', I agree, is typical of the defiant poems justifying Donne's marriage, and it says *the King's reall, or his stamped face* (7); but it may have been written before Elizabeth was dead. The lover has withdrawn from the world, and only knows in general that the heads on coins are usually male ones. However, if we found mention of kings in no other poems but these, it might be significant; so I looked back at the admittedly early *Elegies* for mention of kings, and found plenty. Thus in 'The Perfume' Donne is smelt by the young lady's father while creeping to her bedroom:

> When, like a tyran King, that in his bed
> Smelt gunpowder, the pale wretch shivered.
> Had it beene some bad smell, he would have thought
> That his owne feet...   (43–6)

– a patent reference to the Gunpowder Plot, and also to the disgust excited by James among handsome young courtiers; the case is far stronger than any the editor has adduced. 'Internal evidence' is usually weak, and cannot help being, but sometimes the pointers converge and amount to good evidence. They do not do it here.

A textual point has to be put at the end, after the discussion of 'philosophic' poems, because it can only be understood if you realise that Professor Gardner wants to make Donne copy out the insipid Ebreo.[15] For this purpose she rewrites the text of 'The Extasie', without any manuscript authority at all.

> As our blood labours to beget
>   Spirits, as like soules as it can,
> Because such fingers need to knit
>   That subtile knot, which makes us man:
> So must pure lovers soules descend
>   T'affections, and to faculties
> Which sense may reach and apprehend;
>   Else a great Prince in prison lies.
> To'our bodies turne wee then, that so
>   Weake men on love reveal'd may look...   (61–70)

The editor prints '*That* sense may reach', explaining in her notes (p. 187):

'sense' does not 'reach and apprehend' affections and faculties but 'reaches and apprehends' the objects of perception by means of affections and faculties. If we read 'That' (in order that) the action of the souls parallels the action of the blood.

But surely, the blood produces something higher than itself on the ladder of being, so as to meet the souls, and the souls go down to affections and faculties, where this thing can meet them. It is called 'sense'. Professor Gardner says that the souls must descend 'in order that man's sense organs may become rational', and she quotes Ebreo as saying 'in order that man may approach the objects of sense in the world around him', but these plans are very different. She makes them look less different by depriving the verbs of their direct object, thus producing an impression of tactful guff extremely remote from the style of Donne (as one might say 'corsets that endear' or 'perfumes that fetch'); indeed, since philosophers often try to explain the delusions caused by the senses, I should be inclined to improve the line further, and put 'in order that sense may reach and apprehend pink elephants'.

Professor Gardner is right to say that the verse is about the senses becoming rational; Donne was fascinated by this idea. Wordsworth thought the typical case was the baby at the breast, rightly no doubt, but for Donne it was the high-born lady. Such creatures, owing to their delicacy of feeling, illustrated the mysteries of Nature almost as translucently as an angel would do, and this was a major reason for his craving to know them. It is why Elizabeth Drury's body 'almost thought', and why God had to make better clay for the 'through-shine' body of the Countess of Bedford. Their senses are inter-related with their souls, so that they think 'intuitively', grasping a whole situation at once. What they sense, in fact, turns out to be 'affections and faculties', not 'objects of sense *through* them' – they are not praised, like the princess in the fairy story, for feeling a dried pea under nineteen mattresses.

In any case, Donne's *sense* includes sexual desire, as is needed for the surprise of his argument. We owe our bodies thanks, he says,

> ...because they thus
> Did us, to us, at first convay,
> Yeelded their forces, sense, to us,
> Nor are drosse to us, but allay.   (53–6)

'We could not recognise each other's presence without the use of our senses', unanswerable as far as it goes, insinuates a different meaning 'we could not appreciate one another's characters unless urged forward by sensual desire'. *Affections* was not a technical term; it carried then more suggestion than it does now of bodily weakness and sensual desire, but could already mean love as well. Thus *affections...which sense may reach* could mean simply 'desires in you which are recognised instinctively by desires in me'; though it was sure to mean something more affectionate as well, as the teaching powers of love had been celebrated for so long. Indeed, an eruption of passion was to be expected after the long spiritual ecstasy, as was so often found at revivalist camp meetings. The idea that the story needs explaining away is itself what needs explanation. Professor Gardner maintains that the lovers have been to bed together already, so that at the end of the poem they merely 'recover their senses', or stop being in ecstasy, and are ready to receive the visitor. It is true that the words are not explicit. But when such a master has used all his resources to present an astonishing turn in his logic and his story, the usual presumption is that he means something adequate to the occasion he has created.

One expects almost any good thing to be destroyed now. But I must say I am rather encouraged by this last emendation. It is so obviously wrong.[16] Maybe we will be allowed to keep the text of Donne after all.

CHAPTER 4

Rescuing Donne

In the twenties, when my eyes were opening, it was usual for critics to consider that Donne in his earlier poetry held broad and enlightened views on church and state, that he was influenced by the recent great scientific discoveries, and that he used the theme of freedom in love partly as a vehicle for these ideas to show what the ideological and sociological effects of Paracelsus and Copernicus would turn out to be. A critic of the time wrote: 'His correct interpretation of the effects of the dark beginnings of our modern science places him on a level with Mr H. G. Wells for piercing insight.'[1] I was imitating this Donne, the poet as so conceived, in my own verse at the time with love and wonder, and I have never in later years come across any good reason for the universal change of opinion about him at the start of the thirties. I am anxious not to give too feeble an impression of the loathing with which I regard the present image of him. The habitual mean-mindedness of modern academic criticism, its moral emptiness combined with incessant moral nagging, its scrubbed prison-like isolation, are particularly misleading in the case of Donne; in fact, we are the ones who need rescuing, not the poet. But the text of the love poems does literally need rescuing, at a small number of crucial points, from the recent edition edited by Professor Helen Gardner (*The Elegies and the Songs and Sonnets*, Oxford, 1965). I am of course glad to accept the main results of the massive work which has been put into the manuscripts, but I am chiefly concerned with the interpretation of them. The problem of the manuscripts is still very puzzling, and the simple theory which I propose would at least clear up one of the major difficulties.

It was not until my 'Donne the Spaceman' appeared in *The Kenyon Review* (Summer 1957) that I first realised my colleagues and I disagreed so vehemently on this matter. My 'Donne in the New

Edition' (*Critical Quarterly*) was a reaction to the first shock of reading Professor Gardner, who apparently had felt that she was bringing to ripeness the accepted scholarly conclusions on the subject, and could hardly believe that anyone disagreed with them. Part of my case has been presented in my previous articles, which are concerned mainly with the intellectual interests of the young Donne; here I have focused on the text.

The chief event in the textual field since the Gardner edition of the love poems has been the companion edition of the *Satires* and *Verse Letters* by Wesley Milgate.[2] It has helped my case a good deal, especially by clearing up the subject of manuscript *W*. Donne became famous during his lifetime for poems which he refused to print, so that they gradually got into circulation in a variety of manuscripts. Even as a young man, wanting to become a civil servant and politician (before he was converted and became a parson), he feared that the love poems would stand in his way, and tried to keep them out of manuscript circulation.[3] But the satires could be shown round; they had claims to be grave and moral, and anyway writing satires was considered a respectable pastime. However, manuscripts that provide an early form of the text show that manuscript *W* is not the original version. In Satire IV, line 48, Donne spoiled one of his own jokes out of professional caution. The real text, after remarking that all men are liars but the biggest liars are ecclesiastical historians, instanced one Papist and one Protestant historian; but nearly all the surviving manuscripts give two Papists. This had already been pointed out by Grierson in his magnificent edition of 1912;[4] Mr Milgate presents additional proof that the change was made in 1598 when Donne had just been made secretary to Egerton, for whom he was actually writing another satire to help forward some legal reform. Egerton would need to be assured that Donne was now a staunch Protestant. Mr Milgate's further evidence (p. lviii) is rather hard to summarise but it is strong. I can accept it as an admission by my opponents, since Mr Milgate writes as a loyal disciple of Professor Gardner. For the *Satires*, in this clear case and a number of minor ones, manuscript *W* gives the doctored text. The first part of *W* is held to be not later than 1598, so the debate established by Mr Milgate is crucial; and the poet would have the same reason for a little doctoring of both satires and elegies. Even if lawyer Egerton wanted only satires, Donne would meet a number of important gentlemen with whom he needed to make friends, and many of them would be agog for the elegies. This group of poems, on the whole set pieces written to a dramatic theme, appears to have got into a very limited circulation before he became cautious about showing poems, so that they would be known and asked for; whereas those of the songs and sonnets which were already written were kept secret. He would mull over the elegies, after he had consented to read a few poems after dinner, considering which would do, and occasionally writing a less upsetting word or phrase above the line. Fun with sex would not upset that audience, but a suspicion of heresy (about sex or anything else) would. I cannot say whether the young ladies of Egerton's household were present or not; probably it would not make much difference. Donne would write out and present to Egerton a doctored text of the satires, but need not have written out the doctored elegies at all; in any case, as writing paper was expensive, he kept the old sheets on which he had written corrections, with the first draft plainly visible below. This became the basic source for the manuscripts.

There is only one major crux in the *Elegies*: 'To His Mistris Going to Bed' presents the poet as coaxing a richly dressed lady, the wife of a city businessman, to undress for him. (I agree here with Professor Gardner's note and its cross-reference to 'Loves Usury'.)[5] He makes a series of encouraging comparisons, designed to prove that this is the right thing to do, which amount to erecting personal love into a rival to Christianity. She is America, where one is out of reach of both the queen and the pope, and the first hint comes of making her a habitable planet, presumably requiring a unique relation to the Redeemer. Calvin had ruled that men can only be admitted to heaven by a whim of God, because all men are infinitely unworthy of it; Donne is thus immensely reverential to the lady when he says (using the technical term) that he is one of those allowed by 'imputed grace' to see her revealed. It is all a kind of joke, sure enough, but it tries out a position which might become very serious; so there is no change of tone when he arrives at the tremendous penultimate couplet: 'cast all, yea, this white lynnen hence, / There is no pennance due to innocence.' To call an act of illicit sex 'innocent' might well strike a listener as heretical and might excite embarrassing discussion, so he drew a line through *due to* on his manuscript and wrote *much less* above it, thus ending the poem with an orthodox but ugly sneer. Donne's loyal friend Woodward gladly accepted the improvement, but he could not have put *Here* for *There*, because that helpful accommodation was invented by editorial copyists a long while after. What else, after all, could have happened? The only alternative theory yet proposed is that the line got torn, or smudged, and the copier invented *due to* as a stopgap. But how could this botcher write so much better than the poet had done, in the characteristic manner of the poet? Since Donne's tone was not characteristically sneering, there is very little temptation to assume that he is sneering at this point.

However, to show that the original of *W* is late enough to have been bowdlerised is only half the requirement; the origins of the manuscripts which vote against *W* cannot possibly be *early* enough since there is a gap of a generation and more. The Group V manuscripts appeared to give the text as it was before Donne altered it; this seemed plain in the initial case of *due to* and I began to realise that they did it habitually. In fact, many students of the subject have had this idea before me, some of them earnestly wishing it could be true, but have retired baffled by sheer historical impossibility. Obviously, these critics felt, the Group V manuscripts have no such long pedigree.

Of the five groups, Group I is held to date from 1614; Donne was told by his criminal patron Somerset to print his poems before taking orders (on a promise of immediate preferment from Somerset), as we know because a surviving letter from the poet asks a friend to return some texts.[6] He was much upset by the insolent ruling and was probably tempted to bowdlerise for the occasion, but apparently did not. Somehow he was spared from having to print the poems, but the incident, as well as fathering one of the groups of manuscripts, would leave him a collected and prepared set of his poems, which no doubt he retained after he had taken orders. Grierson wrote indignantly that Donne cannot be supposed to have held on to the early poems even in his last fierce asceticism, but his mind was always complex and statesmanlike. Maybe he genuinely wished he could destroy the early poems, but he knew that other people held copies that they could publish after his death and that they might add worse things than he had written. Furthermore, he spent whole days writing out sermons so his children could publish them, should they need money after his death. He regularly presented himself in sermons as a sinner when young; he might have relished the exposure as a further penance. Besides, I doubt whether he always hated the prospect of eternal fame. I am in agreement with Professor Gardner here; she proposed in her edition of the *Divine Poems* (Oxford, 1952) that 'some time after 1625 Donne must have allowed a copy of the poems in his possession to be taken', and that this copy became the basis of Group II. But some Group II manuscripts had other poems not in Donne's own collection added afterwards, and some of their texts may have recorded early uncorrected versions. Group IV was copied from Donne's own handwriting by his old friend Woodward. The four manuscripts of Group III are also held to derive from one source, but they are very late, two of them were incomplete after the death of the poet, and other manuscripts were collated in preparation for the posthumous edition. It seems obvious that *what* was collated was the Group V manuscripts, or their sources, but this is never said; very little can be summarised about Group V from the discussion of Professor Gardner. There are ten manuscripts, with a leader and three groups of three. They are not considered to derive from one source, and their sources are not believed to be early. They are slovenly and untrustworthy. But they often offer a better alternative, and sometimes they vote all together with a decisive answer to a problem. One finds in examining the detail of Professor Gardner's editing that she pays them a remarkable amount of attention, far more than would be gathered from her introduction. It is an impressive record of good sense retained under the distraction of a wrong theory, and the times when she is being wrenched in this way make the most interesting parts of her paradoxical edition, which still leaves the problem of the Group V manuscripts crying out for a simple factual explanation.

As I combed through the text for evidence that might help to solve the problem, I took for granted that Group V copiers, for whom I at once felt a natural sympathy, had done what I would have done in their situation; it took a great deal of bumbling about before I realised that my assumptions (and I even thought that Professor Gardner had made the same assumptions) amounted to a new theory. It is likely that the Dean finally allowed his poems to be copied, on one occasion for Group II. Therefore he would be likely to allow it again, though only for some special friend, as a great favour, once every few years. A man who was granted this honour would be urged by his more knowing friends to put a copyist to work at once. He would be strictly instructed to ignore the later corrections because the literary world had taken into its head that the heretical ecstasies of young Jack could be retained in this way, whereas the semi-official copies had been gelded by the dean. Perhaps this friend, who would have been put up at the deanery, would beg leave to take the precious documents to his bedroom and mull over them during the night, and then hand them to his accomplice out of the window on the stairs. In any case, surely I cannot be wrong in assuming that interest and suspicion would be very keen about these texts; imagine if W. H. Auden had refused to publish during his lifetime, and was definitely known in at least one case to have sabotaged the great poetry he had written. This sentiment was still strong a generation later, when the Restoration made possible an unhampered edition (the seventh). Although every scrap of fun with sex was dug up from the manuscripts, Group V readings were often adhered to even when (as usual) they gave the duller version of the two. The second edition of Donne's poems, only two years after the first, was already thoroughly infected with Group V readings. I do not know how this was done, but the Group V man would need to have some convincing story. The speed and thoroughness of the movement on the one hand, and its lasting so long on the other, give a very different impression from the flabby incompetence that Professor Gardner describes. In fact, almost certainly one man was at work, not three ancestral copyists; though he could appeal to corroborating documents – other men had done the same job, and their results agreed simply because they had worked on the same principle.

Professor Gardner was very unlikely to have taken this point of view. We must respect her for her endurance, in checking through all those documents, which seemed to her so sordidly unscholarly, and no wonder she regards the writers of them with contempt. Dirty, lazy, and ignorant she expects them to be; but actually plotting against authority among themselves she would regard as inconceivable. I was misled by her note on 'The Good-Morrow', one of the two poems which the poet admittedly altered. One might suppose, she says (pp. 197–8), if the author did not write out a fair copy, that: 'The ancestor of $L74$, Group II, &c., would then be a copy of the original poem; the ancestor of Group III a copy of the corrected version which incorporated most but not all [of] the corrections; and the ancestor of $H40$ and Group I would be a copy that included all the second thoughts. Or it might be held that there were three stages...' She winces at the thought of an independent-minded copyist, but even in considering the possibility she has only envisaged him as an aesthete, choosing the variant he preferred. I think this process did occur, and may well have occurred in Group II, where I do not understand the voting; Group II never seems to provide an interesting reading, anyway. The voting of the manuscripts over whether to read *grow* or *groan* in 'Twicknam Garden' is I think partly of this aesthetic kind, though we can deduce a change by the author in 1614. Lady Bedford had only taken the house in Twickenham a few years before, so the poem was fresh in his mind. He refuses to leave the garden, and pretends to be despairingly in love with the lady – she was sickly, and of inflexible virtue, and appears to have looked rather like a spider, so we may presume that Donne was drawing upon other experiences, though real ones, for his splendid compliment (unless otherwise noted, quotations of poetry are from Grierson's 1912 edition):

> ... Love let mee
> Some senslesse peece of this place bee;
> Make me a mandrake, that I may groane here,
> Or a stone fountaine weeping out my yeare.   (15–18)

Professor Gardner prints *grow* and comments (p. 216): '"Groane", the reading of Groups I and II, could have arisen independently from the strong association of mandrakes with groans. But the mandrake was not held to groan when *in situ*, it only groaned when it was torn up; see Browne...'

She does not actually deny that the poet made the correction himself in 1614, despite her theory of the Groups, so I think she must be breaking one of the rules of scholarly editors – the final text authorised by a poet must be printed, even if he changed the original draft under threat of torture. Evidently Donne had appreciated the professor's objection, and had selected *grow* because it sounds like *groan* but would not be grumbled at (hearing the poem sung, it would be hard to tell which text was used); but then, when it came to print, he permitted himself to write what he had always wanted. Everybody knew that the mandrake was only a kind of emblem, so that what you said about it did not matter, and some of the Group I manuscripts agree with *HK2* here. (Professor Gardner's note admits that she is siding with *HK2*.) I think that Grierson was plainly right, as usual, to print *groan*; it is a glowingly romantic poem, not at all hurt by a little frank absurdity. But the Group V manuscripts are not arty at all; they are vowed to copy the text as it was before it was mucked up, however seductive the alterations may appear.

Professor Gardner has a major objection to treating the Group V manuscripts as a serious source of evidence, to which I must give full weight: they are slovenly, and full of trivial slips. Surely, the reason is that they were made by amateurs; they set out to be unofficial versions, giving the lowdown. It strikes me that the disciplinary attitude of Professor Gardner makes her confuse two different matters here. If I had to do this copying, I too would do it messily; but I would not write down bland tidy nonsense, like the professional scribes of Groups I and II. When Professor Gardner chooses to destroy a poem, remarking with buttoned lips that the authority against Grierson and the first edition (for some killing variant) is overwhelming, I feel I am in the hands of a nurse who says: 'I will not believe you when you tell me the house is burning down, because you have dribbled on your bib.'

This confusion does something to explain a long and earnest section of her Introduction (pp. lxxv–lxxix) which claims to refute any such deduction as I am making from her apparatus. The first four of the ten Group V manuscripts, she says, may sometimes report 'an alternative version,' but only if it is also found in, and derived from, *L74*, a manuscript almost in Group II but partly independent, which may tap early sources (pp. lxxvi–lxxvii):

In the twenty-three lyrics common to *HK2* and *L74*, it is plain that *HK2* contains an inferior version of the text in *L74*. It shares its rare errors and adds to them errors and distinctive readings of its own ... In any of the *Songs and Sonnets* where there are a sufficient number of significant variants to allow the construction of a stemma, *Cy*, *O* and *P* will always be found below *HK2*, and in the remainder it is nearly always clear that their text is a corruption of the text of *HK2*. Their readings are, therefore, valueless in any attempt to construct the original text.

Professor Gardner has objected earnestly that her apparatus, being highly selective, cannot be used backwards as a means of testing her assertions; but surely what it has selected are precisely the errors which are meaningful, as apart from the trivial and careless ones. I have no doubt that her assertions here are based on a careful statistical analysis of the errors, but then the trivial ones are bound to predominate. I still say that her assertions are plainly untrue of the meaningful variants recorded in her apparatus. The sequence *L74*, *Cy*, *O*, *P* does sometimes occur in full, but *HK2* behaves much the same way whether *L74* is present or not, so do *Cy*, *O* and *P* whether *HK2* is present or not; and nearly always, when you get the full sequence, the rest of Group V also behaves consistently. Surely she does not claim that they all derive from *L74*. The fact is, this whole line of argument collapses as soon as you envisage copyists who refused to accept the alterations written above the line. The only reason for needing a 'pedigree' to prove that a variant is early is the presumption that, because a copyist cannot think, he must have been set to copy a page on which the later version had not been written.[7]

There is one case, 'The Curse', which seems refreshingly clear; all agree that the poet thought of a better joke, three lines long [ll. 14–16], and wrote it onto the manuscript to replace his previous joke. The poem was considered almost a satire and allowed entry into *Q*, the early manuscript of the satires that gave Mr Milgate the undoctored text. Professor Gardner's notes give a really impressive proof that Donne thought of the new joke in 1598. Sure enough, *L74*, *HK2* and *P* stick to the old version. But so do all the rest of Group V (except *B*, and *Cy* which omits). And so do all of Group II, though their ancestor must have had Donne's own text available to him because the poem is in Group I. I have just been trying to speak up for the copyists, but do not know what motive I can ascribe to this Group II man; perhaps he thought that the duller joke was the more decorous one. The ancestors of Group V, of course, were acting on their rule.

Coming at last to some examples, I must first try to win a little respect for Group V. In the elegy 'Love's Progress', Donne is explaining that if you want to get to the centre of a woman it is more practical to start caressing her feet:

> How much they erre that set out at the face!
> The hair a Forest is of Ambushes,
> Of springes, snares, fetters and manacles: (40–2)

All manuscripts of Groups I and II write *springs* instead of *springes*, nonsense which does not even scan, and in Group III only manuscript *O'F*, the last stage of the editing process, gets round to the right word; whereas *every one* of the Group V manuscripts, however slovenly and dirty-minded they may be, gets it right. It comes as rather a jolt, after you have learned from Professor Gardner's 'Textual Introduction' that these manuscripts are 'valueless in any attempt to construct the original text', to find that she accepts their ruling without comment, without any note on the passage. It is comforting to find that there was some use, after all, in her labour of collating them.

We find a similar case on the first page of the *Songs and Sonnets*, as she arranges them, and here a note by the professor, with her immense calming dignity, is felt to be needed to put the matter in its right light.

> If thou beest borne to strange sights,
>   Things invisible to see,
> Ride ten thousand daies and nights
>   Till age snow white haires on thee...
>
> ('Song: Goe and catche a falling starre', 10–13)

All manuscripts of Groups I and II omit *to* in the second line, making nonsense which does not even scan, and two of Group III (including the final *O'F*) are still following them, but the other two supply *go*.[8] *S* agrees with this, but all other Group V manuscripts, except *B* before correction, supply our familiar *to*, thus agreeing with the first and all subsequent editions. A block decision of this kind is like a high wind; it sweeps away any discussion of whether we have here one of the 'distinctive readings' of *HK2*, and whether all distinctive readings are bad ones. Professor Gardner offers a bold distraction (p. 153): '*1633* appears to have made an obvious correction of the defective line in Groups I and II. The true reading has possibly been preserved in Group III (*Dob*, *S96*) which reads "goe see", giving an imperative to balance "Ride": "If you are already gifted with the power to see marvels, go and see the invisible." The manuscripts that agree with *1633* may do so accidentally through having made the same correction in the defective line in Group II with which they are all textually connected.' Surely, Professor Gardner must know why this imperative is not a better reading, because otherwise she would print it. The song is a tease for the ladies, pretending to make accusations against them even while sung in their very boudoirs. Hence it requires to be light, and the thudding insistence of two imperatives is not a balance at all; *what* would it balance? I am sure, if I were set to emend that truncated line, I would come up with *go* or some worse verb; I did not appreciate the grace of the construction with *to*, implying somehow that the well-born soul does not need to struggle, till I realised how hard it would be to reinvent. The effect of praising the clumsy wrong invention here is to distract attention from the small triumph of Group V.

Most readers of the edition, indeed, can have no idea of what is going on; it has cost me many a tumble to acquire my uneasy mastery of this tricky technique. After a square bracket, the apparatus does not list the manuscripts which agree with the editor, but only gives a list of variant readings, each followed by its supporting manuscripts (out of a selected list of manuscripts given at the start). It is lucky for her not to have to tell the reader here that only the Group V manuscripts agree with her. As to her last sentence, you must remove *S* and *B* from the ten, and *K* omits the poem, and she has maintained that the sequence *HK2*, *Cy*, *O* and *P* are all derived from *L74*, which is a special Group II manuscript. The apparatus omits *D17*, which is anyway classed with *A25* and *JC*, and these two, the only ones left, are actually said in the 'Textual Introduction' (pp. lxxviii–lxxix) to agree frequently with *HK2*. Professor Gardner's statement is therefore properly covered. But what use is there in making the bad manuscripts sound less disgraceful by saying they have respectable connections, when they are right and their respectable connections wrong? I am drawing attention to a high piece of literary artistry in this note, far more tense and absorbed than anything in the careless song upon which it is supposed to comment.

In both these examples, the handwriting must have made the needed extra letters rather hard to read, though not too hard for each of the Group V ancestor copiers to catch them. They would naturally be more interested and alerted than the professional copiers. There is no question of a change by the author. But evidence is needed for the assumption that the Group V manuscripts often report the text of Donne as it was before correction. The garbling of a copier may be exactly like the first clumsy effort of an author. It might even be doubted whether Donne corrected his poems at all since he liked to speak casually about them; but he often worked over them a great deal. Mr Milgate has shown (Appendix C) that the passage in Satire III about seeking truth 'On a huge hill' (ll. 79–82), which is famous for making the sound fit the sense, was not in its present form until Donne presented his satires to Lady Bedford in 1608, about fourteen years after first writing it. However, there are also cases where a poet changes a word almost at once, as his plan develops, during the original act of writing; and this is likely to give the best evidence, because the poem itself as it goes on makes the rejected word irrelevant; or anyway, one can see that the poet needed to change it. Thus we are told in 'Loves Progress' (ll. 31–2) that Cupid lived underground, like Pluto: 'Men to such Gods, their sacrificing Coals / Did not in Altars lay, but pits and holes.' One manuscript out of each of the three sets of Group V reads 'on Altars'. Clearly, Donne was thinking of altars and forgetting the other half of the antithesis, so he first wrote *on*, but then, when he read the passage over, or maybe at once, saw that he needed another word to cover the case of *holes*.[9] The copyists were not under the same need for invention, and would not think of the mistake three times independently. Then, a lot of the minor variants record doubts whether to use the subjunctive after *if*, and whether to use *which* of a person; the final decision is sometimes more 'correct' and sometimes less, so it is not a matter of a pedantic scribe correcting a careless poet. It may seem a bit surprising that he first wrote in 'Loves Growth': 'Love's not so pure *an* abstract, as they use / To say, *who* have no Mistresse but their Muse' (my italics). This phrase, which states that love is not a refined platonic abstraction, is more philosophic than the final version because Donne came to feel that he needed to sound manly and plain here, so the phrase became 'pure, *and* abstract, as they use / To say, which...' This, by the way, is a good case to test the 'connection' of Group V with Group II through *L74* and *HK2*. Both these manuscripts omit the poem, but *Cy* and *P* bear their witness as usual, and are supported by Group V manuscripts from both other sets – by all of Group V, apart from another omission. The end of 'The Apparition' gives a striking example:

> ...and since my love is spent,
> I'had rather thou shouldst painfully repent,
> Than by my threatnings rest still innocent. (15–17)

I had thought of this as emerging white hot from the anvil, already needing a heavy stress on *thou*, implying 'as I do now', with two great pauses to mark the increasing hammer-blows of '*rest...still...inn–*.' But a first draft 'keep thee innocent' is attested by *Cy, P, A25, JC* (and *L74, HK2* omit the poem). I suppose that too could be pronounced with a heavy irony on *innocent*, and maybe it is a comfort to find that the poet could only slowly cook up the pretence of being so cross. It is fairly strong evidence of revision; here again, one might say that the copyist merely garbled, but two independent sets of Group V would have to garble the same way.

As a rule, Donne's corrections were improvements, and he made extremely few changes for religious, political or sexual security; so most of his changes tell us little. One sometimes finds him misled by a current fashion. Thus, towards the end of that determinedly good-

humoured poem about loss of money, 'The Bracelet', the curse on the
imaginary finder rises for a moment to real solemnity:

> ...love; marriage
> Afflict thee, and, at thy lives last moment,
> May thy swolne sinnes themselves to thee present.
>   But, I forgive; Repent thee honest man:
> Gold is Restorative, restore it then ...   (108–12)

Last is attested by *A25*, *Cy*, *P*, *B* – all three sets of Group V; and
accepted by Grierson and the first edition which prints the poem. But
Professor Gardner prints *latest*, following all the reputable manuscripts. Very likely Donne made the change in 1614, when he had
often been accused of 'deserving hanging for not keeping accent.' In
an effort to appear more decorous, he adopted what we now think
very ugly, a 'Simpsonian rhyme'. This means rhyming an unstressed
syllable with a stressed syllable, as happens without effort if you put
latest; but the ear of Donne had been much better employed in the
first version, where awe and solemn delay turn *moment* into a spondee.
However, maybe neither version is very good, and the reader of
Professor Gardner is more likely to be shocked at the start of 'The
Legacie':

> When I dyed last, and, Deare, I dye,
>   As often as from thee I goe,
>   Thou it be but an houre agoe,
> And Lovers houres be full eternity,
> I can remember yet, that I ...   (1–5)

Professor Gardner omits *but*, with strong authority from Groups I and
II, saying (p. 172) that to add this word 'gives eight syllables at the
cost of sense. The point is that even though it was as long as an hour
ago he can still remember.' This capacity for chop-logic in Professor
Gardner's work seemed to me at first to make her peculiarly unable
to interpret the poems of Donne. 'The point is' that our minds are
endowed with several different ways of experiencing or estimating
time, immensely out of step with one another, so that logic would be
equally satisfied by 'as long as' (I can yet remember) and 'as short
as' (I am already in despair). To convey this idea of the double time-
scale decisively, at the start of a lyric, it is essential to have an
apparent illogic, to have the paradox of *but*. No wonder that the first
edition and Grierson retain *but*, and it is attested by *HK2* (the other

Group V manuscripts seem to fall down here, but *HK2* is the chief of them). However, after giving full weight to this, one must still agree with Professor Gardner that Donne himself cut out *but* in 1614, presumably for the very reason she has given. I now think that she is in close touch with a part of his mind, but one that his editors have been quite right in rejecting, and should continue to reject, because it harms, rather than improves, his poems.

The songs, and as she remarks this poem is 'near to song', make a separate problem because Donne was evidently trying to help the composer, and perhaps coax a particular composer. In 'The Prohibition', I thought at first that Professor Gardner was being merely malignant when she printed for the last lines: 'Then, least thy love, hate and mee thou undoe, / *Oh let mee live, yet love and hate mee too.*' Grierson and the first edition, with sturdy Group V support (*HK2, P, B*), give an ending which (instead of these hideous gasps) can be read with calm pleasure as completing a demonstration: 'Lest thou thy love and hate and mee undoe, / *To let mee live, O love and hate mee too.*' Surely this is what should be printed, but she is probably right in estimating that her version is the final draft that Donne had written on the page. He was envisaging a very operatic performance by a singer; but did composers in the 1590s write in that way? I wish I were less ignorant about this interesting case. No contemporary setting has survived.

The best of the songs, and the first to appear in a songbook, is the 'The Expiration', and here it is illuminating to have available the first stage in the writing, probably altered almost at once, when he added the final couplet of the verse. What it shows is that the poetry depended on a story, which the hearer of the song must guess at, and Donne altered the words to fit when he invented a bit more story:

> So, so, leave off this last lamenting kisse,
>   Which sucks two soules, and vapors Both away,
> Turn thou ghost that way, and let mee turne this,
>   And let our sowles benight our happy day.   (1–4)

I give the first draft, as recorded by Groups III and V, hoping the reader may thus appreciate how strong and consistent it is so far. The legend that a devil sucked out a soul in a kiss gets extended to the idea that each lover is a devil to the other, and the souls thus extracted make a fog, darkening a day previously sunlit. So far they are merely lovers with feelings that drag them into conflict; but then he began inventing a larger and more Byronic story, which starts with the couplet added to the first quatrain. They have run away together, and already on the first day they are both ruined by their mutual love, they find they hate each other; or rather, they find that life has become unendurable, either together or apart. The previous picture or conceit needs now to be blurred or enlarged; it is their wilfulness or their inherent characters, their *selves* and not any trivial superstition, which spoil what ought to be the *happiest* day of their lives. *And let ourselves benight our happiest day.*

To finish this brief survey of the songs, I need to give a clear example of the moral strength of the editor in 'The Message':

> Send home my harmless heart againe,
> Which no unworthy thought could staine,
> But if it be taught by thine
>   To make jestings
>   Of protestings ...   (9–13)

Easy grace takes a lot of struggle, and Donne had evidently (when you see all the trivial variants in the apparatus) worked hard, scribbling above the lines, before he felt content; then he wrote out the verse separately. This in itself would create a puzzle for a committed Group V copier. Feeling now at ease, the poet himself made a slip more usual among copiers; he wrote *which* instead of *but* at the start of the third line, 'catching it up' from the line before. Little did he know that he would encounter the serious side of Professor Gardner (p. 154): 'It is impossible, having regard to the agreement of I, II, *Dob*, *S96*, to regard "But" as anything but an emendation in *Lut* to avoid the repetition that Grierson disliked. The remaining manuscripts rewrite the line to make it conform to l. 3, *HK2* and *A25* showing a first stage in a process completed in *P, B, JC.*' No literary considerations, none of that chop-logic that is her softer side, are interposed here; it is a straight kill. And yet what really happened must be perfectly well known to Professor Gardner; she hardly pretends otherwise. If a copyist had made this mistake, she would have thrown it out at once, feeling that she was putting the man in his place; but when the author does it, she insists that he must eat it. It is interesting to find here that she regards the Group V manuscripts as making contacts across their sets; but perhaps one or two of the ancestors of Group V, when confronted with this difficult case, wrote down one or two alternatives.

Keynes' account of induction says that a theory becomes more probable each time it is verified, but only by a process of multiplication, so that if the probability was zero to start with it remains zero after however many times. Of course I think that my theory has a positive initial probability, but I can hardly hope that these minor examples would ever convince a settled opponent. The following case appears decisive to me because no tolerable alternative theory can be proposed. In 'The Dreame' the poet apologises to the lady for mistaking her for God (as Petrarchan poets do) because he realises now that, since she is better than God, she was insulted by the comparison. All Group V report him saying: 'I do confess, I could not choose but be / Prophane, to think thee anything but thee' (ll. 19–20); and when, in all manuscripts except the Group V ones, he is made to say '*it* could not choose…/*Profaness*…', it is plain that the poet himself got cold feet, and inserted a useless precaution. No one else would have thought that this tiny indirection would be enough to make him safe; and therefore the Group V manuscripts must be reporting his first version.

Another decisive case is found in the elegy 'Natures Lay Ideot' [Gardner: 'Tutelage'], which presents the poet as scolding a girl whom he taught how to make love, with the result that she married a wealthy husband. The husband is jealous and tries to seclude her, so the poet suspects that she has a platoon of lovers, and why is he, the very source of all this busy happiness, not among them? The indignant tutor claims that he has

> with amorous delicacies
> Refin'd thee into a blisful Paradise.
> Thy graces and good words my creatures be;　　　(23–5)

Then Donne waited for a moment, to decide how to finish the couplet. That he has established her in a paradise is the starting point, so she is Eve, and has acquired risky but important knowledge; he is the creator of the woman she has now become – hence the word *creatures*. There is an ambiguity about *paradise*; she has herself become a paradise for men, but also she is enjoying unwonted luxury; he has both changed her into a paradise and led her into one. And so far as he can remember, he selected this dull girl by a pure whim. In fact, he behaved like the God of Calvin, deciding at random which men to send to heaven and which to hell. The crucial debate about whether men are saved by grace (given if you have faith) or by works would thus come to his mind; and, come to think of it, he has a fair claim to be the serpent as well. He drew a line through *words*, writing *works* above it, and could now lay down the clincher: 'I planted knowledge and lifes tree in thee.' In this case, what the page retained was evidence not of a later improvement but of the actual process of composition.

It is pathetic to see in the apparatus how all the prosy manuscripts of Groups I and II give the sexy variant *works*, whereas all the Group V manuscripts give the dull variant *words*. Professor Gardner, to do her justice, can spot which is the dull one, and she is determined to print that, though it is embarrassing to have to agree with Group V. The Restoration editor could also see the point, so he broke with Group V here, thus continuing to disagree with Professor Gardner. Her note says (p. 127): '"Works" would appear to have arisen independently in Group I, *TCC*, and *Dob*, owing to the influence of "graces". The editor of *1633* presumably corrected his Group I manuscript by recourse to his Group II manuscript which read with *TCD*. "Good words" takes us back to l. 13. Taught by him she can now both flatter and praise.' Undoubtedly it takes us back, but a phrase in a poem sometimes needs to take us forward as well as back; and, even if we only look back, the poem insists that her callow flattery would never have caught her this rich husband. Her good works are something she has learned through the implanting of life's tree, and one is tempted to think they are a skill at pleasing men in bed; that indeed is the joke, but the meaning needs to be something larger as well – it was not in bed, presumably, that she first charmed the prospective husband, who must then have thought her pure. I daresay the witty repartee of the traditional barmaid had more to do with it than flattery, and this would allow Donne, when he initially wrote *good words*, to intend a *contrast* with line 13 (which says: 'Remember since all thy words us'd to bee/ To every suitor; *I, 'if my friends agree.'*).

It is wildly improbable that Groups I, II, and III all independently made the same mistake, as Professor Gardner supposes. No doubt one often heard about grace and works in sermons, but here the 'graces' of a young woman are in question, a sufficiently positive idea; the mind would not habitually leap away from that to a highly technical use of the word in the singular. Admittedly, the mind of Donne did it once; but he had a very special reason for such a leap – it felt deliciously absurd to make his own love as capricious as the love of the God of Calvin. Having once thought of the joke, he repeated it; in the first line of the elegy 'Change', where he is saying that he does not expect his mistress to be faithful: 'Although thy hand and faith, and good workes too, / Have seal'd thy love which nothing should undoe...' It has become a boring joke, which he throws away. According to Professor Gardner, Donne could not have thought of this joke, but three copiers, none of them thinking it a joke, wrote it down by a verbal association with a pair of words often heard in church. It may be answered that my view also entails improbability, because at least one of the Group II copiers, with *workes* before him, has to reinvent *words*. But he might well do this to avoid the suggestion of blasphemy, so he need not be supposed to do it by a meaningless verbal association.

Many people, I should say, have at the back of their minds a real moral objection to the earlier Donne love-poems because they regard the poet as a cad who boasts of getting girls into trouble, as in 'Love's Alchymie', a particularly boyish poem: 'I have lov'd, and got, and told...' So far from that, 'Nature's Lay Ideot' ['Tutelage'] shows him feeling confident, in a rough brotherly way, that he is giving the girls a leg up in the world, or doing them good, anyhow. I had felt that the distaste of Professor Gardner for the poet deserved respect if it had this kind of ground, but then I was taken aback by her introductory note (p. 126) to 'Nature's Lay Ideot': 'This Elegy may owe something to Tibullus, I. vi. 5–14, though it is more innocent. Only "Jealousy" among Donne's *Elegies* is concerned with adultery.' Both Grierson and Leishman, whose advice she generally considers, would have told her that the girl is now married. It might be argued that the girl has merely found a rich keeper; but this would only remove the point of the homely story. When Donne first met her she was using charms to learn her future husband's name and negotiating with suitors; now Donne says 'Thou art not by so many duties his' (the man who is trying to keep her in purdah) 'as mine' (because the poet enabled her to achieve her present status). Surely the duties to a husband need to be the other half of the paradox, or it has no bite. Besides, she has enough security of tenure to risk having lovers on the side, and the poet boasts that he brought her to this strong position. Tibullus, I find, writes about one adulterer supplanting another; in the iron marriage market of the grandees of imperial Rome, a girl would not catch a rich husband merely by her charms. Nor would she among Elizabethan grandees, but city life had more room for exceptions. I expect that this girl, as she was living respectably and had advisers, though separated from her family, would be working in a shop. The world described by Donne really is more innocent, though that would hardly be what Professor Gardner meant. Maybe she just thinks that the poet had a lustful daydream after one of his Latin lessons, and never met a girl at all. But the poem breathes a rather comfortable air, belonging to the time when he was spending his inheritance, so we should try to clear our minds of bitter irony. He really did consider that a girl was engaged in good works when she learned how to give men pleasure.

Grierson considered that the first edition was likely to be right, and that corrections from the manuscripts should be made only when a poem required them to restore its beauty.[10] It was essential for Professor Gardner to reduce the authority of this edition, or she could not introduce so many novelties (and, if they are all ugly ones, it is fair to remember that Grierson had first pick). She maintains firmly that the author had no voice in the edition. Obviously Donne should have put his affairs in the hands of a good lawyer, but he was restrained by a mixture of motives, some devotional, some worldly, and probably some just superstitious; so that it is rather hard to guess how he would behave. He was very accustomed to negotiating fine points of conscience, weighing up the opposing claims of immensely diverse influences. Several people, we know, were preparing a text for publication as soon as he died; and they would think this a reason, not for hiding from him, but for obtaining an audience so as to coax him. It would be easy to place their requests on high grounds. The divine poems were of course to be included; and while he was choosing one of his poems to be sung at his funeral, did he consider himself forbidden to get its text right? While he was posing in his coffin for the sculptor, would Donne tell the editor that he was too busy about the Lord's work for earthly vanities? A good deal of elegant affectation of that sort would no doubt be expected and allowed for, but he could probably be coaxed into giving a certain amount of help. Professor Gardner says 'there is no sign' of it, but signs of it would be just what he took care to avoid. Probably an old friend would be primed with a list of specific questions about doubtful passages; it would be easy to compile. Donne, after all, might reasonably have become offended if he had not been approached in this way. But one may suspect that, after cooperating the first time, he refused when a second batch of questions were brought the following week. The editor himself then made some bold decisions, though without this encouragement and annoyance he would not have presumed. We get some bad bold decisions, as Professor Gardner says, but also some good ones; and if we get any good ones we may reasonably expect they come from the author.

The reading *contract*, instead of *extract* at the end of 'The Canonization' seems to me a clear case. After defending his runaway marriage, Donne claims that he and his wife will eventually become saints and apostles of the religion of true love (implying that the pretensions of Christianity to be a religion of love have been exposed, but the dean could simply ignore that part); people will invoke them saying:

> You, to whom love was peace, that now is rage;
> Who did the whole worlds soule contract, and drove
>   Into the glasses of your eyes,
>   (So made such mirrors, and such spies
> That they did all to you epitomize,)
>   Countries, Towns, Courts: Beg from above
>   A patterne of your love!   (39–45)

There is a second change, of *your* to *our* in the last line, but this is also found in two Group I manuscripts. Donne might well have felt in 1614 that this made the covert meaning a bit more tolerable, after wondering perhaps whether he ought to suppress the poem altogether; it says 'Ask God to teach us the kind of love we all need to learn' rather than 'Ask God to teach us to love like you.' So probably this is also a change by the author, though it makes little difference. Professor Gardner's note (p. 204) says that the reading *contract* 'destroys the alchemical metaphor and with it the pun on glasses and makes the verb "drove" unintelligible... The "soul" of the world is extracted and driven into their eyes... by sublimation and distillation, driving it through the pipes of the still into the "glasses", or vessels, in which it is stored. These "glasses" then become mirrors.' Also she refers us to her Introduction (p. lxxxvi) where she says that the alchemical metaphor 'is reduced to the apparently more obvious notion of "contracting" the soul of the "whole world" into the small space of the lovers' eyes. But, on reflection, it can be seen that it is absurd to apply spatial notions to the soul, and that this idea of much in little weakly anticipates the next thought: that the eyes, by this infusion of the *anima mundi*, are made mirrors and spies to epitomize all.' Just so, I expect, would the young man have defended his text, but I still think that the old one was right to change it. What does the thought gain by dragging in the chemistry on top of the optics? They are both only illustrations of the thought of the microcosm, and there is no room for both in one sentence. The 'glasses' have to be grotesquely transformed from containers to lenses the very instant after they have been mentioned ('glasses of your eyes'); the young man would say that this insists upon the full complexity of the thought, and illustrates the compression described, but the old man would call it 'showing off'. The limbeck and the telescope habitually came into the poet's mind together, meaning the same kind of thing, and here they are crudely jammed on top of one another. It is not even as if he used the world-soul when he has got it; the prayer goes 'above', presumably to heaven. To say that the simplification *contract* 'weakly anticipates the next thought' presumes that there is a progress or at least a succession of thoughts, but they are jumbled together within one sentence, one breath. And it is not true that the correction makes the verb *drove* unintelligible; writers on optics habitually say that the lenses *direct* the rays of light, and Donne himself says it in the 'Refusal to Woodward':[11] 'for as / Men force the sunne with much more force to passe, / By gathering his beames with a cristall glasse; / So wee...' (had better only read our own poems). The view of Professor Gardner that light is not spiritual enough to describe the soul, which needs instead a strong brew of organic matter, may be very sound; but surely she would not claim to rewrite every text in which the metaphor occurs. ('I am the Light of the World.') However, I am not sure that these considerations would be the decisive ones. The old Donne had had experience of doctors, and the distilled medicines of Paracelsus were remarkably kill-or-cure; maybe he now realised that pumping stuff like that into lovers' eyes would not convey the detached but universally healing balm that he had intended. I can understand a reader preferring the manuscript version, but surely it is hard to deny that the change for the edition was made by the author.

The variant in 'A Valediction: of the Booke' can also be defended; poems exalting his marriage would no doubt strike the old man as high-minded enough to deserve his attention. Ann's collection of their hasty notes of assignation will become a sacred book, the gospel of the religion of true love, powerful enough to build another civilisation after a new Dark Age. Everything can be extracted from it; statesmen, for instance (says the poem), will understand their occupation from ours, because both love and statecraft are spoiled if they are analysed:

> In both they doe excell
>   Who the present governe well,
>   Whose weaknesse none doth, or dares tell;
>   In this thy booke, such will their something see,
> As in the Bible some can find out Alchimy.   (50–4)

The first edition has *something*, but all manuscripts (except two) have *nothing*. Professor Gardner remarks in her note (p. 195): 'I regard the agreement of *O* and *P* with *1633* in reading "there something" as coincidental. It is an obvious sophistication of an at first sight difficult reading.' In her Introduction (p. lxxxvii), she adds: 'Here we have not only a weak anticipation of the following lines, but also a redundant "there". In this case the edition has the support of two degenerate manuscripts, *O* and *P*, agreeing accidentally with one of their characteristic corruptions.' The verse begins 'Here Statesmen (or of them, they which can reade)'; after that, even for a copier, it cannot be very difficult to think of their art as 'nothing'; one might instead call this fun rather cheap, though fair enough from a poet who has just daffed the world aside. Professor Gardner's complaint about 'weak anticipation' of the next line (not *lines*, as it is the last one of the verse) is puzzling because any comparison (introduced with 'As') must be anticipated by the thing it is compared to; how is this different if you read 'nothing'? I suspect she just means that the word *some* occurs twice with different meanings, but Donne was too concentrated upon the meaning to be distracted by such an echo. Professor Gardner's accusation of redundance is justified if you attach importance to the misspelling of *their*; but surely there must be a lot of other misspellings not recorded in the apparatus. Queried passages were read aloud to Donne, who did not mull over the text, so misspellings probably were often overlooked.

In this poem, Donne is not mainly concerned with distributing contempt. Every skill nurtured within a civilised society has some kind of merit, he is saying, even if a very paltry one, and that merit, even if not derived from, is irradiated by the central belief on which the whole society is constructed. In the new society, when the crucial belief is in sexual love as exemplified by Donne and his wife, the politicians will be bound to understand their odd duties much more clearly; if Donne had gone into the matter further, we might find that some of the worst faults of the profession, if not justified, were at least made to appear in a better light. Speaking in his rough manly way, even while in this mood of charitable casuistry, he might describe the tiny merit of their trade as practically nothing. But he would not agree with the explanatory note of Professor Gardner (p. 195): 'Statesmen will find their own "nothing" in the "nothing" of the lovers in the same way as Alchemists find support for their doctrines in the Bible.' This is neo-Christian cynicism run mad. Donne really does intend to boast about his marriage; you can impute bad motives to him, or lies, and you are within the field of human probability, but if you say he insinuated a bitter irony into the middle of this fighting and defiant praise of the most decisive action of his life you are mistaking him for some other author. The glittering praises of ambition, such as law and politics have to offer, are sure to corrupt, but he drives this home chiefly to heighten the contrast with his own incorruptible love. When Professor Gardner prints with quote-marks 'the "nothing" of the lovers' she implies that Donne himself calls his love nothing; and he does not in this poem, at any rate. He might perhaps imply a defiant recognition that it is nothing in the eyes of the world, but even that would be quite secondary. Does she suppose that he calls the Bible nothing, too?

All the same, it evidently did cross his mind, at some later stage, that the whole passage, beginning with the humorous admission of the mystery of love, might be misunderstood in the way his editor now does; that was why he changed *nothing* to *something*. Also the old man would reflect that he had had a certain amount to do with political decisions, and that the jealous impatience of the young man had rather spoiled the logic of the passage by calling all such work 'nothing'. The change is much more likely to be made by the author, at any rate, than by a printer so innocent that he never heard of jeering at politicians. This much seems clear, and I am rather sorry to risk confusing it by a conjecture; but the testimony of *O* and *P* might be true as well. When Donne was first thrown out of the world, because of his marriage, he was defiant but not sour about the world – he expected to make a come-back. It was only gradually that he lost hope of gaining civil employment by recommending himself to politicians; so he might have written in 'nothing' one later day to express his irritation. But then, 'they which can read' at the beginning of the verse has already a good deal of this cheerful contempt. I only feel that, as Professor Gardner makes unduly heavy demands upon coincidence, they had better be reduced where possible.

I am also emboldened to plead for another case: the beauty of a line in the *Divine Poems* – the only case in that earlier edition where she could be accused of spoiling a line. Following all manuscripts, and rejecting all editions, she printed a line in *Holy Sonnets added in 1635*, number 3, as: 'Because I did suffer'I must suffer paine.' Her note (p. 76) added, as additional reason for rejecting '*Cause*, that 'There is no other example in the *Concordance* of Donne's using this abbreviation.' It was a splendid defiance or declaration of a programme and the only trouble was that she then explained, to comfort us, how the line should be read aloud. Stresses are on *cause, did, suff, must suff, pain*, making six not five but, as I understand, rightly treating *must suff* as a spondee, or a jammed stress. Now, this reading is far too awful: it is the voice of a determinedly cheerful teacher drumming the point into the heads of some hideously thick-witted class. Donne is regarding himself as a predestined victim and speaking with a kind of awe; we do not easily like him for it, but we should allow him to say: 'all those girls gave me hell, now God will give me hell because I tried to please all those girls'. It needs to be read as if liturgically, with almost the same stresses all along – the victim is in a trance. (There are some who maintain that he is lying to God here, just as earlier he lied to his smart young friends, because he never really had any mistresses at all. If this were the case, I myself would think that the pronunciation of the poems hardly mattered.) During his lifetime, Donne was often accused of being metrically rough, but he probably did not intend to be, except in the *Satires*; he just relied on the reader to give the lines the intonation demanded by the meaning, which in itself was often strained. No doubt he was accustomed to make this answer, in a general way; so the questioner would be likely to have such a case on his list. Donne would readily pronounce the line so that the 'be' of *because* though present did not spoil the rhythm, and would be told: 'Yes, but unless you alter it they will go on pronouncing it like this': he would then be made to hear the Gardner intonation and would agree at once even to printing the 'poetical' form '*Cause*, which he would naturally dislike. He assumed that this sacrifice would be enough, and so it was for three centuries, but Professor Gardner got him in the end. The purpose of imagining this little scene is to test whether it feels possible, and it feels to me positively likely. Surely one ought to be very chary of rejecting a variant in the first edition for which such an intelligible motive can be found.

One or two other remarks about rhythm may be fitted in here as general support. Professor Gardner is often wrong when she gives the scansion; for example, in 'A Valediction: of Weeping', 'Weepe me not dead, in thine armes, but forbeare' is given stresses on *weepe, me, dead, thine, armes, beare*. I thought at first the extra stress on *me* was one of the misprints, but she adds: 'The line depends on our giving the metrical stress, which as often in Donne falls on the personal pronouns, sufficient weight.' A stress on *thine* is wanted, I agree, to imply 'It is odd to be in danger when in the arms of any woman, but in yours above all', but what can be the implications of the stress on *me*? 'Weep yourself dead in mine, you pig', or more elaborately: 'I suppose you have a queue of men coming to do this. Well, I'm the one that's going to get away.' Of course she did not intend this, but she does seem to mean by it that the poet was egotistical. The third line of 'The Flea' says 'It suck'd me first, and now sucks thee', thus giving a firm foundation for the metaphysical arguments that follow. Professor Gardner prints 'Me it suck'd', with the note: 'The inversion throws the stress where it is needed, on the two personal pronouns.' But there is no such need; he intends to sound cool here, before he starts to drive home his argument. And Professor Gardner is following *L74, HK2, Cy, P*. The main body of Group I is against her, so she must attach some importance to the choice. However, Group II agrees with her, and indeed the line-up of the manuscripts is rather eccentric; it was his best-known poem, and at such a point a scribe might often ignore the text he was copying. I expect her theory is right here, only she did not draw the conclusion. Her introduction allowed some respect for the combination *L74, HK2* (unlike any of the rest of Group V) as perhaps sometimes reporting an earlier version, later corrected by the poet himself. She was right about the detail 'Me it suck'd'; Donne first wrote in a blaze of comic argument, and later (perhaps as late as 1614) realised that a cooler lead-in gave a better effect. By the rules, surely, Professor Gardner is not allowed to print the author's first thoughts. I think they often ought to be printed, but in this case Donne, by smoothing the dramatic effect, made an actual tiny improvement, which ought to be preserved.

The reputation of Donne as metrically uncivilised still hangs about, and I think nowadays chiefly from the one line, introducing a

splendidly bland and smooth romantic poem ('Twicknam Garden'):
'Blasted with sighs, and surrounded with teares.' *Surround* is from
superundare, and the *Oxford English Dictionary* (1961) tells us that it was
sometimes spelt 'sur-und' even into the eighteenth century. Editors
would be well advised to print 'sur-unded' here, to make plain that
the word was pronounced like 'sur-tax.' I find that this discovery was
anticipated by John Crowe Ransom in *The New Criticism* (Norfolk,
Conn., 1941) and by others; Professor Gardner need not have been
reduced to blaming the line for 'a lack of metrical tact' (p. 215). On
another occasion she does envisage an archaic stress, but needlessly,
I think, in 'A Feaver':

> And yet she cannot wast by this
>   Nor long beare this torturing wrong,
> For much corruption needful is
>   To fuell such a feaver long.   (17–20)

Tormenting instead of *torturing* is read by *HK2, JC, S* (that is, one from
each set of Group V), and in Group III *O'F* corrects *torturing* to
tormenting. Professor Gardner's note says (p. 188): 'If the Latin or
French stress is given the line runs smoothly... With the usual stress
the line is harsh and the reading "tormenting", found in some
manuscripts of weak authority, is an obvious attempt to smooth it
and avoid two successive inverted stresses.' As I understand, a stress
on *ure* in *torture* would have been likely a generation or two earlier, but
Donne was determinedly not an archaist, and would pronounce the
word as Shakespeare or Jonson expected actors to do on stage. (The
Shakespeare Concordance is decisive for the modern intonation.) Donne
first wrote what Group V reports, *tormenting,* and because *long* and
ment stand out this feels like a smooth line. Too smooth for the
meaning, the poet decided when looking it over (but whether a few
minutes later or ten years later I cannot tell), so he wrote *torturing*
above the line (not later than 1614) for the purpose of making the
scansion more strained. There now has to be a jammed stress or
spondee; the stresses are *nor, long bear, tort,* and *wrong,* making the
whole verse very graceful and expressive. *O'F* made the change back
to *tormenting* because *O'F* (here and elsewhere) was becoming
increasingly inclined to think that the bold policy of the Group V
copyists had been the correct one.

The dating of the poems is an important part of rescuing Donne, because it is capable of having great effect on judgment of the poet's character. I should however testify at once that to have the *Songs and Sonnets* put in an order which can be more or less remembered is an immense convenience; going back to the Grierson edition, after using the Gardner, is like having the lights go out.

The 'Refusal to Woodward', as it needs to be called, a verse letter beginning 'Like one who'in her third widdowhood', is crucial here and Mr Milgate's edition has been a great help about it. He agrees with Professor Gardner that it was written in 1597–8, whereas I stick to Grierson's dating of 1603–4, not long after Donne's marriage.[12] It seems to me that my opponents fail to imagine the letter as a real one, conveying a real snub, and therefore do not grasp how damaging to Donne's character their date would be. In 1597, after bringing himself into favourable notice by volunteering for the Islands voyage, and making friends on it with a number of well-placed young men, he and Wotton (as Mr Milgate remarks) 'were securing positions at Court' (p. 225); and early next year Donne became secretary to the Lord Keeper. We have two verse letters to Wotton at this time, which were handed to Woodward for his collection, and they do, I grant, speak with lordly contempt for the great world which he is observing, but they make no bones about his desire to succeed in it. The letter to Woodward, on the other hand, might be from a yogi in a cave, fed by the local peasants; it recommends complete retirement and self-concentration, so that, if a man is still a poet (as Donne is not), he should read only his own poems and not those of his friends. It is a noble poem, fierce and bare, but it is perhaps a bit presuming even when Donne has been thrown out of his worldly job, and would be gross impudence if written when he was just seeking one or settling into one. In the later part of 1597, Donne had sent Woodward a verse letter praising him for having achieved philosophic retirement, and then another (if Mr Milgate puts them in order of composition) thanking him extravagantly for sending a poem which had brought Donne back to life. Woodward must be supposed to ask him for poems in return, and receives this astonishing snub. To strengthen his date, Mr Milgate even accepts a note of manuscript *K*, saying that the poem was written at court. That would make it farcically hypocritical, fit for Dickens. Mr Milgate himself speaks of manuscript *K* with severe contempt, and would certainly not use it for any less desired conclusion (poor *K* was merely remembering one of the letters to Wotton, which says it was written from court). Maybe critics

assume that bad taste must be expected in the metaphysical style, so
that it can be ignored; but, in any style, *manure thyselfe then* is a great
snub: it means 'Roll in your own dung; do not come nosing round
after mine.' (This meaning of the word was fairly new, but Donne
was not a man to ignore it.) Surely it is likely to mark a real break,
with a cause for it, and we know that Woodward was never able to
copy out the songs and sonnets. But he was allowed to copy out the
two letters to Wotton, probably later that year, and the altered text
of the satires the year after.

The main argument of Professor Gardner for this date is that all the
poems in the first section of *W* are not later than 1598, 'with one
explicable exception' (p. lxxii). This is a sonnet to an earl, introducing
a series of holy sonnets, which after being presented to the earl
somehow became available for Woodward to copy, and for no other
copyist. He put the introductory sonnet among his verse letters,
which had had no addition for a long time. Yes, but this explanation,
showing that any verse letter could be added to the list, applies just
as well to the snub from Donne. It is a classic example of the 'proof'
which is a total illusion; but somehow the phrase 'with one explicable
exception', perhaps because it is so hard to pronounce, freezes all
objection upon the lips of the common reader; it is the voice of science
in person. Next we have a real argument, though a slight one: that
most of the manuscripts agree in putting the 'Refusal' near to the
'Storme' and the first two letters to Wotton. But Woodward's
collection was necessarily the only source for the 'Refusal', and
probably for the two letters to Wotton; the copiers did not want any
of the rest of Woodward's collection, the trivial letters of the youthful
Donne to his friends, so these were written out together. I grant that,
on my view, Woodward made a slight break in the order of time,
putting the 'Refusal' before the two Wotton letters, but he was not
committed to any order; he might put this final letter to himself at the
end of the letters to early friends, before starting on letters to
impressive social figures. Or he may have wanted the refusal to look
less like a snub, but quite possibly he never knew he had been
snubbed; in its incidentals, the 'Refusal' is almost unctuously
affectionate, as if Donne felt determined to choke off the demand but
without making an enemy. It was rather a disagreeable job, so he
might not have wanted to keep a copy of the poem, not being at all
a spiteful man. I have last to consider Mr Milgate's argument from
the style. The poet would feel socially embarrassed, and it is natural

that he began in the formless unbuttoned style of his letters when younger; but he soon managed to ride away grandly on his moral high horse, in a uniquely grand use of his later style. This did not have to be written at a date in between them. After the initial verses, both the style and the exalted stoicism, as Grierson remarks, are nearest to a letter written to Goodyer from Mitcham, where Donne went to a cottage with his family in 1605.

Around 1603–4, after a mood of defiant exaltation over his marriage which produced a few poems, Donne had settled into a mood from which the 'Refusal' could be written sincerely. Also Woodward was preparing to go to Venice on the embassy of Wotton, and might well ask for a text of the *Songs and Sonnets*, which would help him to make grand friends. These are strong reasons, but I think more is needed to explain the fierceness of the reply. I think Donne was advised, probably by Wotton who was now in a position to hear such things, that Woodward had shown round his collection of Donne's verse letters too freely, and that this had been bad for Donne's prospects of renewed official employment. He recently had had to defend his marriage, we should remember, by an official assurance that he had not been a seducer of young ladies; no doubt he told his friends (like Byron) that he had been more raped than anybody since the Trojan War, but it would leave his nerves a bit raw. Mr Milgate gives very helpful background notes on the early letters. It turns out that when Donne was 21 he wrote several of them to Woodward's younger brother Tom, aged 17, threatening to die for love of him and suchlike; the collection included an answer from Tom. This poem is very plucky and admiring, and much more like real poetry than what Donne had written to him (it is in Grierson as well as Milgate, tucked away in the notes).[13] It would leave a scandalmonger in no doubt that the two lads had been up to something together, and also it insinuated that the wit of Donne's poetry or the interest of his conversation perhaps derived from secret heretical opinions: 'The nimble fyer which in thy brayne doth dwell / Is it the fyre of heaven or that of hell ...' Indeed, several of the witty comparisons in the surviving letters to young friends would have been considered blasphemous, as we know (Mr Milgate points out) because all of the copyists who accepted these letters omitted the comparisons. One way or another, Donne would find this a peculiarly exasperating corpse to emerge from the glacier just at that time. Maybe the sheer success of Tom's poem was an extra irritant; *O* and

P both copy it out on two separate occasions, and though they of course were written much later, that in itself might be regarded as evidence for a prolonged vogue. So poor Donne need hardly be blamed for his rudeness to Woodward, who may, in any case, have remained confident that the poems were to the credit of all concerned.

Grierson in the apparatus to his text gives some interesting variants in the 'Refusal', mainly from the Group V manuscripts *Cy* and *P*; the Group III manuscripts *S96* and *O'F* sometimes agree with them. Most of these variants seem plainly wrong, and the first edition right; but the second, and later editions, even until *1669*, tend to adopt them; this poem is a particularly striking example of a general trend. This pro-Group V faction at least shows that the problems of text were getting attention. Mr Milgate's apparatus tells us nothing about such matters, as he is a disciple of Professor Gardner. She herself records the Group V variants very fully, as she has sometimes a use for them; but she tells us earnestly that they are valueless. He believes what she says, so he thinks recording them must be a waste of time. As a minor example, consider ('To Mr Rowland Woodward', ll. 25–7):

> You know, Physitians, when they would infuse
> Into any'oyle, the Soules of Simples, use
> Places, where they may lie still warme, to chuse.

Mr Milgate prints 'Soule', and his apparatus says (p. 70): 'Soule MSS: Soules *1633*.' It is literally correct, because he only undertakes to record the variants from a few manuscripts, listed separately for each poem, and habitually excluding Group V. But it is the wrong reading, and the entry is part of a cumulative smear against the first edition. The plural *soules* is needed because different essences or medicines were distilled from different herbs; this might be 'understood', but as Mr Milgate himself makes clear in his note (p. 224), it was the distilled essences, not the untreated herbs, which were kept warm – *they* has to refer to *soules*. Grierson's apparatus has 'Soules *1633–69*, *Cy*, *P*'; it is the one occasion in the poem where the first edition anticipates the swing-over to Group V readings among the six later editions. But some of the Group V readings here are certainly wrong; as when at the beginning of the fourth verse ('For though to use it seeme') has *use* by influence from the beginning of the third ('Though to use, and love poetry'), which weakens the sentence but happens not to make nonsense; this typical copyist's error cannot be Donne's first draft. Nor should we expect that, because the poem could not be taken from one. It appears among the Group I manuscripts, deriving from 1614, whereas the other distinctive verse letters of Woodward do not. One letter to young Tom gets in, perhaps the dullest of them, and a Group I manuscript heads it 'An old letter'. Evidently a copy had just happened to be kept among Donne's papers. Woodward had got hold of one of the *Songs and Sonnets*, 'A Jet Ring Sent', and this did not appear in Group I. So we may be sure that Donne had still not forgiven him in 1614. His fault had been to put unpermitted material into circulation, and he firmly did the same to the poem which snubbed him for it; so Donne could get a copy of his poem in 1614, but not in his own handwriting. He corrected its errors from memory and the resulting document joined his collection, for the use of all subsequent copiers; but here only a fanatical Group V ancestor would reject the corrections, as they were the only part in Donne's handwriting; they were only rejected by the ancestor of *Cy* and *P*. This actual plural was probably not erased by Donne, but merely rather hard to read. We of course have the version in manuscript *W*, copied in old age from the original letter by the man who had received it, but he makes at least one error (line four has to read *too* not *so*), and Donne might be slightly wrong about what he had written ten years before. Still, the survival of *W* is enough to make sure that Donne did not say his Muse was in a chaste *holiness*, which would have been bad taste. I think my theory stands up well to this unusual case.

There is good reason to suppose that the break with Woodward occurred before 1605, when he is known to have been in Venice on Wotton's staff, also that Wotton was concerned in the break, because Woodward was never allowed to copy Donne's verse letter of congratulations to Wotton on becoming ambassador. It is extremely innocuous, so that there could have been no intention of secrecy, or feeling of intimacy in showing it to a subordinate; indeed, it only survives because it was copied into Wotton's Commonplace Book by one of his secretaries. Surely it is remarkable that Woodward could not get a copy, even when on the staff. Elizabethans of course had a keen sense of class, but many habitually crossed class lines. To gratify a cultured inferior by letting him study a piece of one's own grand equipment in public so as to raise him above his colleagues, but playfully as if humouring a foible, was the kind of thing Izaak Walton admired Wotton for knowing just how to do. He would not have missed the opportunity if he had not turned against Woodward shortly after the appointment of this subordinate. Indeed, one might suspect that making Woodward act as courier and spy, a job he does not seem to have been especially good at (he got caught), was a means of getting him out of earshot. He was home again in two years, much battered, and the Government allowed Tom some money for the doctoring.[14]

One might suppose that he was eventually allowed to copy the *Songs and Sonnets*, and they just got removed from manuscript *W*, during its centuries in the earl's library, as the most interesting part. But Grierson remarks that the manuscript is still 'bound in its original vellum',[15] so that if there had been any excisions they would have been visible. However, he did again become an intimate friend of Donne when they were quite old, because he alone was given four Holy Sonnets, first published by Grierson, which were to be hidden from the world though they seem harmless now. Perhaps by that time he was no longer keen to copy out the *Songs and Sonnets*.

The dating of this minor poem throws a considerable spanner into the theory of Professor Gardner; Donne is found writing that his muse is in a chaste fallowness just when she has him in full production for half the *Songs and Sonnets*. He was not at leisure, she thinks, to read Neoplatonic authors till he married for ambition and failed to get the money; the resulting mortification turned his mind to higher things, and though he never experienced fulfilment in love he had a lot of daydreams about it, recorded in poems which appear to be about adultery but are merely the results of sulking to spite his wife. Of course, this habit of reflection upon spiritual matters was gradually leading him towards the church ... I find almost every aspect of the theory detestable, but I feel now that my *Critical Quarterly* article, though mostly right, was wrong in assuming that Donne could not become Neoplatonic. I meant that when he started writing he revolted against the outlook of Spenser, so he would not have discovered Neoplatonism when unemployed. But Plato was widely diffused, and Donne might well go on encountering more of him. A medical man of the time, as C. S. Lewis pointed out, would take *platonic* to mean the belief in middle spirits of earth, air, fire, and water;[16] and it does seem plain that Donne was influenced by Paracelsus, though this has not yet been fully investigated. And then there were the Radical Reformers. The chief support for my position about Donne that has appeared since my 'Donne the Spaceman' is to be found in *The Pursuit of the Millenium* (London, 1957) by Norman

Cohn and *The Everlasting Gospel* (London, 1958) by A. L. Morton, which dug up evidence about the fanatics of Donne's time. Recent critics have tended to despise poems which recommend freedom of love, calling them soft and sentimental (this has been the 'tough' reason for rejecting 'There is no pennance due to innocence'); but when Donne said such things they would sound defiant – that was why he was so keen to restrict the circulation of the songs and sonnets. He is recalling the fanatic position, surely, when he writes: 'as infinite as it' in 'Love's Progress' (l. 38); 'all love is wonder' in 'The Anagram' (l. 25); 'all divinity / Is love or wonder' in 'Valediction: of the Booke' (ll. 28–9). Professor Gardner in her notes generously tells us she cannot trace these to their sources. Donne of course was not himself a Radical Reformer; in a way, he was the opposite, and may have felt that to recall them helped to make an ex-Catholic more acceptable, but anyhow he was alert to the whole theological field. The Reformers were notorious for their sexual as well as their political freedom, and were being stamped out in blood and fire. Though everyone remarked on the ignorance of these low-class fanatics, howling outside in the street, they habitually claimed to have derived their doctrines from Plato.

From the twelfth century onwards, there was a left wing of Christianity in Europe, half quietist and half revolutionary, which maintained that every man may become Christ, may become an avatar of the Logos, as Jesus did. It is the same doctrine as the Hindu 'That art Thou' – 'At bottom, the soul of each man is the soul of the world.' Thus a seventeenth-century writer reports that Harry Nicholas (Morton, *The Everlasting Gospel*, p. 39): 'maketh every one of his Familie of *Love* to be Christ; yea, and God, and himself God, and Christ in a more excellent manner'. At the end of *The Alchemist* one of the disappointed sectarians (Ananias) is jeered off the stage by being called a Harry Nicholas, and Jonson would not have done this unless the sect was familiar to his audience; indeed, Morton assures us that it was well established in England by 1600 (p. 40). Cohn (*The Pursuit of the Millenium*, p. 304), after full documentation for medieval Europe, gives quotations proving that the doctrine was still firmly held in Cromwell's England: 'I do not apprehend that God was onely manifest in the flesh of Christ, or the man called Christ; but that he as really and substantially dwells in the flesh of other men and Creatures, as well as in the man Christ.' Donne in the love poems often presents himself as a Christ of True Love, founding a colony or teaching a school to promulgate his new doctrine; when you realise this, you are no longer tempted to deny the obvious meaning of the lines in 'The Relic': 'Thou shalt be a Mary Magdalen, and I / A something else thereby.' One might almost say, it is inherent in the idea of the microcosm that each man can represent the whole world; and yet it was enough to turn the commonplace into a dangerous idea, liable to persecution. Then again, we can hardly help feeling in 'The Dreame' that Donne is being intellectually facetious, or pointlessly flippant, when he says that his mistress is so much better than God that to mistake her for God would be profane, but some of the adepts of the 'Free Spirit', Mr Cohn tells us, really did entertain this idea, as a result of expecting such a radical improvement (p. 185): 'Once the absolute stillness of the divine Oneness has been reached, neither knowledge nor praise nor even the love of God exist any more. "At the highest point of being, God himself is abandoned by himself in himself"; meaning that the God of Christianity is left behind, in favour of the God of pantheist ecstasy.' The authors do not give an actual source for 'all divinity is love or wonder', but to find oneself turning into God must excite such feelings as the phrase recalls. This is clear in the Ranter Jacob Bottomley, who while serving in Cromwell's army wrote *The Light and Dark sides of God* (Cohn, *The Pursuit of the Millenium*, p. 303): 'if I say I see thee, it is nothing but thy seeing of thy selfe; for there is nothing in me capable of seeing thee but thy self...' At any rate, this religion was certainly not keeping commandments or performing rituals.

'Infinite as it' would be merely a sex joke, and probably a jeer, if it were not such good poetry. The vagina is as infinite as the soul, and the soul has just been compared to the starry heavens (from 'Love's Progress', a rich and mysterious piece of fun). Cupid, we have been told, is an earth-god:

> Men to such Gods, their sacrificing Coles
> Did not in Altars lay, but pits and holes.
> Although we see Celestial bodies move
> Above the earth, the earth we Till and love:
> So we her ayres contemplate, words and heart,
> And virtues; but we love the Centrique part.
>   Nor is the soul more worthy, or more fit
> For love, then this, as infinite as it.
> But in attaining this desired place
> How much they erre; that set out at the face?   (31–40)

A conscientious historian might feel that we ought not to read back the sentiments of D. H. Lawrence into these obscure fanatics; but they were already familiar. Abiezer Coppe was a boisterous Cromwellian Ranter who from early youth had been tormented by a craving to swear, and for him the greatest relief of becoming illuminated was that he might now swear even in his sermons (Morton, *The Everlasting Gospel*, p. 51): '[I] had rather heare a mighty Angell (in man) swearing a full-mouthed Oath...than heare a zealous Presbyterian, Independent or Spirituall Notionist pray, preach, or exercise.' 'Spiritual Notionist' is a phrase that Lawrence would have enjoyed, and it makes just his usual appeal to class sentiment; the white-collar men, Coppe implies, will spoil everything unless they are prevented from doing so. Norman Cohn regards his Millenarians with cold horror, and indeed many of the medieval continental messiahs ended in a ghastly betrayal of their own ideals; but A. L. Morton approves of his Ranters, feeling that they foreshadow the Labour party as well as William Blake. They do often strike a note of sturdy innocence, for example the Ranter who 'hoped to see the poor Devil cleared of a great many slanders that had been cast upon him' (p. 45). Donne of course was always aristocratic in attitude, but he could not use this tone of popular good humour. In any case, it was not at all new to say that the individual soul was as huge as the night sky; Cohn has his mystics saying (p. 173): 'The soul is so vast that all the saints and angels would not fill it, so beautiful that the beauty of the saints and angels cannot approach it. It fills all things.' Also they would earnestly regard a sexual ecstasy as a divine one, to a purified soul. They considered that the third age was dawning, and for its illuminati all laws were abrogated by Jesus. Nakedness and adultery were symbols of the achieved freedom, and 'Some adepts attributed a transcendental quasi-mystical value to the sexual act itself, when it was performed by such as they...[T]he leader of the *Homines intelligentiae* claimed to have a special way of performing the sexual act which was that practised by Adam and Eve in the Garden of Eden' (Cohn, *The Pursuit of the Millenium*, p. 180). He would of course teach it to favoured disciples, just as there is a grave third figure beside each of the couples in Bosch's Garden of Delights; or as a pupil watches the lovers in 'The Ecstasy'. Coppe, says Anthony Wood, 'was accustomed to preach stark naked...and in the night be drunk and lye with a wench that had also been his hearer stark naked' (Morton, *The Everlasting Gospel*, p. 52. Coppe denied this, but some naked preaching seems well attested). The Ranter Clarkson, in his tract *A Single Eye all Light, no Darkness* (1650) actually uses the word *centre* as Donne does (Cohn, *The Pursuit of the Millenium*, p. 315): '... thy body consisting of flesh and bone, is made of the dust of the earth, therefore when thy body is reduced to its centre, then (and not till then) is thy body alive, perfected in its happiness.' In his autobiography, he says he had believed when a Ranter said that 'no man could attain perfection but by this way'. Of course, these figures come later than Donne, but they echo the medieval mystics very closely, and the only reason why we have no such writing from the time of Donne's youth is that it was firmly suppressed. His love poetry has much more solidity if you assume him to have heard of the Family of Love.

If I may turn back now to the theory that Donne never experienced love, but only engaged in daydreams about it after his marriage, so as to sulk and insult his wife. This fancy is not merely an invention of Professor Gardner. She regarded it as an established result of scholarship, and it is indeed typical of modern 'Eng. Lit'. It seems to have been invented by J. B. Leishman in *The Monarch of Wit* (London, 1959), and he is much more disagreeable about it than Professor Gardner. The leering worldliness with which he assures the children that grown-ups only have daydreams seems to me a prime example of: 'Any lie whatsoever so long as it discourages the young people from going to bed together.' He draws his main evidence from 'The Dreame'. Here Donne says that he dreamed about making love, and the critic can suppose that this means a voluntary daydream, not a true dream, and thence that all the poems are only about daydreams.[17] Professor Gardner echoes this with rather too much confidence, during some cosy praise of the poet in her Introduction (p. xxi). She is remarking that he often takes a stock theme but at once transforms it; for example, poems about dreaming of love had long been familiar, but Donne added 'the brilliant stroke of bringing the lady herself into the room just as the dream reaches its climax of joy; and for the sadness of waking there is substituted disappointment in actuality and a return to the pleasures of dreaming'. This is grossly false, and I had better quote the whole verse to leave no doubt:

> Comming and staying show'd thee, thee,
> But rising makes me doubt, that now,
> Thou art not thou.

That love is weake, where feare's as strong as hee;
  'Tis not all spirit, pure, and brave,
If mixture it of *Feare, Shame, Honor*, have.
Perchance as torches which must ready bee,
Men light and put out, so thou deal'st with mee,
Thou cam'st to kindle, goest to come; Then I
Will dreame that hope againe, but else would die.   (21–30)

Comming to his bed at just the right moment showed her to be omniscient, like God, and *staying* was another action worthy of her divine nature; *rising* explains that while staying she got into bed. There is no hint of disappointment so far; it only appears when she goes away again, out of fear that they may be discovered. (Probably she visits him in the morning, shortly before the servants begin coming to the bedrooms; maybe they are both guests at a country house, or perhaps they are in the palace of the Keeper of the Great Seal.) This caution is not ideally heroic of her, but he can praise her whole action if it has a practical aim, of getting him ready to start the work of love at once on the next brief opportunity. If so, he will consent to dream of her again, but only as 'dreaming of hope', preparing for the actuality. Rather than accept a life of mere fantasy, he would kill himself. He seems anxious, one might say pedantically anxious if his precautions had not proved inadequate, to leave no loophole for the misreading of Mr Leishman and Professor Gardner.

She draws attention to a similar movement of thought, and applies to it the same false logic, in a poem she calls 'Image and Dream'. I agree (on second thoughts) that he had probably been reading Ebreo, or some other expert on visionary love (a thing he might do at any date), because otherwise it seems gratuitous to threaten to return her miniature portrait in order to have daydreams about her more comfortably; but this does not prove he is converted to the doctrine. The poem gives a cosy recommendation to the safe and convenient practice of fantasy, but the poem's last six lines amount to a convulsive rejection of dreams. He will keep her picture, he decides at the end, to secure him against this escapism: 'Fill'd with her love, may I be rather grown / Mad with much *heart*, then *ideott* with none.' I don't quite agree with Donne here, in the educational field, at any rate; I would not prevent the children from daydreaming at the cost of their sanity. But the scholarly misrepresentation here of what he meant to say is startling.

Having both the Milgate and Gardner editions available also allows of a convenient statistical check on Professor Gardner's dating of the poems. I think that about a dozen of the poems in her 'Songs and Sonnets II' ought to be put back into I, the group written before marriage, to avoid maligning the poet and allow an intelligible development of his character. There is practically no evidence either way; she relies on a principle that the poems using 'philosophical' ideas about love (some of them very boyish and raw) belong to his later life, when he is beginning to be thoughtful (Anglican); whereas in fact all these ideas, not treated so gravely but treated as familiar, appear in the *Satires*, *Verse Letters*, and *Elegies*, admittedly written some time before his marriage. 'Songs and Sonnets I' does succeed in giving a picture of a rather empty-headed young man, but it is incredible that he should always refrain from using these ideas, which are particularly suitable to the themes of the love-poems, if he is already using them elsewhere.

The word *king*, though not very philosophical, helps to show how artificial the arrangement is. Two of Donne's poems, which mention a king, have been triumphantly dated as written under James, and I agree that they were written after Donne's marriage, though maybe before Elizabeth died. 'Songs and Sonnets I' have been selected so that the word *king* never appears at all. But consider Satire IV, where he describes himself visiting Elizabeth's court; *king* is incessantly repeated, as if he dislikes to admit that he is being ruled by a queen.

Donne, like Dylan Thomas, has only a few philosophical ideas in his poetry, though they are important ones. The microcosm, the new medicine, the new astronomy are about enough. Now, the limbeck of Paracelsus comes into 'The Comparison', an elegy which may be as early as 1594 (Professor Gardner prints it second); and Donne is already feeling wonder at it, even though he only uses it to praise his own mistress as part of a tiresome joke argument:

> Then like the Chymicks masculine equall fire,
> Which in the Lymbecks warme wombe doth inspire
> Into th' earths worthless durt a soule of gold,
> Such cherishing heat her best lov'd part doth hold.   (35–8)

He already assumes that the technique of distillation extracts a soul or essence, and therefore yields profound analogies with human affairs. In Satire IV (l. 95) we gather he has watched the machine working 'as a Still, which staies / A Sembriefe, 'twixt each drop...'

There are references to astronomy in 'Loves Progress', which Professor Gardner puts at about the middle of the *Elegies*, dating them 1593–6. You should start toward the centre of a woman by caressing her feet, not her face, and the celestial spheres can advise us about that, though Cupid is infernal and lives underground:

> For as free Spheres move faster far then can
> Birds, whom the air resists, so may that man
> Which goes this empty and Aetherial way
> Than if at beauties elements he stay. (87–90)

On any theory, the heavenly bodies have to move at speeds unknown in common life; the air cannot extend up to the moon, or the moon would slow down. Donne cannot mention the subject, even for this farcical purpose, without showing that he knows the basic problems about it. With 'The Autumnal' (about 1600), we get him using a technical term 'lation' which staggered the more intelligent copyists; he must have read a good deal in the subject by the time he did that. The thought of space travel, taking us to other habitable planets, is first hinted at in 'Love's War', which Professor Gardner dates back to 1594. The strife of love, says the poet, is better than fighting for one's country, and why? Because patriotic fighting, whether in Ireland, Spain or Flanders, always means getting into a *boat*:

> And ships are carts for executions.
> Yea they are Deaths; Is't not all one to flye
> Into an other World, as t'is to dye? (26–8)

'Another world' might be the New World of America, as it was already called, but a voyage that means death is bound to suggest going to heaven, where the planets are. Of course this is not part of the joke argument, but the poetry often comes from the play of mind all around that. The first idea of a loved woman as a planet comes I think in the elegy 'To His Mistris Going to Bed' (1596 perhaps), but he only recognises it in passing as a theme to be developed later: 'Off with that girdle, like heavens Zone glittering, / But a far fairer world incompassing.' The Milky Way was quite prominent in the sixteenth-century mind; the voyage to India around the cape had found that it really does encircle the heavens, as the ancients had assumed it would. Professor Gardner's note says that this 'zone' is *either* the girdle of Orion *or* the whole orb of the fixed stars (p. 131); but Orion's girdle does not encompass any world, and a complete sphere is not usually said to be a zone. Here as so often she has no contact with the poet's interests. The merit of the Milky Way here is that it would girdle any planet, even of another solar system perhaps; the lady may be far grander than our earthly world, and yet have the same zone. Donne notices, almost in passing, that a firm hold of the old cliché could lead one into an entirely new country.

I had expected the microcosm to have been familiar to Donne in the schoolroom, but there seem to be only two early references, and Mr Milgate dates them unexpectedly late. The letter to Rowland Woodward beginning 'If, as mine is, thy life…' (p. 64) was probably written in August 1597, he decides, while waiting at Plymouth as part of the Islands Voyage:

> If men be worlds, there is in every one
> Some thing to answere in some proportion
> All the worlds riches; And in good men, this,
> Vertue, our formes forme and our soules soule, is.   (29–32)

Maybe he was already getting rather tired of keeping up a high enough moral tone to gratify Woodward; just as, in the other example, he felt he was doing hackwork when he wrote Satire V to please his new employer, Egerton, early in 1598. Donne is labouring to support some proposed change of law, and displays philosophic breadth near the start by saying: 'If all things be in all' (as they must because they are made of the same elements), then each thing 'implies or represents' each other thing – 'then man is a world'. But at once the law courts are compared to a landscape, so that the world is a man, and the moral is (very truly no doubt) that you will be ruined if you go to law. This is sad stuff, and one might think (as I had assumed) that he regarded the idea as commonplace; but he actually does not seem to have mentioned it before. It is tiresome not to be sure whether he had just returned from extensive travel. However, these prosy references are enough to prove that he did not acquire the idea of the microcosm during the retirement after his marriage.

Professor Gardner does not use the term microcosm in her edition, thinking perhaps that too much fuss has been made about it, and also not caring to join in the exaltation of the isolated human couple. However, a particularly grand use of that trope is found in 'A Valediction: Of the Booke'. As I remarked earlier, Donne is boasting that the scribbled notes which passed between himself and Ann during the hectic time before their runaway marriage, if digested into a treatise, could survive the next Dark Age and become the gospel of the next Renaissance. It would be the root from which an entire new civilisation could grow, this time genuinely based upon the religion of love:

> When this booke is made thus,
> Should againe the ravenous
> Vandals and Goths inundate us,
> Learning were safe; in this our Universe
> Schooles might learne Sciences, Spheares Musick,
> Angels Verse. (23–7)

Professor Gardner remarks (p. 194): 'Since "university" was frequently used for "universe" at this period, I assume that Donne regards the words as interchangeable.' Only at Oxford would a don take for granted that the university teaches the angels how to sing before God. So far from intending this cosy picture, the poet must be supposed to presume that the ruins of Oxford are only being inhabited by a few roving predators. A Dark Age is to be expected because the present representatives of a religion of love are busy burning each other alive, and persecuting any genuine lovers they may encounter. The eventual new civilisation will find very little use in their relics and must extract all learning from the one book which has life in it; inventing a new heaven will be quite incidental. Such an outlook is by no means sceptical; it really does believe in the religion of love. But it cannot believe in the uniqueness of the historical Jesus, since any man (or married couple) aware of the truth may be called on to act as messiah, as in America or on the planet Mars, and may do it well enough. Belief in immortality also must become rather dubious, because this particular heaven will be a function of the doctrines worked out by the society from its basic text; but maybe all such societies have a sufficient likeness to give a kind of permanence.

Controversy often strikes the observer as tedious, but the participant feels he is learning all the time. I now realise that I never really appreciated the poems until it became necessary to defend them. What other seventeenth-century author had such a grasp of the historical process that he could envisage, if only for a defiant joke, the invention of a new heaven after a renewed Dark Age? It was not absurd of the twenties, I still think, to compare him to H. G. Wells.

CHAPTER 5

Donne's foresight

The view currently accepted is that Donne became interested in astronomy only after the publication of Galileo's *Sidereal Messenger* (1610, reporting the first discoveries from the use of the telescope); the elaborate joke of *Ignatius his Conclave* (1610) must have been written fast to cash in on the immediate fame of that book, and Miss Marjorie Nicolson considers that, like Donne's other interests, his interest in astronomy lasted only a few years after the initial stimulus.[1] I maintain that he foresaw the coming theological row about life on other planets, from 1600 at the latest, and used the idea in the love-poetry; which indeed seems pretty trivial if you cut the idea out.

The reader may naturally answer: 'But he could not think of it before it had happened; this criticism is unhistorical. Only a very clear statement in the poems would allow us to read into them such an inherently improbable meaning.' It took me a long time to start poking round for historical evidence, knowing I was untrained for such work, but when I was driven to it I found at once that there is plenty of historical evidence for the kind of thing I want to say. The historical argument is all bluff.

The first Part assumed that belief in rational creatures on other planets had raised a problem about the Redeemer. Later on it did, but an opponent might answer that this difficulty had not yet been invented at the relevant time. So I was glad to find that Philip Melanchthon had printed the objection in 1549, only six years after Copernicus had printed, in his *Initia Doctrinae Physicae*. Mr Grant McColley, in an article on 'The Seventeenth-century Doctrine of a Plurality of Worlds' (*Annals of Science*, October 1936), sums up the position as:

The most vital argument to Melanchthon is his last, wherein he states that there is but one Son of God, our Lord Jesus Christ, who was sent into this world, was dead, and was resurrected. He did not appear in other worlds, nor was He dead and resurrected there. Nor is it to be thought that if there are many worlds, something not to be imagined, that Christ was often dead and resurrected. Nor should it be considered that in any other world, without the sacrifice of the Son of God, men could be brought to eternal life. As Melanchthon reasons, to accept a plurality of worlds is to deny or to make a travesty of the Atonement. (pp. 412–13)

For Protestants, the views of Melanchthon, a close adherent of Luther, would be authoritative and well known. However, it might be thought that this view would be unremarkable because almost routine. Cicero [*Academica*, 2, xxxx] had disapproved of belief in rational life in other worlds because he connected it with atoms and Epicurus; St Augustine [*De Civitate Dei*, xii, chap. 11] had denounced it because it ignored the special creation of man. So perhaps Melanchthon himself merely felt that he was putting into incisive terms the traditional objection to a recurrent fantasy; but the effect of being incisive at that time was to confront interpreters of Copernicus with a sharp dilemma. My opponents, as I understand, don't deny that Donne even when young was a great reader of current theological controversy, and would be bound to be aware of this background when he made his lovers colonise a private planet.

One did not have to be a specialist to understand him. *The Wonderfull Woorkmanship of the World*, by Lambertus Danaeus, published in French 1575 and in English 1578, struck me as a rather low-brow work giving healthy plain answers to all questions (I owe the reference to Mr McColley's article, p. 413), and it is fully equipped with the objection of Melanchthon. Chapter 25, 'Whether there be one world or many', reports that, apart from the false belief of Plato in an ideal world, some people fancy

another world like unto ours, and other heavens, and another Sun, and a Moon, and all other things in them as in ours. Wherefore, some of them suppose that there are an infinite number of worlds, some more, some fewer. Among whom are reckoned the followers of the philosophers Epicurus and Democritus… (St Jerome refutes the belief from the Scriptures.) …Moreover, what is their state, order, condition, fall, constancy, Saviour and Jesus, what likewise is their life everlasting, and from whence cometh the salvation of this second or third world, it is nowhere declared, neither in what sort these other worlds were made and created: but all these things are expressed concerning one only.

He means, of course, expressed in the Bible. The discussion is notably free from rancour, though the mild joke about a smaller infinite number of worlds shows where the author's heart lies. Twenty years later, Edward Guilpin [*Skialetheia*, Satyre I] is still jeering at the thought of

> Some halfe a dozen of th' infinity
> Of Anaxarchus' worlds.

Guilpin is often said to be one of the school of satirists founded by Donne, and Donne must have felt ashamed of such followers (one of the reasons, perhaps, why he refused to publish); Guilpin displays the same raucous low-brow contempt for any intellectual stirring that our own Christian authors have made so familiar. Still, even Guilpin had heard of the recent controversy about the plurality of worlds (to imply that no modern knew more than the ancients was of course a standard reactionary ploy), so it is absurd to presume that Donne had not.

A rather similar tone is taken by Ben Jonson about Nicholas Hill (1570?–1610), a man whom Donne was likely to have met. He had been secretary to the flighty Earl of Oxford and in the household of the wizard Earl of Northumberland; but became a Papist and printed *Philosophia Epicurea* in Paris in 1601 (second edition 1619). As well as an atomist, he was a Copernican and accepted the plurality of worlds; also he believed that the human soul and the angels were composed of tenuous matter.[2] Ben Jonson jeers at him for atomism in an epigram to Drummond,[3] and again in an ugly dirty poem about rowing down Fleet Ditch (*Epigram* 133, the final one).[4] The ditch is an open sewer, and the disembodied farts

> in more formes out-started,
> Than all those *Atomi* ridiculous,
> Whereof old DEMOCRITE, and HILL NICHOLAS,
> One said, the other swore, the world consists.
> These be the cause of those thicke frequent mists
> Arising in that place, through which, who goes,
> Must trie th'vn-vsed valour of a nose...

The note to the Collected Edition intelligently remarks: 'The inversion of Hill's Christian name was perhaps suggested by "Harry Nicholas", *Alch.* v. v. 117.'[5] In the play, the name of the founder of the Family of Love is merely used as a familiar insult when dismissing the comic Puritans; the epigram is believed (says the Notes) to have been written at about the same time. The low-class ultra-Protestant fanatic looks to us about as remote as he could be from the courtly Papist scholar, but Jonson realised that all advanced thinkers tended to take much the same position, a Socinian one which impugned the uniqueness of Jesus Christ. I think that the Donne of the love-poetry used both the thoughts of Nicholas Hill and those of the Family of Love, so I am interested to find Jonson, in his coarse hatred, doing the same. Jonson of course (with his especial admiration for 'The Calme' and 'The Flea' [*Ben Jonson*, 1, p. 135]) could no more grasp the special merits of Donne than those of Shakespeare; if he could, his friendship with both would probably have vanished; but he knew what to 'make' of the theories of Nicholas Hill, and could rely upon the same prejudices in his audience.

However, the state of opinion in England was more confused, and to its credit more fertile, than these official snubs would suggest. One should realise that the fantasy of life on other worlds was boiling up before the publication of Copernicus, which happened tacitly to give it an unexpected support. The *Zodiacus Vitae* of Marcellus Palingenius Stellatus was Englished about 1580, and one may take it that a European book had to be pretty best-selling to get Englished then; it carries the haunting even if clod-hopping couplet [quoted in McColley, p. 402]:

> But some have thought yt every starre a worlde we well may call,
> The earth they count a darkned starre, whereas the least of all.

In 1585 the *Diversarum Speculationum* of a respected mathematician, Giovanni Battista Benedetti, 'drew from the heliocentric cosmology the conception that other bodies in our solar system are similar to the Earth, and suggested that, since the centre of the lunar epicycle would scarcely be the only object of creation, the planets are inhabited'. The phrasing is Mr McColley's (p. 409), and does I think convey the feeling that an intellectual would get at that time; there was one coarsely obvious way out of the web of confusion spun by Copernicus, and it was what would strike the plebs as particularly egghead, viz. the belief in life on other worlds. A fair number of references can be scraped up before 1590, apart from the explosive tactlessness of Bruno; but it was a time when the intellectuals were keen not to let the mob know what they were thinking about astronomy, as was said with neurotic intensity by Copernicus himself. I greatly admired *The Sleepwalkers* (1959), by Koestler, but I suspect that he has always generously over-rated the plotting ability of organisations, of the German communists for example, and that he does it again when he imputes wise and statesmanlike motives to the astronomical Jesuits of the sixteenth and early seventeenth centuries. The book argues that there was no need for a quarrel about the new astronomy, because the Jesuits were already working hard to get it accepted tactfully, and that only the extremely disagreeable and deceitful character of Galileo forced a show-down. Above all, there was no intellectual persecution; in fact the intellectuals were treated like sacred cows; why, Galileo had to fight to get even an appearance of being threatened with torture in 1633. As the intellectuals only wrote to each other in a grimly tough way if at all through the open post about the burning alive of Bruno in 1600, that proves they have nothing to be frightened about. This kind of comment is however merely laid on top of the book, which illuminates the scene in depth. Koestler leaves us in no doubt that they were all real calculating men, and if they were as frightened as he shows them to be we need not agree with Koestler that they had calculated wrong; they had much fuller detail to work on than he has. The subject was recognised as an explosive one by learned men during the rather long incubation period between the death-bed publication of Copernicus and the report of what Galileo saw through a telescope. A great deal of thinking and talking went on without direct publication, not only in universities but usually with their connivance. It does not seem to me at all surprising that a young man like Donne, expensively educated and extremely keen to get hold of the latest ideas, should succeed in getting hold of them. Consider, he comes right at the end of the incubation period; the only controversy is about whether he could have heard how things were going ten or twelve years before Galileo produced the evidence. The young Donne would consider it very insulting if he could read these arguments to prove he couldn't possibly have understood what he wrote poems about.

But then again, though you did have this major division of opinion, there was a way out of it. To believe that there were spirits, as apart from men, in the moon and the planets was practically orthodox, and this was all that Science Fiction required. At least, this became the position after the show-down of Galileo's only just adequate telescope; from 1590 to 1610, the darkest hour before the dawn, hardly any literary man except Donne cares to handle the subject; and he refuses to publish until he is dead.

I shall therefore describe a few of the ways out which were found shortly after Donne had written the love-poetry based upon the dilemma; this busy activity, though often rather absurd, does I think show that the problem was already being felt as a crucial one for the mind of Europe when Donne was toying with it. Here then is Campanella, writing a *Defence of Galileo* in prison in 1615; we need not be surprised if he is rather confused, but perhaps we are merely unaccustomed to his line of argument. In a medieval manner, he justifies Galileo by citing previous authorities who had expressed similar beliefs; on top of that, he claims that Galileo and himself have avoided their errors (and even Aquinas had been wrong in calling life impossible at the Equator):

I pass without comment the opinion that Galileo has revived the heresy that Christ must make atonement for the men who inhabit the stars, and die there again; just as formerly it was said that Christ must be crucified a second time in the antipodes, if the men living there were to be saved as we have been saved. The heretic Paracelsus, whom the Jesuit Martin Delrio attacked in his *Discourse on Magic*, placed men, who rightly should participate in heavenly bliss, under the earth, in the air, and within the water, and questioned their redemption...

The learned Cardinal Cusanus accepted the hypothesis [of life in the stars], and acknowledged that other suns and planets move in orbits in the starry heaven. Nolanus, whose errors cannot be named, also supported the theory, as did other philosophers...[6]

– especially the heretics in England [including 'William Gilbert, in his *On the Magnet*, and innumerable other Englishmen'], he believes. The idea that Paracelsus was an authority in favour of life on other planets, or at least in queer places, and that his 'spirits' were really men, is rather hard to place; *A Midsummer Night's Dream*, with Mustardseed rumbling about in the belly of Bottom, may have been an alarmingly Paracelsian affair. The references in a Donne love-poem to Copernicus and Paracelsus would carry the same atmosphere, as both bold and new, in a way which we can no longer feel.

Listing an accusation without any answer, to show that you despise it, seems to have been a rhetorical formula; Campanella does not really despise it, because he comes back to answer it later:

If the inhabitants which may be in other stars are men, they did not originate from Adam and are not infected by his sin. Nor do these inhabitants need redemption, unless they have committed some other sin... In his *Epistle* on the solar spots Galileo expressly denies that men can exist in other stars (as I prove with scientific argument in *Physical Questions*), but affirms that beings of a higher nature can exist there. Their nature is similar to ours, but it is not the same, despite whatever sportful and jocose thing Kepler says at such length in his prefatory discussion to *The Starry Messenger* ... It is obvious how far removed from the insanity of Paracelsus is the doctrine of Galileo. (pp. 66–7)

Indeed, all this defence for Galileo might seem unnecessary, as he was ' one of the few of his period' (says Professor Marjorie Nicolson in *The World in the Moon*, 1936) who denied that there were men on the moon; for the good reason that he had seen no water there. But he reserved judgment about the planets, and the whole movement needed defending. We should also notice that on one occasion he called the belief that the matter of the moon is like the matter of the earth ' a most improbable suggestion'; this may have been protective colouring, which he thought to be needed (and I do not understand how Mr Koestler can know that it wasn't) ;[7] but one can imagine that his mind would fall back on medieval or Ptolemaic ideas very readily. He would agree, when in this frame of mind, that if Donne and his mistress had got onto a private planet, they must be made of some aristocratic material, more refined than our common clay.

Young Wilkins, in *The Discovery of a New World in the Moon* (1638), is safe in England, and on his way to a bishopric so far from fearing jail. But he knows that he must be adroit about calming the opposition; after surveying the controversy, he decides to agree in the main with Campanella, whose book had been smuggled out of prison for publication in 1622, on the crucial issue of lunar redemption.[8]

If they were men, then he [Campanella] thinks they could not be infected with Adam's sin; yet, perhaps, they had some of their own which might make them liable to the same misery with us; out of which, it may be, they were delivered by the same means as we, the death of Christ; and thus he thinks that place of the Ephesians may be interpreted, where the Apostle says, God gathered all things together in Christ, both which are in earth, and which are in the heavens [Eph. 1. 10]. So also that of the same Apostle to the Colossians, where he says, that it pleased the father to reconcile all things unto himself by Christ, whether they be things in earth, or things in heaven. (John Wilkins, *The Mathematical and Philosophical Works*. London: Frank Cass and Co., 1970 [facsimile of 1802 edition], 1, p. 102.)

CHAPTER 6

Copernicanism and the censor

It has been pronounced that there was no censoring of the Copernican Theory under the first Elizabeth, and indeed, no book was suppressed which later became known; but this does not go very far. All books had to be licensed before they could be printed, at least in principle, and a book arguing for an unwelcome belief could be suppressed without any evidence surviving. One cannot prove that the system was never used, and the mere possibility would often prevent a man from writing such a book. Thomas Harriot is reproached in a letter from a friend [Sir William Lower], for losing his priority in a discovery, yet again, by refusing to print it; and still he would not print anything at all. Perhaps he was hoping for better conditions in the next reign; but after five years under James he wrote despairingly to Kepler [13 July 1608, Old Style]:

Things with us are in such a condition that I still cannot philosophize freely. We are still stuck in the mud. I hope almighty God will soon put an end to it.[1]

He had been accused of atheism rather wildly in pamphlets, as part of a political campaign against Ralegh, and suffered a brief imprisonment at the start of the inquiry, and when he wrote had long been acting as agent for Ralegh and Northumberland, who were in the Tower; it may be argued that he was in no real danger, and his troubles had made him neurotic or petulant. Even so, something had happened to turn him against print; his only previous book, reporting the visit to Virginia (*A Briefe and True Report of the New Found Land of Virginia*, London 1588), had been a success. Only one explanation is likely; his next book had been refused the licence to print. The young man was affronted; he made it a point of honour never to expose himself to a censor again. The idea would seem intelligible to his friends then, though it has not done ever since, so it has failed to make the impression he wanted.

The censors would be pleased to hear that they are still invisible to us, as they insisted upon silence. The government wanted to suggest that England, if not actually 'free', was much freer than the mainland [Europe], and that the lions under the throne only emerged when necessary. But they needed also to be feared, and so they were. *The Isle of Dogs*, a play which appeared briefly in 1597, seems to have been a 'revue', a series of skits on prominent courtiers by several hands. There was talk of closing all the theatres for ever. Nashe skipped off, probably to Scotland [actually to Yarmouth], but Jonson insisted upon joining the authors in prison, while denying that he had written any of the play. Anecdotes of this sort we have, because the attempt to imprison all the authors had to be public. But not one phrase from the play survives, not even a sentence explaining why it was considered so wicked. We may be sure there was much gossip, because that might be used later in a court of law. This at least shows that the censorship could be active.[2]

The chief reason why it is now thought to have been inactive about Copernicus lies in a very good book, *Astronomical Thought in Renaissance England*, by Francis R. Johnson (Baltimore: The Johns Hopkins Press, 1937). It found much to praise, and has established its main points permanently. One must agree that the censoring, if any, was of a moderate kind. The only weapon used was a refusal of the licence to print (though the punishment if that were disobeyed might be severe), and it was only deployed against serious arguments in favour of Copernicus, especially rebuttals of the arguments commonly used by his opponents. A large and artful intelligence had decided on the policy here, maybe without needing to think twice about it. The ideas of Copernicus had been made familiar to the general public under Bloody Mary, by Robert Recorde's *Castle of Knowledge* (1556), and had established themselves among the fancies that informed people liked to wonder about (on the whole, they thought the daily rotation of the earth a sensible plan, but saw much less point in its yearly orbit round the sun).[3] To interfere with casual mention of this wondering procedure would be considered tyrannous, and would be sure to be ineffectual; what one could usefully do was make it seem ignorant and rather contemptible – because it never answered the learned objections to such beliefs.

This covers all the cases except the decisively important one, *A*

Perfit Description of the Caelestiall Orbes by Thomas Digges (1576). His brief pamphlet defends the two main theses of Copernicus with majestic eloquence, and adds the thrilling belief that the universe is infinite – or makes the belief prominent, if the master had already intended to hint at it.[4] There were at least six reprints in the next thirty years (some may have failed to survive), with the last under King James (1605), who presumably suppressed it as soon as he realised what was going on. There is a simple explanation of the many reprints; under Elizabeth, the law permitted a book once it had been licenced to be reprinted at will, so long as no change was made. James altered the law, so that a book had to be reconsidered at every reprinting. It is clear from internal evidence, I submit, that Digges was only allowed to reprint an exact copy of his first edition; even numerical errors in computation are scrupulously retained. The text was reset for each reprint, say the bibliographers, so there can have been no convenience here; and surely Digges would want to comment on recent events. The *nova* of 1572 had proved that there can be change in the heavens, the sphere of the fixed stars; Digges wrote a book in Latin about his observations on it [*Alae seu Scalae Mathematicae*, 1573], which was liked by Tycho Brahe, who therefore sent him in 1600 an advance copy of the book adumbrating his new theory [*Astronomiae Instauratae Progymnasmata*], not published till 1602 (in fuller form).[5] He could not attack this work publicly, but it might well sting him into some general reflections. Also, Johnson quotes him talking as if he had a telescope or opera-glass (and Harriot reports that there was one on his ship to Virginia ['a perspective glasse whereby was showed manie strange sightes'], very interesting to the Red Indians). This would have shown Digges that the fixed stars are merely points of light, says Johnson p. 175, whereas their apparent size to the naked eye had long been a major objection to the Copernican theory, since it made them all larger than the sun. Probably his telescope would not make this very clear, nor Galileo's either, but it would surely provide something to add. Of course he may have been reserving all this for a later publication; and he does give a list of projected unfinished works.[6] Johnson explains (p. 179) that he was very busy after 1580 improving the fortifications of Dover, also with a tiresome family lawsuit. But surely he would reach a point, before he died, when he wanted to announce his recent discoveries any way he could. To have a book which is frequently reprinted is a great convenience for such an author; he need only write a page or two, and the publisher would be glad to boast about it on the title-page. Digges died in 1595, and there were reprints in 1592 and 1596; it would be an unusual death which did not allow of some farewell in the posthumous edition, after twenty years. This case proves, I submit, that he could only reprint without recensorship so long as he made no change whatever, and that he knew the censor would insist upon this condition.

How the book got licenced in the first place becomes a question, and it would be enough to suppose that the drive against Copernicus dates from the appointment of Archbishop Whitgift in 1583. He was a determined Calvinist, though of course there had to be a loophole for the queen and her bishops, and Calvin had followed Luther quite early in a firm rejection of the theory. There was a real theological difficulty, usually obscured by arguments about the literal words of the Bible (its text of course had to be interpreted in many other cases). Melanchthon, who was chief intellectual adviser of Luther, said as soon as he had looked over the book: 'Christ died for mankind, not for inhabitants of other planets';[7] it did not take another century to find out that that would be the real issue. Most Anglicans had taken it coolly, but Whitgift would not, and he was prone to gear up the censorship, claiming for example to censor the ballads on broadsheets. The origin would be enough to explain the despair of the ageing Harriot in his letter to Kepler, which is the basic thing requiring explanation; and there need be no doubt that Whitgift increased the pressure. But there was pressure before.

Copernicus had published in 1543. In 1556 Robert Recorde published an elementary book about astronomy (*The Castle of Knowledge*), speaking strongly in favour of Copernicus and promising to write a more detailed account of him, but this was prevented by his death in 1558. An *Ephemeris* [by John Feild] for 1557 (these were calculations of times for near-meetings of planets with fixed stars during the year, chiefly needed by sailors) had a Latin introduction by John Dee, strongly recommending Copernicus; he never did that again, and could have said, thinks Johnson, if an enemy had later recalled this essentially ephemeral publication, that he had not directly expressed belief in the physical reality of the earth-movements (p. 135). (Probably he did believe in them, and kept quiet; but then, he had ambitions on the Continent, and need not have been especially anxious about reactions in England.) In 1559 William Cunningham published a substitute (*The Cosmographical*

Glasse) for the more detailed astronomical work that Recorde had intended, praising the dead man, but saying nothing about Copernicus. In 1561 a book on navigation [*The Arte of Nauigation*], translated from Spanish [*Breve Compendio de la Sphera y de la Arte de navegar*, by Martin Cortes], claimed to refute Copernicus. This looks like a concerted movement, as nothing was published on the other side; the death of Bloody Mary in 1558, succeeded by a Protestant queen, was of course exhilarating to Protestants, and the new Government might naturally follow Luther on this point.

Foreign books of course were not kept out, if admittedly prominent. Ramus [*Proemium Mathematicum*] praised Copernicus in 1567, but complained at his still using eccentric circles and epicycles (Johnson, pp. 143–4). There was much controversy about Ramus in the English universities from 1575, but he was read in Latin. *The Zodiac of Life* (*c.* 1531) by Palingenius, however, was completely translated by 1565, and parts of it in Latin were often used in schools; it is a placid survey, ignoring Copernicus, but recalls in passing the belief of some early Greeks that all the fixed stars are suns, and sustain worlds.[8] Johnson (pp. 147–9) is perhaps rather stretching a point when he takes this to show broad-mindedness, but it may have produced some. This takes us quite near to 1576, the date of Thomas Digges' addition to his father's handbook. The father had died in 1559, without hearing of Copernicus apparently, and Johnson gives his book generous praise. It is a small loosely bound book on coarse paper, called a *Prognostication Everlasting*: that is, for example, it tells you how to work out the hours of high tide at London Bridge for all future time. Johnson does not question its eternal accuracy, but another pamphleteer in 1612, while praising the work of Digges, says that it has become out of date, and gives a yet more everlasting computation (Johnson, p. 253). High-mindedly, it was intended for people of small education, and we should praise the author for that; but the book itself must always have seemed rather absurd. A wise censor would reflect that he had better allow such people to be absurd; they will attract ridicule of their own accord. A censor already convinced that the theory was nonsense, who looked at the make-up and then at one of young Digges' purple passages about infinity, might easily take this view. Of course he was making a mistake, and deserved to be sent to a country curacy, but there was no way of correcting his mistake under the current rules. King James realised this after the publication of 1605, and altered the rule or the law; a reprint had now to be re-censored, and he allowed only old Digges' *Prognostication*, not young Digges' *Perfit Description*.

Other examples need to be given. Thomas Blundeville, another populariser [*M. Blundevile His Exercises*], rejected Copernicus in 1594; so did Thomas Hill [*The Schoole of Skil*] (posthumous publication, 1599). Here Johnson uses a form of charity which becomes habitual to him; he praises the authors (pp. 183, 185, 207) for at least adopting the 'figures' of Copernicus – numbers for the distance of the moon and suchlike. But it would be natural to expect that the later authority had some reason for his changes, and they were generally adopted; probably the censor did not realise the source, and quite possibly the populariser did not either. Richard Bostocke, while writing on Paracelsus in 1585 [*The difference between the aunciant Phisicke . . . and the latter Phisicke*], praises Copernicus as the same kind of discoverer (Johnson, p. 183);[9] but this is incidental, and he does not give arguments, so it would be usual to pass him. In 1596 John Blagrave publishes an account of his 'Uranical Astrolabe', which was an improvement, and he claimed that its mechanical details supported Copernicus. As Johnson explains (pp. 208–10), no mechanical details could support him against Tycho Brahe, whose views were becoming known though not yet published; and anyhow Blagrave was merely an artisan, whose views need not be taken seriously.[10]

Reading King James' *Demonology*, one feels that he expected when he came to England to stiffen the scandalous looseness of the censorship, and incidentally do battle for the firmness of the earth, though he could not see that that was much in danger. The publication of Tycho Brahe's 'theory' [*Progymnasmata*] (1602) relieved the pressure here; it accepted the results of Copernicus and merely said that, for any purpose of calculation, they were quite compatible with a motionless earth. For an astronomer to claim that he disagreed with Tycho, while using all the methods he recommended, became mere wilful rudeness. And yet, probably most of the astronomers were hoping for some physical explanation of what they saw, as Kepler undoubtedly was; the real objection to Tycho's plan, the reason why it was plainly a dodge rather than a theory, was that it killed any such explanation stone dead – the behaviour of the Creator could only be thought insanely whimsical.[11] The reason why Milton in *Paradise Lost* did not let the angel mention Tycho's view is that he thought it too silly; at least, this is quite as likely as that he was ignorant and out-of-date [cf. Johnson, pp. 284–7]. The same impulse became evident in Nicholas Reymers' system, which allows the daily rotation of the earth but keeps it in one place;[12] the book was published early enough (1588) for Tycho to accuse him of having stolen his bright idea (a very obvious idea), so it was not a result of reading Gilbert's *De Magnete*. Many people felt the daily rotation as a positive comfort, because it saved one from imagining a monstrous speed in the fixed stars; but the yearly orbit round the sun offered no corresponding relief. In fact one could see no point in it unless one took the further step of deducing life on Mars.

My account here is too simple. The old view had been that anything beyond the moon was made of the quintessence, the fifth element which was unlike the earthly four, as a circus-horse instead of a cart-horse, or rather as more like a shadow than anything real. Any movement could be ascribed to it. This did not suit the sixteenth-century mind, perhaps because simple machines were more in use, and the artisans who understood them got more attention. The period had great luck in the prominent *nova* of 1572, which plainly kept its place among the fixed stars, and several comets which could be proved to be beyond the moon. This had encouraged the demand for a mechanical explanation; but one need hardly fight for that before it had been invented.

In one case, the rotation of the earth, it had been invented, and was published just before James arrived, in Gilbert's *De Magnete* (1600). The book was greatly praised on the continent, and may be said to have given the scientific work of James' new subjects the recognition that it deserved; besides, he had been intensely loyal and ready with help for ships' pilots. His posthumous book turned out to be insistent for the daily rotation but dumb about the yearly orbit ['Earth's remaining motions'], which was not required for his thesis;[13] well now, the Bible does say that the earth is fixed, but does not positively deny rotation, except by using common phrases. It would have been absurdly tactless for James to lead off by denouncing the recently dead hero, and he was well able to understand that. So, for two reasons, James was quieted down about astronomy; quieting him down about witches took a bit more time. Even though quiet, Harriot considered that he made genuine publication impossible.

It is remarkable that two fiercely pro-Copernican almanac-makers flourished from the start of James' reign; the yearly output of one of them, from 1605 to 1618, has survived, and many almanacs have got lost. They are Edward Gresham and Thomas Bretnor, and no doubt they were testing how much the new king would stand. Johnson (pp. 250–2) praises their learning – they had at least been well advised what books to recommend. The dramatists jeer at them, and Bretnor did accept astrology, but they deserve praise as witness to the truth. Also they were jolly about it, judging from the few quotations given by Johnson, calling the orthodox opinion the 'old dotage' and suchlike.[14] One must remember that this came in an 'almanac', with lists of the days when it was safe to have a bath or cut one's hair. The king, I suggest, was told that such publications had long been allowed, because they brought the new heresy into contempt.

For whatever reason, the treatment of learned books is much more severe, both before and after the change of reign. Gresham College was founded in 1597, a belated recognition that sailors need to learn navigation, and it had professors of astronomy from the first, some of whose lectures survive. None of them saying anything at all about the views of Copernicus. Most of them were 'outright Copernicans', says Johnson, so no doubt 'their ideas were transmitted by the spoken word' (p. 267).[15] Nudges and winks might have come in handy, too; Johnson seems to realise at this stage that he is talking about a censorship, but he still feels it would be a rude thing to mention. The first professor of astronomy at Oxford (John Bainbridge, 1621) was less shy, and had remarked in a book about a comet, while discussing its orbit:

I can hardly keepe within the sphaere of this little Treatise, and scarsely refraine from the Samian Philosophy of *Aristarchus* in the earths motion, were it not I feared another *Aristarchus* his broach: and that I must reserue these mysteries for a more learned language.[16]

He is very easy about it, and does not seem well informed (such things did not get published more easily in Latin); still, his candour is a welcome change. Johnson praises him here because he 'took pains to give his reader a definite hint' that he was a Copernican (p. 270), but he does more than hint at something more. Nathanael Carpenter attacked Aristotelian doctrines in his *Philosophia Libera*, and accepted Gilbert's theory that the earth revolves because it is a magnet, and otherwise, after a full discussion, voted for Tycho (Johnson, p. 274). Small beer enough, but he published this book in Frankfurt (1621), and then in Oxford a year later. Presumably, when the book was already available, he was informed that the Oxford licence would be granted. John Swan in his *Speculum Mundi*, printed at Cambridge in 1635, is 'conservative' and even reactionary but has had to accept a good deal; he adopts Tycho's system and admits that there is no fifth essence in the heavens (Johnson, pp. 276–7). These are all the theoretical writers mentioned by Johnson in the period which almost takes us to the Civil War; we next have Wilkins in the *Discourse concerning a New Planet* (1640), which presumes that the king's censorship has stopped. The persecution of Galileo would also be a recommendation for the new astronomy among Protestants, but it seems clear that most of these English authors were merely waiting for the end of censorship. Johnson remarks (pp. 278–82) that a decisive swing against the dodge of Tycho comes in 1649, but does not remark that the king's head had just been cut off.

A quaint detail, with a spice of mystery, serves to round the story off. Soon after James came to England, around 1607, a Dutch inventor called Cornelis Drebbel made a perpetual motion machine, a specimen of which he presented to the king, disguised as a globe of the fixed stars. So far, it might as well have been a map of the earth, but apparently he said it was worked by 'a fierie spirit' mixed with 'his proper Aire'. So it didn't spin for a magnetic reason, like the earth of Gilbert; and this would be a satisfaction to James. It is part of the politeness of Johnson not to ask tiresome questions, so he does not discuss how either method could produce rotation; but he does let drop that Drebbel was a Copernican (pp. 262–3). The machine lived at Eltham Palace, and perhaps James only stayed there for short periods. This was just about the time when Harriot wrote his despairing letter to Kepler.

Still, though the Stuarts were more exasperating than Elizabeth, in restrictions on science as well as other matters, the evidence implies that she gave her archbishops pretty well all they wanted in that line, with the minimum of public turmoil.

CHAPTER 7

Thomas Digges his infinite universe

In 1576, Thomas Digges (1532?–95)[1] reprinted a book by his father Leonard (d. 1571), *A Prognostication Everlasting*, 85 pages, mostly diagrams and columns of figures, adding at the end 23 pages of his own, mostly letterpress, nearly 10,000 words. His father's part was first published in 1553, and had two reprints before Elizabeth came to the throne; of course, it uses the old astronomy, but the description of that is only a framework; the everlasting forecasts are about such things as the date of Easter and the hours of the tides at the major ports of England ('Ensample: I desire to know the Full Water at London Bridge, in the year of our Lord 1555, the 6 day of February'). All this remains; then the son remarks coolly that the reader had better know the alternative theory of the planets, and his account is an impassioned defence of it.

This arrangement slipped through the net of the censorship, and Thomas had hoped that it would; but he did not foresee that a stiffening of the censorship would for ever prevent any improvement in his essay; some of it is very fine prose, but the end of it seems casual and off the point. Probably he hurried so as to keep the book in print; he could hardly foresee that Whitgift, who was to stiffen the licensing system, would be made Archbishop in the following year. A new star had appeared in 1572, which was held to prove that the heavens were corruptible; though, as Thomas remarked in the book, you would not say a cat was corrupted because it had kittens; and this portent might strike him as an opportunity to open a campaign. Also Dr Gilbert, later to write *De Magnete*, took up a practice in London during 1573; the questions at the end of Thomas' Addition, about the variations from the pole in the magnetic needle; and whether what the sailors tell you can be trusted, continued to be central for the work of Gilbert. He was then about 33, Thomas just over 40, and what was central for the various books of Thomas during his remaining 20 years may be summed up as the technical requirements of England when at war; whereas young Gilbert must have started from a theoretical interest, so the minds of the two men were complementary. Still, though astronomy was not the main interest of Thomas, he was active and fond of arguing; he would not have continued to reprint this very successful book at frequent intervals without taking any part in the subsequent controversy, unless his licence *only* allowed reprinting, and would be forfeited if he altered the work at all. In 1588 Tycho Brahe produced his absurd compromise, not admitting even the daily rotation of the earth, but allowing the solar system to career round it in such a way that one could calculate as if Copernicus was right. Another continental figure, Reymers Bär, published a similar work in the same year, but he allowed the earth a daily rotation; to deny that [motion] had come to seem almost an act of faith, whereas to make the earth stay in the same place while rotating went a long way towards allowing literal acceptance of the crucial texts in the Bible. Surely Thomas Digges would have joined in this debate, having such a convenient instrument to his hand, if it had not meant risking the confiscation of the instrument itself. Most of what I am saying here is familiar, but I have not seen this argument put.

There is a serious claim for Thomas Digges as innovator rather than populariser, which was brought to light by the work of F. R. Johnson and S. V. Larkey ('Thomas Digges, the Copernican System, and the Idea of the Infinity of the Universe in 1576', *Huntington Library Bulletin*, v, April 1934); he would have denied it himself, but that leaves him still a discoverer. He thought that Copernicus regarded the 'sphere' of the fixed stars, not as a smooth firm surface with spangles on it, but as an immensely deep 'outer space' carrying stars at random intervals. Copernicus, as I understand, wrote very dully and clumsily, but before blaming him for this one should realise that it may have been a precaution. There have been strong arguments [to say] that Digges was right about the intention of Copernicus; but even if he was, nobody had recognised this intention before. No wonder he was glad to have a Nova certified as occurring in outer space. And if you believe in deep outer space you find the daily rotation of the earth essential; whether it goes round the sun does not matter nearly so much. He does argue very earnestly, at the start of his Addition, for the sun as the centre, but if you imagine a detached rather ignorant reader, Shakespeare for example, he will tend to think that some odd religion is being recommended. The sun deserves the position,

for not vnfitly it is of some called the lampe or lighte of the worlde, of others the mynde, of others the Ruler of the worlde. (p. 87)

' *Trismegistus* called hym the visible God.'[2] Of course this is copied from Copernicus, and there isn't much else to say if you must leave out the mathematics. But as soon as Digges turns to the rotation, he is very hard-hitting. I feel ignorant here; the apparently inherent knowledge of dynamics which is appealed to must depend on some experience of spinning or swinging bodies, and maybe this became more familiar in the Renaissance than the Middle Ages, but I do not see how. For whatever reason, Digges need only assert, feeling confident that his audience will agree, that there cannot be a daily rotation of the sphere of the fixed stars. Perhaps it is because they had come to regard the stars as real matter, not as a kind of shadow-play. Their minds were not primitive; subtle ideas about space, very like those of modern physicists, were bandied about freely. For example, Digges has to face the argument that we should all be thrown off the earth if it were spinning, and he cannot make the only adequate answer, that we *would* be thrown off if it went faster, if the day was as short as an hour, but we have a comfortable margin; because here he too has no 'mathematics', any more than his ignorant reader. But it is enough for him to say that, if the outermost sphere did the revolution instead of the earth, the effects would be enormously worse. It would be bound to crack apart and pour out to infinity.

But say they without the Heauen there is no body, no place, no emptynes, no not any thinge at all whether heauen should or could farther extende. But this surelye is verye straunge that nothinge shoulde haue sutche efficiente power to restrayne some thinge... (p. 91)

Here he can safely play at being unimaginative, but infinite space is more than even he can bear, so he invents a rule that light fails after a fixed (very great) distance. Otherwise we would see far too many stars, and he is right to think so if he has an unconscious knowledge of the inverse square law. Wilkins can be found accepting this source of comfort, sixty years later. [...]

Never mind, [Digges] is right on the main point he wanted to drive home: the enormous physical scale of the universe, making it impossible that men were the only creatures of God or the only ones attended to by a Redeemer:

Heerein can wee neuer sufficiently admire thys wonderfull & incomprehensible huge frame of goddes woorke proponed to our senses, seinge fyrst thys baull of ye earth wherein we moue, to the common sorte seemeth greate, and yet in respecte of the Moones Orbe is very small, but compared with *Orbis magnus* wherein it is carried, it scarcely retayneth any sensible proportion, so merueilously is that Orbe of Annuall motion greater than this litle darcke starre wherein we liue. But that *Orbus magnus* beinge as is before declared but as a poynct in respect of the immensity of that immoueable heaven, we may easily consider what little portion of gods frame, our Elementare corruptible worlde is, but neuer sufficiently be able to admire the immensity of the Rest. Especially of that fixed Orbe garnished with lightes innumerable and reachinge vp in *Sphæricall altitude* without ende. Of whiche lightes Celestiall it is to bee thoughte that we onley behoulde sutch as are in the inferioure partes of the same Orbe, and as they are hygher, so seeme they of lesse and lesser quantity, euen tyll our sighte beinge not able farder to reache or conceyue, the greatest part rest by reason of their wonderfull distance inuisible vnto vs. And this may wel be thought of vs to be the gloriouse court of ye great god, whose vnsercheable worcks inuisible we may partly by these his visible coiecture, to whose infinit power and maiesty such an infinit place surmountinge all other both in quantity and quality only is conueniente. (pp. 88–9)

[...] Most later astronomers gave up this theory, together with the belief in infinite space for which it was designed. But there were no such palliations when the child Donne first read astronomy; and the many references to life on other planets in his love-poetry, where their main function is just as a symbol of the independent rights of the pair of lovers, always carry some memory of the appalling splendour of this account by Digges.[3]

CHAPTER 8

Godwin's voyage to the moon

('THE MAN IN THE MOONE: OR A DISCOURSE OF A VOYAGE THITHER BY DOMINGO GONSALES, THE SPEEDY MESSENGER')

I

I am now to consider the science-fiction Utopia of Francis Godwin, trying to move its date a little earlier and to grant it an influence when new; but perhaps I need first to defend my belief that so slight a narrative, so near to flippancy, is worth the reader's attention. Well, it received a great deal of attention when at last it was published, being felt to involve questions of importance; and the magical doctrines are also involved in it quite a lot. Anyway, it is a very good piece of writing, all aglow with intelligence and good humour, and taken at a spanking pace. Donne would certainly be influenced by it, if he had the chance; but the chance would only come if he read the manuscript early enough, at the time when he made an important change in the themes and outlook of his poetry. I propose that he read it, soon after it was first drafted, in 1597, preferably before going on the Islands Voyage. (That is, he read most of what we now have, but Godwin inserted a new ending and made a few other changes, to bring the moral of his story up to date, twenty years later.) Perhaps I may explain: I became interested in the dating of *The Man in the Moone* some time ago through a spontaneous exasperation with the absurd arguments for dating it late, and have only recently noticed that the earlier date allows of the influence on Donne. This now seems to me the main interest of the question, and I shall begin the essay with some remarks about it. In any case, I think it important to recognise that the London of the 1590s was full of discussion of new discoveries and ideas, though people were careful not to let it get into print; they were waiting for the old queen to die, but also for the Anglican Church to finish its balancing act. Hence for example the *Songs and Sonnets* of Donne, among the few who were allowed to read them, could readily be taken to mean a good deal. I feel sure of this in any case, but to establish an earlier date for the brief Utopia of Godwin would slightly improve the general probability.

Donne and Godwin were pretty sure to meet in 1597, because they would be going to the same places. Donne had evidently decided to seek for official employment, having spent most of the money left him by his father; volunteering for the Islands Voyage was an early step, but no doubt even before that he had started attending the receptions at which hopeful young men might offer themselves for scrutiny. Godwin was ten years older, and already a clergyman – his father was a bishop, and he had fitted him into some minor post; but he was ambitious, and had been compiling a history of the English bishops, which was printed in 1601, and as a reward he was made Bishop of Llandaff. Presumably he had had to tour the cathedral towns, copying out records, but towards the end he would spend a good deal of time collating the results in Lambeth and Canterbury. By 1597 he would feel that the main donkey-work was behind him, and the reward in sight, if only he played his cards correctly. It seems a natural time to write a gay and expansive fantasy. The two young men would feel no rivalry, as they were in for such different jobs; and Donne would readily appreciate a flow of antiquarian church gossip. It may be thought that Godwin would not show his secret fantasy to anyone, least of all to such an obvious tattle as the young Donne; that might cost him the very bishopric for which he laboured. But the story was designed to be shown round, almost too frankly one might think; the Lunars fall on their knees at every mention of Jesus Christ, and profess a greedy admiration for Queen Elizabeth. A prospective bishop of course could not print a little merriment of this kind, but nobody would object to its being shown privately; I expect Godwin was rather puzzled to know how to get it shown round sufficiently widely.

All this may seem remote from the ecstatic poems which present a couple of lovers colonising a private planet; but the story itself is basically one of adventure – the Spaniard has a staggering amount of nerve, and though ready to boast (e.g. about his rather dubious gentility) takes his virtue for granted; also he is deeply interested in what he finds on the moon, asking the questions which the reader wants to have answered; he is very capable of wonder, though also keen to turn his discoveries to some patriotic use. This part of the wonder belongs to the world of modern science, but Godwin is touched by the older point of view, which would expect any inhabitants of the stars to be nobler than ourselves – that is why the story is a Utopia. In the Hermetic writings, man is an exile from the stars, his natural home; soon after the creation he fell in love with the beauty of the earth, which loved him back, so his fall was not really to his discredit, but he had better disentangle himself as soon as he can. Cornelius Agrippa had better be quoted, echoing this point of view, with acknowledgement, in the *Occult Philosophy*, chapter 59 (I use the graceful translation by John French of 1651). He is discussing Sacrifices, which are 'natural Mediums betwixt the Gods and men':

And these are (as *Orpheus* calls them) keys which open the gates of the elements and the heavens, that by them a man may ascend to the supercelestials; and the intelligences of the heavens, and the demons of the elements, may descend to him. Now men that are perfect, and truly Religious need them not, but only they, who (saith Trismegistus) being fallen into disorder, are made the servants of the heavens and creatures; who because they are subjected to the heavens, therefore think they may be corroborated by the favour of the celestiall vertue, untill they flying higher be acquitted from their presidency, and become more sublime than they. (Book III, chapter 59, pp. 536–7)

The Latin text (1633) was very well known in the sixteenth century, but not considered enough to teach the important secrets. It is plain here that getting in touch with a planet, though smart and perhaps useful, is not particularly holy; and the astronomical poems of Donne give a similar impression. In any case, though exalted, it plainly belonged to a religion other than Christianity, however willing the magicians might be to keep up good relations; so it could be adapted very readily to a religion of earthly love (of course I do not mean that Donne was really praising magic in the love-poems, which would have been irrelevant to them).

Donne writes about the limbeck in poems which are accepted as quite early, and there are early references to astronomy, though slight ones; but he does not seem to have written about the microcosm, the belief that each man contains specimens of everything in the world, or that each human couple inherently colonises its own plantation, before a letter to Rowland Woodward of 1597, while his ship was waiting to sail on the Islands Voyage. Both parts of the idea, having an external adventure and being able to internalise it, were needed to give enough bite to his rather sketchy love-poems about space travel. He mentions choosing the Voyage to escape 'the queasy pain of loving and being loved', which I do not think he would have said unless it had been literally true, though his practical reason for volunteering was to display loyalty and make influential friends so as to get a suitable job. Thus he had all the elements together at that time, if he had Godwin too.

I am only uncertain about the Elegy 'Love's War', which Professor Gardner puts as early as 1594;[1] perhaps there is no need to doubt that such ideas had been knocking about in his mind quite early. He is deciding here not to volunteer for some kind of fighting, probably on land, in Ireland or Belgium perhaps, because there is a basic objection to all patriotic activity – it always starts with getting on a *boat*:

> And ships are carts for executions,
> Yea they are Deaths; Is't not all one to flye
> Into an other World as t'is to dye? (26–8)

On second thoughts, the answer to the question has to be: 'Well, no; they might be quite different'; but we need not deduce that Donne had read Godwin's manuscript, only that he was prepared to be interested in it. 'The Good-Morrow', for so long printed as the first of the *Songs and Sonnets*, seems to mark the actual discovery of the theme; he has already described for a verse and a half his astonishment at the new happiness, his feeling of being reborn into a new life, and then he stumbles upon the idea that they are on a planet of their own. This would be most likely to happen if such an experience was already prominent in his mind, but in quite another context, so that he needed to be searching for an analogy before it could break through. And what else could he have been reading, that would fit the requirement, except the *Man in the Moone*? 'The Sun Rising' belongs to the same period, I think, because it is so brisk and brash; he has reflected a good deal upon this new kind of microcosm, but it is still fresh in his feelings (there is of course not the slightest need for King James to be on the throne). The most impressive poems by Donne using lovers on planets were probably written to his wife after their runaway marriage (December 1601), when the couple were far more really marooned; these poems no doubt express greater depth of feeling but could not, after what the couple had been through, come with so much bounce. The main reason for the dating, generally agreed upon, is that no previous love-affair of Donne had ruined him, so there could be no occasion for them earlier. I believe that the mistresses were real, which some critics have earnestly doubted, because he tells us in 'Love's Growth' that he would have despised himself if they had not been, and tells God they were real in Holy Sonnet XIII. We need therefore to ascribe an earlier date to 'The Good-Morrow', before he had met Ann, and he must have read Godwin before that. This change of tone is the main thing, but also, as part of it, he has a tendency to mock at his old trope or at least express disillusionment with it. I think this is going on in 'A Valediction: of weeping', and it is much required in the 'Nocturnal', where the belief that his wife is dead makes him look back over their courtship with sad amusement. 'We thought we were in great trouble, but in fact, compared to this, we were having a lively time':

> Oft a flood
> Have wee two wept, and so
> Drownd the whole world, us two; oft did we grow
> To be two Chaosses, when we did show
> Care to ought else; and often absences
> Withdrew our soules, and made us carcasses. (22–7)

The vast hyperboles appear as the jargon of a game for children, and then he comes back with a greater one. Of course this is written long after the marriage (very probably in 1611), but it presumes an even longer history for the poetical formula. Debunking critics often reject this type of argument, calling it self-indulgent fantasy, but I answer that they are refusing to read; when a man is writing as well as this, he is long past imputing a bogus bit of history.

Finally, I have an argument to prove that Donne had read *The Man in the Moone* by the time he wrote 'The First Anniversary' (1611). It is not much needed, unless someone thinks that Godwin never showed the manuscript to anyone, but it does clear up an obscure part in the poem. The world is rotting away, Donne is arguing, because Elizabeth Drury was the soul of it, and she is dead; everything is going out of shape, and even astronomy has gone soggy and cheesy. Probably this is because men have been getting too much control over it (260–88). Sure enough, novelties in astronomy are mentioned further down, but the first thing men have done is:

> They have impal'd within a Zodiake
> The free-borne Sun, and keepe twelve Signes awake
> To watch his steps...
> ('An Anatomy of the World: The First Anniversary', 263–5)

and the Goat and Crab keep the sun from running to the Poles. This is a very ancient action by Man, so it gives no evidence for a rapid collapse of the firmament since the death of Elizabeth Drury. It is important, I think, to realise that the famous passage is in part playful, or at least makes a show of being; maybe Donne did expect the world to end soon, but he could not have wanted the buyers in the shop (oh horror!) to jeer at him for superstition. The sun cannot 'perfect a circle' (269), we are next told, but has a serpentine movement; this is presumably the precession of the equinoxes, which was not considered by astronomers to be a new activity of the sun. Next comes:

> And seeming weary with his reeling thus,
> He meanes to sleepe, being now falne nearer us.   (273–4)

Here we do get a prospect of change, and the dauntless Campanella expected the arrival of the sun to bring a millenium, but even that might perhaps involve the destruction of the world by fire. (There was a new estimate of the distance of the sun, which had made it nearer than the old one; Samuel Butler recalls the controversy in *Hudibras* Part II, Canto iii, line 885.)[2] The next lines seem to give more prominence to the harmful activity of man:

> So, of the Starres which boast that they doe runne
> In Circle still, none ends where he begun.
> All their proportion's lame, it sinkes, it swels.
> For of Meridians, and Parallels,
> Man hath weav'd out a net, and this net throwne
> Upon the Heavens, and now they are his owne.
> Loth to goe up the hill, or labour thus
> To goe to heaven, we make heaven come to us.
> We spur, we reine the starres, and in their race
> They're diversly content t'obey our pace.
> But keepes the earth her round proportion still?
> Doth not a Tenarif, or higher Hill
> Rise so high like a Rocke, that one might thinke
> The floating Moone would shipwracke there, and sinke?
>   (275–88)

How we spur and rein the stars I have no idea; perhaps the magicians had made some claim which could be so misinterpreted. But look now, Donne continues, while we fuss about the stars, much worse things are happening down here; the earth is no longer round; it has the Rock of Teneriffe sticking out. The earth does not keep her round proportion 'still', because the Rock 'rises'. Now Donne, I submit, was not a nonsense-writer; he may have wanted to leave the public guessing here, in a cloudy sinister passage, but he would need to feel that, if challenged, he could produce an answer which made sense of the detail about the Peak, as he could about the reeling sun. Had there been a recent increase in the estimated height of the Peak? There had indeed; the hero of Godwin says it is fifty miles high, and this naturally gave his birds a great help in carrying him through the earth's gravitation: they had a rest at the top. At least, he says fifteen leagues high, and Godwin makes him give an estimate of the distance of St Helena from the mainland (of Africa) which is correct if you take his league as the English nautical league, about three and a third miles. A rock fifty miles high could be seen for 360 miles, by a calculation which was already familiar, and this would make Teneriffe a prominent landmark from Madeira, which was only 260 miles away. So this would have been considered a comical gaffe made by young Godwin, and Donne I think remembered it rather affectionately, a dozen years later. He was being deliberately obscure; that is, he could not want the majority of his readers to guess the source, because it would not be solemn enough for them; but he was not 'writing down' to them: as poetry the firm Peak rising higher and higher, as it oozes like a tooth out of the rotting world, gives a positive satisfaction. I owe this interesting quotation to Mr John Webb.

II

I am next to offer reasons from the life of Godwin why he should have drafted his story in 1597. The main reason is a simple one: he needed to do it early, as all his friends would agree, and the latest historical event mentioned is the Battle of the Isle of Pines, in the West Indies (1596).[3] However, the hero returns from the moon in 1601, and fantastically accurate details about the dates of going and returning, with the situation of the planets just then, are given towards the end. One needs to form an estimate of the attitude of Godwin towards his story – it would be very unlike that of a modern novelist. He would feel that it was allowable as a whim, and therefore as a thing done at one stroke; to fuss about improving it would be contemptible. This would not prevent him from having another whim, twenty years later, when he made the hero end in China; but he would not himself add the details about the date, in 1601, when the almanac was available, nor would he twenty years later go and look up the details in a library, though he was accustomed to using libraries. I think one of the friends to whom he had lent the manuscript in 1601 wrote in these details from the almanac, explaining that some astrologer would be sure to need them; and Godwin was pleased to have it done. He would certainly not have invented false details, merely for a literary effect (though here of course my assertion is subject to check).

He lived from 1562 to 1633, so when he drafted the book he was 35. He became DD and acquired some further clerical appointments during that year; plainly, it would have been unwise to put off writing the story any longer. The DNB, with its Victorian gaiety, still tells us that he wrote it while a lad at college, and this is just a literary estimate; it is a young man's book, and Godwin did not remain a young man – he issued very fussy instructions, annoying his clergy-men, as soon as he was made a bishop. However, the scholars of the 1930s revolted against the Victorian cosiness, especially in America, and Grant McColley, whose edition of the story is still the only one likely to be available in a library, proved with great energy that Godwin must have written the story late in life.[4] The moderate view of F. R. Johnson (*Astronomical Thought in Renaissance England*, 1937) allows it to have been written between 1600 and 1610,[5] so I need only fight for three years; but I think both sets of arguments need answering. Anyhow, Donne was in no condition during 1601 to absorb Godwin creatively.

Early promotion is often a bad thing, and what little we know of Godwin's later life is sad. Llandaff was an ill-paid bishopric, and he retained his precentorship at Exeter; this may have been why his clergymen were not enthusiastic about his code of regulations. However, he kept up his historical studies, and in 1615 brought out an improved chronicle of the English bishops, also a history of the early Tudors [*Annals of the Reigns of Henry VIII, Edward VI, and Mary*]; as a reward, James I made him bishop of Hereford. This was nearly as far from London as Llandaff, but it was tolerably well paid, and not in Wales; he would feel he had carried through another successful operation, though it took him till late in 1614 to get hold of the temporalities. He would thus be cheerful and sanguine enough to read two books, printed in Latin on the Continent, which made him feel that a slight change in his old story would adapt it to the modern world; they were the very strange *Confessio* of the Rosicrucians (1614, in Cassel)[6] and the successes of the Jesuits in Peking [*De Christiana Expeditone apud Sinas suscepta ab Societate Jesu*], reported by [Nicholas] Trigault (1615, in Augsburg). This made him complete his masterpiece, but he must already have been approaching a state of delusion. So far as one can gather from the brief but searching article in the DNB (a biography is greatly needed), the complaints against his behaviour as a bishop all come from Hereford. He secluded himself, and then complained that official business had been kept from him; accused of nepotism, he answered that he could not find properly instructed clergymen outside his own family. The years immediately after the appointment to Hereford must have been the last time he could possibly have added to the book without spoiling it; he next came to believe that he had magical powers, and that he was much wronged because the Government would not recognise them. It is very good luck that his addition only brought a ground bass into the book, which makes it stronger; to suppose that he could have written the whole story in later life is sadly absurd.

He invented science fiction, in the practical sense that he was believed to have done it by his imitators in the century after his death; and this branch of literature requires a certain bounce, or readiness to deceive at the moment of salesmanship. It is a very innocent procedure, because the author actually hopes the reader will realise that he is being deceived, and will puzzle over how it can be done. At least, this is so in the foundation case of Godwin, where I can never see the fallacy, but it is very seldom achieved by his followers. In Godwin, the hero is to be carried to the moon by a flock of geese, and I had better attempt a summary. He is a typical Spaniard, skinny, dried-up, dwarfish, and madly plucky. He is a solitary type with a theoretical interest in carrying messages, and while happening to be isolated on St Helena, merely because of ill-health, he trains a flock of geese to carry messages to his negro slave, his only human contact, who is made to live at the other end of the bay merely to receive messages (pp. 9–10). These geese are a peculiarly powerful type called gansas, with one claw like an eagle's, and obviously they could carry him if only they could be made to pull together, each taking a fair share. It is in effect a labour problem, which is supposed to be solved by a mechanical device. He hitches the geese to a system of pulleys, which are shown at work in a handsome picture, together with a fairly long paragraph explaining their mode of action, and somehow one feels sure that all has been explained

(p. 11). Even after rescuing my mind from the hallucination of the technique, I am not sure that no such device is possible; I only know that, if I tried to carry it out, I would find the author to have omitted a crucial part of his secret. The technical impossibility is not huddled out of sight but brought forward as a point of special interest, which is explained to the reader, and he is expected to share in the radiant pleasure of discovering the solution. Only a reader living in the Machine Age would react in the manner expected here, and so I should think Godwin really was using the literary device for the first time. It requires considerable inventiveness of the author, but also, I should say, a certain flippancy; and this quality breaks out again towards the end of his brief survey, telling us what he has learned about life on the moon. There is a hierarchy of more and more superior beings, and at the bottom you find creatures very like men, who of course do the rough work (p. 30); but the grand Lunars have enough genetic skill to know when a worker child is born likely to make trouble when he grows up. Such an infant is sent down to the earth, to get it out of the way; mainly to America, a particularly out-of-the-way place, and this is why the Red Indians smoke, as the grand Lunars are very fond of smoking (p. 40). 'It all fits in', as people say; and here the author in effect throws away the illusion to make his joke, though I do not think he wants to throw it away anywhere else. Even if so far flippant, the joke appeals to a deep kind of interest in the whole topic; after you had found all those Red Indians, so isolated, so completely unexplained, with such un-expected skills and such astonishing gaps in them, you could not reasonably boggle at men on the moon. For that matter, the behaviour of migrating birds, which was beginning to be guessed at, was almost equally incredible; if some birds go halfway across the world to pass the winter, how do you know that others don't go to the moon (p. 18, 26)? This firm logical process of extrapolation has of course regularly been the source of the best Science Fiction. All the same, it is familiar as a means of delusion, so that the reader is in effect asked to play at having allowed himself to be deceived. I think the Victorians were right in feeling that this procedure, now become standard in Science Fiction, could only have been invented by a young man.

Grant McColley, an able historian of science, claimed to have proved (p. xii) that it could not have been written till Galileo had printed what he saw through his telescope (*The Starry Messenger*,

1609). F. R. Johnson decided that the story must have been written before the 1609 publication but after the publication of Gilbert's *Magnet* (1600). McColley lists six points as necessarily taken from seventeenth-century publications:[7]

(1) There are small irregularities on the moon not visible from earth.

Come now, an author is trying to imagine what he would see when flying toward the moon. He knows there are spots on the moon. What would he see next? More spots. McColley asserts that a man could not possibly think of this without knowing what Galileo saw through the telescope.

(2) The diurnal rotation of the earth would be visible from the moon.

But a *relative* rotation of the earth, when not hidden by cloud, would *necessarily* be visible from the moon, on any theory, even the most primitive. I cannot invent anything sensible for McColley to mean here.

(3) and (4) Gravitation on the earth is a loadstone effect, and the same effect would be found on the moon.

Yes, indeed, the book says this plainly, and Gilbert did not publish his *Magnet* (1600) till near the end of his life (1540–1603). But he had been showing his collection at his grand house in London for twenty years; he was keen to induce returned pilots to come and give him more information about the loadstone, so he had no temptation to make a secret of it. Gilbert only printed (leaving incomplete some of his lines of research) because he decided that the queen was dying; so he had to give up everything else, closing his house never to return, and doctor her till she died; which she did three years later (steadfastly refusing, it appears, to accept any doctoring), and he died himself shortly after. The publication of the book marked the end of the time when it was easy to learn from Gilbert about his loadstones. Scholars are prone to believe that knowledge can only be conveyed by printed books, and this is a particularly absurd example of the delusion. I do not think that F. R. Johnson gave any other reason for dating Godwin's book after 1600.

The idea that gravitation is like magnetism needs a word of comment. Gilbert must have known several ways in which they are unlike, and what did he gain by calling them alike? Falling in itself is too familiar to suggest any theory; to say that you are being pulled by the whole earth sounds a mythical way to describe it. And any belief in action at a distance, even the influence of the moon on the tides (which Julius Caesar had allowed himself to be told about before invading Britain), seemed to Galileo a medieval superstition.[8] His opponents were lucky to be able to appeal to the loadstone, with its great prestige as a source of naval power, because you could actually bring a magnet forward and take it away again, as you could not do with the Earth, and plainly this magnet was what was attracting the bit of scrap iron, from a distance, though a short one. The new conception of gravitation would otherwise have been far harder to put over; so Godwin and Kepler might well use it independently.

(5) The attraction of the larger earth is greater than that of the smaller moon.

This was an intelligent guess, whoever made it first, but not an astonishing one. Copernicus had already started to generalise the idea of falling, saying that things have 'a certain natural striving...so that by assembling in the form of a sphere they may join together in their unity and wholeness';[9] but he did not think of these spheres as attracting one another, and nor does Godwin. Once you have accepted the basic idea – 'Copernicus has shown that the earth moves like the planets, so probably they are alike in other ways; but we know they are of different sizes' – then it is not hard to think 'how else do they differ?', and not recklessly imaginative to suppose that a bigger one has a stronger pull. Galileo and Kepler had nothing to add here.

(6) Attraction varies with distance as well as with mass or size.

Godwin expected the attraction of a planet to stop altogether at a definite height, and remain steady till that height was reached; there seems to be a layer where the attraction falls off very rapidly. Without this theory, the poor geese would have far too much work. They flew up carrying the hero to the Peak of Teneriffe 'with might and maine', for about an hour, and had a short rest at the top, 'panting and blowing'. Then 'they strooke bolt upright, and never did linne towring upward' for another hour or so, and then 'mee thought I might perceive them to labour lesse and lesse', till 'O incredible thing, they forbade moving any thing at al!' Even now, they would sometimes use their wings to increase their velocity, but velocity once gained was never lost, so they could rest most of the time (pp. 17–18). The hero hardly ever expresses surprise during his travels, and is never again anything like so much surprised. (The geese are not surprised, as they migrate to the moon every year.) On the moon, the edge of gravitation is much nearer the surface; a Lunar can easily jump fifty or sixty feet into the air, and then he is already beyond the moon's field, so he can float about (p. 30). It is not clear when the idea 'came in' that gravitation needed to be a continuous function, therefore operating even at great distances though to an incredibly tiny degree; but Kepler remarks [*Astronomia Nova*] that when the stone moves towards the earth, the earth also moves towards the stone, and this hits the required note of paradox.[10] Godwin is simply unregenerate here, quite out of touch with the seventeenth-century mind.

F. R. Johnson, I have to report, accepts the delusion of his forerunners here (his page 234):

[Gonsales] says that when he and his geese reached the point where the earth's attraction was exactly balanced by that of the moon they stood poised in the heavens without any effort whatsoever, because they were then totally lacking in weight.

Godwin does not. But H. W. Lawton ('Bishop Godwin's *Man in the Moone*', 1931), comparing Cyrano de Bergerac [*Voyage to the Moon*] with Domingo, had said, 'at a certain point on their transit, both swing round with their feet where the heads had been'.[11] They do it, Lawton takes for granted, at the point where the attractions of earth and moon exactly balance. But no; Domingo Gonsales finds that neither attraction is working, for nearly all the way. When the hero arrives at the moon we hear nothing of a swing-over, and should not expect to, because the geese land him on 'a very high hill' (p. 25), where the attraction of the moon would be almost unnoticeable. We do hear of one as he returns to the earth (pp. 43–4):

For the first 8 dayes my birds flew before, and I with the Engine was as it were drawne by them. The Ninth day, when I began to approach unto the Clouds, I perceived myself and mine Engine to sincke towards the Earth, and goe before them.
  I was then horribly afraid...

– so he used his magic stone [the Ebelus, a sovereign slimming aid], a gift from the Chief Lunar, and then his weight was not too much for the reduced number of birds to carry [three of the gansas had expired on the moon]. His carriage is literally drawn by the birds when they increase the speed with their wings, and when they are resting it just remains behind them. He takes only nine days to return, two days less than the journey out; and I must not conceal that he makes a rather unwise conjecture here (p. 43):

No thing stayed my journey any whit at all: Whether it was the earnest desire of my *Birds*, to return to the Earth, where they had missed one season, or that the attraction of the Earth, so much stronger than that of the Moone, furthered their labour; so it came to passe, although now I had 3 *Birds* wanting of those I carried forth with mee.

He seems to have forgotten that the attraction of the earth does not work beyond sixty miles up. Godwin might intend him to be confused; he is not a theoretical type. But he may well be thinking only of the time after the earth's field began its terrifying work, so that he had to slow his fall by magic; he must have come down those sixty miles pretty fast, whereas the geese had had to struggle to carry him up them. And, of course, they would reach the top already too exhausted to get up their full speed on the way to the moon. (It gives a great increase in credibility, if the reader can be made to feel that he understands the situation better than the narrator does.) In any case, whatever Domingo thinks about the matter, it does not alter the theory of Godwin, which we learn from his descriptions.

Godwin assumes that there was breathable air all the way to the moon, as his story required; whereas Kepler, even while admitting that his story can be only a dream, feels he has to offer a feeble palliative against the lack of air in outer space (damp cloth round the nose).[12] No doubt, if Godwin had read Kepler, he might decide to burke the topic; but this is no proof that he had done. Even without reading Kepler, he probably knew he was fudging over the air, because Donne already knew it in a poem written about 1595, probably two years before he read Godwin's manuscript. This is the Elegy 'Love's Progress', arguing that a man who starts caressing a woman's feet, not her head, arrives more rapidly at her centre:

> ... as free spheares move faster far than can
> Birds, whom the ayre resists, so may that man ...   (88–9)

Quite likely Godwin knew of this objection, and merely chose to ignore it.

On the other hand, there is a conjecture about astronomical distances to which he seems positively attached. When he is flying towards the moon he notices that the stars seem bigger than on earth, but that (p. 20):

no starres appeared but on that part of the Hemispheare that was next the Moone, and the neerer to her the bigger in Quantity they shewed.

No more is said at the time, but when he has learned a good deal about life on the moon he reports that the long half-month night of the backside of the moon, though lacking sunlight reflected from the earth, is not so bad as you might expect since it has some light (p. 34):

which it seemeth the propinquitie of the starres and other Planets (so much neerer unto them then us) affoordeth.

This, we now realise, was the kindly plan which the author had in mind when he gave the hero his unexpected observation. The monstrosity of the empty gulfs demanded by any workable scheme for the planets, let alone by the Copernican theory, has never oppressed his mind; it is a deliberate rejection, I think, as the astronomers of the time are rather prone to rhetoric about these distances.

McColley has a subtle bit of detective work (p. 73) purporting to prove that Godwin learned the distance of the moon from Kepler's *Dream*, and therefore must have written after 1610. The *Dream* was not published till both authors were dead, but seems to have been available from about 1610 to a few people in manuscript. Here Kepler mentions the distance in German miles, and ignorant Godwin assumed these to be English miles, so he took the moon to be only 50,000 miles away.[13] (According to the OED, the German mile could cover anything from three to six times the English mile, so Kepler's estimate would include the *exact* distance to the moon.) But neither Godwin nor his hero make any estimate at all. The hero says, soon after entering the long no-gravity stretch between the earth and the moon (pp. 18–19):

But the next thing that did most trouble me, was the swiftnesse of Motion, such as did even almost stop my breath; if I should liken it to an Arrow out of a Bow, or to a stone cast downe from the top of some high tower, it would come farre short, and short.

Later on, when they are approaching the moon, he again expresses astonishment at the birds' speed, saying: 'I thinke they gained not so little as Fifty Leagues in every hower' (p. 21). This guess, made in empty space, does not give much encouragement to calculation. And the speaker is a Spaniard, likely to use a foreign measure of length. Thirdly, even if Godwin did intend the reader to calculate the distance of the moon from this casual remark (taking the league as $3\frac{1}{2}$ miles, and assuming the pace is kept up for eleven days), we already know that he was inclined to shorten the vast distances of astronomy. And sure enough, fourthly, the sum works out at about 45,000, not at 50,000. I think this particular proof that he had read Kepler had better rest in peace.

Casting a new light on a detail already used, McColley says that 'a diurnal rotation of heavenly bodies proved by the movement of their spots' is another thing that Godwin could not have invented for himself. Galileo in 1612 reported seeing spots that revolved on the sun and on Jupiter, and this (McColley implies) was what made Godwin's hero see Africa and America revolve.[14] But the cases are not logically parallel. Many people were still arguing that the surface of the earth stands still, and that all the heavenly bodies revolve round it in an elaborate manner, but nobody had ever maintained this about the surface of the sun, or of Jupiter. Godwin never speaks of any heavenly body as rotating, other than the earth.

One might indeed think, as I did myself, that the author means the hero to appear naive about the argument; he says he knows the earth revolves, because he saw it revolve (p. 22), whereas he can only mean, one may reflect with logical superiority, that his geese continued to aim directly at the moon. The same appearance would be produced whichever was revolving, though Godwin might want us to feel that the naive man was being more sensible than the classical astronomers. But no, the hero is not presented as naive (pp. 20–1):

I perceived my selfe still to be alwaies directly betweene the Moone and the earth. Whereby it appeareth, not only that my *Gansa's* took none other way than directly toward the Moone, but also, that when we rested (as at first we did for many howers,) either we were insensibly carryed (for I perceived no such motion) round about the Globe of Earth, or else that (according to the late opinion of *Copernicus*,) the Earth is carried about, and turneth round perpetually...

It is just possible, I suppose, that the air halfway to the moon moves with the lunar sphere, and this caused sufficient wind-drag to keep the geese directed towards the turning moon even when they were not aiming at it; but Godwin does not propose the idea, and indeed he probably did not want to draw attention to the physical consequences of this vast bulk of air. Instead, a distraction technique is employed; the air is so good that he does not need food or drink, but some 'Illusions of Devills and wicked spirits' come and talk to him on his first day in space, making generous offers (p. 19); he asks for food and drink, expecting that he will need them, and what is brought tastes very good, but when he gets to the moon, where he really is hungry, his devil-brought stores have all gone rotten (p. 26). (The devils had warned him to take plenty, as they wouldn't be able to come back 'till the next Thursday', and perhaps not even then, and nor they did. Next Thursday is a very eerie touch, in the vacant glare of the eternal sun.) In a medieval narrative, one may reflect, this would be a fatal test; even one bite would bring disaster; but here we are left to reflect that the ignorant sailor must have been slandering these good spirits of nature, who cannot have meant him any harm. The geese did not need food in that good air, either. It leaves an impression of asking the reader's indulgence, or at least of jollying him along through a difficult patch; it is very unlike the keen logic of the Copernican passage just quoted.

I must now consider another aspect of that passage, and may well be told that it is enough to refute my whole thesis. Godwin takes for granted the First Law of Newton, that a body retains constant motion in a straight line unless acted on by a force (whether due to impact or at a distance). This was certainly not known to Kepler, who assumes in the *Dream* that a spirit has to push the human traveller all the way, till he starts falling onto the moon.[15] It is accepted as one of the great discoveries of Galileo, yet there is so much difficulty in finding where Galileo enunciated it that one may suspect he never did. He came to treat it as obvious. Having found, by timing the motion of balls on inclined planes, that a steady force causes a steady acceleration, he no longer thought of a steady motion as requiring a force; that was just another place where Aristotle had been wrong. My opponents never point out which book by Galileo could have taught this to Godwin; indeed, they never seem to realise that the point is important. I think they are right, in a way; Godwin did not need to be taught this piece of common sense. But we have a serious difficulty here, in trying to estimate what the pre-scientific mind could do.

The Elizabethans had several bits of scholarly wisdom, often said to be Aristotle's, which they would sometimes bring out earnestly but at other times assume to be false. For example, mothers were not related to their children, since heredity worked only through the father; and it was a mistake to suppose you needed lamps, after dark, because light proceeds from the human eye to the object viewed. No doubt they needed practice in treating a belief casually, since their religious beliefs were so liable to become lethal. Well then, among these half-comic pseudo-beliefs came the belief that nothing can move without being pushed, so that when you throw a ball through the air the wind of its own passing must somehow push it forward. Kepler seems to have taken this belief fairly seriously, but he was a mathematician who liked paradoxes, and had had a horrible childhood during which he can seldom have played catch; nobody could take it seriously while playing catch. So it could not be at all hard for Godwin to say (in effect) 'On the contrary' when he invented his liberating fantasy of enterprise and daring; after all, the first thing he had set himself was to invent some plausible scheme for flying to the moon, and plainly one of the basic needs would be a power to sustain one's own velocity. The aside in Donne's comic sex-poem is enough to prove that such thoughts were not impossible; though it was a nuisance for Godwin to have to assume air all the way. The best thing one could do with the air was turn it into magic ether, also efficient as a food; and this at least suited the mood of exhilaration.

There seems to have been another difficult patch, on the way to the moon, where Godwin pulled his foot out only just in time; and the case does have a quaint likeness to the great *Dialogue* of Galileo, though my opponents do not care to claim it. As the geese rise into the empyrean the hero is fascinated by the great spectacle of the revolving globe; the land mass of Africa looks dark as he gazes, then the Atlantic is 'a great shining brightnesse' (p. 22), then America looks dark again. He sees the same kind of thing on approaching the moon, and only then does he spell out, as it were, what he is saying:

So that same Splendor appearing unto us, and giving light unto our night, appeareth to be nothing else but the reflexion of the Sun beames returned unto us out of the water, as out of a glasse...

But, on second thoughts, this won't do at all, because it is definitely not what we see on the moon. If the moon had a sea, a large sheet of water, we would at times get the sun reflected in it; a small but brilliant white star would appear on the surface of the yellow moon. For his Utopia on the moon, Godwin needs to have plenty of water, so he begins talking his way out of this snag at once; what earth-bound people see when they look at the moon isn't the real thing (p. 24):

The first difference that I found betweene it and our earth, was, that it shewed it selfe in his naturall colours: ever after I was free from the attraction of the Earth; whereas with us, a thing removed from our eye but a league or two, begins to put on that lurid and deadly colour of blew.

This is enough to let the story continue, but does not explain how he could see the great shining light on the Atlantic, even though looking at it through the corrupt atmosphere of the world. Obviously, Godwin is not copying an accepted theory when he rescues himself like this. [See Appendix on Galileo.]

I need to go into rather more detail about Kepler's *Dream*. A manuscript of this work may have become available in England about 1610, and there have been suggestions that it influenced Donne. But this would be too late for any useful influence on Donne, who by 1610 was becoming afraid of the new astronomy as heretical; so I was glad, when an English edition of this work, very fully edited, came out in 1967, to find it so crabbed and uninspiring. Kepler himself says that Donne must have read it before laughing at Kepler in *Ignatius his Conclave*, but the editor decides that he could not have done.[16] The first draft was written as a college exercise in 1593, to show what an astronomer on the moon would observe, but rejected as Copernican; then in 1609 Kepler added the dream-talk at top and tail, a perfunctory attempt to make it an adventure story, no doubt with some other changes, and gave copies of the manuscript to some friends; then he wrote lengthy notes explaining it, between 1622 and 1630; and it was printed in 1632, after his death. Galileo was never intimate with Kepler, and evidently did not tell him of his suspicion that there is no large sheet of water on the moon;[17] but Kepler realised for himself that any surface water would be likely to evaporate during the grim fortnight of the lunar day. He expects life to be pretty grim anywhere, with the pleasure of astronomy as its only cheerful feature. The Privolvans (the creatures on the backside of the moon, who are especially pitiable because they never see the earth),

have no fixed abode, no established domicile. In the course of one of their days they roam in crowds over their whole sphere, each according to his own nature; some use their legs, which far surpass those of our camels; some resort to wings; and some follow the receding water in boats...[18]

Surely it is rather absurd to suppose that the gentlemanly Utopia of Godwin was influenced by this Bosch-like stuff. But there is one detail where the influence has been called obvious. Godwin too realises that the lunar day would be hot, and explains that the working-class Lunars, who are like men, hibernate; they sleep in underground chambers. No doubt the rulers lead sheltered lives anyhow. The hero himself, though he does not wish to be classified with these Yahoos, cannot resist hibernation as the long day draws on (pp. 33–5). Kepler, on the other hand, says there is a particularly bad region where all the inhabitants are dead at the end of a day, but many are brought back to life again; he supports this by recalling some grim East-European superstition.[19] This is very unlike Godwin. I agree (if that is the idea) that Kepler probably thought first of hibernation, not death, and only afterwards decided that a vampire-legend would be more of a thrill. But I doubt whether Godwin would trouble to analyse Kepler's vampire-legend; more likely, he would think it low. Anyhow, when considering how life could be carried on under wild conditions, they might well think of hibernation independently, because they both had genuinely scientific minds. Within their terms of reference, the idea was a fairly obvious one, and neither of them found it much use.

This I think deals with the main arguments for a late date, as regards the journeys to and from the moon, though not about the end of the story. The hero succeeds in returning to earth but finds himself in China, and I agree with Lawton and McColley that this part was written after the publication, in 1615, of a selection from the memoirs of the Jesuit missionary Ricci, edited by another missionary Trigault, as a report on recent work in Peking. It is quite possible, indeed, that Godwin might have got the few bits of information that he uses by some earlier route, being well placed to hear such things, but there is no reason to suppose he would; he was not keen on Papist missionaries. Both my opponents speak with some contempt of the theory of revision, Lawton calling it 'a facile and unsatisfactory device';[20] and I agree that Godwin would not be likely to tinker with the book without some definite reason, probably internal to it (and not a matter of censorship); but this can be supplied.

We may be sure that something has gone wrong with the text at this point, because there is an evident break in the story. One moment (as already quoted) the hero is coming down onto a sea of cloud, and hurriedly fetching out his magic jewel because his weight has become too much of a strain on the geese; evidently, he is very alert to his situation. Then he is on the ground, and not in fog, so he must have emerged below the cloud blanket and seen a bit of countryside. It is of great importance to him to know whether he is landing among enemies, and how is he to tell what country this is from the air? The next paragraph begins (p. 44):

China is a Country so populous, as I thinke there is hardly a peece of ground to bee found ... though but thrice a mans length, which is not most carefully manured.

So naturally a crowd has gathered even before he lands, and he must think of a trick to secure his lunar jewels (a clumsy trick, not likely to have succeeded). Perhaps the sudden crowding is rather a good literary effect, but Godwin is not an artful novelist, like Joyce; whereas he does have the solid merit of keeping the reader inside the mind of the narrator, interested in his reactions. His sons printed the story, with other signs of haste, five years after his death. I suggest that the first paragraph of the new material had got lost, and they did not bother to hunt for it. Or, I have no need to deny, Godwin may just have written here below his usual standard (after all, his readers would not be accustomed to the modern novel); but this too should have a reason for it; it might well happen in the first sentence after a gap of twenty years.

There is also a curious detail about the dates. The hero tells us all about the date when he left the earth, the day of the month, the day of the week, the phase of the moon, its relation to the zodiac, and the year (1599); the same for the date of arrival, twelve days later. Perhaps he thought the information might be needed by some astrologer. Presumably it was taken from a real calendar, and nobody keeps old calendars, so this bit was probably written in the year named. During its first year or two the manuscript would be much borrowed and commented upon, so that minor improvements, such as information for astrologers, would easily get written in – this would be quite compatible with a first main draft in 1597. But, just before leaving the moon, at the end of March 1601, Domingo recalls these dates, and to each of them he has added ten days (p. 42). He is now using the Gregorian Calendar, a reform which had been accepted by all Papists, so that Domingo was sure to use it all along; but the young Godwin had not thought of this, while copying the details out of an English [Julian] calendar. Of course, when he did correct this slip, he would want to alter his earlier page too, so that a later revision is not a sufficient explanation of the failure; but it makes the failure less improbable.[21] Probably by 1617 there were several copies of the manuscript, and Godwin only wrote his corrections onto one of them, which got partially neglected by his sons, twenty years later again. In the first writing there would be only one text, so that a correction written onto it could not be mislaid. It may seem absurd to suppose that Godwin would fuss about these fictitious dates, but he was a historian, accustomed to be meticulous about time, and here a game of pedantry was being played, to give an illusion of sober conscientiousness. He would have been much irritated to know they had been printed wrong.

These two scraps of internal evidence would not be decisive, but they combine with the argument from the details about China. The Jesuit missionaries had not yet arrived in Peking by 1597, and there is a brief mention of them late in the book (necessarily, since they have smuggled the manuscript out of China), so for my thesis I positively need one revision.[22] But I still say that Godwin would not have added this part unless it made a point which his story had come to need during the intervening twenty years. The description of a Utopia of course carried a moral (here as often an undemocratic one), but the Science Fiction side of the book had another moral – the need for England to keep abreast of foreign inventions. Godwin was himself an inventor, and considered that his work was being neglected. In 1597 he was not yet disappointed but already eager, and his story ended with a grim threat: at any moment Domingo will hand over his discoveries to the Spanish Government, as he tells us he will do, thus greatly increasing the power of our implacable enemy. In 1617 there was no threat from Spain, and Domingo after his long silence will not be expected to emerge. Suppose then that his report had been smuggled out of China by the Jesuits, and soon after that the Chinese Government had become suspicious of him, so that he has been rotting twenty years in a Chinese jail. The only record of his achievement would be this brief tantalising document, proving yet again that mankind has vast powers which lie grossly unused. For that matter, the inventor Godwin himself has been rotting all that time in Wales. As Christopher Hill has shown, a general feeling of frustration, of the blocking of progress, set in about 1615 and lasted till the explosion of the Civil War;[23] the private gamble of Godwin might find an echo in many readers, and at least the change made the story contemporary again. Besides, it completed the survey, giving us a glance all round the world. I expect he was thinking of showing his old joke to new friends, in Hereford. If he enquired about publication, I think he would be told that the church preferred not to have these painful difficulties stirred up.

If the end in China was added in 1617, it is natural to agree that the interview granted to the hero by the Grand Lunar, who was inquisitive and helpful to his remote visitor but could not allow himself to be seen (p. 37), was adapted from the report of Ricci's negotiations with an invisible Emperor of China. Once alteration had begun, a few other parts of the book would be altered. Maybe the Bishop had already had an unsatisfactory interview with the King, begging support for his inventions and for large-scale research upon them, so his interest in the scene would be very direct. (The oriental technique of royal seclusion had long been famous, but there was little reason why Godwin should think of it here till he was thinking about China.) However, the Grand Lunar really is a superior being, and is technically competent to devise a means of seeing without being seen, besides being generous-minded; Godwin would think him very unlike the neurotic frustrating Emperor [of China], or even our own James. This difference is not observed by McColley, who apparently regards Godwin as a secret Catholic and the whole book as an allegory glorifying the work of Ricci. Ricci and Domingo Gonsales were born in the same year, he points out, with the menacing comment: 'Such relationships are too close to be pure coincidence.'[24] How fiercely Godwin would rebut this peculiarly malignant canard; he had never mentioned the Papist once, he would retort with justified indignation. I think he decided to use the royal interview, though anyway he had become interested in such events, because it allowed of the gift of the magic jewel. Quaintly enough, this would make the story seem more credible to the reader of 1617. Readers of the manuscript had often told him that he was too boyishly casual about the mighty terror of interplanetary gulfs; you can believe in the geese getting away from the earth, somehow, but to believe they could bring him down again was too hard. So he added the magic to fit the less confident age he had survived into. I have to suppose, rather reluctantly, that the passage about the language of the Lunars also belongs to the revision; they talk purely by musical tones (pp. 36–7), thus outdoing the Chinese, who have managed to hold on to a few consonants; so when the hero gets to Peking he considers the language there pretty ordinary. But maybe the young Godwin had invented it for the first draft; he had a genuinely theoretical mind.

Dark forces of ambition worked under this bright surface, and I had best quote in full a very early paragraph which must partly belong to the revision. It fits so well into the rhetoric of the whole sequence, indeed, that some of it would be needed there from the first; but surely not with such exultation. The hero, recounting his past, explains that he was forced to go to sea because he had been wronged by a cheat; and so we enter the main story (pp. 6–7):

his covetousnesse was like to bee my utter undoing, although since it hath proved a meanes of eternizing my name for ever with all Posteritie, (I verily hope) and to the unspeakeable good of all mortall men, that in succeeding ages the world shall have, if at the leastwise it may please God that I doe returne safe home againe into my Countrie, to give perfect instructions how those admirable devices, and past all credit of possibilitie, which I have light upon, may be imparted unto publique use. You shal then see men to flie from place to place in the ayre; you shall be able, (without moving or travailing of any creature,) to send messages in an instant many Miles off, and receive answer againe immediately; you shall be able to declare your minde presently unto your friend, being in some private and remote place of a populous Citie, with a number of such like things: but that which far surpasseth all the rest, you shall have notice of a new World, of many most rare and incredible secrets of Nature, that all the Philosophers of former ages could never so much as dreame off. But I must be advised, how I be over-liberall, in publishing these wonderfull mysteries, till the Sages of our State have considered how farre the use of these things may stand with the Policy and good government of our Countrey, as also with the Fathers of the Church, how the publication of them, may not prove prejudiciall to the affaires of the Catholique faith and Religion, which I am taught (by those wonders I have seen above any mortall man that hath lived in many ages past) with all my best endeavours to advance, without all respect of temporall good, and soe I hope I shall.

What this presumes, though a reader might not notice it, is that the writer is sure that the short document he is now writing will be read by friends at his home, but that he is not sure he will ever come home and be able to teach them to construct these wonderful engines. Thus it is planned to fit the ending in China. But there is nothing in the story about his being taught such things by the Lunars; of course he cannot report all his conversations on the moon, but we seem for a moment to be hearing a different story, about a man in China who has had his passport removed. He feels he has had exasperatingly bad luck. It is a sadly familiar tone of voice, and Godwin was to strike it again, in his own person, using these very phrases. Perhaps I should have made clear that there is no strong reason for the revision to have been made in 1617 – that merely seems the most natural time; it could have been done at any time during the next ten years; but not, I am afraid, during the remaining five years of his life, because he had gone mad.

Even as a young man he had been keen on ways of sending messages, as we can be sure because the original story required an extreme keenness on it from Domingo, who began teaching his geese to carry weights merely for this purpose (p. 11). The topic continued to grow in Godwin's mind, and in 1620–1 he and his son Thomas laid before the Government a document of which only the title [a digest or prospectus] survives: 'Statement of a Project for Conveying Intelligence into Besieged Towns and Fortresses, and receiving Answers therefrom under condition specified'. Maybe the son was needed, already, to save the bishop from giving a crazy impression, but the father would be sure he was helping the boy to a career. Evidently nothing came of this, and Charles was even less likely than his father James to invest in such experiments, so finally the old man, still insisting that he would only tell his secret to a responsible authority, advertised it over the heads of the Government to all Europe, writing in Latin (*Nuncius Inanimatus*, 1629). A not un-sympathetic translation was made in Restoration times, reading somewhat like Nietzsche when in the euphoria that immediately preceded his madness. The sons must have realised that too obvious madness would cost them the salary of the bishopric, and perhaps he arranged this publication by a trick; it is his last break-out. The sons are described as nursing him through 'a low and languishing disease' before his death, which I hope only means that they kept him from exposing himself in public again. He knew himself that the book made him an object of curiosity, when he wrote into it that he was not a *black* magician, though he had a 'genius' (p. 67) – which would easily mean a 'familiar'.

The author of the *Nuncius*, like those of similar books in earlier times, cannot be blamed for being obscure – he intends to be; he boasts that he is not telling his secrets. But he needs to make specific enough offers to the prospective client. I estimate (looking at the summaries towards the end) that the 'first method' is pure fantasy, and dates from early childhood, but it may well also reflect indignation at a recent confinement (p. 61):

Let nobody come near him, secure the body in a prison, let the hands be bound, hoodwink the face... and he shall understand the words of his absent friends, if this liberty be not taken away from him, that he may be able to do those things which are wont sometimes to be done by Freemen, or may do them without fear or danger.

Surely there is something infantile about this abrupt withdrawal into insinuating suggestion. But the 'second method' feels more impressive because it is a prevision of our familiar telegraph poles (p. 65):

for each mile it will cost five pounds more or less, if it be designed for perpetual use, and nothing can be done without the countenance and authority of the Magistrate...

The 'third method' really is impressive, directing the lightning. It is the radio (p. 65):

truely it requireth no great charge, but it must be observed, that he that doth act, be setled in a place without danger... and here we must not deny, that the condition of him that sends in, than of him that sends out is the worst.

I quote the Restoration translator, because it is interesting to hear him feel that the text is nonsense, whereas to us it seems very proper to say that the receiver of such a shock might be in greater danger than the transmitter. These passages excite awe, as some of the prophecies of Nostradamus do, because (though as usual quite useless) they seem to be evidence of direct prevision. Godwin had a powerful mind, which might have been thinking of something quite different, but I have no idea what else it could be.

At the beginning of the section I am quoting from, Godwin reflects that, exhaustive though his experiments have been, he had left out one of the senses, that of touch, though all ought to be considered; so he will pronounce on telegraphy by fumbling (p. 61):

we should say a little about touching, by the help of which sense that any thing should be signified to them that are afar off, especially without a Messenger is not yet asserted of any one as I think, neither doth it seem credible, but for my part I dare say that it may be done, and that with ease, at the distance of a mile or perchance two, although I have not tryed the verity thereof by any experiment, and I list not to say whether it will be worth our labour for the future.

Here it is plain, I submit, that we see a powerful mind working in a vacuum. Squeers, while impressing some parents at Dotheboys Hall, sometimes says (more or less) 'it's all philosophy; well, there may be a bit of metaphysics in it, but not much', and the masterly hesitation of Godwin as to whether he could fumble at two miles' distance, or only one, gives a similar impression. All the same, whether he was deceitful or crazy when he wrote the book, he would probably (a little earlier) have made an inspiring and effective director of research.

I may be told that he cannot have been mad by the standards of his time, because nobody said so. Well, they were right to treat the old man with respect; but the printed remarks of young John Wilkins are sufficiently transparent. His *Mercury* of 1641 is a thoroughly sensible book about codes and signalling, which he says was inspired by Godwin's book – he needed a bishop as an authority for the new intellectual freedom. The book invents dull but harmless explanations for several of Godwin's wild flights. But, if Godwin meant only that, many of his assertions are plainly untrue, and his book becomes a deceitful inflation, presumably for gain. Wilkins let drop some rather firm phrases to the effect that we ought not to misunderstand the bishop, as he has so good a reputation. 'Our bishop', he was prone to say at first, while excusing some absurd remark, but he soon came to feel that this was not tactful enough. He seems to understand the position well. Godwin has been driven somewhat crazy by the frustration of his period, whereas lucky Wilkins had emerged from college just at the right time. I hope this does not sound like debunking Godwin. I think he becomes a much more determined and coherent character if we realise that, not content with inventing a short whimsy about the moon, he died in an ecstatic belief that he had invented the wireless. He lived to the age of 71, after a considerable success in his profession, and largely gratified his affection for his children; and I daresay his delusion was a great deal more upsetting to the rest of his household than it was to himself. All the same, once you realise that the old man was mad, it does seem rather unlikely that he wrote a gay and flippant little book about a trip to the moon.

As the difference of tone is my chief argument, I have delayed another quotation from the *Voyage* to make the contrast here; Domingo is asking his Lunar master for permission to return home, and this bit comes from the first draft (42):

> Hee much disswaded mee, laying before mee the danger of the Voyage, the misery of that place from whence I came, and the abundant happinesse of that I now was in; But the remembrance of my Wife and Children overweighed all these reasons, and to tell you the truth, I was so farre forth moved with a desire of that deserved glory, that I might purchase at my return, as me thought I deserved not the name of a *Spanyard*, if I would not hazard 20 lives rather than loose but a little possibility of the same. Wherefore I answered him, that my desire of seeing my Children was such, as I knew I could not live any longer, if I were once out of hope of the same.

We know that Swift admired the *Voyage* very much, and this is the part of Godwin's prose style that he imitated. But the young Godwin is not blaming the Spaniard at all; he admires the whole arrangement, and thinks a pretended affection for children an entirely proper excuse for a patriotic motive – Domingo wants to help Spain with his discoveries, that is the next impulse after wanting glory in Spain; though he would obviously begin complaining of his wrongs very soon if he succeeded in helping Spain but did not get a solid reward as well. The coolness here about Domingo, though friendly to him, feels entirely different from the passionate identification with him in my previous quotation, ascribing to Domingo word for word some of the inventions which Godwin claimed to have made himself. The older Godwin, when he makes Domingo renounce all prospect of worldly gain, speaks as he does in person in the *Nuncius*; but the young Godwin is aware that this procedure would be comically transparent. Even without the other evidence, it would be hard to believe that these two passages were written at the same time.

Publication came as soon as the sons of Godwin realised that it had become permissible. In 1638 John Wilkins, a future bishop who had just taken orders at the age of 24, printed as his first book *Discovery of a World in the Moone*, with the licence from the Bishop of London in person. It is a brief but well-packed survey, with many references to classical authors and a firm grasp of the recent debate, maintaining that there is no reason not to expect life on the moon, which Copernicus has shown to be probable. There was of course a theological objection, voiced by Melanchthon [*Initia Doctrinae Physicae*, 1567] as soon as Copernicus published his great work: that rational beings living on other stars would be out of reach of the Redeemer (I am grateful to McColley for this important bit of information).[25] Wilkins treats this objection very coolly but makes no attempt to gloss it over, quoting at length from the conjectures of Campanella in *The Defence of Galileo*; perhaps, for example, the men on the moon have never fallen. It is not likely that Wilkins and his Broad Church party were at all keen on the uniqueness of the Redeemer, even at so early a date; but he had to speak with great caution. Be that as it may, a clergyman did not have to be a secret heretic before he could follow the new trend, as is clear when Bishop Juxon himself signs the licence for the book (ten years later, Juxon went on praying with the king for hours in the banqueting hall, till at last the parliament men were ready for him to step out of the window and have his head cut off). It is perhaps rather surprising that Wilkins should have a royalist patron, as he would not like their absolutism, in religion as well as politics, nor their much-suspected leaning to Rome; but then, he was Erastian, and would not care to be ruled by Calvinist ministers.[27] Probably he was already conscious of the great powers of balance; and he knew it was a good time for such a book – a second edition was called for the same year; and, evidently, the church was willing to have the subject discussed.

The change of policy might occur without getting special attention. The year 1638 marked the end of the stalemate which the king was able to secure so long as he managed not to call a parliament. The Covenant was signed that year in Scotland, and as soon as Charles had to fight the Scots he needed a parliament to vote him money. Milton returned to England in 1638, renouncing his visit to Palestine because he might be needed at home; it was the end of a period of irritating stagnation. The king remained optimistic, finds Miss Wedgwood in *The King's Peace*; he was much pleased that year by *The Religion of Protestants*, an early work by the Cambridge Platonist Chillingworth, for its serene and philosophic tolerance, and marked the author down for preferment. He really did believe that the Anglican *via media* deserved this high claim, even while he and his Archbishop were destroying their safe position by persecution. To allow life on other worlds might seem to him a particularly harmless way to show his liberality; and the Anglican position was inherently freer than those of both north and south Europe, because it was bound neither by a tradition of interpretation (like Rome) nor by the literal words of the Bible (like the Protestants). But the main reason why the change took place now, I submit, was a simple one, which involved no profound rethinking of the matter; it was becoming clear, in spite of all the hush-up, that Rome had made a fool of herself over Galileo, thus giving the Anglicans a pleasant opportunity. His trial was in 1632, but the first Latin edition of the *Dialogue* did not become available till 1635.

The sons of Godwin rushed out an edition of his book five months after the appearance of the first edition of Wilkins (I learn this from H. W. Lawton ['Bishop Godwin's *Man in the Moone*', p. 42], but am not sure whether he merely deduced it from the dates of registration). The book was registered as translated from the Spanish by Edward Mahon of Christ Church, a pseudonym already used by Godwin himself in his *Nuncius* (this was not registered, and the title-page says it was published 'in Utopia', but Wilkins treats the authorship as an open secret). The *Voyage* is given a short preface, mainly concerned to assure the reader that the book is up-to-date in thought though old in the detail of the story, and serious in thought though the story is not true. This preface has the initials 'E. M.' at the end, though the title-page says the author of the book is 'Domingo Gonsales'. McColley gives a quaint argument, with his familiar tone of moral outrage, to prove that the preface *must* have been written by Godwin, so he *must* have written the whole book after Galileo's *Messenger*; because no executor could be so wicked as to steal the pseudonym of a legatee. It would be interesting to see him trying to explain this to the son of Godwin concerned, who would consider that he was securing his father's posthumous fame in a decorous manner. Then, in 1641, Wilkins brought out his third edition, adding a whole chapter to discuss how we may expect to go to the moon and meet its inhabitants, with mention of Kepler's *Dream* on this topic. Right at the end of the added chapter, he says innocently:

Having thus finished this discourse, I chanced upon a late fancy to this purpose, under the fained name of *Domingo Gonsales*, written by a late reverend and learned Bishop: In which (besides sundry particulars wherein this later chapter did unwittingly agree with it) there is delivered a very pleasant and well contrived fancy concerning a voyage to this other world.[27]

Wilkins is always radiantly open, seeming merely talkative till you realise he is talking everyone round, a Broad Church negotiator of great ability and public spirit, whose special powers were particularly needed at that time. Possibly indeed his death at the age of 58 was a disaster, because if he had had twenty years as Archbishop of Canterbury he would have left the Church of England Unitarian (there is a most instructive Life of him by Barbara Shapiro, 1969). However, Archbishop Tillotson was his disciple, and maybe if the policy had been carried further it would have ended in a damaging backlash. Here, though so young, Wilkins already salutes his rival as a respectable ally, and makes only a tiny manœuvre to make sure of keeping his own dignity. He had not read Godwin's *Voyage* before writing his first edition, but he had read it, and been inspired by it, before writing the added chapter for his third. He took the precaution to check some of its details in the modern authorities, and the results seemed all right; he gave footnote references, to prove his own reading. But here he was comically betrayed by his ignorance. Naturally, as he wants a flight to the moon, he must encourage the idea that gravity stops about twenty miles up, so he tells us about its 'true nature' (p. 114):

'Tis such as respective mutual desire of union, whereby condensed bodies, when they come within the sphere of their own vigour, do naturally apply themselves one to another by attraction or coition. But being both without the reach of either's virtue, they then cease to move...

A footnote refers us to Note 66 of Kepler's *Dream*, which may be quoted in full:[28]

I define 'gravity' as a force of mutual attraction, similar to magnetic attraction. But the power of this attraction in bodies near to each other is greater than it is in bodies far away from each other. Hence they offer stronger resistance to being separated from each other when they are still close together.

Even after agreeing that intensity of light varied as the inverse square, Kepler remained doubtful about the rule for gravitation; a simple inverse perhaps; but anyway he expected some continuous rule, suited to calculation.[29] I do not know that Wilkins could have found any source other than Godwin for his theory of gravity.

He could, however, have claimed strong collateral support from Gilbert, who believed the same thing about magnetism; but Wilkins made it too general. He gives a picture of a sphere, furry to show that it is giving something out – magnetism, or gravitation, or light. There is a concentric circle outside it, with more than twice but less than three times the radius, and this is called 'the orb that doth determinate the virtue' of the emitting body. The reference is to Gilbert's *Magnet* II. 7, and there he does say: 'a magnet only excites magneticks at a convenient distance from it.'[30] Gilbert had no means of estimating the intensity of a magnetic force; his book does not contain any calculations about the magnetic field, comparable to weighing: his concern is the compass on board a ship. And, as to light, surely it is the first thing we learn about our eyes that they tell us about things further away than our other senses do, and that a light carried away in the dark dwindles to a tiny speck. It shows an astonishing lack of direct experience for Wilkins to choose light as a familiar illustration of his theory. The following quotation from Gilbert, I think, proves that he did not believe in even a remote cut-off mechanism for vision (VI. 3):

there is no one gifted with excellent sight who does not, when the Moon is dark and the air at its rarest, discern numbers and numbers dim and wavering with minute lights on account of the great distance: hence it is credible both that these are many and that they are never all included in any range of vision. How immeasurable then must be the space which stretches to those remotest of fixed stars![31]

Digges in his *Prognostication Everlasting* (1576) does apparently speak of such a cut-off, during the grand peroration which closes the book, but then Digges believed the heavens to be infinite, and perhaps had an intuitive realisation that it would be fatal to look at an infinite mass of stars at finite density, a terrifying idea anyhow; whereas sober Gilbert believed the heavens to be finite, so had no need to cry for mercy there. [But see Introduction, p. 43 above.] Wilkins would be pretty sure to glance at the famous old book of Digges. But anyhow he is not at home in physics, as is plain when he reports a man who had intended to say: 'Hardness is not a result of close packing, because ice floats on water.' It is plain to Wilkins that dramatic overstatement is always liable to excite resistance on committees, so, because he is in favour of this man and wants to help him forward, he rephrases the doctrine as: 'There is no significant difference between the densities of ice and water.'[32] No wonder he could bring himself to marry a daughter of Cromwell who was considered shockingly ugly;[33] one feels he has never poked his nose outside his study and his

committee-room. But what he said about the sources of Godwin has
been somehow congenial to subsequent literary historians.

There are other arguments which I have not answered, but I do
not think I have neglected any which deserve answers. However, a
broader question may well arise. Granting that Godwin was writing
or at least planning his long-short story before 1600, but at the same
time was an ambitious churchman, or at least determined to get hold
of a good salary by research into church history, surely he would not
have shown this story, which he never dared to print in his lifetime,
to the poet Donne, ten years younger, a scandalous young tattle? Oh
yes, he would; it is rather bleakly planned to be suitable for all private
readers. The snobbery of the period in favour of manuscript, and not
print, is rather hard for us to grasp and we may be sure the rules were
not always obvious for young climbers at the time, but it allowed a
fair amount of latitude. Godwin wanted a bishopric, and yet kicking
up his heels in this way could be positively in his favour, short of the
ridicule of actual public print. He had so written his story that it
could be shown round to his profit even in the very highest quarters.
All ruling-type characters, we must realise, would at once think that
his fable raised the fundamental challenge: if there is life on other
planets, how can we maintain a unique claim for Jesus? The
prospective bishop leaps into action here; he is ruthless about
asserting his orthodoxy. The hero on reaching the moon at first
encounters common Lunars, who are like men; a meeting with a
group of superior Lunars takes them a bit of time to arrange. Some
of these are twelve feet high, some twenty, and the top-class ones 'at
least twenty-seven'; he crosses himself and says 'Jesus Maria', maybe
to express surprise rather than pray for help. 'No sooner was the word
Iesus out of my mouth, but young and old, fell all downe upon their
knees' (p. 28). A Protestant reader may deduce that they did not
wait for the word 'Maria'; indeed, the next time the hero has such an
audience he tries out a list of saints' names on them, to see which
make them fall down – he is always an experimenter; they only fell
down for 'Martin', which might have meant Luther, but he found
afterwards that this was their general term for 'God' (p. 31). They
would not be prone to worship anyone with the appearance of a man,
since they use men as domestic animals. The hero has a special status
as a visitor, but he is forbidden to have any dealings with the servants
who look after men, and is not trusted with the Jewel of Invisibility,
because men are not fit to be given such powers. As he describes the

higher Lunars, they really do have a great moral superiority to mankind; it seems they cannot even fall in love twice, and though he sets out to describe their legal arrangements he gives up in despair: 'Alas what need is there of Exemplary punishment, where there are no offences committed' (p. 40). Here I suppose Godwin leaves open another theory which was considered theologically tolerable; that the Lunars, never having fallen, are not in need of the Redeemer. He does not report himself as asking them how they came to hear about Jesus, or indeed how they got any of their information about mankind; though he believes himself to be the first man who has reached the moon. Later on, however, while reporting that they send to the earth any low-class babies who are expected to be recalcitrant, he adds that they are swapped for particularly good human babies (pp. 39–40). If this operation is carried out efficiently, they must have a very thorough knowledge of mankind. I mentioned this detail at the start of this essay as an example of boyish fun, and I still think it strikes that note, but perhaps the author was calculating a little. It had occurred to him that the Lunars needed some regular contact with the earth, to make their knowledge of Jesus at all convincing; and he saddled them with the challenging legend as a ready-made convenience.

It would work out as a very different picture. At first they seemed immensely high and pure, and benevolent so far as their aloofness permitted, but then, as their secrets began to leak out under his steady questioning, we find them to be malignant imps, spying on us, lurking outside the nursery window. One might protest in defence of Godwin that this is no more contradictory than the gods of Homer. Men have always given their gods a double function; entirely remote and ideal, and yet very dependent on us, always nosing round our affairs and emotionally involved. But Godwin had set out to describe Utopians; it was only a secondary intention, that of making his story completely innocuous to the Anglican Church, which involved them in a close, sordid, undercover relation with mankind. McColley remarks crossly (*The Man in the Moone*, p. 74):

The courageous manner in which Bishop Godwin disposes of the highly controversial question of how inhabitants of other worlds would be saved has, I regret to say, been entirely overlooked...

I find this a typical neo-Christian utterance; a snooty obscurantism not based on any discoverable opinion. I agree that, no doubt, it does take a bit of nerve to think of a story so absurd that it makes you absolutely safe, and then tell it unflinchingly, because that means risking the contempt of your friends. What other kind of courage can McColley impute to Godwin here, except the courage of impudence? He is made to sound like a secret Deist. Probably he just became aware of another tricky patch of his story, where it was hard to please all, and decided not to explain away the improbability, relying on it to feel eerie.

Having gone so far in showing loyalty to the church, he could comfortably show it to the queen as well. To be sure, this was even more absurd. Jesus may actually have visited the moon, and at least the Lunars have had plenty of time to learn about Christianity. But to suppose them fully abreast of the latest developments in European diplomatic history, leaning over the bars of Heaven to catch the very whispers in the lobbies – that had to be reserved till the Spanish hero was just about to fly away. Then the local ruler who had befriended him charges him to convey his salutations to Queen Elizabeth (p. 43):

whom he tearmed the great *Queene of England*, calling her the most glorious of all women living, and indeed hee would often question with mee of her, and therein delighted so much, as it seemed hee was never satisfied in talking of her...Though I account her an enemy of *Spayne*, I may not faile of performing this promise as soone as I shall bee able so to doe.

Surely the report of Domingo, one of her enemies, cannot have been the sole source of information for this Lunar? We are not expected to be at all puzzled. The author steps outside the frame of Science Fiction for a moment to pay a courtly compliment, a thing which was especially admired for being 'deft', that is, apparently easy though totally extravagant. And, if so, the passage was necessarily written while the queen was still alive, and even with some hope of showing the manuscript to influential people who might mention it to her. Lawton ('Bishop Godwin's *Man in the Moone*', p. 37) suggested that Godwin had written it to annoy Charles I, but this feeble procedure would not strike Godwin as enough reason for making nonsense of his story. None of the arguments about books that he 'must have read', I submit, has anything like the force of this one, which also proves that he would not be at all anxious to hide the manuscript from his friends.[34]

Appendix on Galileo

The dialogue form inherently expects a certain amount of evasion, as the author is felt to be rather crude if he identifies himself with one of the characters; but Galileo was a deciding type of man, not to say brash, and it is very unlikely he had no opinion up his sleeve about the first 'Day' of the great *Dialogue* which caused his trial. So much would be agreed, but most people, at any rate in the seventeenth century, felt sure that he believed in life on other stars, and led the reader to the very edge of that forbidden belief without literally expressing it. No doubt he intended people to think so, and did believe in life on other planets in general; but he had found there could not be life on the moon, and this had become an embarrassing secret, which he was determined to hide lest it give comfort to the enemy.

Nearly all of the first 'Day' of the *Dialogue* is occupied with what might seem a minor question – what we would expect to see, looking at the moon, according to the various theories about it. There are three taking part: Salviati who speaks for the author, Sagredo who is intelligent and open-minded, and Simplicio who is an Aristotelian, wrong-headed and foolish. At first Simplicio talks at some length (as the reader must first learn what needs refuting); he says that the moon is a perfect sphere, perfectly smooth, and that its seas would reflect the sun to a distant observer.[1] Salviati denies that 'the reflection of the moon is made in the manner of a mirror', and recalls that Galileo has already refuted this idea in two previous works. Salviati tells his servant to bring out a flat mirror, to the sunlit courtyard where they are sitting, and points out that it reflects the sun in a bright patch on the opposing wall; then he orders a spherical mirror to be brought out, but the others do not notice when it has come (p. 75), because though it reflects the sun in every direction it does not produce a bright patch. Indeed, says Salviati, a perfect sphere would actually be invisible, because the reflecting area would be infinitely small. Now, this is all right as a joke against the Aristotelian ideal, though it presumes a point source of light not the broad sun, but it does not help us to decide whether there are seas on the moon. A sea always waves or ripples, and the reflection of the sun from a cliff is always to some extent blurred. It is not denied that a reflection could be seen in this spherical mirror, even when it subtended as small an angle at the eye as the moon does; and the change of scale should make no difference in itself. A modern astronomer might find some technical snag, but from what Galileo tells us, and looking at the matter as he did, there seems no doubt that, if there were any large sheet of water on the moon, we would occasionally see, at any rate with the help of a telescope, a small bright star shining out from that area of the yellow moon. I submit that Galileo had been calculating when it would appear, and looking for it in his telescope, when he wrote privately in 1615 that he was now sure there were no seas on the moon. Yet in the *Dialogue* the only hint of this conclusion is allotted to silly Simplicio (p. 76):

I am afraid that you have introduced some trickery. Yet I see, in looking at that mirror, that it gives out a dazzling light that almost blinds me, and what is more significant, I see it all the time, wherever I go, changing place on the surface of the mirror according as I look at it from this place or that; a conclusive proof that the light is reflected very vividly upon all sides, and consequently upon the entire wall as upon my eyes.

And why should not this 'dazzling light that almost blinds me' be reflected by the seas of the moon? Salviati says he has explained the point already (p. 77):

that very small part of it which can reflect the image of the sun to the eyes of any individual would remain invisible, because of the great distance, as already explained.

But he only said it when considering the paradox of the infinitely smooth sphere. Why did he bring out his spherical mirror at all, if a consideration merely of scale makes it useless as a guide? We already knew it was not as big as the moon. I think he must have known he was fudging here.

On page 97 they are still discussing the question – I suppose the reader had to be convinced that it had been treated exhaustively. Good-natured Simplicio admits he was wrong to think that the seas on the moon would look brighter than the land, and Salviati has to make a welcoming answer, so that he almost implies an actual belief in these seas; but the subjunctive is still used:

the reflection of light coming from the seas would be less than that coming from the land. I mean here its general reflection, for as to the specific reflection from a quiet sea toward one certain place, I have no doubt that anyone located at that place would see from the water a very strong reflection. But from all other places, the surface of the water would seem darker than the land. And to show this to your own senses, let us go into that hall and pour a little water on the pavement...

– and thus we are given a second experiment to make all plain. Here the author seems quite reckless; one might think he was positively trying to give the game away. And indeed Salviati now ends the first Day with very sober remarks about the moon, refusing to say that there is no life there, but pointing out that there are at any rate no clouds, so that the long hot day must be expected to destroy all life as we know it. 'Very different and wholly unimaginable' is what the life on the moon must be, if there is any; and yet this conclusion was taken to be exalted rather than depressing. No one could say that Galileo had cheated as a scientist; to a fit reader, he might feel, his opinion ought to have been plain. But it does seem to have remained impenetrable for his adherents.

John Wilkins, for example, in his *Discovery of a New World in the Moon* (1638), regards Galileo as a stalwart for the belief; and Wilkins, however weak as a physicist, would always know the current tone of opinion. To be sure, Julius Caesar had asserted from personal knowledge that Kepler and Galileo were only being facetious when they pretended so; but we need not believe that any more, says Wilkins: 'if it had been but a jest, Galileo would never have suffered for it so much as afterwards he did' (or, in 1640, 'as report saith afterwards he did'). Kepler might say there was hardly any water on the moon, or air on the way to it, but Galileo, who in fact believed there was none of either, had endured for the faith. He must have come to a decision in 1615, one would think, when he wrote in a private letter that he was now certain there was no water on the moon. In the same year, Campanella brought out his *Defence of Galileo*, praising him especially for having explained the Biblical phrase 'waters above the firmament', a great worry at the time, by deducing that he had seen fog at the rim of the moon. Maybe this was what decided him; everything that happened to Campanella was so horrible, and his courage was so unbreakable, and to rob him of the moon would be so like cutting off the baby's arm, that he would prove a strong motive for silence. And a strong motive was needed at that time, because it was just when the first edict was signed forbidding Galileo to express belief in Copernicanism. Reasoning beings on other planets had all along been the real point of incompatibility with the Christian system, raised by Melanchthon as soon as Copernicus published, read out among the heresies of Bruno just before he was burned alive; Galileo would have been in a position to bargain if he had pronounced the moon uninhabitable. It is sometimes felt that his recantation was less than heroic, though probably he had a high motive for it – hoping to protect the church from the worst consequences of her folly; but to go through the forms of shame while holding up his sleeve a much more practical recantation – that is up to the standard which all right-thinking people came to expect of him. It is pedantry at her most splendid. 'And yet', he may have muttered to himself, 'nothing moves there'.[2]

Notes

PREFACE

1 WE, letter to Ian Parsons, 4 November 1972 (Chatto and Windus). In 1958 he had told Parsons that his next book would include 'essays on Donne Milton Fielding Joyce and a few extras, aiming at the general point that the neo-Christian movement has greatly upset the natural and traditional way of reading such authors; so that there has to be a certain air of challenge about the book'. But he was not at that time thinking of determining the canon of his essays.
2 WE, letter to Ian Parsons, 21 October 1975 (Chatto and Windus).
3 WE, letters to Christopher Ricks, 22 November 1981 and 10 September 1982.
4 WE, letter to Terence Moore, 4 September 1982.
5 WE, letter to Ian Parsons, postmarked 16 January 1973 (Chatto and Windus).

INTRODUCTION

1 WE, letter to Christopher Ricks, 1 March 1966 (Christopher Ricks).
2 John Carey, 'Creating Cannon Fodder', Sunday Times, 26 November 1989, p. G3. Frank Kermode's essay on Empson appeared first as a review of the posthumous The Royal Beasts, ed. John Haffenden, 'On a Chinese Mountain', in London Review of Books, 20 November 1986; he reprinted it in An Appetite for Poetry, London: William Collins, 1989, as 'William Empson: The Critic as Genius', for two excellent reasons:

First, at a time when there are so many models and techniques that can be got up and assiduously applied, there are individual and eccentric gifts which remain the prerequisite of the best criticism; and Empson possessed them in the degree of genius. Second, there are at the moment attempts to enlist him posthumously in the ranks of a theoretical avant-garde; one sees why, but he does not belong there, and would have said so with his customary asperity and emphasis. It seems desirable to resist this kidnap attempt. (pp. 3–4)

Of Empson's interpretation of Donne's mind and poetry, he believes: 'Though it may take a bourgeois professor to say so, Empson was wrong about Donne and the New Philosophy. Donne knew about Copernicus and made jokes about Kepler and Tycho Brahe and Galileo, but he habitually thought about the world in pre-Copernican terms.' (pp. 127–8).

3 John Carey, *John Donne: Life, Mind and Art*, London: Faber and Faber, 1981, p. 252.

4 'Preface to 1974 edition', *Some Versions of Pastoral* (1935), London: Chatto and Windus, 1974.

5 *Ibid.*, pp. 73, 75.

6 *Ibid.*, pp. 78, 82–4; Empson is slightly (tellingly?) misquoting Jonson's reported remark to Donne, 'if it had been written of ye Virgin Marie it had been something' (*Ben Jonson*, ed. C. H. Herford and P. Simpson, 1, Oxford: Clarendon Press, 1925, p. 133). Edward W. Tayler accuses Empson of committing the cardinal sin of symbolism: 'With respect to The Anniversaries, William Empson appears to have inaugurated the anachronistic enterprise in 1935 by roundly declaring that "the only way to make the poem sensible is to accept Elizabeth as the Logos"' (*Donne's Idea of a Woman: Structure and Meaning in 'The Anniversaries'*, New York: Columbia UP, 1991, p. 9). That charge, which has some point here, would have made Empson boil with outrage.

7 *Ben Jonson*, ed. C. H. Herford and P. Simpson, Oxford: Clarendon Press, 1925, 1, p. 133.

8 James Smith, 'On Metaphysical Poetry', *Scrutiny*, 2:3, December 1933, pp. 228, 227.

9 *Some Versions of Pastoral*, pp. 80–1.

10 Unpublished TS in Empson Papers.

11 Smith, 'On Metaphysical Poetry', p. 225.

12 T. S. Eliot, 'Donne In Our Time', in Theodore Spencer (ed.), *A Garland for John Donne*, Oxford: OUP, 1932, pp. 11–12.

13 Allen Tate, 'A Note on Donne' (1932), *Selected Essays 1928–1955*, Cleveland and New York: Meridian Books, 1955, p. 238.

14 WE, letter to D. A. Shankar, n. d. (Empson Papers).

15 Cf. Deborah Aldrich Larson, who argues that while Tuve's work may serve its purpose as 'a rebuff to the New Critics' it overemphasises the poet's traditionalism: 'it leaves unanswered the question of why Donne *seems* so different from his contemporaries' (*John Donne and Twentieth-Century Criticism*, London and Toronto: Associated University Presses, 1989, pp. 108–109). Joseph Anthony Mazzeo likewise rebuked Tuve's 'almost deterministic view of the influence of logic and rhetoric' ('A Critique of Some Modern Theories of Metaphysical Poetry', *Modern Philology*, 50, November 1952; reprinted in Arthur L. Clements (ed.), *John Donne's Poetry*, 2nd edn., New York and London: W. W. Norton, 1992, p. 170).

16 Frank Kermode, *John Donne* (1957), revised edn, Harlow, Essex: Longman, 1978, pp. 11, 18.

17 Frank Kermode, letter to WE, 26 January 1958 (Empson Papers).

18 Smith, 'On Metaphysical Poetry', p. 224.

19 Kermode, *John Donne*, p. 24.
20 Charles Monroe Coffin, *John Donne and the New Philosophy* (1937), New York: The Humanities Press, 1958, p. 150.
21 Herbert J. C. Grierson, *The Poems of John Donne*, Oxford: Clarendon Press, 1912, II, p. 90.
22 It is now understood that Elegy XIX 'circulated in manuscripts with other elegies that we know from their association and circulation with early verse letters were composed before the marriage' (M. Thomas Hester, 'Donne's (Re)Annunciation of the Virgin(ia Colony) in *Elegy XIX*', *South Central Review*, 4:2, Summer 1987, p. 51).
23 Frank Kermode, letter to WE, 1 May 1958 (Empson Papers).
24 WE, letter to Frank Kermode, 24 November 1957 (copy in Empson Papers). John T. Shawcross, in the foremost modern edition of Donne, prints 'There is no pennance due to innocence'; and yet his gloss seems to overlook the strategic argument of the poem: 'You will not receive penance for remaining innocent of sin or me, or for remaining in your virginal white; you should not wear penitential vestment (as white clothing was considered), for innocence does not require penance.' (*The Complete Poetry of John Donne*, New York: Anchor Books, 1967, p. 58.) A. J. Smith admits on principle, 'The textual evidence for the *1669* reading is weaker, and I print the other one for that reason alone' (*The Complete English Poems*, Harmondsworth, Middlesex: Penguin, 1971, p. 451).
25 J. B. Leishman, *The Monarch of Wit* (1951), 6th edn, London: Hutchinson, 1962, p. 122.
26 See, for example, Barbara Everett's acute and salutary judgment that

> Donne re-works Ovid as radically and as originally as he reworked Horace, Persius, and Juvenal in his figurative narrative. He seems to be learning something both from the early comic Shakespeare and from the brilliant Marlowe of the poems, as he creates here and there an almost purely comical relation between the sober and judicious voice of the narrator and the foolish presence of his own zany desires, or of his mistress's body.

> The 'cool and amused element' in the Elegies offsets 'that more prevalent image of Donne as the lewd seducer that takes support from the more apparently simply sensual of the Elegies... [F]ew first readers of "Going to Bed" have not, I imagine, been surprised to realize when the poem ends that the proposed event has yet to begin, and that the speaker has so far managed to undress no one but himself' ('Donne: A London Life', *Poets in Their Time: Essays on English poetry from Donne to Larkin*, London and Boston: Faber & Faber, 1986, pp. 8–9).

27 Carey, *John Donne*, p. 99.
28 Carey, *John Donne*, pp. 188, 38.
29 Helen Gardner (ed.), John Donne, *The Elegies and The Songs and Sonnets*, Oxford: Clarendon Press, 1965, p. li. Cited hereinafter as *ESS*.
30 Carey, *John Donne*, pp. 116, 124. *Cf.* Larson: 'Carey has been severely censured for this distorted reading of a poem most find delightfully

erotic, but the point here is that he has merely carried to extremes the kind of treatment possible when only one side of Donne's mind is emphasised and, incidentally, when little or no distinction is made between *persona* and poet' (*John Donne and Twentieth-Century Criticism*, p. 138). Philip Smallwood believes for some reason that the effect of Carey's critical biography 'is to protect, not undermine, Donne': '*John Donne* is a work of confirmatory criticism; a sanctification of what has long been a leading orthodoxy of twentieth-century literary taste. Thanks to this book it is likely to remain so' (*Modern Critics in Practice: Critical Portraits of British Literary Critics*, Hemel Hempstead, Herts.: Harvester Wheatsheaf, 1990, p. 87). His judgment is less askew when he concludes: 'In *John Donne*, the journalist supplies the stylistic *élan* and eye for sensation; the academic tailors them both to the needs of the critical *status quo*' (p. 89).

31 Thomas Docherty, *John Donne, Undone*, London and New York: Methuen, 1986, pp. 81–2. (Carey himself slates Docherty's putatively 'post-structuralist' procedures in 'Afterword 1990', *John Donne*, new edn., 1990.) R. V. Young argues that the woman in the poem most certainly has a value, but not what you might think: a 'lust for gold and power, rather than sexual desire', is the principal theme of the *Elegies*, it seems; so that 'the signifier/signified relationship of the imperialist tropes is inverted, and the aporia between missionary piety and lust for gain and conquest is discovered and laid bare as surely as the gold mines of America or the body of a submissive mistress' ('"O my America, my new-found-land": Pornography and Imperial Politics in Donne's *Elegies*', *South Central Review*, 3:2, Summer 1987, pp. 36, 45). M. Thomas Hester argues that 'this complex literary event' is at once 'a hyperbolic send-up of Renaissance epithalamia and ... an equivocal rewriting of the English myth of America...The act of "going to bed"...is being compared throughout the poem to the discovery of America and to "knowing" the Virgin Mary. Thus, the unvoiced word that lay behind the poem from the beginning was the English name of the English colony in America – *Virgin*(ia).' Furthermore, in what amounts to a proper hermeneutic stew, Hester seeks to show that Elegy XIX 'is even more blasphemous or outrageous than critics have therefore supposed'. Donne's 'amphibolous wit', he claims, extends to 'a critique of the Establishment poet [Spenser] and patron [Ralegh] who were rivals of his coterie'; and yet he disarmingly concedes after all: 'I must admit that I do not know where the mockery of Ralegh's adoration of the Virgin Queen (and its personal motives) begins and Donne's delightful play with the dynamics of the bedroom leaves off.' In any event, Hester is happy to reveal the secret of line 46, 'There is no pennance due to innocence', by way of a jocose pun: 'we should not overlook the full thrust of Donne's blasphemy here – the comparison of the speaker's sexual partner to the Virgin Mary' – who 'surely requires "no pennance".' (M. Thomas Hester, 'Donne's (Re)Annunciation of the

Virgin(ia Colony) in *Elegy XIX*', *South Central Review*, 4:2, Summer 1987, pp. 52, 59, 61, 53, 55, 56.)

Ilona Bell takes exception to the idea that Donne does not achieve 'an empathetic, imaginative, and varied response to the lady's point of view' – though admittedly she does not consider the Elegies ('The Role of the Lady in Donne's *Songs and Sonets*', *Studies in English Literature 1500–1900*, 23:1, Winter 1983, pp. 113–29).

32 Empson, '"There Is No Penance Due to Innocence"' (a review of *John Donne: Life, Mind and Art*, by John Carey), *The New York Review of Books*, 28:19, 3 December 1981, p. 42.

33 *Ibid.*, pp. 42–43. 'I agree that the poem…is pornographic', Empson acknowledged; 'it describes the greatest bit of luck in this kind that a male reader can imagine, and eggs him on to be pleased. But it is not sadistic' (p. 42). He wrote to Christopher Ricks on 22 November 1981: 'Perhaps I had been coarsely rude [about Carey], I rather feared, so I was relieved to hear that you didn't.'

According to Arthur F. Marotti, 'Donne's lover plays with his mistress emotionally and intellectually more than sexually: the erotic gestures are accompanied by humorous commentary, so there is little sensuousness or prurience in the poem' (*John Donne, Coterie Poet*, Madison, Wisconsin: University of Wisconsin Press, 1986, p. 54). Ignoring the stunning crux of the poem, Marotti judges that the only surprise reserved for the end is that the speaker is already naked.

34 Carey, *John Donne*, p. 100. *Cf.* Kermode, *An Appetite for Poetry*, p. 130. George Parfitt, who remarks upon Carey's 'coarseness of response', observes that Elegy XIX involves no 'drastic metonomy. Here the woman at least remains the sum of her bodily parts…and there is a rapturous erotic response to the imagined undressing and sexual activity which this prompts and releases.' Just so. And yet Parfitt goes on to allege that the woman 'remains essentially passive, to be discovered and explored – and the more precisely Donne makes language enforce this equation between colonisation and Woman the more firmly the latter is dehumanised'. (*John Donne: A Literary Life*, London: Macmillan Press, 1989, pp. 36, 128.) Parfitt seems to contradict himself again when he observes, 'In Donne's lyrics…as has often been noted, there is little sense of the female as body…Yet it would be inaccurate to say that Donne's lyrics disembody Woman…There is often a strong physical presence.' (*Ibid.*, p. 75.) It looks like playing safe, this flinching from the radical feminists. Clay Hunt, who was clearly not hag-ridden, observes that Elegy XIX extols 'the sheer physical pleasure of sexual intercourse' (*Donne's Poetry: Essays in Literary Analysis*, New Haven: Yale UP, 1954, p. 27).

35 Theodore Redpath (ed.), *The Songs and Sonets of John Donne*, 2nd edn, London: Methuen, 1983, p. 262. Cited hereinafter as *SS*.

36 Gardner, *ESS*, p. xxix.

37 WE, letter to D. A. Shankar, n. d. (copy in Empson Papers).

38 Gardner, *ESS*, p. 222.

39 Redpath, *SS*, p. 286.

40 Helen Gardner, letter to WE, 19 October 1956 (Empson Papers).

41 WE, letter to Gardner, 26 October 1956 (copy in Empson Papers).

42 Helen Gardner, letter to WE, 28 October 1956 (Empson Papers).

43 WE, letter to Helen Gardner, Guy Fawkes' Day 1956 (copy in Empson Papers). John T. Shawcross gives 'A something else' the gloss 'perhaps a Christ' (*The Complete Poetry of John Donne*, p. 142); A. J. Smith notes that the phrase signifies 'possibly "a Jesus Christ"', if the "mis-devotion" denies his resurrection; but more probably one of Mary Magdalen's lovers in her riotous youth. Christopher Ricks points out that "a Jesus Christ" and "a something else" are metrically equivalent' (*The Complete English Poems*, p. 398). I believe Professor Ricks will allow that Empson had taken that observation for granted. James S. Baumlin has recently remarked upon the outrageousness of 'the poet's own implicit apotheosis, his claim to become "a something else" – that is, a resurrected Christ to the lady's Mary Magdalen'. *Pace* Helen Gardner, he poses good questions: 'Does "mis-devotion" reign *because* of an age's superstitious belief in relics and miracles? Or might this relic and the "miracles" (22) of love be curative to an age's misdevotion?' (*John Donne and the Rhetorics of Renaissance Discourse*, Columbia and London: University of Missouri Press, 1991, p. 173.)

44 *Cf.* Empson's pre-emptive observation in *Some Versions of Pastoral*, p. 75: 'if Christ went to all the planets his appearances on each take on a different character; it is a more symbolical matter, and you can apply the ideas about Christ to any one who seems worthy of it'.

45 C. S. Lewis, letter to WE, 29 September 1957 (Empson Papers).

46 Coffin, *John Donne and the New Philosophy*, p. 263. WE commented, in his notes: 'Coffin is mainly concerned [with] (and very good on) the complications around 1610; whereas the most interesting part of Donne's thought about the matter had happened earlier.' (Empson Papers.)

47 Michael Francis Moloney, *John Donne: His Flight from Mediaevalism*, New York: Russell and Russell, 1965, p. 210.

48 Frank Kermode, letter to WE, 26 January 1958 (Empson Papers).

49 Frank Kermode, letter to WE, 1 May 1958 (Empson Papers).

50 Transcript of a recorded conversation between WE and Frank Kermode (copy in Empson Papers). This was a trial run for the script of *John Donne – An Illumination*, a show devised by Empson, Kermode, Roy Strong, and Andrew Hilton, and performed at the Mermaid Theatre, London, 2–8 October 1972. Neither Empson nor Kermode appeared in person, the 'agreed' text of their discussion being delivered by actors. Empson explained in a letter to the French cultural attaché on 13 January 1973,

it was part of the backstairs work for arranging a performance. I wrote many pages recommending what should be done and said in the performance, and what should be shown, and then I did this recording, just to do all I could before I had to fly to Canada. I am thankful for my safety when the terrible struggle of devising the performance went on for a sheer fortnight as I am told. But you should realize that in this recording both Kermode and I were pulling our punches, we were *imitating* a discussion, trying to sketch what had better occur in the play. As it went on, it almost broke through into being real, but never on my side and nor I expect on Kermode's.

(Copy in Empson Papers.) Richard Holmes noticed it: 'The *Illumination* is semi-dramatic, with... George Benson and Antony Brown as a pair of faintly buffoon-like modern critics in spectacles and leather armchairs' (*The Times*, 3 October 1972). Kermode's regretful account of the affair is in *An Appetite for Poetry*: 'The piece was hardly a success, and I am glad to think the Empson scholars are unlikely to trace *that* manuscript' (p. 129). Sorry, Frank.

51 Leishman, *The Monarch of Wit*, pp. 179, 188, 190–1.
52 Note in Empson Papers. Roma Gill, who bows to Gardner in remarking that Donne 'cannot hide his contempt for the women he is using as mere sexual objects', yet reckons that it is a mistake to overemphasise the extent to which Donne lifted from the Latin poets; she writes, of Elegy XIX: 'Donne's sense of blessedness "in this discovering thee" owes more to Drake and Hawkins, who made possible the pun in "discovering", than to Ovid and Propertius' ('*Musa Iocosa Mea*: Thoughts on the Elegies', in A. J. Smith (ed.), *John Donne: Essays in Celebration*, London: Methuen, 1972, pp. 55, 64).
53 Leishman, *The Monarch of Wit*, pp. 215, 221.
54 Draft of the text for *John Donne – An Illumination* at the Mermaid Theatre, October 1972 (TS in Empson Papers).
55 Theodore Redpath, *SS*, p. 230; letter to WE, 24 February 1957 (Empson Papers).
56 Helen Gardner (ed.), John Donne, *The Divine Poems*, Oxford: Clarendon Press, 1952, p. 76. Cited hereinafter as *DP*.
57 Carey, *John Donne*, p. 50.
58 Gardner, *DP*, pp. 75–6. Empson sometime wrote in his notes: 'I had not realised that *I am a little world* was written, on her theory, just before or after Galileo published. Absurd to say he [Donne] didn't know.' (Empson Papers)
59 WE, draft of a discussion document (copy in Empson Papers).
60 WE, *Some Versions of Pastoral*, London: Chatto and Windus, 1935, p. 75.
61 WE, letter to Frank Kermode, n. d. (copy in Empson Papers).
62 WE, draft of a discussion document (copy in Empson Papers).
63 Robert Hues, one of 'the three Magi' retained by the Earl of Northumberland (the others being Walter Warner and Thomas Harriot), published a work on the use of the terrestrial and celestial globes, *Tractatus de Globis et Eorum Usu*, in 1594.
64 Leishman, *The Monarch of Wit*, p. 200.
65 Redpath, *SS*, p. 231.
66 Gardner, *ESS*, p. 199.
67 Gardner, *ESS*, p. liv. R. E. Pritchard ably argues that the poem speaks for a 'new, ideal and transforming relationship', a 'unique love [that] will be a catalytic miracle, cancelling the effect of the Fall': '"The Good

Morrow" presents a new love, different from ordinary sexuality, that is associated with the discovery of reality, the establishment of the true faith, a replacement of the familiar world, an image of perfection and eternity, that recalls an original happy state, and involves an activity unlike that consequent upon the Fall' ('Dying in Donne's "The Good Morrow"', *Essays in Criticism*, 35:3, July 1985, p. 220). *Cf.* Aers and Kress, 'Vexatious Contraries: A Reading of Donne's Poetry', in David Aers, Bob Hodge, Gunther Kress, *Literature, Language and Society in England 1580–1680*, Dublin: Gill and Macmillan, 1981, pp. 52–7.

68 *Cf.* an anonymous review of *The Elegies and The Songs and Sonnets*, ed. Helen Gardner: 'on the question of dating [Empson] has an irrefragable case ... [A]bove all, he is right in contending that if the poems of the second group are attributed to the period of Donne's marriage, it becomes impossible to suggest for many of them a psychologically plausible explanation' (*TLS*, 6 April 1967, pp. 279–80).

69 *Letters*, p. 147; *Selected Prose*, p. 127.

70 Leishman, *The Monarch of Wit*, p. 41.

71 Gosse, *The Life and Letters of John Donne*, London: William Heinemann, 1899, II, p. 48. Joan Bennett likewise cites this letter to illustrate the constancy and the quality of Donne's love for his wife ('The Love Poetry of John Donne', in *Seventeenth-Century Studies Presented to Sir Herbert Grierson*, Oxford: Clarendon Press, 1938; reprinted in Clements, *John Donne's Poetry*, p. 181); so does R. C. Bald (*John Donne: A Life*, London: OUP, 1970, p. 326). See Larson, *John Donne and Twentieth-Century Criticism*, for a survey of the divergent views of the letters; 'to support his assessment of Donne's character, Carey must emphasize the egotistical, ambitious elements in the letters' (p. 88).

72 Gardner, *ESS*, p. xxviii–xxix.

73 Gardner, *ESS*, p. li.

74 Carey, *John Donne*, p. 91.

75 Kermode, *John Donne*, p. 14.

76 Gardner, *ESS*, p. vii.

77 Carey, *John Donne*, p. 251; Lower quoted in John W. Shirley, *Thomas Harriot: A Biography*, Oxford: Clarendon Press, 1983, p. 399.

78 Marjorie Nicolson, 'The "New Astronomy" and English Literary Imagination', *Studies in Philology*, 32, 1935, pp. 428, 449, 459.

79 *Ibid.*, p. 449.

80 Coffin, *John Donne and the New Philosophy*, p. 97.

81 *Ibid.*, p. 159.

82 Kermode, *John Donne*, pp. 13–14.

83 Coffin, *John Donne and the New Philosophy*, p. 210.

84 *Ibid.*, p. 211.

85 Carey, *John Donne*, p. 250.

86 Coffin, *John Donne and the New Philosophy*, p. 213. Nor did Gosse detect jeering in *Ignatius his Conclave*: 'Donne is completely captivated by the recent epoch-making discoveries in the science of astronomy.' (*The Life and Letters of John Donne*, I, pp. 257–8.)

87 Carey, *John Donne*, p. 253.
88 Carey, *John Donne*, p. 250.
89 J. L. E. Dreyer, *History of the Planetary Systems from Thales to Kepler* (Cambridge, 1906), pp. 363–64. See also Kristian P. Moesgaard, 'Copernican Influence on Tycho Brahe', in Jerzy Dobrzycki (ed.), *The Reception of Copernicus' Heliocentric Theory*, Dordrecht, Holland: D. Reidel, 1972, pp. 31–55; Victor Thoren, *The Lord of Uraniborg: A Biography of Tycho Brahe*, Cambridge: CUP, 1991; and John W. Shirley's summary of the controversy aroused by the conception of 'celestial phenomena which could discredit the ideas of perfection and circular motion' (*Thomas Harriot: A Biography*, pp. 393–4).
  Cf. Anthony Low's remark that 'Donne may not have accepted the literal details of Copernican theory, since "The Progresse of the Soule" (1612) pictures Elizabeth Drury reaching heaven through Tycho Brahe's system' ('Love and Science: cultural change in Donne's *Songs and Sonnets*', *Studies in the Literary Imagination*, 22:1, Spring 1989, p. 14). Low credits John T. Shawcross (*The Complete Poetry of John Donne*, p. 296n) with solving the problem of 'Donne's curious ordering of the spheres in that poem'. But Empson actually deserves the credit for being the first to suggest that Donne may have settled for Tycho's system.
90 John Hayward (ed.), John Donne, *Complete Poetry and Selected Prose*, London: The Nonesuch Press, 1929, p. 674.
91 See Grant McColley, 'Nicholas Hill and the *Philosophia epicurea*', *Annals of Science*, 1939, pp. 390–405 (Empson's probable source). For a very good exposition of Hill's opinions, see Jean Jacquot, 'Harriot, Hill, Warner and the New Philosophy', in John W. Shirley (ed.), *Thomas Harriot: Renaissance Scientist*, Oxford: Clarendon Press, 1974.
92 For a description of Donne's copy of *Philosophia Epicurea*, see Geoffrey Keynes, *A Bibliography of Dr John Donne*, 4th edn., Oxford: Clarendon Press, 1973, pp. 270–1. In 1930 Evelyn M. Simpson produced a limited edition of *Catalogus Librorum Aulicorum Incomparabilium et non Vendibilium* (it was first published by John Donne the younger in the poor text of *Poems*, 1650) under the more tame title *The Courtier's Library*. 'Only 750 copies were published, and the edition was sold out within a fortnight', Mrs Simpson explained in 1948. 'Hence there has been little opportunity for it to become widely known among Donne students.' Empson must be counted among those whom it escaped in 1930. Simpson then reprinted a large part of the introduction to her Nonesuch Press edition of *Catalogus Librorum* in the second edition of *A Study of the Prose Works of John Donne* (Oxford: Clarendon Press, 1948, pp. 149–58); but unfortunately Empson had studied only her first edition of 1924.
93 Hugh Trevor-Roper, 'Nicholas Hill, the English Atomist', *Catholics, Anglicans and Puritans: Seventeenth-century Essays*, London: Martin Secker and Warburg, 1987, pp. 3–4.
94 *Ibid.*, pp. viii–ix, 2.
95 Carey, *John Donne*, p. 18. On Donne's anxieties about censorship, see Annabel Patterson, 'Misinterpretable Donne: The Testimony of the

Letters', *John Donne Journal*, 1, 1982, pp. 39–53; M. Thomas Hester, *Kinde Pitty and Brave Scorn: John Donne's Satyres*, Durham, North Carolina: Duke University Press, 1982.

96 Francis R. Johnson and Sanford V. Larkey, 'Thomas Digges, the Copernican System, and the Idea of the Infinity of the Universe in 1576', *Huntington Library Bulletin*, v, April 1934, p. 69. Grant McColley cast doubt on the Johnson–Larkey claims for Digges ('The Seventeenth-century Doctrine of a Plurality of Worlds', *Annals of Science*, 1:3, 1936); Alexander Koyré, another historian of astronomy, was opposed to them: 'Thomas Digges puts his stars into a theological heaven; not into an astronomical sky' (*From the Closed World to the Infinite Universe*, Baltimore: The Johns Hopkins Press, 1957, p. 38).

97 *Ibid.*, pp. 72, 78.

98 *Ibid.*, p. 95.

99 *Ibid.*, p. 111. Johnson and Larkey explain more fully on p. 95 that 'Digges consistently made a practice of printing summaries of the most important features of his unfinished works in the form of short treatises annexed to new editions of his other works'; accordingly:

> In his *An Arithmeticall Militare Treatise, named Stratioticos* (1579), Digges lists the 'Bookes Begon by the Author, heereafter to be published', and among them is *Commentaries* vpon the *Reuolutions of Copernicus*, by euidente Demonstrations grounded vpon late *Obseruations*, to ratifye and confirme hys *Theorikes* and *Hypothesis*, wherein also Demonstratiuelie shall be discussed, whether it bee possible vpon the vulgare *Thesis* of the Earthes *Stabilitie*, to delyuer any true *Theorike* voyde of such irregular Motions, and other absurdities, as repugne the whole *Principles* of *Philosophie* naturall, and apparant groundes of common *Reason*'.

100 *Ibid.*, pp. 73, 115.

101 *Ibid.*, pp. 95–6.

102 Colin A. Ronan, 'The origins of the reflecting telescope', *Journal of the British Astronomical Association*, 101:6, 1991, pp. 335–42; and private information from Mr Ronan. *The Daily Telegraph*, on 31 October 1991, blazoned a report of Mr Ronan's lecture under the front-page headline, 'Now it can be told: British scientists beat Galileo by 33 years'; sadly, the science correspondent misreported Ronan's case with the claim that 'a diagram that Thomas Digges drew in 1576 showing planetary orbits round the Sun as described by Copernicus 40 years before ... was never published. Mr Ronan tracked down part of the manuscript in the British Library.' Suffice it to say that Colin Ronan's address is much sounder than the embarrassingly misplaced patriotism of that misleading story.

103 Émile Namer, *Giordano Bruno, ou l'Univers Infini comme fondement de la Philosophie Moderne* (1966), quoted in Antoinette Mann Paterson, *The Infinite Worlds of Giordano Bruno*, Springfield, Ill.: Charles C. Thomas, 1970, p. 198.

104 The idea that Nicolaus of Cusa 'despised science', Empson wrote in his notes, 'is mere propaganda' (Empson Papers).

105 Quoted in Dorothea Waley Singer, *Giordano Bruno: His Life and Thought* (1950), New York: Greenwood Press, 1968, pp. 76, 107.

106 *De l'Infinito Universo et Mondi* (Lagarde), 1, pp. 318–19; cited in McColley, 'The Seventeenth-century Doctrine of a Plurality of Worlds', p. 414.

107 Maria Rita Pagnoni Sturlese, 'Su Bruno e Tycho Brahe', *Rinascimento*, second series, 30, 1985, p. 311. Tycho Brahe also referred to Bruno as 'Iordanus Nullanus' (p. 310); John Bossy conflates the two sneers as 'Nolanus Nullanus' in his otherwise clear-sighted *Giordano Bruno and the Embassy Affair*, New Haven and London: Yale UP, 1991, p. 138n.

108 Paterson, *The Infinite Worlds of Giordano Bruno*, p. 24.

109 R. McNulty, 'Bruno at Oxford', *Renaissance News*, 13, 1960, pp. 300–305; and Frances A. Yates, *Giordano Bruno and the Hermetic Tradition*, London: Routledge and Kegan Paul, 1964, pp. 207–11.

110 See Hilary Gatti, *The Renaissance Drama of Knowledge: Giordano Bruno in England*, London and New York: Routledge, 1989, pp. 99–100.

111 See Bossy, *Giordano Bruno and the Embassy Affair*, pp. 57–8; and an exemplary essay by David Farley-Hills, 'The "Argomento" of Bruno's *De gli eroici furori* and Sidney's *Astrophil and Stella*', *Modern Language Review*, 87:1, January 1992, pp. 1–17.

112 See Edward Rosen, 'Harriot's Science: The Intellectual Background', in John W. Shirley (ed.), *Thomas Harriot: Renaissance Scientist*, pp. 22ff; and John W. Shirley, *Thomas Harriot: A Biography*, pp. 189–200. Ralegh, when about to embark on the islands Voyage in 1597, significantly left to Harriot 'all my bookes' (M. C. Latham, 'Sir Walter Raleigh's Will', *RES*, n.s. 22, 1971, p. 131).

113 In a draft study of *A Midsummer Night's Dream* (Empson Papers).

114 But *cf.* S. Schoenbaum, *Shakespeare's Lives*, Oxford: Clarendon Press, 1970, p. 737: 'The whole superstructure of theory...rests upon an insecure foundation. There is no evidence to link Chapman directly with Ralegh, and the phrase "School of Night", spoken by the King of Navarre [in *Love's Labour's Lost*], may be a textual corruption, perhaps of "suit of night". From such fragile threads are recondite hypotheses spun.'

115 Ted Hughes, *A Choice of Shakespeare's Verse*, 2nd edn, London: Faber and Faber, 1991, pp. 166–7, 169; see also Hughes, *Shakespeare and the Goddess of Complete Being*, London: Faber and Faber, 1992.

116 According to Aubrey's *Brief Lives*, Harriot discredited 'the old storie of the Creation of the World' – '*ex nihilo nihil fit*,' he would say – and made 'a Philosophical Theologie; wherin he cast-off the Old Testament, and then the New-one would (consequently) have no Foundation. He was a Deist.'

117 John W. Shirley dismisses the romantic myth of a 'School of Night': 'from all the manuscripts left by Harriot, it appears that his connections with the Earl directly were tenuous... [I]t appears certain that there was never a formal association surrounding either Ralegh or Northumberland' (see *Thomas Harriot: A Biography*, pp. 360–79).

118 Quoted in G. B. Harrison (ed.), *Willobie His Avisa*, London, 1926, p. 210. See also William Urry, *Christopher Marlowe and Canterbury*, London and Boston: Faber and Faber, 1988, pp. 70–7, and Stephen Greenblatt's subtle reading of Harriot's subversiveness: 'Invisible Bullets', *Shakespearean Negotiations: The Circulation of Social Energy in Renaissance England*, Oxford: Clarendon Press, 1988, pp. 21–39.

119 Shirley, *Thomas Harriot: A Biography*, p. 317.

120 Bald, *John Donne*, p. 133.

121 John Sampson suggested that it may have been George Gerrard (or Garrett), a close friend of Donne and a putative member of the Earl's household, who introduced Donne to Northumberland ('A Contemporary Light upon John Donne', *Essays and Studies*, VII, Oxford: Clarendon Press, 1921, pp. 94–5).

122 Bald, *John Donne*, pp. 228–9.

123 Edward Rosen (ed.), *Kepler's 'Somnium': The Dream, or Posthumous Work on Lunar Astronomy*, Madison, Milwaukee and London: The University of Wisconsin Press, 1967, Appendix E: 'Kepler and Donne', pp. 212–13. *Cf.* Dennis Flynn's proposal that Donne made use of Northumberland's books while writing *Ignatius His Conclave*, and so must have visited the Earl during his confinement in the Tower beginning in 1606. Moreover, Northumberland purchased a copy of *Conclave Ignati* in February 1611; since it was unusual for the Earl to buy works by English authors, that acquisition may well suggest a strong personal interest ('Donne's *Ignatius His Conclave* and Other Libels on Robert Cecil', *John Donne Journal*, 6:2, 1987, pp. 163–83).

   Donne was to take the opportunity to meet Kepler in Linz, where he journeyed with the embassy of Lord Doncaster (Northumberland's son-in-law) in 1619; see Wilbur Applebaum, 'Donne's Meeting with Kepler: A Previously Unknown Episode', *Philological Quarterly*, 50:1, January 1971, pp. 132–4.

124 Marjorie Nicolson, 'Kepler, the *Somnium*, and John Donne', *Journal of the History of Ideas*, 1:3, June 1940, pp. 273–5.

125 *Cf.* Ben Jonson, who in 1619 said that Donne had written 'all his best pieces err he was 25 years old' (*Ben Jonson*, I, p. 135).

126 Peter J. French, *John Dee: The Life of an Elizabethan Magus*, London: Routledge and Kegan Paul, 1972, p. 171, 99; Robert Hugh Kargon, *Atomism in England from Hariot to Newton*, Oxford: Clarendon Press, 1966; Saverio Ricci, 'Giordano Bruno e il "Northumberland Circle" (1600–1630)', *Rinascimento*, second series, 25, 1985, p. 336.

127 Shirley, *Thomas Harriot: A Biography*, pp. 386–7.

128 McColley, 'The Seventeenth-century Doctrine of a Plurality of Worlds', p. 411. See also Shirley, *Thomas Harriot: A Biography*, p. 401; Gatti, *The Renaissance Drama of Knowledge*, pp. 54–6.

129 McColley, *ibid.* Cf. Alexander Koyré, 'The New Astronomy Against the New Metaphysics: Johannes Kepler's Rejection of Infinity', *From the Closed World to the Infinite Universe*, pp. 58–87.

130 Joannis Kepleri, *De Stella Nova*, in *Werke*, 1, München, 1938, p. 253;
    Harriot in British Library, Add. mss. 6188, fol. 67ᵛ; quoted in Singer,
    Giordano Bruno, pp. 189, 68. Harriot's note was apparently discovered
    by Ethel Seaton, who referred to it in an unpublished lecture to the
    Elizabethan Literary Society in 1933; see Frances Yates, *A Study of
    Love's Labour's Lost*, Cambridge: CUP, 1936, pp. 92–3.

131 Gatti, *The Renaissance Drama of Knowledge*, pp. 51–2, 199–200. Gatti's
    study is most impressive when dealing with the influence of Bruno on
    Northumberland and his associates; less so when she proposes that a
    substantial element of Bruno's influence can be traced in both *Dr
    Faustus* and *Hamlet*.

132 Daniel Massa, 'Giordano Bruno's Ideas in Seventeenth-century
    England', *Journal of the History of Ideas*, 38:2, 1977, pp. 241–2. See also
    David A. Hedrich Hirsch, 'Donne's Atomies and Anatomies: Decon-
    structed Bodies and the Resurrection of Atomic Theory', *Studies in
    English Literature 1500–1900*, 31:1, Winter 1991, pp. 69–94; Giovanni
    Aquilecchia, 'Bruno's mathematical dilemma in his poem *De minimo*',
    Renaissance Studies, 5:3, September 1991, pp. 315–26.

133 *Philosophia Epicurea* (1601), p. 92; cited in Massa, 'Giordano Bruno's
    Ideas in Seventeenth-century England', p. 236; Gatti, *The Renaissance
    Drama of Knowledge*, pp. 53, 200.

134 Saverio Ricci, 'Giordano Bruno e il "Northumberland Circle"
    (1600–1630)', pp. 341, 343.

135 Bodleian Library, MS Rawlinson B. 158; quoted in Trevor-Roper,
    'Nicholas Hill, the English Atomist', p. 11.

136 Grant McColley first drew attention to the fact that in a section of *De
    Mundo* entitled 'De motu Solis & Terrae' Gilbert took time specifically
    to consider Bruno's cosmological ideas under the headings 'Alius
    movendi modus Nolani cum esset junior' and 'Alius modus juxta
    Nolanum' ('William Gilbert and the English Reputation of Giordano
    Bruno', *Annals of Science*, 2:3, 1937, pp. 353–4). Ricci follows that cue
    in 'Giordano Burno e il "Northumberland Circle" (1600–1630)',
    pp. 338–40, and *La Fortuna del Pensiero di Giordano Bruno, 1600–1750*
    (Florence, 1990).

137 Gad Freudenthal, 'Theory of Matter and Cosmology in William
    Gilbert's *De magnete*', *Isis* (Official Journal of the History of Science
    Society), 74:271, March 1983, pp. 34–5.

138 Arthur O. Lovejoy, *The Great Chain of Being: A Study in the History of an
    Idea*, Cambridge, Mass.: Harvard UP, 1936, p. 116. *Cf.* Johnson and
    Larkey:

> When Bruno's cosmological ideas finally became familiar to the English people,
> they merely confirmed the notion, already deeply implanted in their minds,
> that the infinity of the physical universe was an integral part of the Copernican
> hypothesis. The hold which this idea had upon English astronomers is
> strikingly illustrated by the attitude of Thomas Harriot and his group of friends
> and pupils, who were...using telescopes as early as, or perhaps earlier than,

Galileo. When Kepler, in his book *De Stella nova in pede Serpentarii* (1606), attempted to disprove the theory of the infinite universe, and the varying distances of the stars (which Kepler, not knowing Digges' work, credited to Gilbert and Bruno), Harriot and his associates rose to the defense of this idea, and exposed the flaws in Kepler's arguments.

('Thomas Digges, the Copernican System, and the Idea of the Infinity of the Universe in 1576', p. 116). See also Robert S. Westman, 'Magical Reform and Astronomical Reform: The Yates Thesis Reconsidered', in Westman and J. E. McGuire, *Hermeticism and the Scientific Revolution*, University of California, Los Angeles: William Andrews Clark Memorial Library, 1977 (pp. 1–91): 'Bruno was the first to attempt to connect a new ontology of space, homogeneous and infinitely extended...with the Copernican reordering of the planets' (p. 69).

139 Bossy, *Giordano Bruno and the Embassy Affair*, p. 38.
140 WE, untitled review of F. A. Yates, *A Study of 'Love's Labour's Lost'*, *Life and Letters Today*, 15, Autumn 1936, p. 204. See also M. C. Bradbrook, *The School of Night: a Study in the Literary Relationships of Sir Walter Ralegh*, Cambridge: CUP, 1936.
141 Lovejoy, *The Great Chain of Being*, pp. 108–9; citing Thomas Paine, *The Age of Reason*, London, 1794, p. 45.
142 Wesley Milgate (ed.), John Donne, *The Satires, Epigrams and Verse Letters*, Oxford: Clarendon Press, 1967, p. 243.
143 Lovejoy, *The Great Chain of Being*, p. 109.
144 WE, draft of a discussion document with Frank Kermode, 1972 (copy in Empson Papers).
145 McColley, 'The Seventeenth-century Doctrine of a Plurality of Worlds', pp. 412–13. *Cf.* Robert S. Westman, 'The Melanchthon Circle, Rheticus, and the Wittenberg Interpretation of the Copernican Theory', *Isis*, 66, 1975, pp. 165–93. On the influence of 'Melanchthon's circle' and the 'Wittenberg Interpretation', Westman remarks: 'The effects of this informal scientific group on the early reception of the Copernican theory cannot be underestimated. Thanks to its efforts, the realist and cosmological claims of Copernicus' great discovery failed to be given full consideration' (p. 168).
146 Helen Gardner, letter to WE, 19 October 1956 (Empson Papers).
147 WE, draft letter to *Critical Quarterly*, 1967 (copy in Empson Papers).
148 John Hayward (ed.), *Complete Poetry and Selected Prose*, p. 514; cited in McColley, 'The Seventeenth-century Doctrine of a Plurality of Worlds', p. 422; Nicolson, 'The "New Astronomy" and English Literary Imagination', p. 459.
149 Coffin, *John Donne and the New Philosophy*, pp. 215–16.
150 J. L. Mosheim, *An Ecclesiastical History, Ancient and Modern* (London, 1806), IV, p. 484.
151 Nigel Smith, *Perfection Proclaimed: Language and Literature in English Radical Religion 1640–1660*, Oxford: Clarendon Press, 1989, pp. 146–7.

See also Alastair Hamilton, *The Family of Love*, Cambridge: James Clark and Co., 1981.

152 French, *John Dee*, p. 124 note 2.

153 Paterson, *The Infinite Worlds of Giordano Bruno*, p. 125.

154 WE, letter to Frank Kermode, n. d. (copy in Empson Papers). 'Having to inform himself about theologies in the course of clearing his honor, and having much curiosity, Donne would be sure to learn the opinions of the radical reformers of his time', Empson wrote elsewhere; 'and perhaps he ought to have joined the Family of Love... But this would have excluded him from all worldly advancement, and the company would have been too low-class to be comfortable for him; besides, he could be more effective in a larger world if he spoke merely as an ex-papist, and only by hints' ('"There Is No Penance Due to Innocence"', p. 48).

155 John Sparrow, letter to WE, 13 August 1972 (Empson Papers).

156 Gardner, *ESS*, p. lii.

157 *Cf*. Baumlin, *John Donne and the Rhetorics of Renaissance Discourse*, pp. 284–9.

158 Redpath, *SS*, p. 178.

159 Gardner, *ESS*, p. lxiv.

160 Gardner, *ESS*, p. xci.

161 Gardner, *ESS*, p. 209.

162 Redpath, *SS*, p. 179.

163 Theodore Redpath, letter to Haffenden, 17 March 1990.

164 Gardner, *ESS*, p. 210.

165 Redpath, *SS*, p. 179.

166 Gardner, *ESS*, p. 210.

167 See Mark Roberts, 'The New Edition of Donne's Love Poems', *Essays in Criticism*, 17, 1967, p. 277.

168 Redpath, *SS*, Appendix IV, pp. 315–17.

169 Mark Roberts, 'If It Were Done When 'Tis Done', *Essays in Criticism*, 16:3, July 1966, p. 318; Roberts discusses Gardner's inconsistency vis-à-vis 'The Dreame' on p. 317.

170 Roberts, 'If It Were Done When 'Tis Done', p. 326. Roberts later judged that Group III:

seems much further from Donne's papers than either of the other two... In general, I take it that the Group I tradition represents the earliest substantive version of the *Songs and Sonets* that comes down to us; that Group II represents what may be called a revision... and that Group III, though commonly closer to the 'revised' version, presents a number of readings from an early version or versions of which we have no substantive record' ('Problems in Editing Donne's Songs and Sonets', in A. H. de Quehen (ed.), *Editing Poetry from Spenser to Dryden*, New York and London: Garland Publishing, 1981, p. 27).

171 Redpath, *SS*, p. 101.

172 Redpath, *SS*, 317.

173 Gardner, *ESS*, p. 210. Empson spotted the problem: 'Why not?' he

observed in his notes. Gardner '[w]on't let us know which these MS are.' (Empson Papers).

174 Redpath, *SS*, p. 315. It should be noted, however, that Shawcross' textual apparatus includes the entry: 'Profanenes *C57, TCD, Dob, O'F* (> Profane)' (*The Complete Poetry of John Donne*, p. 452).

175 Gardner, *ESS*, p. 133.

176 WE, letter to W. D. Maxwell McMahon, 21 August 1973 (copy in Empson Papers). He wrote to Christopher Ricks on 1 March 1972, 'Of course I admit that plenty of arguing-away can still go on, after starting from her text, but it still feels foul even when a decent meaning has been argued out of it.'

177 WE, letter to Christopher Ricks, 'Good Friday' (Christopher Ricks). Ricks later complimented Empson as Donne's 'best twentieth-century critic', though he also gently criticised certain points of Empson's interpretation (especially over the line 'There is no pennance due to innocence') while prosecuting his own argument that Donne is revolted by the anticlimax of love. 'Donne's postcoital malaise degrades the poems' own deepest understandings,' he insists ('Donne After Love', in Elaine Scarry (ed.), *Literature and the Body: Essays on Populations and Persons*, Baltimore and London: Johns Hopkins UP, 1988, pp. 33–69). Despite her all-embracing brief – *John Donne and Twentieth-Century Criticism* (1989) – Deborah Aldrich Larson takes no account of Empson's writings. The only recent critic to support his case is David Norbrook: 'Whatever his eccentricities of argument, Empson does seem to me to have located a genuine radical impulse in these poems, and to have been justified in objecting to the mean-mindedness of neo-Christian critics of the Cold War epoch who tried to bring the lyrics back in line with a conservative cultural pessimism' ('The Monarchy of Wit and the Republic of Letters: Donne's Politics', in Elizabeth D. Harvey and Katharine Eisaman Maus (eds.), *Soliciting Interpretation: Literary Theory and Seventeenth-Century English Poetry*, Chicago and London: University of Chicago Press, 1990, p. 13).

178 John Crowe Ransom, letter to WE, 18 January 1957 (Empson Papers).

179 Helen Gardner, letter to WE, 15 September 1956 (Empson Papers). 'A lot in Grierson is just slightly unreliable', Helen Gardner added, 'and people will go on arguing on the basis of statements which are not true'.

180 A. L. French, 'Dr Gardner's Dating of the *Songs and Sonnets*', *Essays in Criticism*, 17, 1967, p. 119.

181 Ted-Larry Pebworth, 'Manuscript Poems and Print Assumptions: Donne and His Modern Editors', *John Donne Journal*, 3:1, 1984, pp. 12–17.

182 WE, 'Correspondence', *Critical Quarterly*, 9, 1967, p. 89; Helen Gardner, 'Correspondence', *Critical Quarterly*, 8, 1966, p. 376.

183 WE, letter to the Editors of *Critical Quarterly*, n. d. (copy in Empson Papers).

184 From a commonplace book, Malone MS. 14, in the Bodleian Library;

quoted by Michael Milgate, 'The early references to John Donne', *Notes and Queries*, 195, 8 July 1950, p. 292.

CHAPTER 1: DONNE AND THE RHETORICAL TRADITION

1 Drummond, 'Conversations', in Herford and Simpson, *Ben Jonson*, Oxford: 1925, I, p. 133.
2 'Donne is a "personality" in a sense in which Andrewes is not: his sermons, one feels, are a "means of self-expression"' (T. S. Eliot, *For Lancelot Andrewes: Essays on Style and Order* (1928), London: Faber and Faber, 1970, pp. 24–5).
3 Painted in 1591, when Donne was eighteen. 'The Spanish motto "Antes muerto que mudado" is adapted by a change of gender from a line in the first song of Montemayor's *Diana*. Donne has taken as a boast of his constancy ("Sooner dead than changed") the protestation of a fickle mistress' (Helen Gardner, (ed.), John Donne, *The Elegies and The Songs and Sonnets*, Oxford: Clarendon Press, 1965, p. 266).

CHAPTER 2: DONNE THE SPACE MAN

1 'Donne is a "personality" in a sense in which Andrewes is not: his sermons, one feels, are a "means of self-expression"' (T. S. Eliot, *For Lancelot Andrewes: Essays on Style and Order* (1928), London: Faber and Faber, 1970, pp. 24–5).
2 Drummond, 'Conversations' in Herford and Simpson, *Ben Jonson*, Oxford: 1925, I, p. 133.
3 See 'Donne and the Rhetorical Tradition', footnote 3, above.
4 Meg Lota Brown has recently endorsed the view that Donne's persona in "The Sunne Rising" 'argues for a new definition of authority, claiming that his exceptional love constitutes the standard against which political structures and social values should be measured... Together, the lovers hypostatize the ideal.' In further confirmation of Empson's argument, Brown observes: 'It is appropriate that the speaker addresses a Ptolemaic sun. Donne was well aware of "the new philosophy", and his self-conscious sophistry is all the more apparent in that it assumes a cosmology that has been called into doubt.' (Meg Lota Brown, '"In that the world's contracted thus": Casuistical Politics in Donne's "The Sunne Rising"', in Claude J. Summers and Ted-Larry Pebworth (eds.), '*The Muses Common-Weale': Poetry and Politics in the Seventeenth Century*, Columbia: University of Missouri Press, 1988, pp. 24, 30, 31.)
5 Theodore Redpath (ed.), John Donne, *The Songs and Sonets*, London: Methuen, 1956, pp. 109–10.
6 Pierre Legouis, *Donne the Craftsman: An Essay upon the Structure of the Songs and Sonnets*, Paris: Henri Didier; London: Humphrey Milford and Oxford University Press, 1928, p. 70 note 40. Payne refers to F. W. Payne, who made Ann More the heroine of the poem (*John Donne and His Poetry*, London: George G. Harrap, 1926, pp. 94–5).

7 Legouis, *Donne the Craftsman*, p. 69 n. 39.
8 Cf. Empson's earlier remark in *Some Versions of Pastoral* (1935): 'M. Legouis may be right in saying that [Donne] set out merely to dramatise the process of seduction; it is only clear that he found the argument fascinating and believed that it had some truth in some cases' (p. 135).
9 Marius Bewley, 'Religious Cynicism in Donne's Poetry', *Kenyon Review*, 14:4, Autumn 1952, pp. 619–46. 'What *The Anniversaries* are, in effect, celebrating – albeit *secretly* celebrating – is Donne's apostasy from the Roman Catholic Church' (p. 622).
10 Clay Hunt, *Donne's Poetry*, New Haven and London: Yale University Press, 1954, p. 99. Further references are given in parentheses in the text.
11 Empson noted in a letter of *c.* February 1961:

A gossiping letter of February 1609, given in *Donne's Prose* by E. M. Simpson, reports that he had applied to become Secretary to the Virginia Colony. About this time Donne applied to be Ambassador to Venice, and also the Low Countries, but King James would not let him have any employment unless he took orders, and the needs of his family were increasingly great. As the Virginia Company was private, in some sense, he might think the King could not prevent his becoming its Secretary. The recent edition of William Strachey's *History of Travel into Virginia Britannia*, however, remarks in the preface that Strachey became Secretary after his belated arrival at Jamestown (May 1610) as a result of the drowning of Matthew Scrivener, the previous Secretary [see William Strachey, *The Historie of Travell into Virginia Britannia*, ed. Louis B. Wright and Virginia Freund, London: Hakluyt Society, second series, no. CIII, 1953, pp. xx–xxi]. It does not say when this drowning happened, how it is known, and whether it could have been known in England in February 1609. If it couldn't, the story in the letter becomes hard to believe because there was simply no vacancy; assuming that Donne had tried to join the supply fleet which sailed in May 1609, not the expedition to establish the colony which sailed in December 1606, since the letter claims to give the latest news. Also it looks as if King James could have stopped this appointment too; he controlled appointments to the Council in Virginia, which stayed at home. [See W. F. Craven, *The Southern Colonies in the Seventeenth Century 1607–1689*, Louisiana State University Press, 1949, where 'His Majesty's Council of Virginia' is discussed on pages 90–91; also the following observation, which is germane to Empson's argument, on p. 97: 'The Sea Adventure, which unfortunately was carrying all the leading men on whom the company depended for inauguration of its new venture – Admiral Somers, Governor Gates, William Strachey, newly appointed secretary of the colony... – lost contact with its consorts.'] I wish one could believe in the story; it makes Donne adventurous and keen not to become the great penitent preacher, which meant a great nervous upset of course; but one can hardly believe it without knowing more.

Eager to show that Donne very likely sought to escape his destiny as a cleric, Empson also drafted this later (undated) notice:

The story that Donne tried to go to America is usually called a bit of gossip, but it is less flimsy than that. The letters of John Chamberlain (*The Letters of John Chamberlain*, ed. Norman Egbert McClure, *Memoirs of the American Philosophical Society*, vol. XII, 1939, parts I and II) were unofficial but regular and very well-informed reports from London to the Ambassador at the Hague; historians seem to accept him as trustworthy, and he tells us other things about Donne correctly, for example his visit to France with Sir Robert Drury in 1611. Chamberlain was interested in the Virginia Colony from several angles, and his will bequeathes separately any holdings he may have there at his death. The letter of 23 January 1609 says:

> Here is likewise a ship newly come from Virginia with some petty commodities and hope of more (*Letters*, Part 2, p. 283);

then on 14 February:

> Newes here is none at all but that John Dun seekes to be preferred to be secretarie of Virginia. (*Ibid.*, p. 284)

The *History of Travel into Virginia Britannia* by William Strachey tells us that Strachey got his job later in 1609, after his arrival in Yorktown. He had sailed with the supply fleet, but his ship was wrecked at the Bermudas so that he arrived some months late. The previous secretary had been drowned, it turned out; we are not told when. Thus it is quite possible that the ship which got to England in January reported that the post was already vacant.

It has been suggested that Donne would only want to become secretary of the Company in London, but this is not how Chamberlain uses the term on 3 December 1618:

> But the greatest newes I have is that Master Pory is in the way of high preferment, for yesterday he was chosen Secretarie of Virginia for three yeares, and is upon his departure thether the end of this weeke with the new governor Sir George Yardly, who maried his cousen germain as he tells me: no question but he will become there a sufficient sober man seeing there is no wine in all that climat.

In 1616 we heard that he had been for some years secretary to the Ambassador at Constantinople, and in 1617 Chamberlain wrote of sending Master Pory as messenger to the Hague, 'and when you have him there you may do with him as you see cause' (*ibid.*, p. 87). He lasted for five years in Virginia, and then we hear (30 August 1623):

> Master Porie is come home very poore, and the best helpe he can get or hope for from his friends is to procure him a protection from his old debts. (*Ibid.*, p. 514)

Pory is rather impressive to a modern reader, but Chamberlain invariably regards him as a sordid comic. The letters are written in a sardonic style not easy for us to interpret, at least as regards the social standing of the characters. But we may expect that there is an irony when he says that Donne 'seeks to be preferred' – for a leading scholar whose conversation had impressed the King, this was a very odd job to regard as a prize. The point is of some importance, I think, because it shows how far Donne was willing to go, to what depths he would sink, in order to feed his wife and children without becoming a parson. But no doubt he may also have seen it as an adventure.

12 Redpath, *The Songs and Sonets*, p. 51; Grierson, *The Poems of John Donne*, II, 31: 'By "showne" he does not mean "revealed" – an adjectival predicate "larger" or "greater" must be supplied from the verb

"enlarg'd". "The stars at sunrise are not really made larger, but they are made to seem larger." It is a characteristically elliptical and careless wording of a characteristically acute and vivid image. Mr Wells has used the same phenomenon with effect:

> He peered upwards. 'Look!' he said.
> 'What?' I asked.
> 'In the sky. Already. On the blackness – a little touch of blue. See! The stars seem larger. And the little ones and all those dim nebulosities we saw in empty space – they are hidden.'
> Swiftly. steadily the day approached us. *The First Men in the Moon.* (Chap. vii. Sunrise on the Moon.)'.

13 'Wandering stars differ from each other in magnitude, but this magnitude depended, for the time before telescopes, on the light that they reflected from the sun since they have no light of their own. Is not Donne thinking here of the planets, which are specially "wandering stars"? If he is, the line becomes intelligible, and no further explanation is needed.' (Charles Singer, memorandum in Empson Papers, 12 December 1956.)

14 This was not really a very arcane piece of information. As Hugh Sykes Davies told Empson, Bernard Sylvester (as reported by Neckham) reckoned on a lunar causation of tide; and there is even a tide table for 'fflod at london brigge', with hours of moonlight set down in a column, reputed to date from the thirteenth century: Cotton Julius D. 7. fol. 45vo. (Letter to WE, 12 February 1957.)

15 *Devotions*, in John Hayward (ed.), *Complete Poetry and Selected Prose*, London: Nonesuch Press, 1929, p. 538; Neil Rhodes (ed.), *Selected Prose*, Harmondsworth, Middlesex: Penguin, 1987, p. 126.

16 This line from Holy Sonnet III ('O might those sighes and teares returne again') is discussed more extensively in 'Rescuing Donne' below.

17 See Redpath, *The Songs and Sonets*, Appendix III, pp. 140–4.

18 Hugh Sykes Davies wrote to WE on 12 February 1957, in response to this observation:

> not quite that: – their love [is] presented as being less involved in the need for physical expression – after all, on the violets, it's Donne who's doing the persuading, as in A[ir]&A[ngels] too – he's not defending his virtue against her. What he says is something like this: 'I want you to understand that the way you love me is indeed the way I love you (they are both air), but just as air, without being adulterated by grosser elements, may be densified and thickened to the point of being a kind of body, so my love has a body, and needs one, and achieves it without grossness, simply by making the same kind of transformation in what you know as love for me.' – That's a careless and clumsy version, but it's on the lines of what I mean. (Empson Papers.)

Hugh Sykes Davies later published his arguments in 'Text or Context', *REL* 6, 1965, pp. 93–107. See also Redpath, Appendix v, *The Songs and Sonets*, 2nd edn., pp. 318–22.

19 Richard Sleight, 'John Donne: A Nocturnall Upon S. Lucies Day, Being the Shortest Day', in John Wain (ed.), *Interpretations*, London: Routledge and Kegan Paul, 1955, pp. 46, 48, 49–50, 53.

20 Redpath suggests that 'us two' means 'we were the whole world' (*The Songs and Sonets*, p. 73).

21 While W. K. Wimsatt, Jun. is primary author of *The Verbal Icon: Studies in the Meaning of Poetry* (University of Kentucky Press: 1954), Empson omits to note that 'The Intentional Fallacy' was co-authored by Wimsatt and Monroe C. Beardsley.

22 Marjorie Nicolson, 'The "New Astronomy" and English Literary Imagination', *Studies in Philology*, 32, 1935, p. 449.

23 *Ibid.*, p. 459.

24 '[Hughes's] essay … marks a turning point in scholarship on the poet, no less important than Eliot's essay "The Metaphysical Poets"…' (Deborah Aldrich Larson, *John Donne and Twentieth-Century Criticism*, London and Toronto: Associated University Presses, 1989, p. 116).

25 Merritt Y. Hughes, 'Kidnapping Donne' (1934), reprinted in John R. Roberts (ed.), *Essential Articles for the study of John Donne's Poetry*, Hassocks, Sussex: Harvester Press, 1975, p. 47. All references are to this reprint.

26 Hughes cites Donne's sermon at St Paul's on Easter Day 1627 ('Kidnapping Donne', p. 44).

27 *Paradoxes and Problems* (ed. Keynes, p. 64); cited in Hughes, 'Kidnapping Donne', p. 51.

28 J. B. Leishman, *The Monarch of Wit* (1951), 6th edn, London: Hutchinson, 1962, p. 175–6.

CHAPTER 3: DONNE IN THE NEW EDITION

1 F. W. Payne, *John Donne and His Poetry*, London: George G. Harrap and Co., 1926, p. 164.

2 Marjorie Nicolson, 'The "New Astronomy" and English Literary Imagination', *Studies in Philology*, 32, 1935, p. 459.

3 See Grant McColley, 'The Seventeenth-century Doctrine of a Plurality of Worlds", *Annals of Science*, 1:3 (October 1936), pp. 412–13.

4 T. S. Eliot, 'Donne In Our Time', in Theodore Spencer (ed.), *A Garland for John Donne*, Oxford: OUP, 1931, pp. 11–12.

5 'Tennyson and Browning … do not feel their thought as immediately as the odour of a rose. A thought to Donne was an experience; it modified his sensibility … In the seventeenth century a dissociation of sensibility set in, from which we have never recovered.' (T. S. Eliot, 'The Metaphysical Poets' (1921), in *Selected Essays*, 3rd edn., London: Faber and Faber, 1951, pp. 287–8). And ten years later: 'in Donne, there is a manifest fissure between thought and sensibility, a chasm which in his poetry he bridged in his own way' ('Donne in Our Time', in T. Spencer (ed.), *A Garland for John Donne*, London: OUP, 1931, p. 8). Empson wrote in an undated letter (*c.* 1973) to Roger Sale: 'I don't believe, and

never have believed, that a social and literary "dissociation of sensibility" ever occurred...Eliot merely threw the idea out in passing when young, and is not responsible for its proliferation since' (copy in Empson Papers).

6 WE remarked, in his notes: 'She divides copyists into sheep and goats, so the idea of considering the motives for a variant cannot occur. This is chiefly due to a failure of character; she hardly feels safe unless she is expressing contempt.' (Empson Papers)

7 'To the Countesse of Huntington' ('That unripe side of earth, that heavy clime'), ll. 2–3.

8 'The Relique', l. 30.

9 W. Milgate (John Donne, *The Satires, Epigrams and Verse Letters*, Oxford: Clarendon Press, 1967, p. 230) sees 'no reason to doubt' that 1598 is the correct date.

10 Ted-Larry Pebworth has recently argued, most persuasively, that the Bridgewater volume (*B*) may represent authorial readings ('Manuscript Poems and Print Assumptions: Donne and His Modern Editors', *John Donne Journal*, 3:1, 1984, pp. 10–12).

11 Cf. Mark Roberts, 'Problems in Editing Donne's Songs and Sonets', in A. H. de Quehen (ed.), *Editing Poetry from Spenser to Dryden*, New York and London: Garland Publishing Inc., 1981, pp. 34–41.

12 'The Application of Thought to Textual Criticism' (1921); in A. E. Housman, *Collected Poems and Selected Prose*, ed. Christopher Ricks, Harmondsworth, Middlesex: Penguin, 1989, p. 335.

13 'About Donne there hangs the shadow of the impure motive; and impure motives lend their aid to a facile success. He is a little of the religious spellbinder, the Reverend Billy Sunday of his time, the flesh-creeper, the sorcerer of emotional orgy' (T. S. Eliot, *For Lancelot Andrewes* (1928), London: Faber and Faber, 1970, p. 16). According to Helen Gardner, Eliot's supercilious opinion of Donne the sermoniser was given 'not, I think, on the basis of a very intimate acquaintance with his sermons' ('Donne the Preacher', in *A City Tribute to John Donne*, London: Eyre and Spottiswoode, 1972).

14 H. I. Fausset, *John Donne: a study in discord*, London: Jonathan Cape, 1924, p. 229.

15 Cf. Deborah Aldrich Larson: 'Helen Gardner's "The Argument about 'The Extasy'"' illustrates what can happen when scholars approach a Donne poem with their own ideas of what the poem means and what traditions – in this case Neoplatonism – helped shape it' (*John Donne and Twentieth-Century Criticism*, London and Toronto: Associated University Presses, 1989, p. 124.

16 Cf. Mark Roberts: 'Grierson's reading "Which" is the reading of every manuscript and every edition. Dr. Gardner's "That" is pure editorial conjecture, the necessity for which arises from nothing more substantial than her own dissatisfaction with the line' ('If It Were Done When 'Tis Done', *Essays in Criticism,* 16, 1966, p. 321).

CHAPTER 4: RESCUING DONNE

1 F. W. Payne, *John Donne and His Poetry*, London: George Harrap and Co., 1926, p. 164.
2 John Donne, *The Satires, Epigrams and Verse Letters*, ed. W. Milgate, Oxford: Clarendon Press, 1967.
3 Cf. Ted-Larry Pebworth, 'Manuscript Poems and Print Assumptions: Donne and His Modern Editors', *John Donne Journal*, 3, 1984, pp. 1–27; and Alan MacColl, 'The Circulation of Donne's Poems in Manuscript', in A. J. Smith (ed.), *John Donne: Essays in Celebration*, London: Methuen, 1972, pp. 28–46.
4 Herbert J. C. Grierson (ed.), *The Poems of John Donne*, Oxford, 1912, II, p. 120.
5 'The initial address "Come, Madame, come" and the fact that she is obviously very expensively dressed suggests that she is one of the "cities quelque choses" ("Love's Usury", l. 15).' (Gardner, *ESS*, p. 133.)
6 Quoted in Gardner, *DP*, pp. lxiv–lxv.
7 Empson's protestations have recently received outstanding support from Ted-Larry Pebworth, who argues that Gardner's

> weddedness to the monolithic view of the groups causes her in practice to treat manuscripts of composite origins as if they had single origins. Thus both Gardner and Milgate treat British Library MS Lansdowne 740 [*L74*], for example, as a member of Group II. But in a recent detailed examination of the artifact itself, Ernest W. Sullivan II found that the volume contains paper having eleven different watermarks and that its contents were entered by at least twelve people over a period of more than a century. Specifically, its fifty Donne poems were copied in at least two hands on paper with four different watermarks. In Sullivan's words, 'it would seem very unlikely that the Lansdowne 740 texts all came from the same manuscript'. In placing Lansdowne 740 among the Group II manuscripts with no qualifications, then, Gardner and Milgate have obscured the fact that its several parts – no doubt deriving from a number of sources – may well represent various different steps in the textual histories of the Donne poems that it contains

('Manuscript Poems and Print Assumptions: Donne and His Modern Editors', *John Donne Journal*, 3:1, 1984, pp. 17–18).
8 Empson was misreading here: *Dob* and *S96* (from Group III) read 'goe see', but *O'F* does not figure in the list of manuscripts which drop 'to'; he had probably picked up a reference to *O'F* from another note just below.
9 So far from straining his grammar to embrace the underworld, writes R. V. Young (not without some cause), Donne is actually signifying sexual organs: 'the crude equation of vaginal orifice and mine shaft can be read as savage ridicule of piously veiled lust for America's buried wealth' ('"O my America, my new-found-land": Pornography and Imperial Politics in Donne's *Elegies*', *South Central Review*, 4:2, Summer 1987, p. 42).

10 Grierson, II, p. cxxi.
11 The verse letter 'To Mr Rowland Woodward' ('Like one who'in her third widdowhood doth professe'), *The Satires, Epigrams and Verse Letters*, p. 69. Empson is coining a title which he seeks to justify later in this essay.
12 Grierson, II, p. 147.
13 Milgate (pp. 211–12) conjectures that 'T.W.' could be Rowland Woodward's brother Thomas, who was christened on 16 July 1576, but points out that he has not been able to make a positive identification of 'T.W.', whose putative reply to 'To Mr J.D.' is printed on p. 212. Grierson had no hesitation in identifying 'T.W.' as Thomas Woodward, *The Poems of John Donne*, II p. 147; he published 'To Mr J.D.' on page 166. Empson commented on the poem, in his notes: 'Very sweet... No wonder Donne writes so hypocritically to Tom's elder brother afterwards.' (Empson Papers)
14 'Mr. Pearsall Smith... establishes [in *Life and Letters of Sir Henry Wotton*] that Woodward was at Venice with Wotton in 1605; during his residence there he was sent as a spy to Milan and imprisoned by the Inquisition. In 1607, while bringing home despatches, he was attacked by robbers in France and left for dead. On February 2, 1608, £60 was paid to his brother Thomas for Rowland's "surgeons and diets".' (M. C. Deas, 'A Note on Rowland Woodward, the friend of Donne', *Review of English Studies*, 7:28, October 1931, p. 454).
15 Grierson, *The Poems of John Donne*, II, p. lxxx.
16 C. S. Lewis, *English Literature in the Sixteenth Century excluding Drama*, Oxford: Clarendon Press, 1954, p. 10.
17 J. B. Leishman, *The Monarch of Wit* (1951), 6th edn, London: Hutchinson, 1962, p. 187.

CHAPTER 5: DONNE'S FORESIGHT

1 See Marjorie Nicolson, 'The "New Astronomy" and English Literary Imagination', *Studies in Philology*, 32, 1935, esp. pp. 448–60.
2 See Grant McColley, 'Nicholas Hill and the *Philosophia Epicurea*', *Annals of Science*, 1939, pp. 390–415 (Empson's probable source); Jean Jacquot, 'Harriot, Hill, Warner and the New Philosophy', in John W. Shirley (ed.), *Thomas Harriot: Renaissance Scientist*, Oxford: Clarendon Press, 1974; and Hilary Gatti, *The Renaissance Drama of Knowledge: Giordano Bruno in England*, London and New York: Routledge, 1989, pp. 51–2, 199–200. The best modern account of Hill is by Hugh Trevor-Roper, 'Nicholas Hill, the English Atomist', *Catholics, Anglicans and Puritans: Seventeenth-century Essays*, London: Martin Secker and Warburg, 1987, pp. 1–39.
3 '[A]ne English man who had mentioned democritus opinion of atomes, being old wrott a book to his son (who was not then Six years of age) in which he left him arguments to maintain and answer objections, for all that was in his book' ('Ben Jonson's Conversations with William

Drummond of Hawthornden', *Ben Jonson*, ed. C. H. Herford and P. Simpson, I, Oxford: Clarendon Press, 1925, p. 145).

4 *Ben Jonson*, ed. C. H. Herford, P. and E. Simpson, VIII, Oxford: Clarendon Press, 1947, p. 87.

5 *Ben Jonson*, ed. C. H. Herford, P. and E. Simpson, XI, Oxford: Clarendon Press, 1952, p. 32. Trevor-Roper, in correcting a contemporary account of Hill ('He... is mentioned in Ben Jonson's *Alchymist*') by Robert Hues, misses this connexion ('Nicholas Hill, the English Atomist', p. 11).

6 *The Defense of Galileo of Thomas Campanella*, trans. by Grant McColley, *Smith College Studies in History*, 22:3–4, April–July 1937, pp. 8, 11. It is notable that Tobias Adami, in a preface to the published text of *Apologia pro Galileo* (Frankfurt, 1622), cited Nicholas Hill among earlier advocates of a heliocentric universe.

7 Arthur Koestler, *The Sleepwalkers* (1959), Harmondsworth, Middlesex: Penguin, 1986, pp. 485–6.

8 Cf. Grant McColley, 'The Debt of Bishop John Wilkins to the *Apologia pro Galileo* of Tommaso Campanella', *Annals of Science*, 4:2, 15 April 1939, pp. 150–68. Wilkins also directly quoted Nicholas Hill's arguments for a heliocentric universe; he had probably been drawn to Hill by Adami's preface to *Apologia pro Galileo*.

CHAPTER 6: COPERNICANISM AND THE CENSOR

1 Jean Jacquot, 'Thomas Hariot's Reputation for Impiety', *Notes and Records of the Royal Society*, 9, 167; quoted in Christopher Hill, *Intellectual Origins of the English Revolution*, Oxford: Clarendon Press, 1965, pp. 32–3 (Empson's immediate source). Hill agrees with Empson that the 'negative pressures of Church and conservative opinion' were most likely 'oppressive', and suspects that there must have been 'a silent censorship':

We might have expected things to improve after the defeat of the Armada had made Protestantism and English independence secure; but this did not happen. The external danger had forced radicals to remain loyal to Elizabeth for fear of a worse alternative: the removal of this unifying factor roused the Queen and the conservatives to a flurry of repressive activity. With Leicester and Walsingham dead and Ralegh in disgrace in the fifteen-nineties, the bishops began a determined drive against Puritanism and free thought. This was not checked by the accession of James I... Under James the two leading patrons of science after Leicester, Ralegh and the Earl of Northumberland, both found themselves in the Tower. (pp. 31–2)

Cf. Edward Rosen's argument that it was not Harriot's 'acceptance of the Copernican astronomy that drew the unwelcome attention of the investigating authorities to him. Rather, it seems to have been his favorable attitude towards the atomic theory' ('Harriot's Science: The Intellectual Background'); and Jean Jacquot's detailed essay, 'Harriot,

Hill, Warner and the New Philosophy'; both in John W. Shirley (ed.), *Thomas Harriot: Renaissance Scientist*, Oxford: Clarendon Press, 1974). Empson studied this symposium, though possibly only after drafting the present essay, and was most interested in Rosen's remark that 'Harriot's observation of the moon with a 6 power glass on 26 July 1609, is, I feel, his first telescopic observation' (p. 32 note 13); there is no evidence that Empson managed to read Shirley's *Thomas Harriot: A Biography* (Oxford: Clarendon Press, 1983).

2 For an account of the little that is known of *The Isle of Dogs* affair, see Charles Nicholl, *A Cup of News: The Life of Thomas Nashe*, London: Routledge and Kegan Paul, 1984, pp. 242–56; David Riggs, *Ben Jonson: A Life*, Cambridge, MA: Harvard UP, 1989, pp. 32–4; Janet Clare, '*Art made Tongue-Tied by Authority': Elizabethan and Jacobean Dramatic Censorship*, Manchester and New York: Manchester UP, 1990, pp. 51–4.

3 See also John L. Russell, 'The Copernican System in Great Britain', in Jerzy Dobrzycki (ed.), *The Reception of Copernicus' Heliocentric Theory*, Dordrecht, Holland: D. Reidel, 1972, pp. 189–91. Cited hereinafter as: Russell, 'Copernican System'.

4 Cf. Alexander Koyré, *From the Closed World to the Infinite Universe*, Baltimore: The Johns Hopkins UP, 1957, pp. 35–9.

5 Francis Johnson, *Astronomical Thought in Renaissance England: A study of the English Scientific Writings from 1500 to 1645*, Baltimore: Johns Hopkins University Press, 1937, pp. 158, 224; Russell, 'Copernican System', pp. 192–3.

6 Cf. Colin A. Ronan, 'The origins of the reflecting telescope', *Journal of the British Astronomical Association*, 101:6, 1991, pp. 335–42.

7 Empson is paraphrasing Grant McColley's report of Melanchthon's views in *Initia Doctrinae Physicae*, 1567 ('The Seventeenth-century Doctrine of a Plurality of Worlds', *Annals of Science*, 1:4, 1936, pp. 412–13).

8 See also Foster Watson, *The Zodiacus Vitae of Marcellus Palingenius Stellatus*, London, 1908.

9 *Apud* Russell, Johnson is 'hardly justified' in claiming that 'Bostocke was obviously a Copernican' ('Copernican System', pp. 196–7).

10 *Cf.* Russell, 'Copernican System', p. 195: 'Johnson is…exaggerating when he says that "with the publication of Blagrave's *Astrolabium Uranicum Generale*, sound information about the mechanical details of the new heliocentric astronomy became readily available to all his countrymen". The instrument did, however, graphically illustrate the fact that the two rival theories of a rotating heaven and a rotating earth were observationally equivalent.'

11 See also Kristian Peder Moesgaard, 'Copernican Influence on Tycho Brahe', in Jerzy Dobrzycki (ed.), *The Reception of Copernicus' Heliocentric Theory*, Dordrecht, Holland: D. Reidel, 1972, pp. 31–55.

12 See Francis R. Johnson and Sanford V. Larkey, 'Thomas Digges, the Copernican System, and the Idea of the Infinity of the Universe in

1576', *Huntington Library Bulletin*, 5 (April 1934), p. 97 note 1; and Gad Freudenthal, 'Theory of Matter and Cosmology in William Gilbert's *De Magnete*', *Isis* (Official Journal of the History of Science Society), 74:271, March 1983, p. 34.

13 Johnson, p. 216. *Cf.* McColley, 'The Seventeenth-century Doctrine of a Plurality of Worlds', p. 410: 'It is perhaps an irony of history that, where Gilbert accepts the diurnal rotation and the infinite universe of Copernicus, he should not advocate the annual motion, and that Kepler, staunch friend of this movement and the diurnal rotation, should reject and attack the conception of an infinite cosmos.' See also Russell, 'Copernican System', pp. 203–9; and *cf.* Freudenthal, 'Theory of Matter and Cosmology in William Gilbert's *De Magnete*', p. 33: 'Gilbert's theory, constructed as it was around the notion of a single element, earth, endowed with a natural rotational motion, was in fact entirely irrelevant to any annual revolution, for which it did not offer even the slightest physical or, in particular, magnetic account...Gilbert chose not to discuss the annual revolution at all.' Nevertheless, Freudenthal argues (p. 34), 'There are good reasons to think that Gilbert in fact believed in the heliocentric universe.'

14 Thomas Bretnor, *A Newe Almanacke and Prognostication for the yeare of our Lord God 1615* [London], sig. C2ᵛ, quoted also in Russell, 'Copernican System', p. 213.

15 *Cf.* Russell, 'Copernican System', p. 216.

16 John Bainbridge, *An Astronomicall Description of the late Comet*, London, 1618, p. 5; quoted in Johnson, *Astronomical Thought*, 271. 'Surely this *says* he is restrained by censorship', Empson remarked in his notes for this essay (Empson Papers). Russell, 'Copernican System' (p. 218), supports Empson's judgment of Bainbridge: 'He was obviously attracted by "the Samian philosophy" but was afraid to expound it in a popular treatise. And in spite of his 22 years as a professor of astronomy, he never published anything more on it, even in Latin.' (Aristarchus of Samos (*c.* 300–230 BC) is renowned for having anticipated the heliocentric cosmology of Copernicus.)

CHAPTER 7: THOMAS DIGGES HIS INFINITE UNIVERSE

1 Digges' date of birth is reckoned by Francis R. Johnson and Sandford V. Larkey to be 'about 1545' ('Thomas Digges, the Copernican System, and the Idea of the Infinity of the Universe in 1576', *Huntington Library Bulletin*, 5, April 1934, p. 105). Mark Eccles has established that Leonard Digges was buried in September 1558, so Thomas 'must have been born about 1545' ('Brief Lives: Tudor and Stuart Authors', *Studies in Philology*, LXXIX: 4, Fall 1982, p. 44).

2 "Trimegistus [*sic*] visibilem deum" (N. Copernicus, *De Revolutionibus Orbium Caelestium*, Thorn, 1873, p. 30). See also Frances A. Yates, *Giordano Bruno and the Hermetic Tradition*, London: Routledge and Kegan

Paul, 1964, p. 154; and Peter J. French, *John Dee: The World of an Elizabethan Magus*, London: Routledge and Kegan Paul, 1972, pp. 102ff.

3 Cf. Grant McColley, who doubts the proposition that Digges 'was the first to advance the idea of an infinite universe as a corollary to the Copernican system' ('The Seventeenth-Century Doctrine of a Plurality of Worlds', *Annals of Science*, 1:3, 1936, p. 409); and Alexander Koyré, *From the Closed World to the Infinite Universe*, Baltimore: The Johns Hopkins UP, 1957, pp. 35–9. Empson wrote in an undated letter to Frank Kermode, 'About Digges, I only meant that the plugging oppressive rhythms are alike [i.e. like passages in Donne's prose]; this kind of earnestness wasn't all on the reactionary side. I think the Digges passage... is very magnificent' (copy in Empson Papers).

CHAPTER 8: GODWIN'S VOYAGE TO THE MOON

1 Helen Gardner (ed.), John Donne, *The Elegies and The Songs and Sonnets*, Oxford: Clarendon Press, 1965, p. 128.

2 Cf. Frank Manley (ed.), *John Donne: The Anniversaries*, Baltimore: The Johns Hopkins Press, 1963, p. 150.

3 As Empson pointed out in his notes for this essay, there would be 'no need [for Godwin] to insert or hark back to the battle near the Isle of Pines 1596' if he was in fact writing the story a good many years later.

4 Grant McColley (ed.), *The Man in the Moone and Nuncius Inanimatus*, Smith College Studies in Modern Languages, 19:1, October 1937. All further references to this edition are given in parentheses in the text. (An acceptably abbreviated version of Godwin's fiction is available in Faith K. Pizor and T. Allan Comp (eds.), *The Man in the Moone' and other Lunar Fantasies*, New York: Praeger Publishers, 1971.)

5 Francis R. Johnson, *Astronomical Thought in Renaissance England: A Study of the English Scientific Writings from 1500 to 1645*, Baltimore: The Johns Hopkins Press, 1937, p. 233.

6 In connection with both *The Man in the Moone* and *Nuncius Inanimatus* (which he discusses later in the essay), Empson has in mind passages such as this from the Rosicrucian manifesto *Confessio Fraternitatis*: 'Were it not excellent you dwell in one place, that neither the people which dwell beyond the River Ganges in the Indies could hide anything, nor those which live in Peru might be able to keep secret their counsels from thee?' (Frances A. Yates, *The Rosicrucian Enlightenment*, London: Routledge and Kegan Paul, 1972, p. 253.) Empson explained in an undated letter to John Webb:

It does seem quite possible that Godwin had read the *Confessio* before he wrote the additions to his voyage (in 1615, after Elizabeth had gone to Germany), and (as your note says) it was quite as easy to get hold of as the book about Jesuits in Peking. It would be what made him put in the excited paragraph about discoveries of messages, though merely as a revival of an old interest. He is not really thinking of himself as the inventor, but still writing in character, though he does seem to identify himself as never before with this line of ambition. Whether he read the *Confessio* or not, he was crazy on the subject by the time he wrote his own Messenger, making specific incredible claims – or don't you agree?

Likewise, in a note on Yates' book, he remarked: 'Suppose Godwin was influenced by them, he was still *mad*, wasn't he? The others say these things *can* be done, not that they have done them.' (Empson Papers)

7 Grant McColley, 'The Date of Godwin's *Domingo Gonsales*', *Modern Philology*, 35:1, August 1937, pp. 47–60. Empson is paraphrasing the 'scientific or pseudoscientific conceptions' that McColley enumerates.

8 Galileo reckoned that Kepler, who held that the moon had 'dominion over the waters', had given heed 'to occult properties, and to such puerilities'. (Galileo Galilei, *Dialogue Concerning the Two Chief World Systems – Ptolemaic & Copernican*, trans. Stillman Drake, Berkeley and Los Angeles: University of California Press, 1953, p. 462)

9 Copernicus, *Revolutions*, I, 9; quoted in Edward Rosen, *Kepler's Somnium: The Dream, or posthumous work on lunar astronomy*, Madison, Milwaukee & London: University of Wisconsin Press, 1967, Appendix H ('Kepler's Concept of Gravity'), p. 218.

10 Rosen, *Kepler's Somnium*, p. 221.

11 H. W. Lawton, 'Bishop Godwin's *Man in the Moone*', *Review of English Studies*, 7:25, January 1931 (23–55), p. 48.

12 Rosen, *Kepler's Somnium*, p. 16.

13 'Fifty thousand German miles up in the ether lies the island of Levania' (Rosen, *Kepler's Somnium*, p. 15); 'in my *Hipparchus* I prove, and in my *Epitome of Copernican Astronomy* I deduce a priori, that the moon at its apogee is about 59 earth-radii away. Multiplying 59 by 860 yields 50,740 miles' (*ibid.*, pp. 62–3).

14 McColley, 'The Date of Godwin's *Domingo Gonsales*', pp. 53–5.

15 Kepler's 'rejection of Newton's First Law, which is assumed as common sense by Godwin, was peculiarly extravagant', wrote Empson in a draft of the essay;

he argued that matter wants to lie still, and always stops moving as soon as you stop pushing it. Sometimes it appears not to, but then there is always a spiritual cause at work:

From the soul of anyone who throws pebbles an emanation of motion adheres to the pebbles, by which they are carried forward even when the thrower has taken his hand away from them.

The Daemon at the start of the Dream who explains how he carries men to the moon does not seem to be theorising, but this theory is taken for granted:

After the first stage of the trip is finished, the passage becomes easier. At that time we expose their bodies to the open air and remove our hands. Their bodies roll themselves up, like spiders, into balls which we carry along almost entirely by our will alone, so that finally the bodily mass proceeds toward its destination of its own accord. But this onward drive is of very little use to us, because it is too late. Hence it is by our will, as I said, that we move the body swiftly along, and we forge ahead of it from now on lest it suffer any harm by colliding very hard with the moon. (Rosen, *Kepler's Somnium*, p. 16.)

Kepler's own notes, written some time later, make this so much more intelligible that one feels rather suspicious, but there is no reason to doubt that he understood it when he wrote. When the body is near the moon 'the moon's magnetic force is…predominant' over that of the earth (*ibid.*, p. 73), so it begins falling onto the moon, and no longer needs pushing but only guarding against a crash. Thus at both points, the disbelief in impetus and the belief in remote gravitational forces, Kepler is at odds with Godwin.

16 Rosen, *Kepler's Somnium*, Appendix E ('Kepler and Donne'), pp. 212–13.
17 'In his *Sidereal Message* Galileo said that the moon's "brighter part most fitly represents its land surface, but its darker part the watery surface", and that "the moon has its own atmosphere surrounding it"…This opinion of Galileo was known to Kepler, an avid reader of the *Sidereal Message*, in 1610. Six years later, in a private letter, Galileo denied that there is water on the moon (Galileo, *Opere*, XII, 240:20–21). But this private letter was not made public during Kepler's lifetime. In fact, it was first published in an edition of Galileo's collected works (Florence, 1718, III, 474–75) which appeared nearly a century after Kepler's death. Hence Kepler did not know that Galileo denied the existence of water on the moon' (Rosen, *Kepler's Somnium*, p. 109 note 276).
18 Rosen, *Kepler's Somnium*, p. 27.
19 Rosen, *Kepler's Somnium*, pp. 28, 133; and Appendix M ('The People of Lucumoria'), pp. 236–9.
20 Lawton, 'Bishop Godwin's *Man in the Moone*', p. 37.
21 Cf. McColley, *The Man in the Moone*, p. 76:

The explanation for Godwin's change in calendars is, I believe, a simple one. A number of his hero's adventures among the lunars, as well as those which followed in China, were adapted from events described in Trigault's *De Christiana Expeditione*. As a Roman Catholic Trigault employed the calendar which Gregory had established by papal decree in 1582. Godwin's change may have proceeded from a desire to avoid the inconvenience of thinking in terms of two calendars, or from a realization that his Catholic hero, like Trigault and Father Ricci, would use the calendar of his church.

But compare these notable observations by Cay Dollerup, who also remarks upon 'the consistent internal chronology' of Gonsales' story:

He is involuntarily lifted towards the Moon on 9 September 1599, and leaves again Thursday 29 March 1601 '3 dayes after my awakening from the last Moones light' (p. 37). At this stage, Gonsales has informed us that he sleeps during the long Moon day, and that it starts in the Moon's first quarter and ends in its last quarter (p. 30). Dr. Einecke of the Astronomical Observatory, University of Copenhagen, has kindly informed me that the Moon entered its last quarter 25–27 March 1601. It seems as if Godwin had been watching the Moon and taken down the correct date.

('The earliest Space Voyages in the Renaissance, Heliocentric Solar System', in Luk de Vos (ed.), *Just the Other Day: Essays on the Suture of the Future*, Antwerp: Restant, 1985, p. 113). Like Empson, Dollerup is keen on an early date, and argues that the original text could well have been finished by 1603 – 'and, at all events, hardly after 1605' (p. 106).

22 The Jesuits arrived in China in 1601, and wrote home about it in 1602. As Cay Dollerup remarks, however, neither McColley nor Lawton can explain why Godwin never refers to the leader of the Jesuit mission, Matteo Ricci, but only to a priest named 'Pantoja'; information about the Jesuits in China would have been available to Godwin in England well before the publication of Nicholas Trigault's *De Christiana expeditione apud Sinas suscepta ab Societate Jesu* (Augsburg, 1615). In any event, Collerup saliently notes, it would not have been at all wise for Godwin, an Anglican bishop, to write about the Jesuits after 1605 when Henry Garnett was executed for his part in the Gunpowder Plot (*ibid.*, p. 112).

Godwin's sources possibly included, in addition to Trigault, Samuel Purchas' *Purchas His Pilgrimes* (London, 1625), Richard Hakluyt's *The Principal Navigations, Voiages, Traffiques and Discoveries of the English Nation* (London, 1598–1600), and Richard Eden's *The History of Travayle in the West and East Indies* (London, 1577). But everything Godwin might have learned about China from Purchas was already available to him in Hakluyt: 'it is fairly safe to assume that Godwin relied on both Hakluyt and Purchas or either'. Furthermore, Godwin refers to Peking as *Suntien* – a term which he almost certainly took from *The Historie of the Great and Mightie Kingdome of China* (London, 1588), by Juan Gonzalez de Mendoza. (Takau Shimada, 'Gonzalez de Mendoza's Historie as a possible source for Godwin's *The Man in the Moone*', *Notes and Queries*, II. s. 34:2 [232], pp. 314–15.) Thus his principal published sources, with the sole exception of Trigault, were available to him by 1600 – only a very little later than Empson would wish.

Empson independently observed in his notes for this essay: 'Less than 20 lines at the end given to the Jesuits. No mention of Ricci' (Empson Papers).

23 Christopher Hill, *Intellectual Origins of the English Revolution*, Oxford: Clarendon Press, p. 11.

24 McColley, 'The Date of Godwin's *Domingo Gonsales*', p. 52.

25 Grant McColley, 'The Seventeenth-century Doctrine of a Plurality of Worlds', *Annals of Science*, 1:3 (October 1936), pp. 412–13.

26 'Wilkins was either a moderate Anglican of the Fuller or Ussher variety or a Puritan in the Erastian mold... Latitudinarianism, rather than Anglicanism or Puritanism, seems to be the key feature of his religious outlook.' (Barbara J. Shapiro, *John Wilkins 1614–1672: An Intellectual Biography*, Berkeley and Los Angeles: University of California Press, 1969, pp. 61, 69.)

27 John Wilkins, *The Mathematical and Philosophical Works* [a facsimile of the 1802 edition], London: Frank Cass and Co., 1970, pp. 128–9.

28 See Rosen, *Kepler's Somnium*, p. 71; and Appendix H, 'Kepler's Concept of Gravity'.

29 'Quantitatively, Kepler measured the force of gravitation as the product of a weight times a distance. He believed that gravitational force, like magnetic force and his solar force, was inversely proportionate to the distance, diminishing directly with the simple distance, while light was attenuated with the square of the distance' (Rosen, *Kepler's Somnium*, p. 221).

30 *William Gilbert of Colchester, Physician of London, On the Magnet, Magnetick Bodies also, and on the Great Magnet the Earth: a New Physiology, Demonstrated by Many Arguments and Experiments*, translated from the Latin by a Committee of the Gilbert Club, London: The Chiswick Press, 1900, pp. 76–7. 'William Gilbert's *De Magnete* seems to me a very disappointing book', wrote Empson in his notes.

31 *Ibid.*, p. 215.

32 Empson is paraphrasing Wilkins' observation that water 'does not differ in respect of gravity, when it is frozen, and when it is fluid... [F]rozen waters... are not properly condensed, but congealed into a harder substance, the parts being not contracted closer together, but still possessing the same extension.' (Wilkins, *The Mathematical and Philosophical Works*, p. 215.)

33 See Shapiro, *John Wilkins 1614–1672*, pp. 111–13.

34 Cay Dollerup agrees with Empson that it is 'suggestive that the lunar prince asks Gonsales to greet Elizabeth, "the most glorious of all women living" (p. 36). She died 24 March 1603, and it would definitely have been in place if there was a greeting to her successor as well – especially as Godwin himself dedicated his enlarged history of the English bishops to James I, when it came out in 1615' ('The earliest Space Voyages in the Renaissance, Heliocentric Solar System', p. 112).

APPENDIX ON GALILEO

1 *Dialogue Concerning the Two Chief World Systems – Ptolemaic & Copernican*, trans. Stillman Drake, Berkeley and Los Angeles: University of California Press, 1953, p. 70. Subsequent references are given in the text.

2 Cf. Arthur O. Lovejoy, *The Great Chain of Being*, Cambridge, Mass.: Harvard UP, 1936, pp. 121–2.

Index

Abbott, George, 36
Adami, Tobias, 283
Aers, David, 266
Agrippa, Cornelius, 222
Alphonsus of Castille, 18–19
Anaximander, 35
Applebaum, Wilbur, 270
Aquilecchia, Giovanni, 271
Aquinas, St Thomas, 54, 143, 205
Aristarchus of Samos, 214, 285
Aristotle; and Aristotelianism, 26, 29, 42, 113, 155, 214, 236, 256
Aubrey, John, 31, 37, 269
Augustine, St, 201

Bacon, Francis, 38
Bainbridge, John, 214, 285
Bald, R. C., 38, 40, 266
Baldwin, T. W., 63
Bär, Reymers, 217
Bateson, F. W., 54
Batman Upon Bartholeme, 155
Baudelaire, Charles, 152
Baumlin, James S., 264
Beardsley, Monroe C., 279
Bedford, Countess of, *see* Harrington, Lucy
Bell, Ilona, 263
Benedetti, Giovanni Battista, 203
Bennett, Joan, 266
Bennett, Roger E., 152
Bentley, R., 133
Bergerac, Cyrano de, 232
Bewley, Marius, 88–9, 276
Bible, The, 103, 111, 181–2, 201, 206, 213, 257
Blagrave, John, 212, 284
Blake, William, 94, 151, 193
Blundeville, Thomas, 212
Bosch, Hieronymus, 193, 239
Bossy, John, 269
Bostocke, Richard, 212, 284

Bottomley, Jacob, 192
Bradbrook, M. C., 272
Brahe, Tycho, 25, 28–9, 34–5, 41, 113, 125, 209, 212–15, 217, 260, 267, 269
Bretnor, Thomas, 214
Brown, Meg Lota, 275
Browne, Sir Thomas, 90
Bruno, Giordano, 27, 31–2, 34–7, 41–4, 48–9, 76, 78, 81–3, 113, 124, 130, 203–5, 258, 269, 271–2
Butler, Samuel, *Hudibras*, 225

Calvin, John, 174, 176, 210
Campanella, Tommaso, 205–6, 225, 248, 257–8, 283
Carey, John, xiii, 1–2, 10–12, 18–19, 21–6, 28–9, 40–1, 51, 58, 261–3, 266
Carpenter, Nathanael, 214
Carr, Robert, Earl of Somerset, 134, 146–7, 162
Chamberlain, John, 276–7
Chapman, George, 37, 269
Charles I, King, 254
Chaucer, Geoffrey, 115
Chillingworth, William, 248
Christianity, 2–9, 13–15, 19–20, 24, 27–8, 35–6, 44–9, 70–1, 75–6, 79–94, 102, 108–14, 124, 129–30, 141, 143, 152, 161, 178, 191–2, 199–201, 203–6, 210, 222, 252–3, 258–9, 264
Cicero, 201
Clarkson, Laurence, 194
Clavius, Christopher, 18–19, 46
Coffin, C. M., 8, 15, 27–9, 47, 122, 264
Cohn, Norman, 190–4
Coleridge, Samuel T., 79–80, 119
Copernicus, Nicholas, and Copernicanism, 2, 5, 6, 18, 25–6, 28–30, 32–3, 36, 41–2, 44–6, 48, 69, 76, 78, 81–2, 84, 98, 100, 110, 113–14, 122–6, 129–30, 138, 159, 201–5, 207–15, 217–18, 231,